Visit classzone.com and get connected

Online resources for students and parents

ClassZone resources provide instruction, practice, and learning support.

eEdition Plus ONLINE

This interactive version of the text encourages students to explore science.

Content Review Online

Interactive review reinforces the big idea and key concepts of each chapter.

SciLinks

NSTA-selected links provide relevant Web resources correlated to the text.

Chapter-Based Support

Math tutorials, news, resources, test practice, and a misconceptions database help students succeed.

Now it all clicks!™

McDougal Littell

McDougal Littell Science

Earth's Surface

biosphere

sedimentary rock

EROSION

geosphere

EARTH SCIENCE

A ▶ Earth's Surface
B ▶ The Changing Earth
C ▶ Earth's Waters
D ▶ Earth's Atmosphere
E ▶ Space Science

PHYSICAL SCIENCE

A ▶ Matter and Energy
B ▶ Chemical Interactions
C ▶ Motion and Forces
D ▶ Waves, Sound, and Light
E ▶ Electricity and Magnetism

LIFE SCIENCE

A ▶ Cells and Heredity
B ▶ Life Over Time
C ▶ Diversity of Living Things
D ▶ Ecology
E ▶ Human Biology

Acknowledgments: Excerpts and adaptations from *National Science Education Standards* by the National Academy of Sciences. Copyright © 1996 by the National Academy of Sciences. Reprinted with permission from the National Academies Press, Washington, D.C.

Excerpts and adaptations from *Benchmarks for Science Literacy: Project 2061.* Copyright © 1993 by the American Association for the Advancement of Science. Reprinted with permission.

ISBN: 0-618-33419-X 5 6 7 8 VJM 08 07 06 05

Internet Web Site: http://www.mcdougallittell.com

Science Consultants

Chief Science Consultant

James Trefil, Ph.D. is the Clarence J. Robinson Professor of Physics at George Mason University. He is the author or co-author of more than 25 books, including *Science Matters* and *The Nature of Science*. Dr. Trefil is a member of the American Association for the Advancement of Science's Committee on the Public Understanding of Science and Technology. He is also a fellow of the World Economic Forum and a frequent contributor to *Smithsonian* magazine.

Rita Ann Calvo, Ph.D. is Senior Lecturer in Molecular Biology and Genetics at Cornell University, where for 12 years she also directed the Cornell Institute for Biology Teachers. Dr. Calvo is the 1999 recipient of the College and University Teaching Award from the National Association of Biology Teachers.

Kenneth Cutler, M.S. is the Education Coordinator for the Julius L. Chambers Biomedical Biotechnology Research Institute at North Carolina Central University. A former middle school and high school science teacher, he received a 1999 Presidential Award for Excellence in Science Teaching.

Instructional Design Consultants

Douglas Carnine, Ph.D. is Professor of Education and Director of the National Center for Improving the Tools of Educators at the University of Oregon. He is the author of seven books and over 100 other scholarly publications, primarily in the areas of instructional design and effective instructional strategies and tools for diverse learners. Dr. Carnine also serves as a member of the National Institute for Literacy Advisory Board.

Linda Carnine, Ph.D. consults with school districts on curriculum development and effective instruction for students struggling academically. A former teacher and school administrator, Dr. Carnine also co-authored a popular remedial reading program.

Sam Miller, Ph.D. is a middle school science teacher and the Teacher Development Liaison for the Eugene, Oregon, Public Schools. He is the author of curricula for teaching science, mathematics, computer skills, and language arts.

Donald Steely, Ph.D. serves as principal investigator at the Oregon Center for Applied Science (ORCAS) on federal grants for science and language arts programs. His background also includes teaching and authoring of print and multimedia programs in science, mathematics, history, and spelling.

Vicky Vachon, Ph.D. consults with school districts throughout the United States and Canada on improving overall academic achievement with a focus on literacy. She is also co-author of a widely used program for remedial readers.

Content Reviewers

John Beaver, Ph.D.
Ecology
Professor, Director of Science Education Center
College of Education and Human Services
Western Illinois University
Macomb, IL

Donald J. DeCoste, Ph.D.
Matter and Energy, Chemical Interactions
Chemistry Instructor
University of Illinois
Urbana-Champaign, IL

Dorothy Ann Fallows, Ph.D., MSc
Diversity of Living Things, Microbiology
Partners in Health
Boston, MA

Michael Foote, Ph.D.
The Changing Earth, Life Over Time
Associate Professor
Department of the Geophysical Sciences
The University of Chicago
Chicago, IL

Lucy Fortson, Ph.D.
Space Science
Director of Astronomy
Adler Planetarium and Astronomy Museum
Chicago, IL

Elizabeth Godrick, Ph.D.
Human Biology
Professor, CAS Biology
Boston University
Boston, MA

Isabelle Sacramento Grilo, M.S.
The Changing Earth
Lecturer, Department of the Geological Sciences
San Diego State University
San Diego, CA

David Harbster, MSc
Diversity of Living Things
Professor of Biology
Paradise Valley Community College
Phoenix, AZ

Richard D. Norris, Ph.D.
Earth's Waters
Professor of Paleobiology
Scripps Institution of Oceanography
University of California, San Diego
La Jolla, CA

Donald B. Peck, M.S.
Motion and Forces; Waves, Sound, and Light; Electricity and Magnetism
Director of the Center for Science Education (retired)
Fairleigh Dickinson University
Madison, NJ

Javier Penalosa, Ph.D.
Diversity of Living Things, Plants
Associate Professor, Biology Department
Buffalo State College
Buffalo, NY

Raymond T. Pierrehumbert, Ph.D.
Earth's Atmosphere
Professor in Geophysical Sciences (Atmospheric Science)
The University of Chicago
Chicago, IL

Brian J. Skinner, Ph.D.
Earth's Surface
Eugene Higgins Professor of Geology and Geophysics
Yale University
New Haven, CT

Nancy E. Spaulding, M.S.
Earth's Surface, The Changing Earth, Earth's Waters
Earth Science Teacher (retired)
Elmira Free Academy
Elmira, NY

Steven S. Zumdahl, Ph.D.
Matter and Energy, Chemical Interactions
Professor Emeritus of Chemistry
University of Illinois
Urbana-Champaign, IL

Susan L. Zumdahl, M.S.
Matter and Energy, Chemical Interactions
Chemistry Education Specialist
University of Illinois
Urbana-Champaign, IL

Safety Consultant

Juliana Texley, Ph.D.
Former K–12 Science Teacher and School Superintendent
Boca Raton, FL

English Language Advisor

Judy Lewis, M.A.
Director, State and Federal Programs for reading proficiency and high risk populations
Rancho Cordova, CA

Teacher Panel Members

Carol Arbour
Tallmadge Middle School,
Tallmadge, OH

Patty Belcher
Goodrich Middle School,
Akron, OH

Gwen Broestl
Luis Munoz Marin Middle School,
Cleveland, OH

Al Brofman
Tehipite Middle School,
Fresno, CA

John Cockrell
Clinton Middle School,
Columbus, OH

Jenifer Cox
Sylvan Middle School,
Citrus Heights, CA

Linda Culpepper
Martin Middle School,
Charlotte, NC

Kathleen Ann DeMatteo
Margate Middle School,
Margate, FL

Melvin Figueroa
New River Middle School,
Ft. Lauderdale, FL

Doretha Grier
Kannapolis Middle School,
Kannapolis, NC

Robert Hood
Alexander Hamilton Middle School,
Cleveland, OH

Scott Hudson
Covedale Elementary School,
Cincinnati, OH

Loretta Langdon
Princeton Middle School,
Princeton, NC

Carlyn Little
Glades Middle School,
Miami, FL

Ann Marie Lynn
Amelia Earhart Middle School,
Riverside, CA

James Minogue
Lowe's Grove Middle School,
Durham, NC

Joann Myers
Buchanan Middle School,
Tampa, FL

Barbara Newell
Charles Evans Hughes Middle School,
Long Beach, CA

Anita Parker
Kannapolis Middle School,
Kannapolis, NC

Greg Pirolo
Golden Valley Middle School,
San Bernardino, CA

Laura Pottmyer
Apex Middle School,
Apex, NC

Lynn Prichard
Booker T. Washington Middle Magnet
School, Tampa, FL

Jacque Quick
Walter Williams High School,
Burlington, NC

Robert Glenn Reynolds
Hillman Middle School,
Youngstown, OH

Stacy Rinehart
Lufkin Road Middle School,
Apex, NC

Theresa Short
Abbott Middle School,
Fayetteville, NC

Rita Slivka
Alexander Hamilton Middle School,
Cleveland, OH

Marie Sofsak
B F Stanton Middle School,
Alliance, OH

Nancy Stubbs
Sweetwater Union Unified School District,
Chula Vista, CA

Sharon Stull
Quail Hollow Middle School,
Charlotte, NC

Donna Taylor
Okeeheelee Middle School,
West Palm Beach, FL

Sandi Thompson
Harding Middle School,
Lakewood, OH

Lori Walker
Audubon Middle School & Magnet Center,
Los Angeles, CA

Teacher Lab Evaluators

Andrew Boy
W.E.B. DuBois Academy,
Cincinnati, OH

Jill Brimm-Byrne
Albany Park Academy,
Chicago, IL

Gwen Broestl
Luis Munoz Marin Middle School,
Cleveland, OH

Al Brofman
Tehipite Middle School,
Fresno, CA

Michael A. Burstein
The Rashi School,
Newton, MA

Trudi Coutts
Madison Middle School,
Naperville, IL

Jenifer Cox
Sylvan Middle School,
Citrus Heights, CA

Larry Cwik
Madison Middle School,
Naperville, IL

Jennifer Donatelli
Kennedy Junior High School,
Lisle, IL

Melissa Dupree
Lakeside Middle School,
Evans, GA

Carl Fechko
Luis Munoz Marin Middle School,
Cleveland, OH

Paige Fullhart
Highland Middle School,
Libertyville, IL

Sue Hood
Glen Crest Middle School,
Glen Ellyn, IL

William Luzader
Plymouth Community Intermediate School,
Plymouth, MA

Ann Min
Beardsley Middle School,
Crystal Lake, IL

Aileen Mueller
Kennedy Junior High School,
Lisle, IL

Nancy Nega
Churchville Middle School,
Elmhurst, IL

Oscar Newman
Sumner Math and Science Academy,
Chicago, IL

Lynn Prichard
Booker T. Washington Middle Magnet
School, Tampa, FL

Jacque Quick
Walter Williams High School,
Burlington, NC

Stacy Rinehart
Lufkin Road Middle School,
Apex, NC

Seth Robey
Gwendolyn Brooks Middle School,
Oak Park, IL

Kevin Steele
Grissom Middle School,
Tinley Park, IL

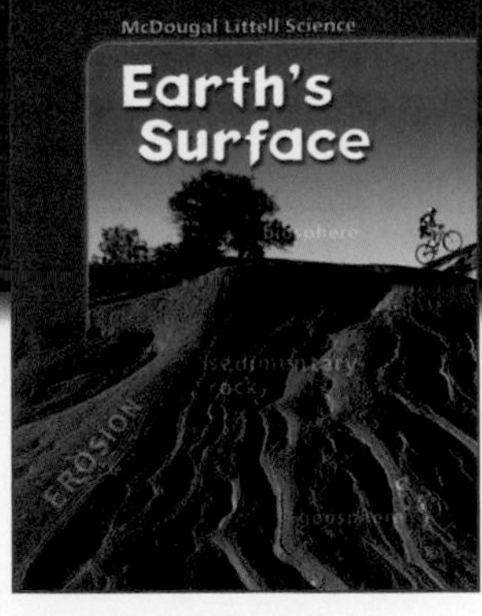

Earth's Surface

Unit Features

SCIENTIFIC AMERICAN

1 Views of Earth Today 6

the BIG idea

Modern technology has changed the way we view and map Earth.

2 Minerals 40

the BIG idea

Minerals are basic building blocks of Earth.

Why can gold be separated from other minerals and rocks in a river? page 40

How long will these rocks remain as they are? page 72

Features

Visual Highlights

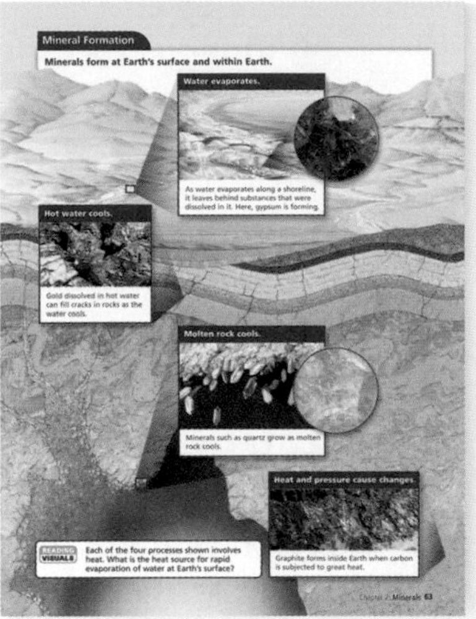

Mineral Formation
Minerals form at Earth's surface and within Earth.
Water evaporates.
Hot water cools.
Molten rock cools.
Heat and pressure cause changes.

Internet Resources @ ClassZone.com

INVESTIGATIONS AND ACTIVITIES

EXPLORE THE BIG IDEA

Chapter Opening Inquiry

CHAPTER INVESTIGATION

Full-Period Labs

EXPLORE

Introductory Inquiry Activities

INVESTIGATE

Skill Labs

Standards and Benchmarks

Each chapter in **Earth's Surface** covers some of the learning goals that are described in the *National Science Education Standards* (NSES) and the Project 2061 Benchmarks for Science Literacy. Selected content and skill standards are shown below in shortened form. The following National Science Education Standards are covered on pages xii-xxvii, in Frontiers in Science, and in Timelines in Science, as well as in chapter features and laboratory investigations: Understandings About Scientific Inquiry (A.9), Understandings About Science and Technology (E.6), Science and Technology in Society (F.5), Science as a Human Endeavor (G.1), Nature of Science (G.2), and History of Science (G.3).

Content Standards

1 Views of Earth Today

National Science Education Standards

A.9.d Technology is used to gather more detailed and accurate data to help scientists in their investigations.

D.1.a Earth consists of an inner and outer core, a mantle, and a crust.

E.6.c Technology allows scientists to observe or measure phenomena that would otherwise be beyond scientists' reach.

Project 2061 Benchmarks

1.C.6 Computers speed up and extend scientists' ability to collect, store, compile, analyze, and prepare data.

4.B.2 Earth is a rocky planet surrounded by a thin blanket of air, with water covering nearly three-quarters of its surface. The planet supports a wide variety of life.

9.C.3 The spherical Earth is distorted when projected onto a flat map.

9.C.5 It takes two numbers to locate a point on a map.

11.A.2 Thinking about things as systems means looking at how each part relates to the others.

2 Minerals

Project 2061 Benchmarks

4.B.10 The ability to recover valuable minerals is just as important as how abundant or rare they are in nature. As minerals are used up, obtaining them becomes more difficult.

4.C.3 Sand, smaller particles, and dissolved minerals form solid rock.

3 Rocks

National Science Education Standards

D.1.d In the rock cycle, old rocks at Earth's surface weather and become sediments. The sediments are buried, then compressed and heated to form new rock. If the new rock layers are pushed to the surface, the cycle begins again.

D.1.k Living organisms have produced some types of rocks.

Project 2061 Benchmarks

4.C.3 In the rock cycle, sediments are buried and cemented together by dissolved minerals to form solid rock again.

4.C.4 Rocks bear evidence of the minerals, temperatures, and forces that formed them in the rock cycle.

Weathering and Soil Formation

National Science Education Standards

D.1.e Soil consists of weathered rocks, decayed organic plant and animal matter, and bacteria. Each layer of soil has a different composition and texture.

D.1.k Living organisms have contributed to the weathering of rocks.

Project 2061 Benchmarks

4.C.6 Soil composition, texture, and fertility are influenced by plant roots and debris and by organisms living in the soil.

Erosion and Deposition

National Science Education Standards

D.1.c Landforms are shaped by weathering and erosion.

Project 2061 Benchmarks

4.C.2 Earth's surface is shaped in part by the motion of wind and water over very long times.

4.C.6 Soil's resistance to erosion is influenced by organisms living in the soil and by plant roots and debris.

Process and Skill Standards

National Science Education Standards

A.1 Identify questions that can be answered using scientific methods.

A.2 Design and conduct a scientific investigation.

A.3 Use appropriate tools and techniques to gather and analyze data.

A.4 Use evidence to describe, predict, explain, and model.

A.5 Use critical thinking to find relationships between results and interpretations.

A.7 Communicate procedures, results, and conclusions.

A.8 Use mathematics in scientific investigations.

E.1 Identify a problem to be solved.

E.2 Design a solution or product.

E.3 Implement the proposed solution.

E.4 Evaluate the solution or design.

Project 2061 Benchmarks

9.A.3 Write numbers in different forms.

9.B.2 Use mathematics to describe change.

9.B.3 Use graphs to show relationships.

11.B.1 Use models to think about processes.

11.C.4 Use equations to summarize change.

11.D.2 With complex systems, use summaries, averages, ranges, and examples.

12.B.3 Calculate volumes of rectangular solids.

12.B.5 Estimate distances and travel times from maps.

12.B.7 Determine, use, and convert units.

12.C.3 Use and read measurement instruments.

12.D.3 Read, interpret, and describe tables and graphs.

12.D.4 Understand graphs and charts.

12.D.5 Use coordinates to find locations on maps.

Introducing Earth Science

Scientists are curious. Since ancient times, they have been asking and answering questions about the world around them. Scientists are also very suspicious of the answers they get. They carefully collect evidence and test their answers many times before accepting an idea as correct.

In this book you will see how scientific knowledge keeps growing and changing as scientists ask new questions and rethink what was known before. The following sections will help get you started.

What Is Earth Science?

Earth science is the study of Earth's interior, its rocks and soil, its atmosphere, its oceans, and outer space. For many years, scientists studied each of these topics separately. They learned many important things. More recently, however, scientists have looked more and more at the connections among the different parts of Earth—its oceans, atmosphere, living things, and rocks and soil. Scientists have also been learning more about other planets in our solar system, as well as stars and galaxies far away. Through these studies they have learned much about Earth and its place in the universe.

The text and pictures in this book will help you learn key concepts and important facts about earth science. A variety of activities will help you investigate these concepts. As you learn, it helps to have a big picture of earth science as a framework for this new information. The four unifying principles listed below will give you this big picture. Read the next few pages to get an overview of each of these principles and a sense of why they are so important.

- **Heat energy inside Earth and radiation from the Sun provide energy for Earth's processes.**
- **Physical forces, such as gravity, affect the movement of all matter on Earth and throughout the universe.**
- **Matter and energy move among Earth's rocks and soil, atmosphere, waters, and living things.**
- **Earth has changed over time and continues to change.**

the BIG idea

Each chapter begins with a big idea. Keep in mind that each big idea relates to one or more of the unifying principles.

UNIFYING PRINCIPLE

Heat energy inside Earth and radiation from the Sun provide energy for Earth's processes.

The lava pouring out of this volcano in Hawaii is liquid rock that was melted by heat energy under Earth's surface. Another, much more powerful energy source constantly bombards Earth's surface with energy, heating the air around you, and keeping the oceans from freezing over. This energy source is the Sun. Everything that moves or changes on Earth gets its energy either from the Sun or from the inside of our planet.

What It Means

You are always surrounded by different forms of energy, such as heat energy or light. **Energy** is the ability to cause change. All of Earth's processes need energy to occur. A process is a set of changes that leads to a particular result. For example, **evaporation** is the process by which liquid changes into gas. A puddle on a sidewalk dries up through the process of evaporation. The energy needed for the puddle to dry up comes from the Sun.

Heat Energy Inside Earth

Underneath the cool surface layer of rock, Earth's interior is so hot that the solid rock there is able to flow very slowly—a few centimeters each year. In a process called **convection,** hot material rises, cools, then sinks until it is heated enough to rise again. Convection of hot rock carries heat energy up to Earth's surface, where it provides the energy to build mountains, cause earthquakes, and make volcanoes erupt.

Radiation from the Sun

Earth receives energy from the Sun as **radiation**—energy that travels across distances in the form of certain types of waves. Visible light is one type of radiation. Radiation from the Sun heats Earth's surface, making bright summer days hot. Different parts of Earth receive different amounts of radiation at different times of the year, causing seasons. Energy from the Sun also causes winds to blow, ocean currents to flow, and water to move from the ground to the atmosphere and back again.

Why It's Important

Understanding Earth's processes makes it possible to

- know what types of crops to plant and when to plant them
- know when to watch for dangerous weather, such as tornadoes and hurricanes
- predict a volcano's eruption in time for people to leave the area

Physical forces, such as gravity, affect the movement of all matter on Earth and throughout the universe.

The universe is everything that exists, and everything in the universe is governed by the same physical laws. The same laws govern the stars shown in this picture and the page on which the picture is printed.

What It Means

What do the stars in a galaxy, the planet Earth, and your body have in common? For one thing, they are all made of matter. **Matter** is anything that has mass and takes up space. Rocks are matter. You are matter. Even the air around you is matter. Matter is made of tiny particles called **atoms** that are too small to see through an ordinary microscope.

Everything in the universe is also affected by the same physical forces. A **force** is a push or a pull. Forces affect how matter moves everywhere in the universe.

- One force you experience every moment is **gravity,** which is the attraction, or pull, between two objects. Gravity is pulling you to Earth and Earth to you. Gravity is the force that causes objects to fall downward toward the center of Earth. Gravity is also the force that keeps objects in orbit around planets and stars.
- **Friction** is the force that resists motion between two surfaces that are pressed together. Friction can keep a rock on a hillside from sliding down to the bottom of the hill. If you lightly rub your finger across a smooth page in a book and then across a piece of sandpaper, you can feel how the different surfaces produce different frictional forces. Which is easier to do?
- There are many other forces at work on Earth and throughout the universe. For example, Earth has a magnetic field. A compass needle responds to the force exerted by Earth's magnetic field. Another example is the contact force between a rock and the ground beneath it. A contact force occurs when one object pushes or pulls on another object by touching it.

Why It's Important

Physical forces influence the movement of all matter, from the tiniest particle to you to the largest galaxy. Understanding forces allows people to

- predict how objects and materials move on Earth
- send spacecraft and equipment into space
- explain and predict the movements of Earth, the Moon, planets, and stars

Matter and energy move among Earth's rocks and soil, atmosphere, waters, and living things.

When a wolf eats a rabbit, matter and energy move from one living thing into another. When a wolf drinks water warmed by the Sun, matter and energy move from Earth's waters into one of its living things. These are just two examples of how energy and matter move among different parts of the Earth system.

What It Means

Think of Earth as a huge system, or an organized group of parts that work together. Within this system, matter and energy move among the different parts. The four major parts of Earth's system are the

- **atmosphere,** which includes all the air surrounding the solid planet
- **geosphere,** which includes all of Earth's rocks and minerals, as well as Earth's interior
- **hydrosphere,** which includes oceans, rivers, lakes, and every drop of water on or under Earth's surface
- **biosphere,** which includes all the living things on Earth

Matter in the Earth System

It's easy to see how matter moves within the Earth system. When water in the atmosphere falls as rain, it becomes part of the hydrosphere. When an animal drinks water from a puddle, the water becomes part of the biosphere. When rainwater soaks into the ground, it moves through the geosphere. As the puddle dries up, the water becomes part of the atmosphere again.

Energy in the Earth System

Most of the energy you depend on comes from the Sun and moves among the four major parts of the Earth system. Think again about the puddle that is drying up. Sunlight shines through the water and heats the soil, or geosphere, beneath the puddle. Some of this heat energy goes into the puddle, moving into the hydrosphere. As the water evaporates and becomes part of the atmosphere, it takes the energy that came from the Sun with it. The Sun provides energy for all weather and ocean currents. Without the Sun, life could not exist on Earth's surface.

Why It's Important

Understanding how matter and energy move through the Earth system makes it possible to

- predict how a temperature change in ocean water might affect the weather
- determine how clearing forests might affect rainfall
- explain where organisms on the ocean floor get energy to carry out life processes

UNIFYING PRINCIPLE

Earth has changed over time and continues to change.

You see Earth changing all of the time. Rain turns dirt to mud, and a dry wind turns the mud to dust. Many changes are small and can take hundreds, thousands, or even millions of years to add up to much. Other changes are sudden and can destroy in minutes a house that had stood for many years.

What It Means

Events are always changing Earth's surface. Some events, such as the building or wearing away of mountains, occur over millions of years. Others, such as earthquakes, occur within seconds. A change can affect a small area or even the entire planet.

Records of Change

What was the distant past like? Think about how scientists learn about ancient people. They study what the people left behind and draw conclusions based on the evidence. In a similar way, scientists learn about Earth's past by examining the evidence they find in rock layers and by observing processes now occurring.

By observing that water breaks down rocks and carries the material away to other places, people learned that rivers can slowly carve deep valleys. Evidence from rocks and fossils along the edges of continents shows that all continents were once joined and then moved apart over time. A **fossil** is the trace of a once-living organism. Fossils also show that new types of plants and animals develop, and others, such as dinosaurs, die out.

Change Continues Today

Every year, earthquakes occur, volcanoes erupt, and rivers flood. Continents continue to move slowly. The Himalayan Mountains of Asia push a few millimeters higher. **Climate**—the long-term weather patterns of an area—may also change. Scientists are studying how changes in climates around the world might affect Earth even within this century.

Why It's Important

Understanding the changing Earth makes it possible to

- predict and prepare for events such as volcanic eruptions, landslides, floods, and climate changes
- design buildings to withstand shaking during earthquakes
- protect important environments for plants and animals

The Nature of Science

You may think of science as a body of knowledge or a collection of facts. More important, however, science is an active process that involves certain ways of looking at the world.

Scientific Habits of Mind

Scientists are curious. They ask questions. A scientist who finds an unusual rock by the side of a river would ask questions such as, "Did this rock form in this area?" or "Did this rock form elsewhere and get moved here?" Questions like these make a scientist want to investigate.

Scientists are observant. They look closely at the world around them. A scientist who studies rocks can learn a lot about a rock just by picking it up, looking at its color, and feeling how heavy it is.

Scientists are creative. They draw on what they know to form possible explanations for a pattern, an event, or an interesting phenomenon that they have observed. Then scientists put together a plan for testing their ideas.

Scientists are skeptical. Scientists don't accept an explanation or answer unless it is based on evidence and logical reasoning. They continually question their own conclusions as well as the conclusions suggested by other scientists. Scientists only trust evidence that can be confirmed by other people or other methods.

Scientists use seismographs to observe and measure vibrations that move through the ground.

This scientist is collecting a sample of melted rock from a hot lava flow in Hawaii.

Science Processes at Work

You can think of science as a continuous cycle of asking and seeking answers to questions about the world. Although there are many processes that scientists use, all scientists typically do the following:

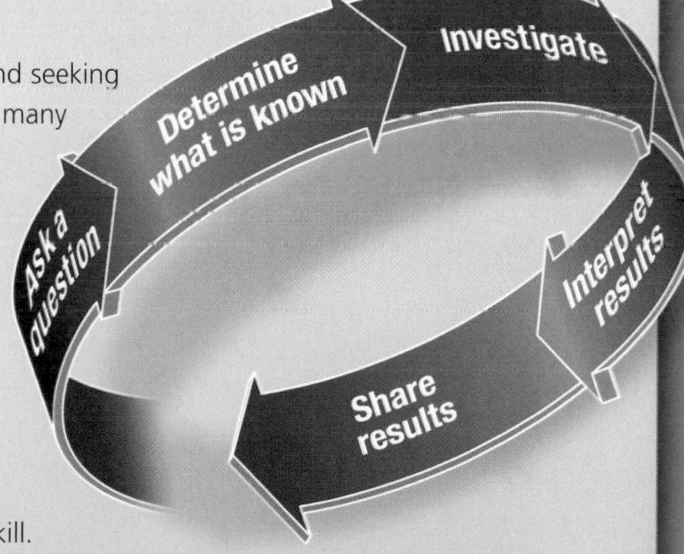

- Observe and ask a question
- Determine what is known
- Investigate
- Interpret results
- Share results

Observe and Ask a Question

It may surprise you that asking questions is an important skill. A scientific investigation may start when a scientist asks a question. Perhaps scientists observe an event or a process that they don't understand, or perhaps answering one question leads to another.

Determine What Is Known

When beginning an inquiry, scientists find out what is already known about a question. They study results from other scientific investigations, read journals, and talk with other scientists. The scientist who is trying to figure out where an unusual rock came from will study maps that show what types of rocks are already known to be in the area where the rock was found.

Investigate

Investigating is the process of collecting evidence. Two important ways of doing this are experimenting and observing.

An **experiment** is an organized procedure to study something under controlled conditions. For example, the scientist who found the rock by the river might notice that it is lighter in color where it is chipped. The scientist might design an experiment to determine why the rock is a different color on the inside. The scientist could break off a small piece of the inside of the rock and heat it up to see if it becomes the same color as the outside. The scientist would need to use a piece of the same rock that is being studied. A different rock might react differently to heat.

A scientist may use photography to study fast events, such as multiple flashes of lightning.

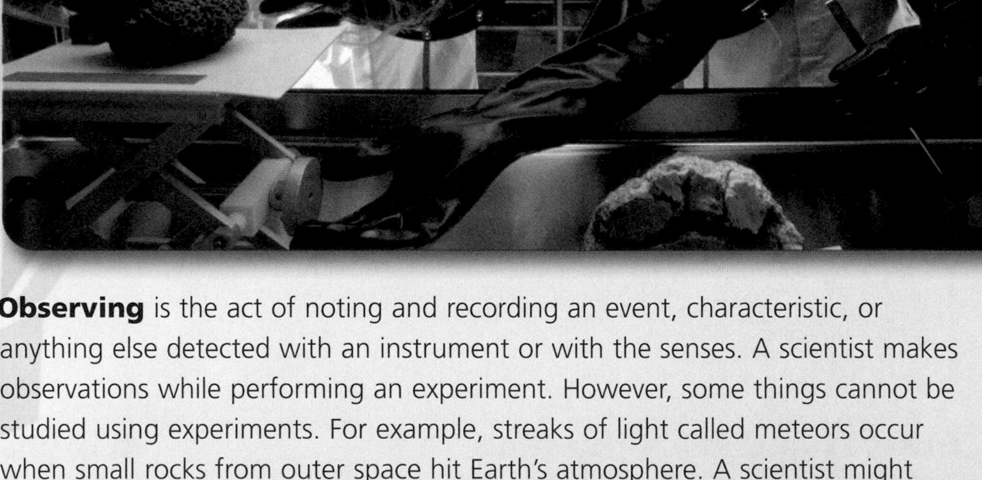

Rocks, such as this one from the Moon, can be subjected to different conditions in a laboratory.

Observing is the act of noting and recording an event, characteristic, or anything else detected with an instrument or with the senses. A scientist makes observations while performing an experiment. However, some things cannot be studied using experiments. For example, streaks of light called meteors occur when small rocks from outer space hit Earth's atmosphere. A scientist might study meteors by taking pictures of the sky at a time when meteors are likely to occur.

Forming hypotheses and making predictions are two other skills involved in scientific investigations. A **hypothesis** is a tentative explanation for an observation or a scientific problem that can be tested by further investigation. For example, the scientist might make the following hypothesis about the rock from the beach:

The rock is a meteorite, which is a rock that fell to the ground from outer space. The outside of the rock changed color because it was heated up from passing through Earth's atmosphere.

A **prediction** is an expectation of what will be observed or what will happen. To test the hypothesis that the rock's outside is black because it is a meteorite, the scientist might predict that a close examination of the rock will show that it has many characteristics in common with rocks that are already known to be meteorites.

Interpret Results

As scientists investigate, they analyze their evidence, or data, and begin to draw conclusions. **Analyzing data** involves looking at the evidence gathered through observations or experiments and trying to identify any patterns that might exist in the data. Scientists often need to make additional observations or perform more experiments before they are sure of their conclusions. Many times scientists make new predictions or revise their hypotheses.

Scientists use computers to gather and interpret data.

Scientists make images such as this computer drawing of a landscape to help share their results with others.

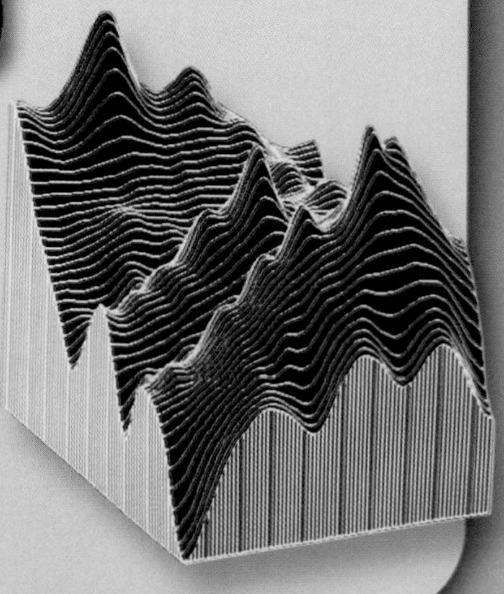

Share Results

An important part of scientific investigation is sharing results of experiments. Scientists read and publish in journals and attend conferences to communicate with other scientists around the world. Sharing data and procedures gives scientists a way to test each others' results. They also share results with the public through newspapers, television, and other media.

The Nature of Technology

When you think of technology, you may think of cars, computers, and cell phones. Imagine having no refrigerator or radio. It's difficult to think of a world without the products of what we call technology. Technology, however, is more than just devices that make our daily activities easier. Technology is the process of using scientific knowledge to design solutions to real-world problems.

Science and Technology

Science and technology go hand in hand. Each depends upon the other. Even a device as simple as a thermometer is designed using knowledge of the ways different materials respond to changes in temperature. In turn, thermometers have allowed scientists to learn more about the world. Greater knowledge of how materials respond to changes in temperature helped engineers to build items such as refrigerators. They have also built thermometers that could be read automatically by computers. New technologies lead to new scientific knowledge and new scientific knowledge leads to even better technologies.

The Process of Technological Design

The process of technological design involves many choices. What, for example, should be done to protect the residents of an area prone to severe storms such as tornadoes and hurricanes? Build stronger homes that can withstand the winds? Try to develop a way to detect the storms long before they occur? Or learn more about hurricanes in order to find new ways to protect people from the dangers? The steps people take to solve the problem depend a great deal on what they already know about the problem as well as what can reasonably be done. As you learn about the steps in the process of technological design, think about the different choices that could be made at each step.

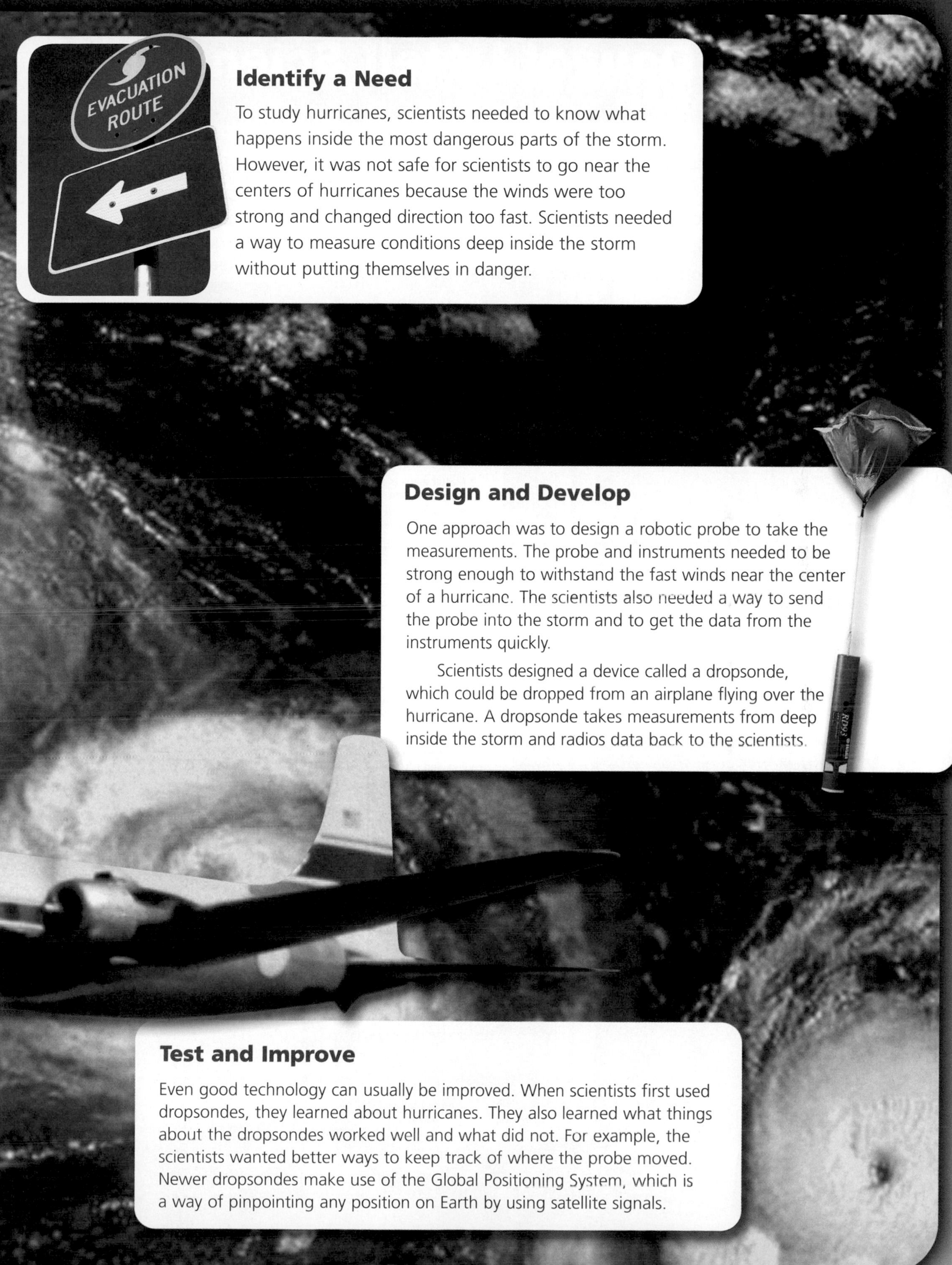

Identify a Need

To study hurricanes, scientists needed to know what happens inside the most dangerous parts of the storm. However, it was not safe for scientists to go near the centers of hurricanes because the winds were too strong and changed direction too fast. Scientists needed a way to measure conditions deep inside the storm without putting themselves in danger.

Design and Develop

One approach was to design a robotic probe to take the measurements. The probe and instruments needed to be strong enough to withstand the fast winds near the center of a hurricane. The scientists also needed a way to send the probe into the storm and to get the data from the instruments quickly.

Scientists designed a device called a dropsonde, which could be dropped from an airplane flying over the hurricane. A dropsonde takes measurements from deep inside the storm and radios data back to the scientists.

Test and Improve

Even good technology can usually be improved. When scientists first used dropsondes, they learned about hurricanes. They also learned what things about the dropsondes worked well and what did not. For example, the scientists wanted better ways to keep track of where the probe moved. Newer dropsondes make use of the Global Positioning System, which is a way of pinpointing any position on Earth by using satellite signals.

Using McDougal Littell Science

Reading Text and Visuals

This book is organized to help you learn. Use these boxed pointers as a path to help you learn and remember the **Big Ideas** and **Key Concepts**.

Take notes.

Use the strategies on the **Getting Ready to Learn** page.

Read the Big Idea.

As you read **Key Concepts** for the chapter, relate them to **the Big Idea.**

CHAPTER 2 Mi

the BIG idea

Minerals are basic building blocks of Earth.

Key Concepts

SECTION 2.1 **Minerals are all around us.** Learn about the characteristics all minerals share.

SECTION 2.2 **A mineral is identified by its properties.** Learn how to identify minerals by observing and testing their properties.

SECTION 2.3 **Minerals are valuable resources.** Learn how minerals form, how they are mined, and how they are used.

Internet Preview

CLASSZONE.COM

Chapter 2 online resources: Content Review, Visualization, three Resource Centers, Math Tutorial, Test Practice

A 40 Unit: Earth's Surface

CHAPTER 2

Getting Ready to Learn

CONCEPT REVIEW

- Earth has four main layers: crust, mantle, outer core, and inner core.
- Matter exists in the forms of gas, liquid, and solid.
- People use maps to show many different features of Earth.

VOCABULARY REVIEW

atom *See Glossary.*

geosphere p. 12

CONTENT REVIEW

CLASSZONE.COM

Review concepts and vocabulary.

TAKING NOTES

SUPPORTING MAIN IDEAS

Make a chart to show each main idea and the information that supports it. Copy each blue heading. Below each heading, add supporting information, such as reasons, explanations, and examples.

VOCABULARY STRATEGY

Place each vocabulary term at the center of a **description wheel**. On the spokes write some words explaining it.

See the Note-Taking Handbook on pages R45–R51.

SCIENCE NOTEBOOK

Minerals have four characteristics.
Minerals form naturally.
All minerals are solids.
Each mineral is always made of the same element or elements.
All minerals have crystal structures.
formed by all minerals
atoms joined in a repeating 3-D pattern
CRYSTAL

A 42 Unit: Earth's Surface

Read each heading.

See how it fits into the outline of the chapter.

KEY CONCEPT

2.1 Minerals are all around us.

Remember what you know.

Think about concepts you learned earlier and preview what you'll learn now.

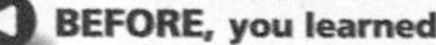

BEFORE, you learned
- Earth is made of layers
- Earth's outermost rocky layer is the crust

NOW, you will learn
- What the characteristics of minerals are
- How minerals are classified into groups
- Which mineral group is most common

VOCABULARY
mineral p. 43
element p. 45
crystal p. 46

Try the activities.

They will introduce you to science concepts.

EXPLORE Minerals

What are some characteristics of a mineral?

PROCEDURE

1. Sprinkle some table salt on a sheet of colored paper. Look at a few grains of the salt through a magnifying glass. Then rub a few grains between your fingers.
2. In your notebook, describe all the qualities of the salt that you observe.
3. Examine the rock salt in the same way and describe its qualities in your notebook. How do the two differ?

MATERIALS
- colored paper
- table salt
- rock salt
- magnifying glass

WHAT DO YOU THINK?
Salt is a mineral. From your observations of salt, what do you think are some characteristics of minerals?

Minerals have four characteristics.

You use minerals all the time. Every time you turn on a microwave oven or a TV, you depend on minerals. The copper in the wires that carry electricity to the device is a mineral. Table salt, or halite (HAYL-YT), is another mineral that you use in your everyday life.

Minerals have four characteristics. A **mineral** is a substance that
- forms in nature
- is a solid
- has a definite chemical makeup
- has a crystal structure

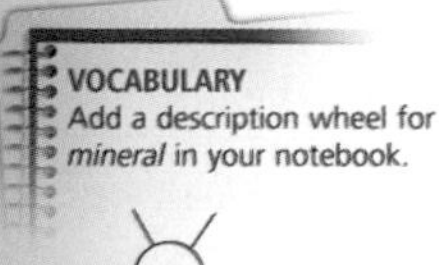

VOCABULARY
Add a description wheel for *mineral* in your notebook.

Learn the vocabulary.

Take notes on each term.

Reading Text and Visuals

Study the visuals.

- Read the title.
- Read all labels and captions.
- Figure out what the picture is showing. Notice colors, arrows, and lines.

Minerals in Rocks

Most rocks are made up of minerals.

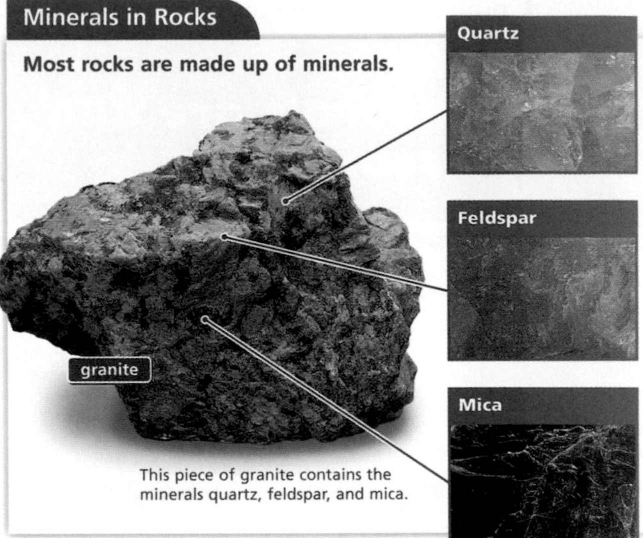

This piece of granite contains the minerals quartz, feldspar, and mica.

Answer the questions.

Check Your Reading questions will help you remember what you read.

You might think that minerals and rocks are the same things. But a mineral must have the four characteristics listed on page 43. A rock has only two of these characteristics—it is a solid and it forms naturally. A rock usually contains two or more types of minerals.

READING TIP
Proportions show relationships between amounts. For example, a quartz crystal always has two oxygen atoms for every silicon atom.

Two samples of the same type of rock may vary greatly in the amounts of different minerals they contain. Minerals, however, are always made up of the same materials in the same proportions. A ruby is a mineral. Therefore, a ruby found in India has the same makeup as a ruby found in Australia.

CHECK YOUR READING How are minerals different from rocks?

Read one paragraph at a time.

Look for a topic sentence that explains the main idea of the paragraph. Figure out how the details relate to that idea. One paragraph might have several important ideas; you may have to reread to understand.

Formed in Nature

Minerals are formed by natural processes. Every type of mineral can form in nature by processes that do not involve living organisms. As you will read, a few minerals can also be produced by organisms as part of their shells or bones.

READING TIP
Molten rock refers to rock that has become so hot that it has melted.

Minerals form in many ways. The mineral halite, which is used as table salt, forms when water evaporates in a hot, shallow part of the ocean, leaving behind the salt it contained. Many types of minerals, including the ones in granite, develop when molten rock cools. Talc, a mineral that can be used to make baby powder, forms deep in Earth as high pressure and temperature cause changes in solid rock.

A 44 Unit: Earth's Surface

Doing Labs

To understand science, you have to see it in action. Doing labs helps you understand how things really work.

① Read the entire lab first.

② Follow the procedure.

③ Record the data.

CHAPTER INVESTIGATION

MATERIALS
• numbered mineral samples
• hand lens
• streak plate
• copper penny
• steel file
• magnet
• dilute hydrochloric acid
• eyedropper
• Mohs scale
• Mineral Identification Key

Mineral Identification

OVERVIEW AND PURPOSE In this activity, you will observe and perform tests on minerals. Then you will compare your observations to a mineral identification key.

Procedure

1 Make a data table like the one shown in the notebook on the next page.

2 You will examine and identify five minerals. Get a numbered mineral sample from the mineral set. Record the number of your sample in your table.

3 First, observe the sample. Note the color and the luster of the sample. Write your observations in your table. In the row labeled "Luster," write metallic if the mineral appears shiny like metal. Write nonmetallic if the sample does not look like metal. For example, it may look glassy, pearly, or dull.

step 3

4 Observe the sample through the hand lens. Look to see any signs of how the crystals in the mineral broke. If it appears that the crystals have broken along straight lines, put a check in the row labeled "Cleavage." If it appears that the sample has fractured, put a check in the appropriate row of your table.

step 4

5 CAUTION: Keep the streak plate on your desktop or table while you are doing the streak test. A broken streak plate can cause serious cuts. Rub the mineral sample on the streak plate. If the sample does not leave a mark, the mineral is harder than the streak plate. Write no in the row labeled "Streak." If the sample does leave a mark on the streak plate, write the color of the streak in that row.

step 5

A 58 Unit: Earth's Surface

6 Test each sample for its hardness on the Mohs scale. Try to scratch the sample with each of these items in order: a fingernail, a copper penny, and a steel file. In the Mohs scale, find the hardness number of the object that first scratches the sample. Write in the table that the mineral's hardness value is between that of the hardest item that did not scratch the sample and that of the item that did scratch it.

7 Test the sample with the magnet. If the magnet is attracted to the sample, put a check in the row labeled "Magnetic."

step 7

8 Repeat steps 2 through 7 for each of the other numbered samples.

Observe and Analyze
Write It Up

1. INTERPRET DATA Use the Mineral Identification Key and the information in your data table to identify your samples. Write the names of the minerals in your table.

2. COLLECT DATA CAUTION: Before doing the acid test, put on your safety glasses, protective gloves, and lab apron. Acids can cause burns. If you identified one of the samples as a carbonate mineral, such as calcite, you can check your identification with the acid test. Use the eyedropper to put a few drops of dilute hydrochloric acid on the mineral. If the acid bubbles, the sample is a carbonate.

Conclude
Write It Up

1. COMPARE AND CONTRAST How are the minerals calcite and halite alike? Which property can you use to test whether a sample is calcite or halite?

2. INTERPRET Look at the data in your table. Name any minerals that you could identify on the basis of a single property.

3. APPLY Examine a piece of granite rock. On the basis of your examination of granite and your observations of the samples, try to determine what the light-colored, translucent mineral in the granite is and what the flaky, darker mineral is.

INVESTIGATE Further

Specific gravity is another property used to identify minerals. The specific gravity of a mineral is determined by comparing the mineral's density with the density of water.

Find the specific gravity of an unknown mineral chosen from your teacher's samples. Attach your mineral with a string to a spring scale. Record its mass and label this value M1. Then suspend the mineral in a beaker of water. Record the measurement of the mineral's mass in water. Label this value M2. To determine the mineral's specific gravity, use the following equation:

M1 / (M1 − M2) = specific gravity

Do all the other steps to identify the sample. Does the specific gravity you measured match the one listed for that mineral in the identification key?

Mineral Identification
Table 1. Mineral Properties
Property
Sample Number
1 2 3 4 5
Color
Luster
Cleavage
Fracture
Streak
Hardness
Magnetic
Acid test
Name of mineral

Chapter 2: Minerals 59 A

④ Analyze your results.

⑤ Write your lab report.

Using Technology

The Internet is a great source of information about up-to-date science. The ClassZone Website and SciLinks have exciting sites for you to explore. Video clips and simulations can make science come alive.

Look for red banners.

Go to **ClassZone.com** to see simulations, visualizations, resources centers, and content review.

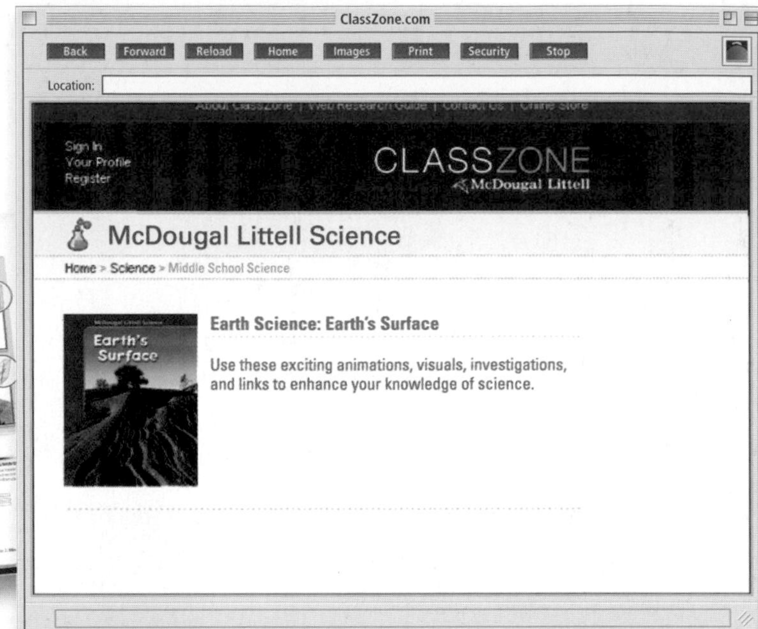

Watch the videos.

See science at work in the **Scientific American Frontiers video.**

Look up SciLinks.

Go to **scilinks.org** to explore the topic.

Earth's Spheres **Code: MDL013**

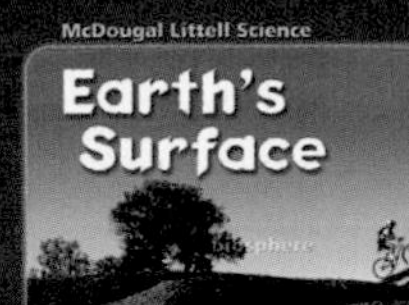

Earth's Surface Contents Overview

Unit Features

FRONTIERS IN SCIENCE Remote Sensing 2
TIMELINES IN SCIENCE History of the Earth System 108

1 Views of Earth Today 6

the BIG idea

Modern technology has changed the way we view and map Earth.

2 Minerals 40

the BIG idea

Minerals are basic building blocks of Earth.

3 Rocks 72

the BIG idea

Rocks change into other rocks over time.

4 Weathering and Soil Formation 112

the BIG idea

Natural forces break rocks apart and form soil, which supports life.

5 Erosion and Deposition 142

the BIG idea

Water, wind, and ice shape Earth's surface.

REMOTE SENSING

Technology high above Earth's surface is giving scientists a whole new look at our planet. This image is of Jasper Ridge, near Palo Alto, California.

SCIENTIFIC AMERICAN FRONTIERS

View the video segment "All That Glitters" to learn how explorers use remote sensing and other methods to find valuable materials.

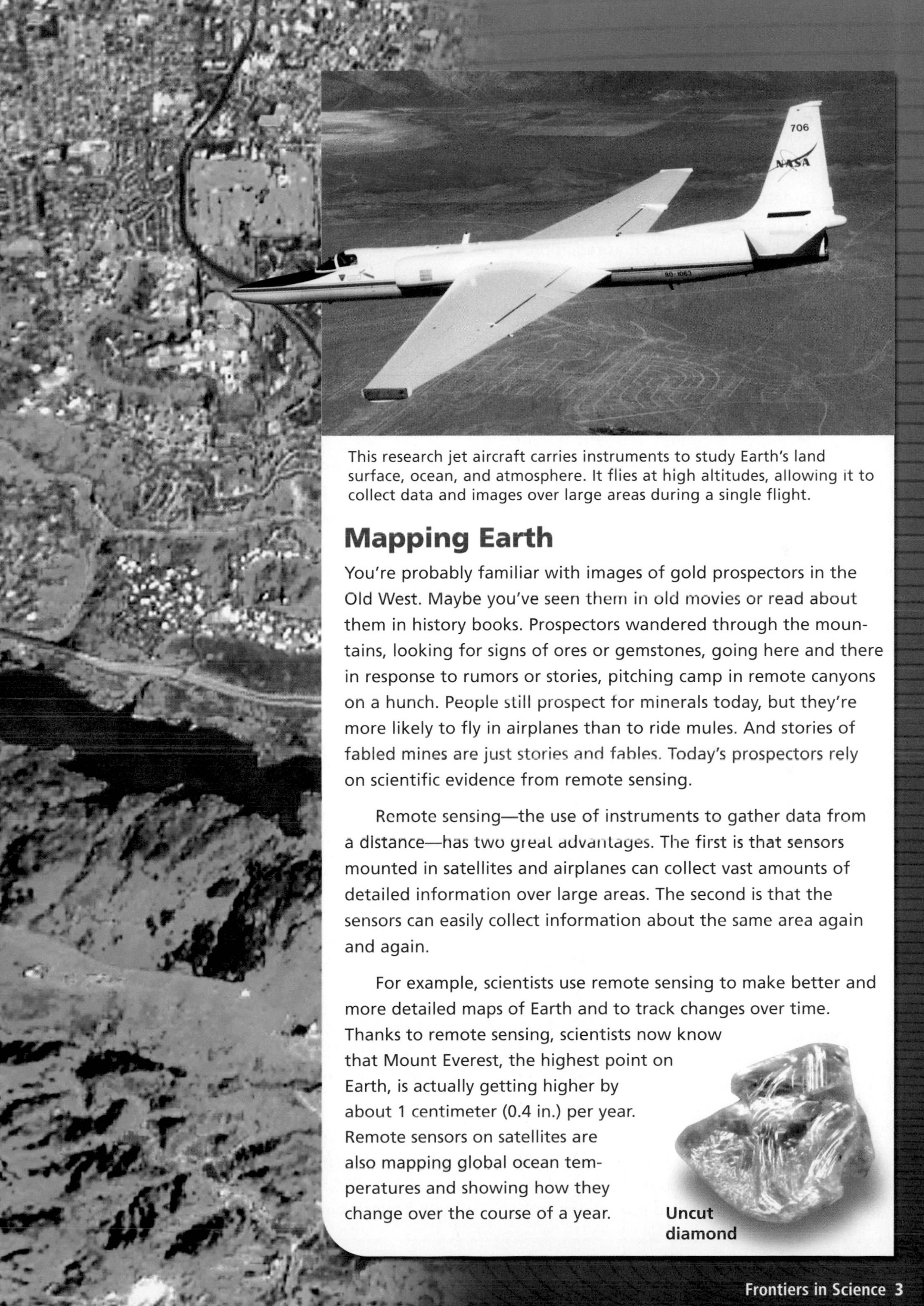

This research jet aircraft carries instruments to study Earth's land surface, ocean, and atmosphere. It flies at high altitudes, allowing it to collect data and images over large areas during a single flight.

Mapping Earth

You're probably familiar with images of gold prospectors in the Old West. Maybe you've seen them in old movies or read about them in history books. Prospectors wandered through the mountains, looking for signs of ores or gemstones, going here and there in response to rumors or stories, pitching camp in remote canyons on a hunch. People still prospect for minerals today, but they're more likely to fly in airplanes than to ride mules. And stories of fabled mines are just stories and fables. Today's prospectors rely on scientific evidence from remote sensing.

Remote sensing—the use of instruments to gather data from a distance—has two great advantages. The first is that sensors mounted in satellites and airplanes can collect vast amounts of detailed information over large areas. The second is that the sensors can easily collect information about the same area again and again.

For example, scientists use remote sensing to make better and more detailed maps of Earth and to track changes over time. Thanks to remote sensing, scientists now know that Mount Everest, the highest point on Earth, is actually getting higher by about 1 centimeter (0.4 in.) per year. Remote sensors on satellites are also mapping global ocean temperatures and showing how they change over the course of a year.

Uncut diamond

Detecting Minerals from Above

One of the many uses of remote sensing is to find new sources of valuable minerals, such as diamonds. To detect minerals from airplanes or satellites, remote sensors make use of the energy in sunlight. Sunlight reaches Earth as radiation, which travels in the form of waves. All objects absorb some types of radiation and reflect others. The particular wavelengths absorbed or reflected depend upon the materials that make up the objects. Each kind of material has a unique "fingerprint" of the wavelengths it absorbs and the wavelengths it reflects.

Energy from the Sun reflects at different wavelengths from materials at Earth's surface. Instruments on the jet analyze the reflected energy and map the surface.

When sunlight strikes Earth's surface, some of it is reflected back into the sky. Some of the radiation is absorbed by rocks and other objects and then emitted, or given off, in a different form. Remote sensors in airplanes and satellites collect the reflected and emitted radiation and analyze it to determine which types of rocks and minerals lie on the surface. The remote sensing systems collect so much data that computer processing and analysis are difficult and expensive. Still, the data are usually clear enough to show the types of minerals located in the regions scanned. However, minerals that are buried cannot be detected by remote sensing from aircraft or satellites. The sensors receive only energy from or near the surface.

SCIENTIFIC AMERICAN FRONTIERS

View the "All that Glitters" segment of your *Scientific American Frontiers* video to see how finding certain common minerals can indicate the presence of a valuable mineral like diamond.

IN THIS SCENE FROM THE VIDEO **a mineral prospector searches for diamonds in a cylinder of rock drilled from beneath Earth's surface.**

SEARCHING FOR DIAMONDS People used to think that North America did not have many diamonds. However, northern Canada is geologically similar to the world's major diamond-producing areas: southern Africa, Russia, and Australia. A few diamond prospectors kept searching, using remote sensing and other techniques. The prospectors looked for more common minerals that form under the same conditions as diamonds. They made maps showing where these minerals were most plentiful and used the maps to search for diamond-rich rock. Once the prospectors realized that the glaciers of the last ice age had moved the minerals, they looked for and found diamonds farther northward. Canada is now a big producer of diamonds.

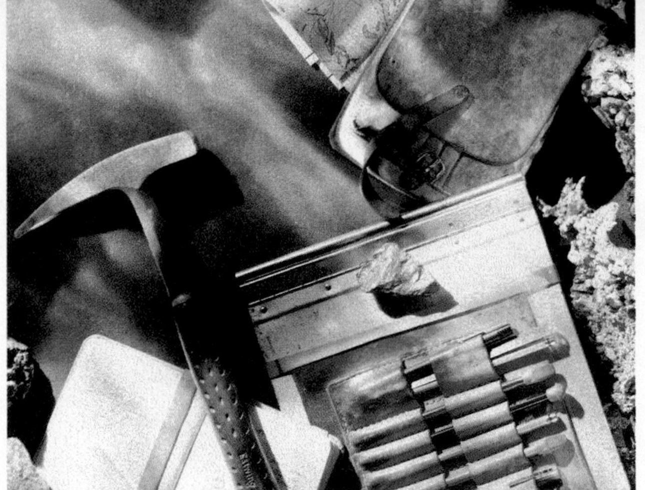

Remote sensing can show the presence of minerals that occur with diamonds, but people must still use older methods to collect samples for further analysis.

Prospecting for Diamonds

One of the major regions of mineral exploration in which remote sensing is used is in the Northwest Territories of Canada, where the first diamond mine began operating in 1998. The Canada Centre for Remote Sensing has helped develop sensing equipment that can fit easily onto light airplanes and computer equipment to analyze results quickly. The sensing equipment is used to detect certain types of minerals that are often found along with diamonds.

Using remote sensing to locate minerals associated with diamonds or valuable ores is only a beginning. The data cannot show how far the minerals or ores extend underground. Prospectors must still explore the area and take samples. However, remote sensing gives mineral prospectors an excellent idea of where to start looking.

UNANSWERED Questions

As scientists use remote sensing to study Earth's land surface, ocean, and atmosphere, they work to answer new questions.

- Can remote sensing be used to locate sources of iron, platinum, or gold in areas that are difficult to explore on foot?
- How do changes in water temperature at the ocean surface affect long-range weather patterns and the health of ocean organisms?
- How do different types of clouds affect the amount of sunlight reaching Earth's surface and the average temperature of the surface?

UNIT PROJECTS

As you study this unit, work alone or with a group on one of the projects listed below.

Hiker's Guide Video

Like prospectors, wilderness hikers must be able to read maps that show the shape of the land. Prepare a video to teach hikers how to choose hiking and camping areas by reading maps.

- Obtain a topographic map of a wilderness area in a national or state park.
- Write a script outlining what you will teach and how you will videotape it.
- Present your video and display the maps you used.

Diamond Mine Model

Diamonds can be carried toward Earth's surface by kimberlite pipes. Show how diamonds are mined from kimberlite.

- Build a model of a diamond-mine tunnel that passes through kimberlite.
- Present your model to your class. Explain the relationship between kimberlite and diamonds.

Glacier Photo Essay

Make a photo essay showing how glaciers reshape Earth's surface as they move and melt.

- Find images of areas that are or have been affected by glaciers. Write captions for them.
- Present the images as a photo essay on a poster or in a portfolio.

Learn more about careers in mineralogy.

CHAPTER

Views of Earth Today

the BIG idea

Modern technology has changed the way we view and map Earth.

Key Concepts

SECTION

1.1 Technology is used to explore the Earth system.
Learn how technology has changed people's view of Earth.

SECTION

1.2 Maps and globes are models of Earth.
Learn how to locate any place on Earth and how Earth's sphere is portrayed on flat maps.

SECTION

1.3 Topographic maps show the shape of the land.
Learn about representing the features of Earth's surface on flat maps.

SECTION

1.4 Technology is used to map Earth.
Learn how satellites and computers are used to provide more detailed maps of Earth.

Internet Preview

CLASSZONE.COM

Chapter 1 online resources: Content Review, Simulation, Visualization, three Resource Centers, Math Tutorial, and Test Practice

What do all these views show about Earth?

Swirling clouds over North and South America: NASA Terra satellite data

Warm and cool ocean-surface temperatures: NASA satellite image

Chlorophyll levels (green) on land and sea: SeaStar spacecraft image

Earth's rocky surface without the oceans: NASA satellite data

EXPLORE the BIG idea

Earth's Changing Surface

Go outside and find evidence of how wind, water, or living things change the surface of Earth. You might look in alleyways, parks, wooded areas, or backyards. For example, you might find a path worn through a grassy area near a parking lot.

Observe and Think What changes do you observe? What do you think caused the changes?

Using Modern Maps

Find a map of a city, a bus or rail system, or a state. Study the names, colors, and symbols on the map and any features of interest.

Observe and Think Which direction on the map is north? What do the symbols mean? How do you measure the distance from one point to another?

Internet Activity: Mapping

Go to **ClassZone.com** to learn more about mapping Earth from space. Find out about a NASA mission to develop the most accurate map of Earth ever made.

Observe and Think Why do you think scientists need different maps produced from satellite data?

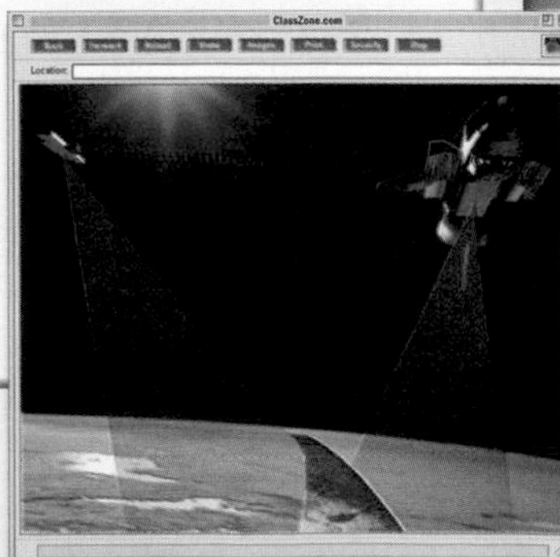

Earth's Spheres Code: MDL013

CHAPTER 1

Getting Ready to Learn

CONCEPT REVIEW

- Earth, like all planets, is shaped roughly like a sphere.
- Earth supports a complex web of life.
- The planet consists of many parts that interact with one another.

VOCABULARY REVIEW

See Glossary for definitions.

energy

matter

planet

satellite

CONTENT REVIEW

CLASSZONE.COM

Review concepts and vocabulary.

TAKING NOTES

MAIN IDEA AND DETAIL NOTES

Make a two-column chart. Write the main ideas, such as those in the blue headings, in the column on the left. Write details about each of those main ideas in the column on the right.

VOCABULARY STRATEGY

Draw a **word triangle** diagram for each new vocabulary term. On the bottom line write and define the term. Above that, write a sentence that uses the term correctly. At the top, draw a picture to show what the term looks like.

See the Note-Taking Handbook on pages R45–R51.

SCIENCE NOTEBOOK

MAIN IDEAS	DETAIL NOTES
1. The Earth system has four main parts.	1. Atmosphere = mixture of gases surrounding Earth 1. Hydrosphere = all waters on Earth

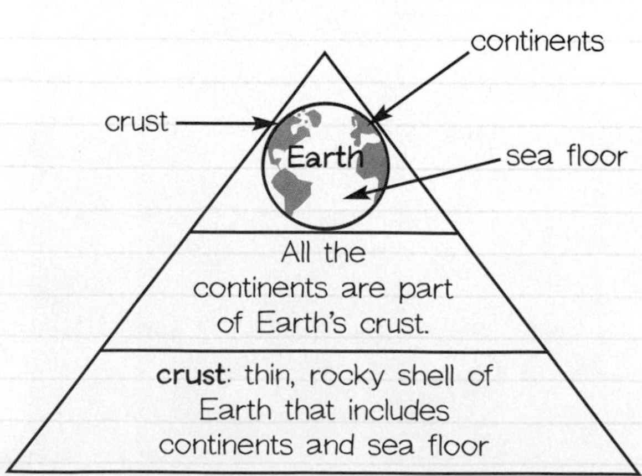

continents
crust
Earth
sea floor
All the continents are part of Earth's crust.
crust: thin, rocky shell of Earth that includes continents and sea floor

KEY CONCEPT

Technology is used to explore the Earth system.

BEFORE, you learned

- Earth has a spherical shape and supports a complex web of life
- Earth's environment is a system with many parts

NOW, you will learn

- About the Earth system and its four major parts
- How technology is used to explore the Earth system
- How the parts of the Earth system shape the surface

VOCABULARY

system p. 9
atmosphere p. 10
hydrosphere p. 10
biosphere p. 11
geosphere p. 12

THINK ABOUT

How do these parts work together?

Look closely at this terrarium. Notice that the bowl and its cover form a boundary between the terrarium and the outside world. What might happen to the entire terrarium if any part were taken away? What might happen if you placed the terrarium in a dark closet?

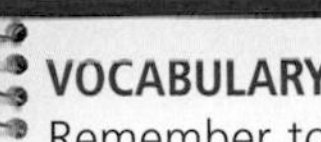

VOCABULARY
Remember to draw a word triangle in your notebook for each vocabulary term.

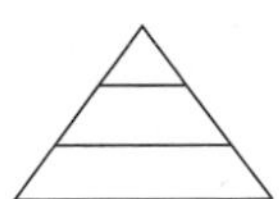

The Earth system has four major parts.

A terrarium is a simple example of a **system** —an organized group of parts that work together to form a whole. To understand a system, you need to see how all its parts work together. This principle is true for a small terrarium, and it is true for planet Earth.

Both a terrarium and Earth are closed systems. They are closed because matter, such as soil or water, cannot enter or leave. However, energy can flow into or out of the system. Just as light and heat pass through the glass of the terrarium, sunlight and heat enter and leave the Earth system through the atmosphere.

Within the Earth system are four connected parts: the atmosphere (Earth's air), the hydrosphere (Earth's waters), the biosphere (Earth's living things), and the geosphere (Earth's interior and its rocks and soils). Each of these parts is an open system because both matter and energy move into and out of it. The four open systems work together to form one large, closed system called Earth.

Atmosphere

READING TIP

The names of the Earth system's four parts contain Greek prefixes. *Atmo-* refers to vapor or gas. *Hydro-* refers to water. *Bio-* refers to life, and *geo-* refers to earth.

The **atmosphere** (AT-muh-SFEER) is the mixture of gases and particles that surrounds and protects the surface of Earth. The most abundant gases are nitrogen (about 78%) and oxygen (nearly 21%). The atmosphere also contains carbon dioxide, water vapor, and a few other gases.

Before the 1800s, all studies of the atmosphere had to be done from the ground. Today, scientists launch weather balloons, fly specially equipped planes, and view the atmosphere in satellite images. The data they collect show that the atmosphere interacts with the other parts of the Earth system to form complex weather patterns that circulate around Earth. The more scientists learn about these patterns, the more accurately they can predict local weather.

Hydrosphere

The **hydrosphere** (HY-druh-SFEER) is made up of all the water on Earth in oceans, lakes, glaciers, rivers, and streams and underground. Water covers nearly three-quarters of Earth's surface. Only about 3 percent of the hydrosphere is fresh water. Nearly 70 percent of Earth's fresh water is frozen in glaciers and polar ice caps.

Over 400 cones make this weather balloon more stable as it gathers data about the atmosphere.

Scientists need special diving equipment to study Earth's oceans.

In the past 50 years, scientists have used deep-sea vehicles, special buoys, satellite images, and diving suits, such as the one shown on page 10, to study the world's oceans. They have discovered that the oceans contain several layers of cold and warm water. As these layers circulate, they form cold and warm ocean currents. The currents interact with wind patterns in the atmosphere and affect Earth's weather.

How does the hydrosphere affect the atmosphere?

Biosphere

The **biosphere** (BY-uh-SFEER) includes all life on Earth, in the air, on the land, and in the waters. The biosphere can be studied with a variety of technologies. For example, satellite photos are used to track yearly changes in Earth's plant and animal life. As the photograph below shows, special equipment allows scientists to study complex environments, such as rain forests, without damaging them.

MAIN IDEA AND DETAILS
As you read this section, use this strategy to take notes.

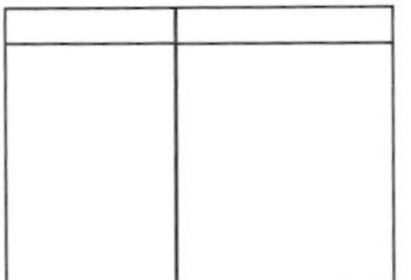

Scientists have learned a lot about how the biosphere interacts with the other parts of the Earth system. For example, large forests act as Earth's "lungs," absorbing carbon dioxide and releasing oxygen into the atmosphere. When dead trees decay, they return nutrients to the soil.

CHECK YOUR READING Name one way the biosphere and the atmosphere interact.

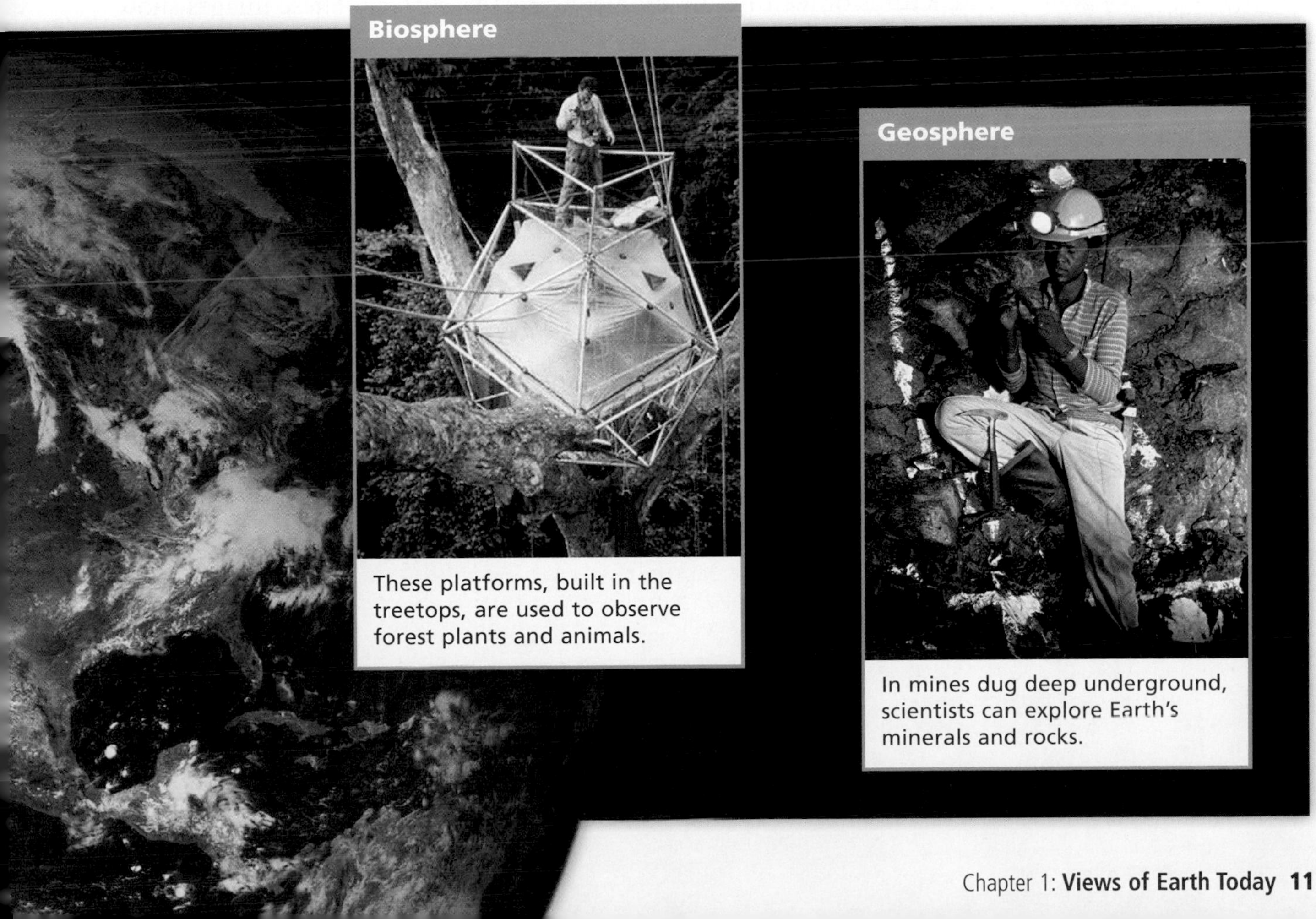

Biosphere

These platforms, built in the treetops, are used to observe forest plants and animals.

Geosphere

In mines dug deep underground, scientists can explore Earth's minerals and rocks.

Geosphere

The **geosphere** (JEE-uh-SFEER) includes all the features on Earth's surface—the continents, islands, and sea floor—and everything below the surface. As the diagram illustrates, the geosphere is made up of several layers: crust, mantle, and outer and inner core.

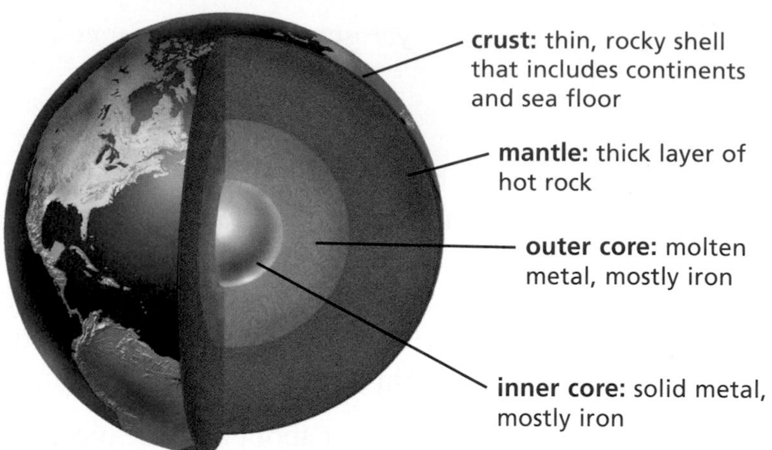
crust: thin, rocky shell that includes continents and sea floor
mantle: thick layer of hot rock
outer core: molten metal, mostly iron
inner core: solid metal, mostly iron

People have studied the surface of the geosphere for centuries. Not until the 1900s, however, were people able to study Earth from space or to explore deep within the planet. Today, scientists use satellite images, sound waves, and computer modeling to develop accurate pictures of features on and below Earth's surface. These images show that Earth constantly changes. Some changes are sudden—a volcano explodes, releasing harmful gases and dust into the air. Other changes, such as the birth of new islands, happen over millions of years.

CHECK YOUR READING Give an example of matter moving from the geosphere to the atmosphere.

Earth's continents have many unique landforms such as these rock towers in Cathedral Valley, Utah.

INVESTIGATE Geosphere's Layers

How can you model the geosphere's layers?

PROCEDURE

1. To model the layers of the geosphere, you will be using a quarter of an apple that your teacher has cut. Note: NEVER eat food in the science classroom.
2. Hold the apple slice and observe it carefully. Compare it with the diagram of the geosphere's layers on page 12.
3. Draw a diagram of the apple and label it with the names of the layers of the geosphere.

WHAT DO YOU THINK?

- What are the four parts of the apple slice?
- What major layer of the geosphere does each part of the apple resemble?

CHALLENGE What other object do you think would make a good model of the geosphere's layers? What model could you build or make yourself?

SKILL FOCUS
Modeling

MATERIALS
apple slice

TIME
15 minutes

All four parts of the Earth system shape the planet's surface.

Earth's surface is worn away, built up, and reshaped every day by the atmosphere, the hydrosphere, the biosphere, and the geosphere. Here are some of the ways they affect the surface.

Atmosphere and Hydrosphere Not even the hardest stone can withstand wind and water. Over millions of years, rain, wind, and flowing water carve huge formations such as the Grand Canyon in Arizona or the rock towers of Utah, shown on page 12.

Geosphere Landmasses pushing together have set off earthquakes and formed volcanoes and mountain ranges around the world.

Biosphere Plants, animals, and human beings have also changed Earth's surface. For instance, earthworms help make soils more fertile. And throughout human history, people have dammed rivers and cleared forests for farmland.

You are part of this process, too. Every time you walk or ride a bike across open land, you are changing Earth's surface. Your feet or the bike's tires dig into the dirt, wearing away plants and exposing soil to sunlight, wind, and water. If you take the same route every day, over time you will wear a path in the land.

READING TIP

Landmass is a compound word made up of the words *land* and *mass*. Landmass means "a large area of land."

Mudslide in California
Atmosphere and Hydrosphere Heavy winter rains soak the ground until it cannot absorb any more water.
Biosphere People who build on fragile hillsides remove plants whose roots help hold the soil in place.
Geosphere With nothing to hold the water-soaked ground, it slides downhill, leaving a deep trench.

The photograph above shows a good example of how the four parts can suddenly change Earth's surface. A mudslide like this one can happen in a matter of minutes. Sometimes the side of a mountain may collapse, becoming a river of mud that can bury an entire town.

The four parts of the Earth system continue to shape the surface with every passing year. Scientists will continue to record these changes to update maps and other images of the planet's complex system.

CHECK YOUR READING Find three examples on pages 13 and 14 that show how the parts of the Earth system shape the planet's surface.

1.1 Review

KEY CONCEPTS

1. Define *system.* Compare an open and a closed system.
2. Name the four parts of the Earth system. List one fact about each part that scientists learned through modern technology.
3. Give two examples of how the Earth system's four parts can interact with each other.

CRITICAL THINKING

4. **Apply** One day you see that plants are dying in the class terrarium. What part might be missing from its system?
5. **Infer** You visit a state park and see a thin rock wall with a hole, like a window, worn through it. Which of the four parts of the Earth system might have made the hole? Explain.

CHALLENGE

6. **Predict** Imagine that a meteorite 200 meters wide strikes Earth, landing in a wooded area. Describe one way that this event would affect the biosphere or the geosphere. **Hint:** A meteorite is traveling several thousand kilometers per hour when it strikes the ground.

KEY CONCEPT

Maps and globes are models of Earth.

BEFORE, you learned

- The Earth system has four main parts: atmosphere, hydrosphere, biosphere, and geosphere
- Technology is used to study and map the Earth system
- The Earth system's parts interact to shape Earth's surface

NOW, you will learn

- What information maps can provide about natural and human-made features
- How to find exact locations on Earth
- Why all maps distort Earth's surface

VOCABULARY

relief map p. 16
map scale p. 17
map legend p. 17
equator p. 18
latitude p. 18
prime meridian p. 19
longitude p. 19
projection p. 20

EXPLORE Mapping

What makes a good map?

PROCEDURE

1. Draw a map to guide someone from your school to your home or to a point of interest, such as a park, statue, or store, near your school.
2. Trade maps with a classmate. Is his or her map easy to understand? Why or why not?
3. Use feedback from your partner to revise your own map.

MATERIALS

- paper
- pencil or pen

WHAT DO YOU THINK?

What visual clues make a map easy to understand and use?

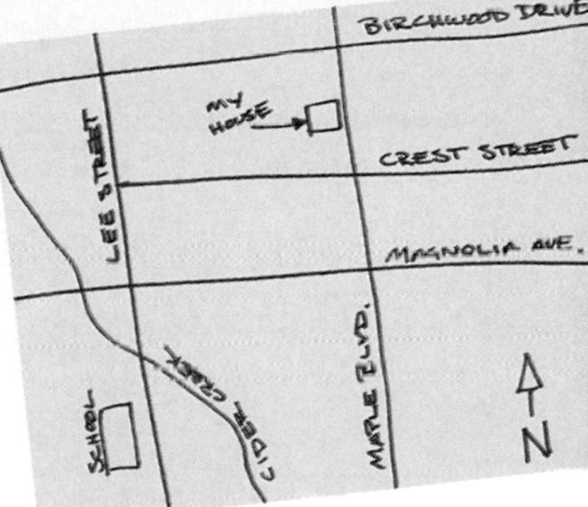

Maps show natural and human-made features.

Have you ever drawn a map to help someone get to your home? If so, your map is actually a rough model of your neighborhood, showing important streets and landmarks. Any map you use is a flat model of Earth's surface, showing Earth's features as seen from above.

On the other hand, a globe represents Earth as if you were looking at it from outer space. A globe is a sphere that shows the relative sizes and shapes of Earth's land features and waters.

In this section you will learn how maps and globes provide different types of information about Earth's surface. They can show everything from city streets to land features to the entire world.

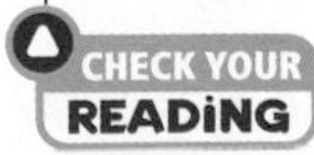

How are maps and globes alike? How are they different?

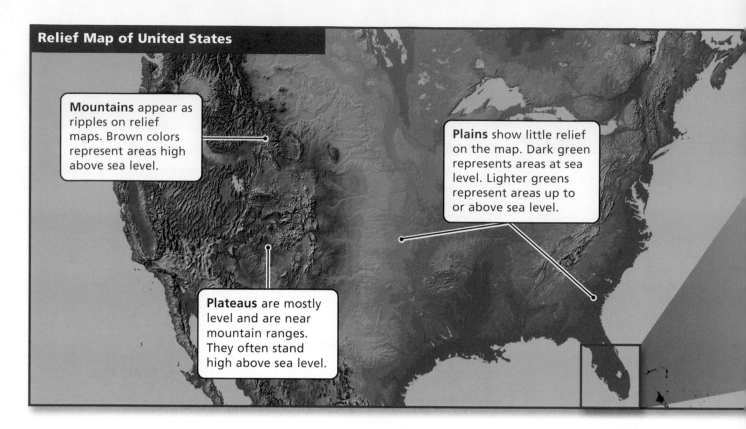

Relief Map of United States

Mountains appear as ripples on relief maps. Brown colors represent areas high above sea level.

Plains show little relief on the map. Dark green represents areas at sea level. Lighter greens represent areas up to or above sea level.

Plateaus are mostly level and are near mountain ranges. They often stand high above sea level.

Land Features on Maps

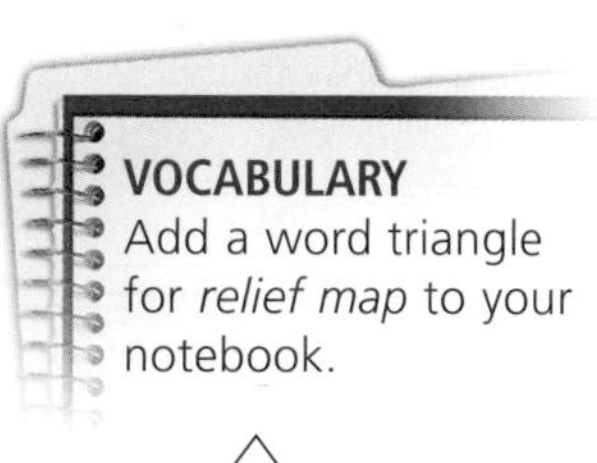

VOCABULARY
Add a word triangle for *relief map* to your notebook.

When scientists or travelers want to know what the landscape of an area actually looks like, they will often use a relief map. A **relief map,** such as the one above, shows how high or low each feature is on Earth. A mapmaker uses photographs or satellite images to build a three-dimensional view of Earth's surface. A relief map shows three main types of land features: mountains, plains, and plateaus.

Mountains stand higher than the land around them. A mountain's base may cover several square kilometers. A group of mountains is called a mountain range. Mountain ranges connected in a long chain form a mountain belt. The Rocky Mountains in the United States are part of a huge mountain belt that includes the Canadian Rockies and the Andes Mountains in South America.

Plateaus have fairly level surfaces but stand high above sea level. Plateaus are often found near large mountain ranges. In the United States, the Colorado Plateau is about 3350 meters (11,000 ft) above sea level. This plateau includes parts of Arizona, Colorado, New Mexico, and Utah.

Plains are gently rolling or flat features. The United States has two types of plains—coastal plains near the eastern and southeastern shores, and interior plains in the center of the nation. The interior Great Plains cover the middle third of the United States.

CHECK YOUR READING How is a plateau different from either a mountain or a plain?

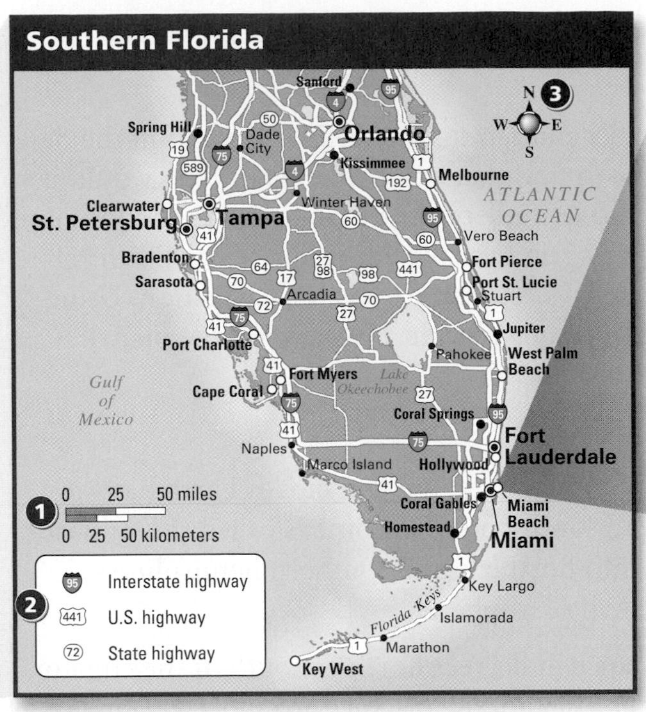

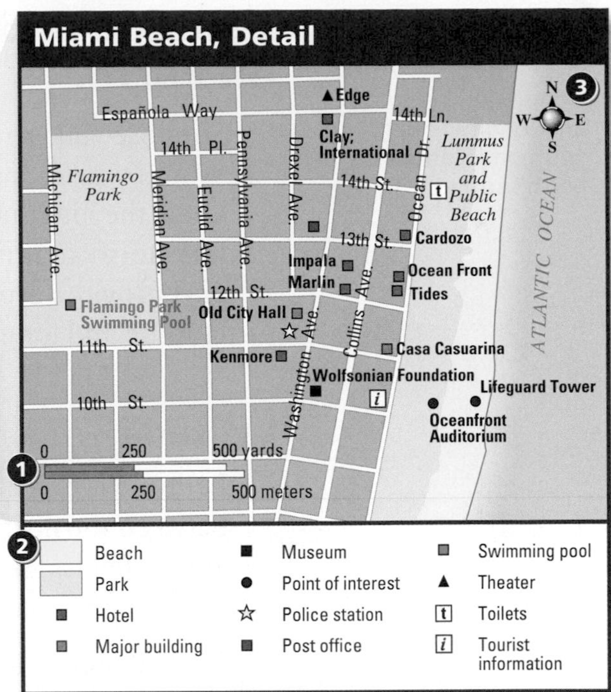

Scale and Symbols on Maps

The maps most people use are road and city maps like the ones above. These maps provide information about human-made features as well as some natural features. To use these maps, you need to know how to read a map scale and a map legend, or key.

1 A **map scale** relates distances on a map to actual distances on Earth's surface. Notice that on the map of southern Florida above, the scale is in kilometers and miles. On the Miami Beach map, the scale is in meters and yards. The smaller the area a map shows, the more detail it includes.

The scale can be expressed as a ratio, a bar, or equivalent units of distance. For example, a ratio of 1:25,000 means that 1 centimeter on the map represents 25,000 centimeters (0.25 kilometer) on Earth.

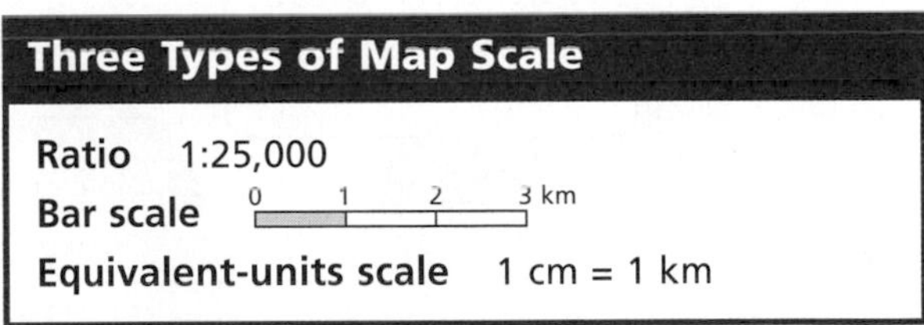

Three Types of Map Scale

Ratio	1:25,000
Bar scale	0 1 2 3 km
Equivalent-units scale	1 cm = 1 km

2 A **map legend,** also called a key, is a chart that explains the meaning of each symbol used on a map. Symbols can stand for highways, parks, and other features. The legend on the Miami Beach map shows major points of interest for tourists.

3 A map usually includes a compass rose to show which directions are north, south, east, and west. In general, north on a map points to the top of the page.

READING TiP

As used here, *legend* does not refer to a story. It is based on the Latin word *legenda,* which means "to be read."

CHECK YOUR READING What information do map scales and map legends provide?

Explore how latitude and longitude help you find locations on Earth's surface.

Latitude and longitude show locations on Earth.

Suppose you were lucky enough to find dinosaur bones in the desert. Would you know how to find that exact spot again? You would if you knew the longitude and latitude of the place. Latitude and longitude lines form an imaginary grid over the entire surface of Earth. This grid provides everyone with the same tools for navigation. Using latitude and longitude, you can locate any place on the planet.

Latitude

READING TIP

Hemi- is a Greek prefix meaning "half."

Latitude is based on an imaginary line that circles Earth halfway between the north and south poles. This line is called the **equator,** and it divides Earth into northern and southern hemispheres. A hemisphere is one half of a sphere.

Latitude is a distance in degrees north or south of the equator, which is 0°. A degree is 1/360 of the distance around a full circle. If you start at one point on the equator and travel all the way around the world back to that point, you have traveled 360 degrees.

The illustration below shows that latitude lines are parallel to the equator and are evenly spaced between the equator and the poles. Also, latitude lines are always labeled north or south of the equator to

Latitude and Longitude

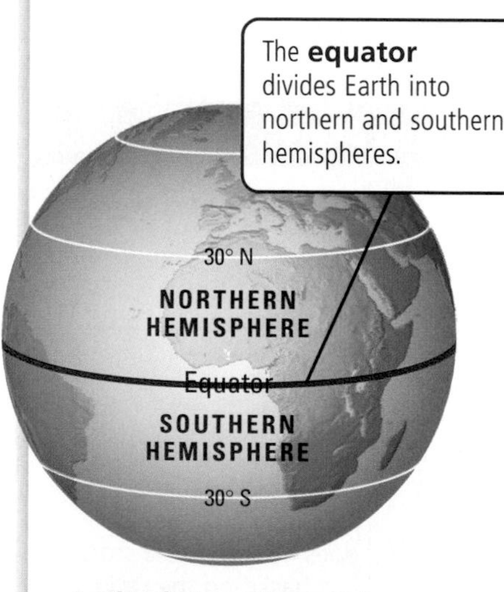

Latitude is a distance in degrees north or south of the equator.

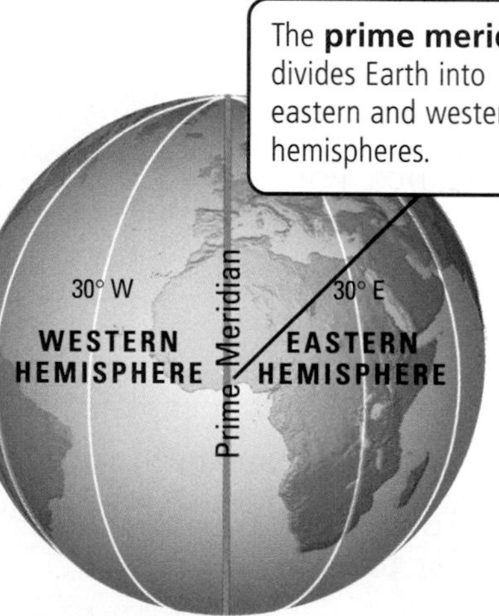

Longitude is a distance in degrees east or west of the prime meridian.

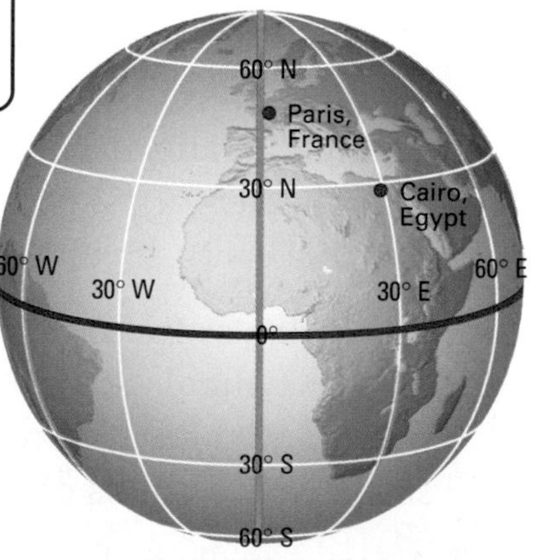

You can find a location by noting where latitude and longitude lines cross.

READING VISUALS What are the approximate latitudes and longitudes of Cairo, Egypt, and Paris, France?

show whether a location is in the northern or southern hemisphere. For instance, the North Pole is 90° north, or 90°N, while the South Pole is 90° south, or 90°S. Latitude, however, is only half of what you need to locate any spot on Earth. You also need to know its longitude.

Longitude

Longitude is based on an imaginary line that stretches from the North Pole through Greenwich, England, to the South Pole. This line is called the **prime meridian.** Any place up to 180° west of the prime meridian is in the Western Hemisphere. Any place up to 180° east of the prime meridian is in the Eastern Hemisphere.

READING TIP

There is an easy way to remember the difference between latitude and longitude. Think of longitude lines as the "long" lines that go from pole to pole.

Longitude is a distance in degrees east or west of the prime meridian, which is 0°. Beginning at the prime meridian, longitude lines are numbered 0° to 180° west and 0° to 180° east.

Longitude lines are labeled east or west to indicate whether a location is in the eastern or western hemisphere. For example, the longitude of Washington, D.C., is about 78° west, or 78°W. The city of Hamburg, Germany, is about 10° east, or 10°E. If you understand latitude and longitude, you can find any spot on Earth's surface.

CHECK YOUR READING: Why do all cities in the United States have a north latitude and a west longitude?

Global Positioning System

The Global Positioning System (GPS) is a network of satellites that are used to find the latitude, longitude, and elevation, or height above sea level, of any site. Twenty-four GPS satellites circle Earth and send signals that are picked up by receivers on the surface. At least three satellites need to be above the horizon for GPS to work. A computer inside a receiver uses the satellite signals to calculate the user's exact location—latitude, longitude, and elevation. GPS is an accurate, easy method for finding location.

GPS devices are used by many people, including pilots, sailors, hikers, and map makers. Some cars now have GPS receivers and digital road maps stored in their computers. A driver types in an address, and the car's computer finds the best way to get there.

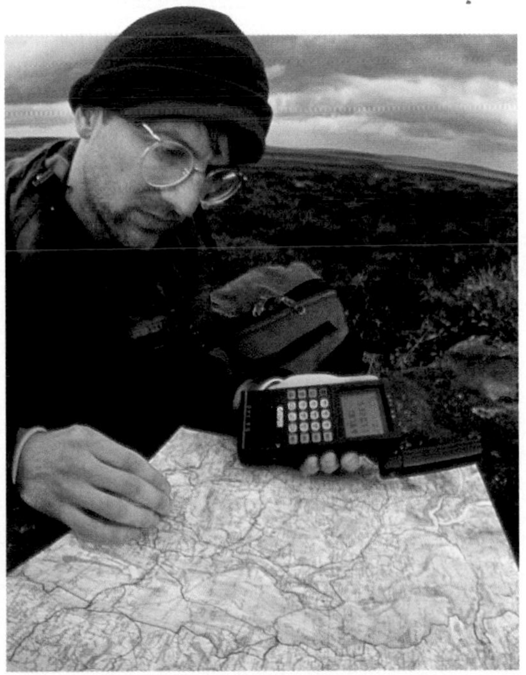

Never be lost again. This hiker turns on his GPS unit to find out his current latitude and longitude. He then locates these data on his map to pinpoint his exact location.

CHECK YOUR READING: Explain how GPS can help someone find their exact location.

Map projections distort the view of Earth's surface.

The most accurate way to show Earth's surface is on a globe. A globe, however, cannot show much detail, and it is awkward to carry. People use flat maps for their detail and convenience. A **projection** is a way of representing Earth's curved surface on a flat map. Mapmakers use different types of projections, all of which distort, or misrepresent, Earth's surface in different ways.

Cylindrical Projection

The Mercator projection shows Earth as if the map were a large cylinder wrapped around the planet. The outlines of the landmasses and seas are then drawn onto the map. As shown in the diagram on page 21, the cylinder is unrolled to form a flat map. Latitude and longitude appear as straight lines, forming a grid of rectangles.

The Mercator projection is useful for navigating at sea or in the air. It shows the entire world, except for regions near the poles, on one map. Sailors and pilots can draw a straight line from one point to

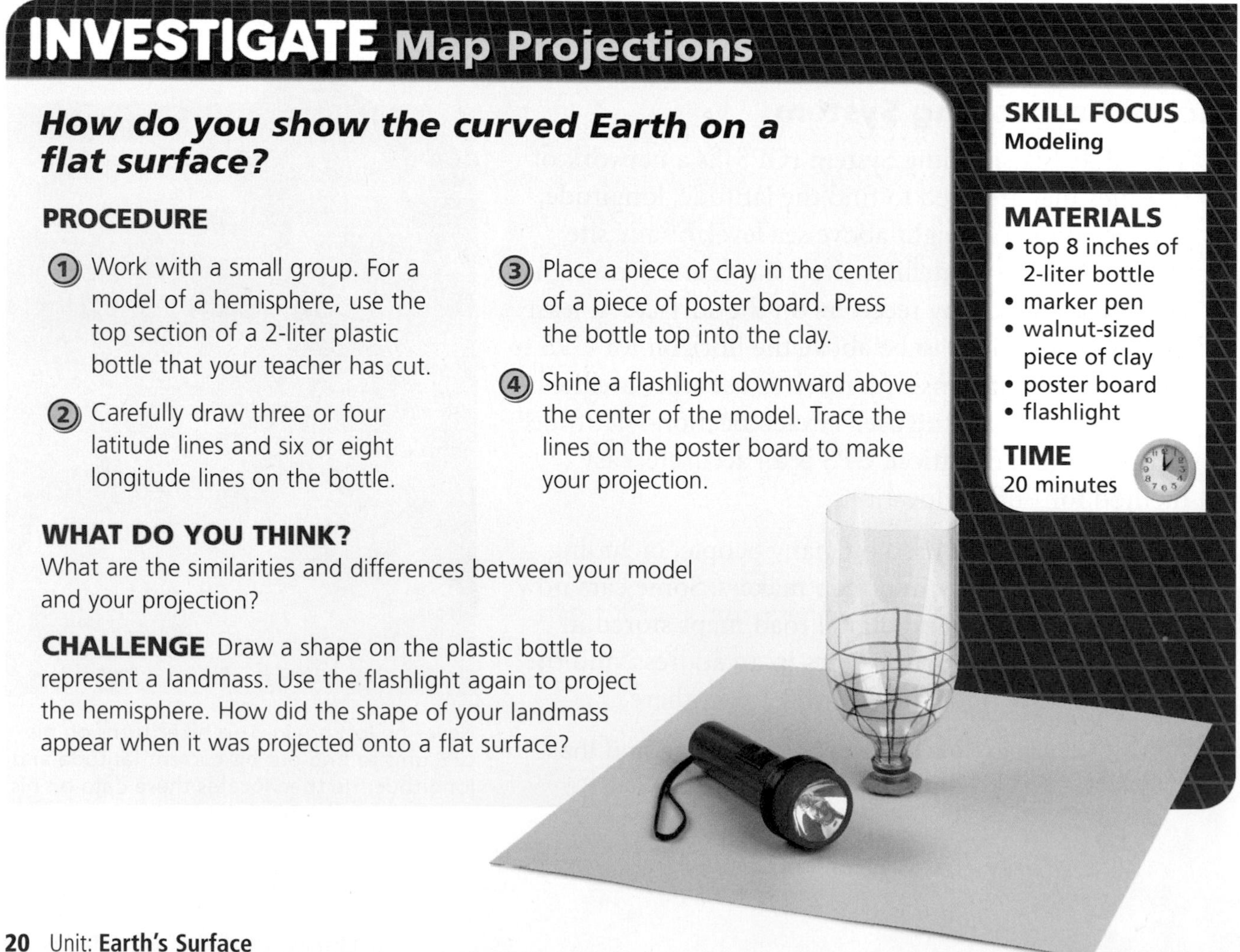

INVESTIGATE Map Projections

How do you show the curved Earth on a flat surface?

PROCEDURE

1. Work with a small group. For a model of a hemisphere, use the top section of a 2-liter plastic bottle that your teacher has cut.
2. Carefully draw three or four latitude lines and six or eight longitude lines on the bottle.
3. Place a piece of clay in the center of a piece of poster board. Press the bottle top into the clay.
4. Shine a flashlight downward above the center of the model. Trace the lines on the poster board to make your projection.

WHAT DO YOU THINK?
What are the similarities and differences between your model and your projection?

CHALLENGE Draw a shape on the plastic bottle to represent a landmass. Use the flashlight again to project the hemisphere. How did the shape of your landmass appear when it was projected onto a flat surface?

SKILL FOCUS
Modeling

MATERIALS
- top 8 inches of 2-liter bottle
- marker pen
- walnut-sized piece of clay
- poster board
- flashlight

TIME
20 minutes

another to plot a course. The problem with Mercator maps is that areas far away from the equator appear much larger than they really are. On the map below, Greenland looks bigger than South America. In reality, South America is about eight times larger than Greenland.

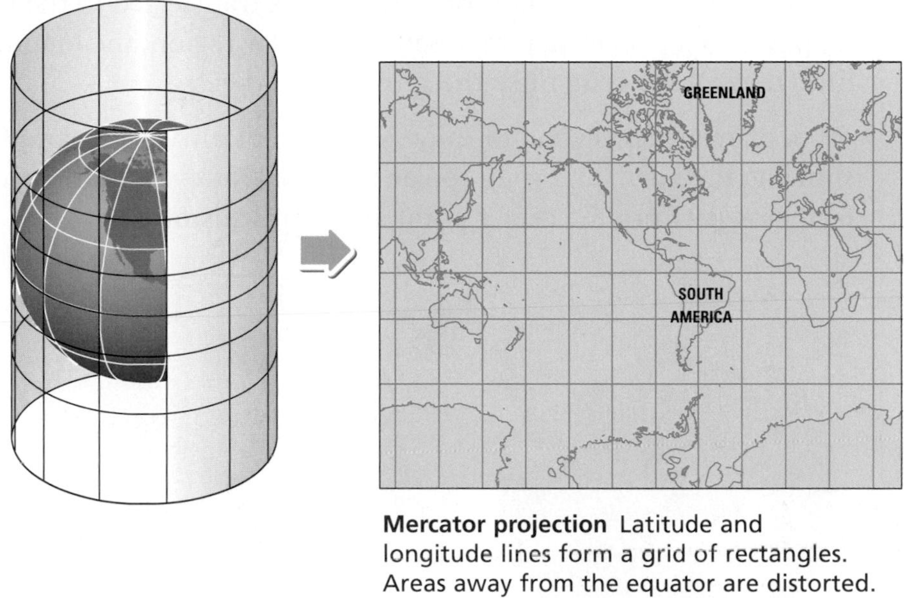

Mercator projection Latitude and longitude lines form a grid of rectangles. Areas away from the equator are distorted.

Conic Projections

Conic projections are based on the shape of a cone. The diagram below shows how a cone of paper might be wrapped around the globe. The paper touches the surface only at the middle latitudes, halfway between the equator and the North Pole.

When the cone is flattened out, the latitude lines are curved slightly. The curved lines represent the curved surface of Earth. This allows the map to show the true sizes and shapes of some landmasses.

Conic projections are most useful for mapping large areas in the middle latitudes, such as the United States. However, landmasses near the equator or near the north or south pole will be distorted.

CHECK YOUR READING What are the main uses of Mercator and conic projections?

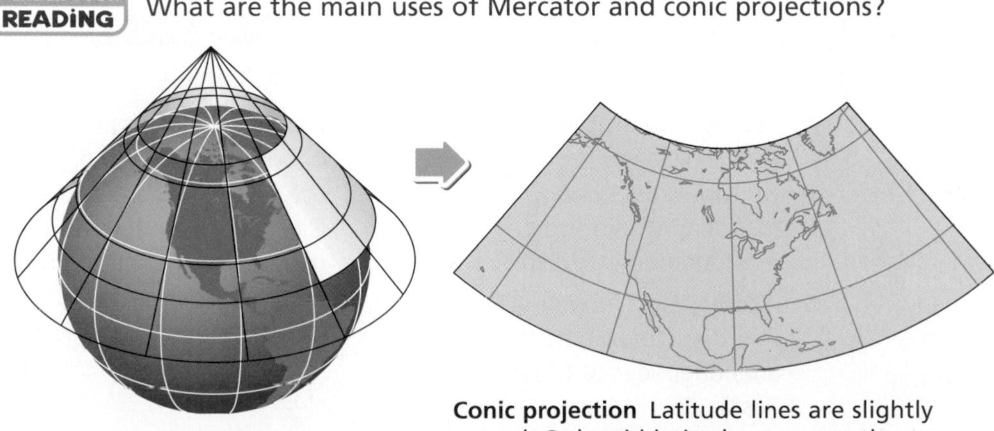

Conic projection Latitude lines are slightly curved. Only mid-latitude areas are the correct size and shape.

Planar Projections

Find out more about map projections and how they are used.

Planar projections were developed to help people find the shortest distance between two points. They are drawn as if a circle of paper were laid on a point on Earth's surface. As you look at the diagram below, notice how the shape of the sphere is transferred to the flat map. When a planar map represents the polar region, the longitude lines meet at the center like the spokes of a wheel.

A planar map is good for plotting ocean or air voyages and for showing the north and south polar regions. However, landmasses farther away from the center point are greatly distorted.

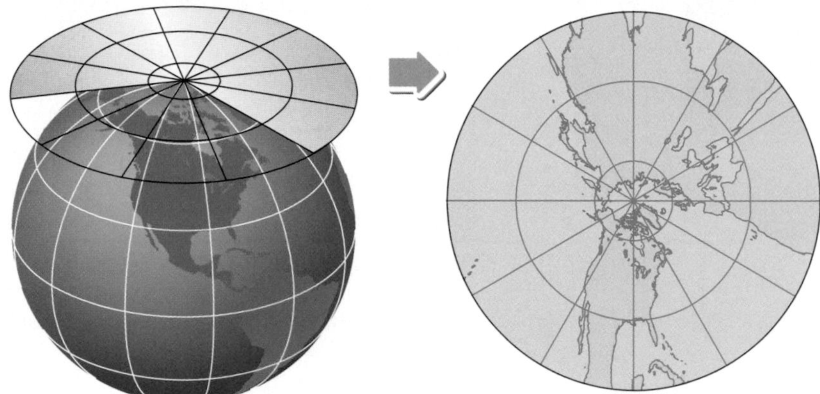

Planar projection Only areas near the center point are the correct size and shape.

The Mercator, conic, and planar projections are all attempts to solve the problem of representing a curved surface on a flat map. Each projection can show certain areas of the world accurately but distorts other areas.

What areas does the planar projection show accurately?

1.2 Review

KEY CONCEPTS

1. What natural and human-made features can maps show? Give two examples of each.
2. Explain how latitude and longitude can help you locate any place on Earth.
3. Why do all flat maps distort Earth's surface?

CRITICAL THINKING

4. **Provide Examples** Imagine that your family is on a long car trip. What symbols on a road map would you pay the most attention to? Explain.
5. **Apply** Use a world map to find the approximate latitudes and longitudes of Moscow, Russia; Tokyo, Japan; Denver, Colorado; and La Paz, Bolivia.

CHALLENGE

6. **Apply** Working with a partner or with a small group, select the shortest airline route from Chicago to London, using a globe and a Mercator map. **Hint:** Notice that as you go farther north on the globe, the longitude lines become closer together.

MATH in SCIENCE

SKILL: USING PROPORTIONS

MATH TUTORIAL
CLASSZONE.COM
Click on Math Tutorial for more help with solving proportions.

How Far Is It?

A science class is visiting Chicago and is using the map on the left to walk to the lakefront museums. Remember, a map scale shows how distances on the map compare to actual distances on the ground.

Buckingham Fountain

Example

In this case, the map scale indicates that 1 centimeter on the map represents 300 meters on the ground. The map scale shows this as equivalent units. By using these units to write a proportion, you can use cross products to determine actual distances.

What distance does 3 cm on the map represent? Set up the problem like this:

$$\frac{1\text{ cm}}{300\text{ m}} = \frac{3\text{ cm}}{x}$$

(1) $1\text{ cm} \cdot x = 3\text{ cm} \cdot 300\text{ m}$

(2) $x = 3 \cdot 300\text{ m}$

(3) $x = 900\text{ m}$

ANSWER 3 centimeters on the map represents 900 meters on the ground.

Use cross products and a metric ruler to answer the following questions.

1. The science class divides into two groups. Each group starts at Buckingham Fountain. How far, in meters, will one group walk to get to the Adler Planetarium if they follow the red dotted line?
2. How far, in meters, will the other group walk to get to the end of Navy Pier if they follow the blue dotted line?
3. The group that walked to Adler decides to take a boat to join the other group at Navy Pier. How far, in meters, is their boat ride along the red dotted line?

CHALLENGE What is the total distance, in kilometers, that the two groups traveled? Set up the problem as a proportion. **Hint:** There are 1000 meters in a kilometer.

SION T
LAKE SHORE DR
AVE
SUPERIOR ST
MICHIGAN
ND AV
NAVY PIER
Chicago River
RANDOLPH ST
DR
MS ST
Art Institute of Chicago
KSON
DR
Buckingham Fountain
Chicago Harbor
CONGRESS PKWY
LAKE SHORE DR
Lake Michigan
MICHIGAN AVE
COLUMBUS
Shedd Aquarium
ROOSEVELT RD
Adler Planetarium
Field Museum of Natural History
Northerly Island
LAKE SHORE DR
LAKEFRONT TRAIL
AVE
18TH ST
N W E S
RMAK RD
MICHIGAN
MC CORMICK PLACE
0 150 300 meters
1 cm = 300 m

KEY CONCEPT

1.3 Topographic maps show the shape of the land.

BEFORE, you learned

- Different maps provide information about natural and human-made features
- Latitude and longitude are used to find places on Earth
- All flat maps distort Earth's surface

NOW, you will learn

- How contour lines show elevation, slope, and relief
- What rules contour lines follow
- What common symbols are used on topographic maps

VOCABULARY

topography p. 24
contour line p. 25
elevation p. 25
slope p. 25
relief p. 25
contour interval p. 26

EXPLORE Topographic Maps

How can you map your knuckles?

PROCEDURE

1. Hold your fist closed, knuckles up, as shown in the photo.
2. Draw circles around the first knuckle. Make sure the circles are the same distance from each other.
3. Flatten out your hand. Observe what happens. Write down your observations.

WHAT DO YOU THINK?

- How does the height of your knuckles change when you clench your fist, then flatten out your hand?
- What do you think the circles represent?

MATERIAL

washable colored pen

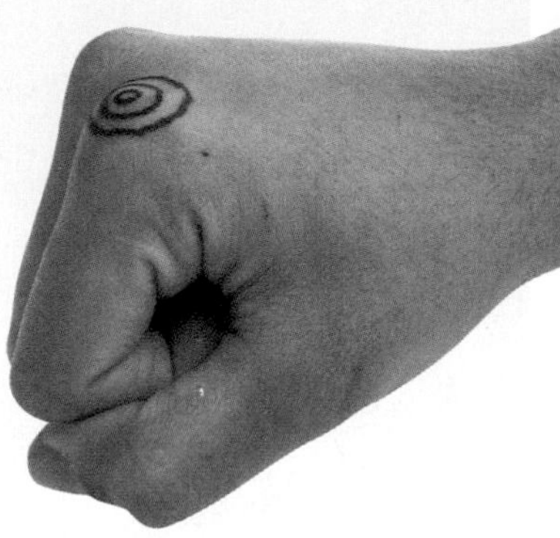

Topographic maps use contour lines to show features.

VOCABULARY
Add a word triangle for *topography* to your notebook.

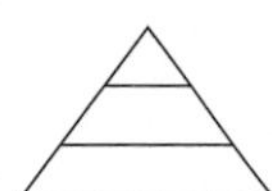

Imagine you are on vacation with your family in a national park. You have a simple trail map that shows you where to hike. But the map does not tell you anything about what the land looks like. Will you have to cross any rivers or valleys? How far uphill or downhill will you have to hike?

To answer these questions, you need to know something about the topography of the area. **Topography** is the shape, or features, of the land. These features can be natural—such as mountains, plateaus, and plains—or human-made—such as dams and roads. To show the topography of an area, mapmakers draw a topographic map.

A topographic map is a flat map that uses lines to show Earth's surface features. Distance and elevation can be given in feet or meters. Take a look at the topographic map of Mount Hood on this page. The wiggly lines on the map are called **contour lines,** and they show an area's elevation, slope, and relief.

1. The **elevation** of a place is how high above sea level it is. An area can range from a few meters to several thousand meters above sea level. The numbers on the contour lines show the elevations of different points in the Mount Hood area.

2. The **slope** of a landform or area is how steep it is. The more gradual the slope, the farther apart the contour lines on the map. The steeper the slope, the closer together the contour lines.

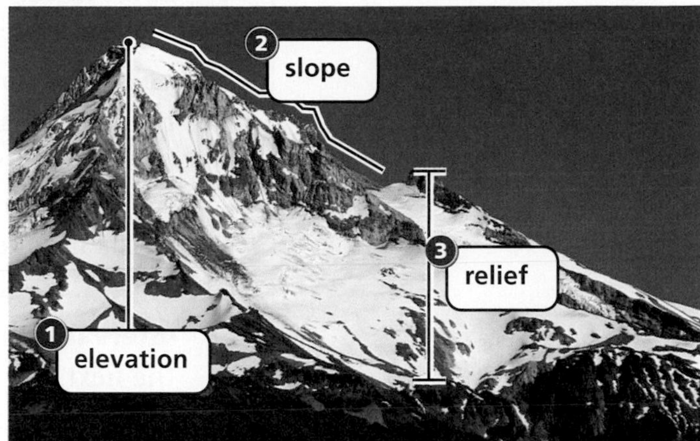

3. The **relief** of an area is the difference between its high and low points. For example, subtracting the lowest elevation on the map from the highest gives you a measure of the area's relief.

What is the difference between elevation and slope?

Mount Hood Topographic Map

A topographic map shows the land as if you were above the land looking down on it.

WILDERNESS

MOUNT HOOD

3426

Lamberson Butte

1750

1500

South Fork

Fork

36

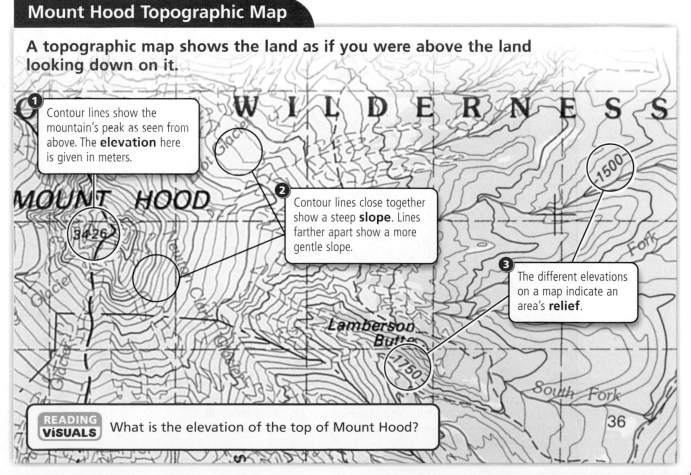

1. Contour lines show the mountain's peak as seen from above. The **elevation** here is given in meters.

2. Contour lines close together show a steep **slope**. Lines farther apart show a more gentle slope.

3. The different elevations on a map indicate an area's **relief**.

READING VISUALS What is the elevation of the top of Mount Hood?

Contour lines follow certain rules.

MAIN IDEA AND DETAILS Use your main idea and details chart to take notes on the rules for reading a topographic map.

Contour lines on topographic maps can help you visualize landforms. Think of the following statements as rules for reading such maps:

- **Lines never cross.** Contour lines never cross, because each line represents an exact elevation.
- **Circles show highest and lowest points.** Contour lines form closed circles around mountaintops, hilltops, and the centers of depressions, which are sunken areas in the ground. Sometimes, the elevation of a mountain or hill is written in meters or feet in the middle of the circle.
- **Contour interval is always the same on a map.** The **contour interval** is the difference in elevation from one contour line to the next. For example, the contour interval on the map below is 10 feet. This means that the change in elevation between contour lines is always 10 feet. The contour interval can differ from map to map, but it is always the same on a particular map.

Ely, Minnesota, Topographic Map

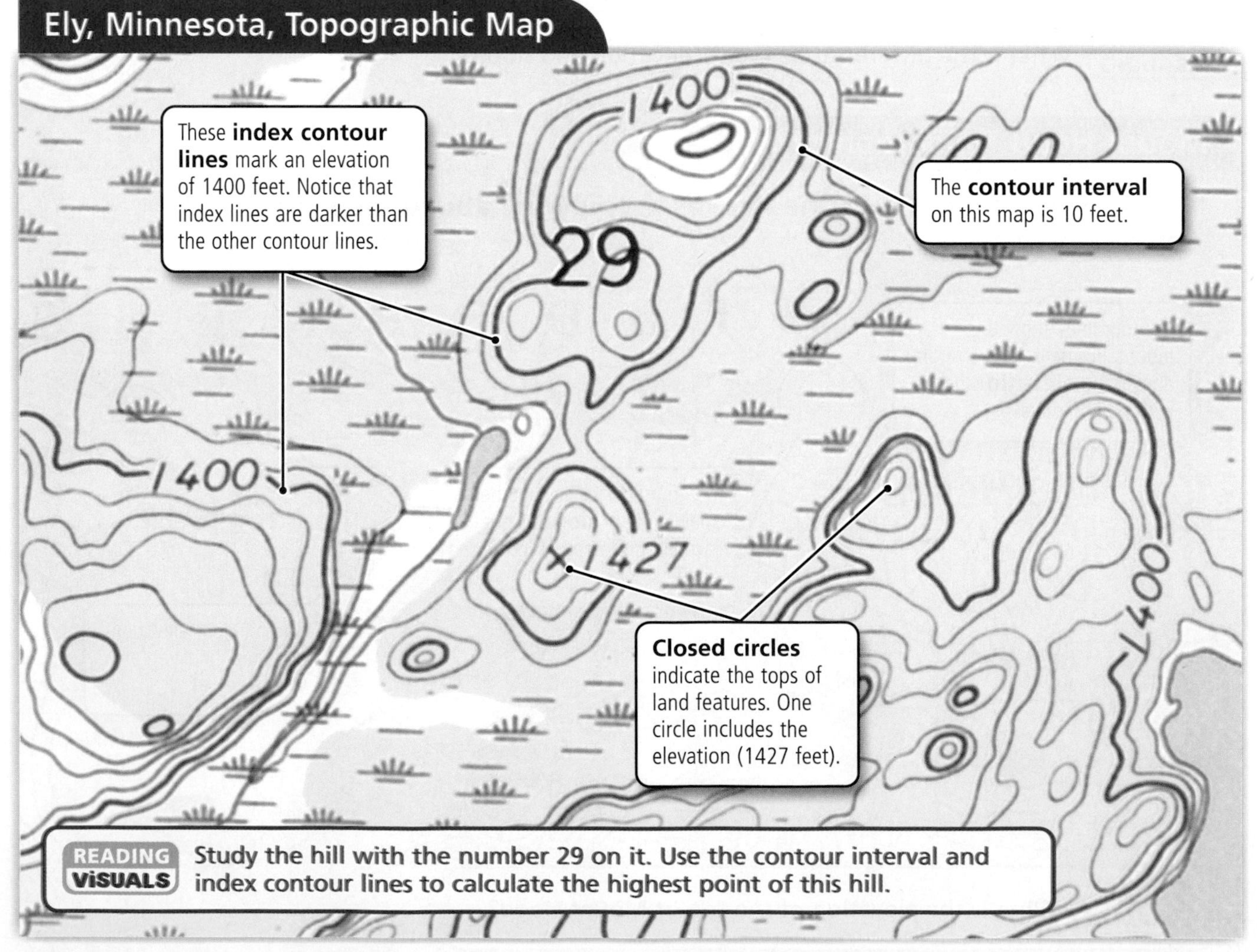

These **index contour lines** mark an elevation of 1400 feet. Notice that index lines are darker than the other contour lines.
The **contour interval** on this map is 10 feet.
1400
29
1400
1427
1400
Closed circles indicate the tops of land features. One circle includes the elevation (1427 feet).

READING VISUALS **Study the hill with the number 29 on it. Use the contour interval and index contour lines to calculate the highest point of this hill.**

- **Index contour lines mark elevations.** The darker contour lines on a map are called index contour lines. Numbers that indicate elevations are often written on these lines. To calculate higher or lower elevations, simply count the number of lines above or below an index line. Then multiply that number by the contour interval. For instance, on the Ely map, one index line marks 1400 feet. To find the elevation of a point three lines up from this index line, you would multiply 10 feet (the contour interval) by 3. Add the result, 30, to 1400. The point's elevation is 1430 feet.

Discover the relationship between topographic maps and surface features.

What information do index contour lines provide?

Besides contour lines, topographic maps also contain symbols for natural and human-made features. Below are some common map symbols that the United States Geological Survey (USGS) uses on its topographic maps.

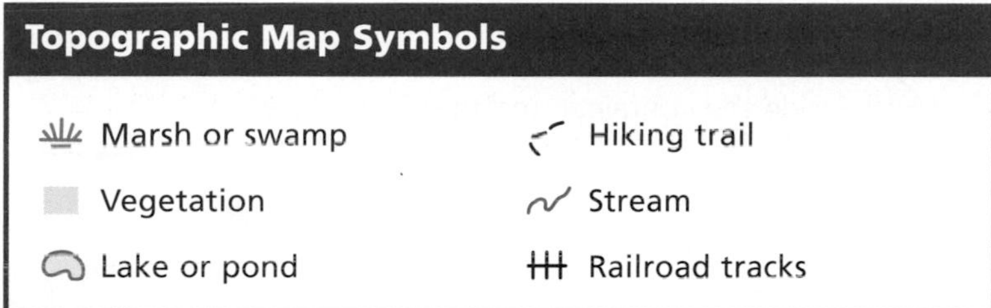

Topographic Map Symbols

Marsh or swamp	Hiking trail
Vegetation	Stream
Lake or pond	Railroad tracks

The USGS provides topographic maps for nearly every part of the United States. These maps cover urban, rural, and wilderness areas. Hikers and campers are not the only ones who use topographic maps. Engineers, archaeologists, forest rangers, biologists, and others rely on them as well.

1.3 Review

KEY CONCEPTS

1. How do contour lines show elevation, slope, and relief?
2. Why do contour lines never cross on a topographic map?
3. How would you show the top of a hill, an area of vegetation, or a hiking trail on a topographic map?

CRITICAL THINKING

4. **Apply** For an area with gently sloping hills and little relief, would you draw contour lines close together or far apart? Explain why.
5. **Compare and Contrast** How would a road map and a topographic map of the same area differ? What information would each provide?

CHALLENGE

6. **Synthesize** Work with a group to make a topographic map of the area around your school. First decide how big an area you will include. Then choose a contour interval, a map scale, and symbols for buildings, sports fields, and other features. Let other students test the map's accuracy.

CHAPTER INVESTIGATION

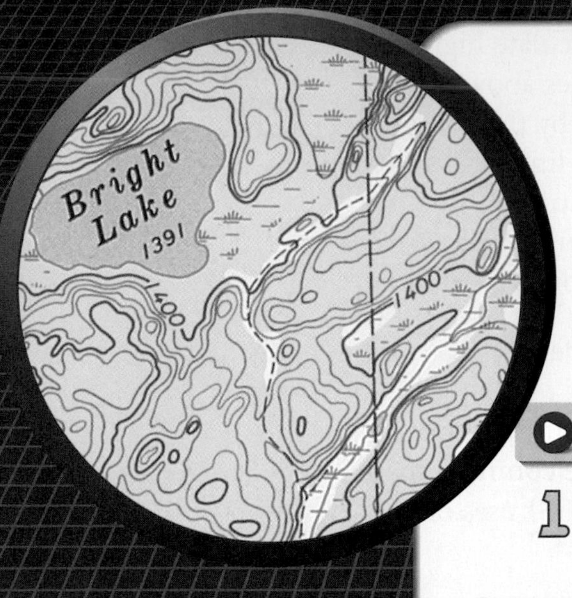

Investigate Topographic Maps

OVERVIEW AND PURPOSE Topographic maps show the shape of the land. In this lab you will use what you have learned about how Earth's three-dimensional surface is represented on maps to

- make a terrain model out of clay
- produce a topographic map of the model

MATERIALS

- half-gallon cardboard juice container
- scissors
- modeling clay
- clear plastic sheet (transparency or sheet protector)
- cellophane tape
- ruler
- water
- food coloring
- box of spaghetti
- erasable marker pen

Procedure

1. Build a simple landscape about 6–8 cm high from modeling clay. Include a variety of land features. Make sure your model is no taller than the sides of the container.

2. Place your model into the container. Stand a ruler upright inside the container and tape it in place.

3. Lay the clear plastic sheet over the container and tape it on one side like a hinge. Carefully trace the outline of your clay model.

4. Add 2 cm of colored water to the container.

5. Insert spaghetti sticks into the model all around the waterline. Place the sticks about 3 cm apart. Make sure the sticks are vertical and are no taller than the sides of the container.

6. Lower the plastic sheet back over the container. Looking straight down on the container, make a dot on the sheet wherever you see a spaghetti stick. Connect the dots to trace the contour line accurately onto your map.

7. Continue adding water, 2 cm at a time. Each time you add water, insert the sticks into the model at the waterline and repeat step 6. Continue until the model landscape is underwater. Carefully drain the water when finished.

step 3

step 5

Observe and Analyze

1. Compare your topographic map with the three-dimensional model. Remember that contour lines connect points of equal elevation. What do widely spaced or tightly spaced contour lines mean? What does a closed circle mean?
2. Make a permanent record of your map to keep in your **Science Notebook** by carefully tracing the contour lines onto a sheet of white paper. To make reading the map easier, use a different color for an index contour line.
3. What is the contour interval of your model landscape? For example, each 2 centimeters might represent 20 meters in an actual landscape. Record the elevation of the index contour line on your map.

Conclude

1. **INFER** How would you determine the elevation of a point located halfway between two contour lines?
2. **EVALUATE** Describe any errors that you may have made in your procedure or any places where errors might have occurred.
3. **APPLY** Explain how you would use a topographic map if you were planning a hiking trip or a cross-country bike race.

INVESTIGATE Further

CHALLENGE Choose one feature on a topographic map—such as the map on page 26—to translate into a cross-sectional diagram.

1. Lay a piece of ruled paper across the center of the topographical feature.
2. Mark each of the contour lines on the ruled paper and label each mark with the elevation.
3. Mark the same elevations on the side of the paper, as shown in the example.
4. Use a ruler to draw a straight line down from each mark to the matching elevation on the side of the paper.
5. Connect the points to draw a profile of the landform.

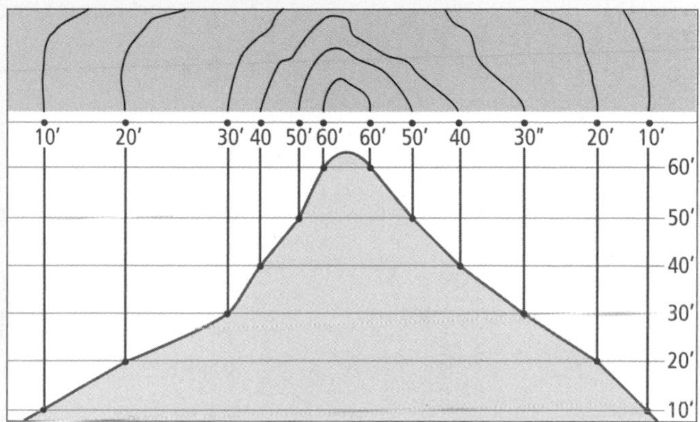

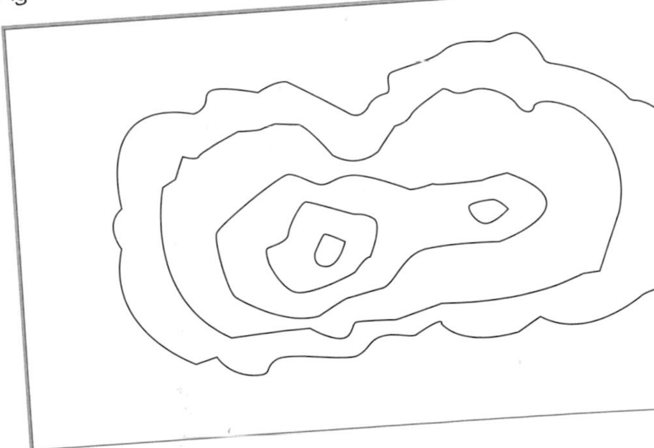

INVESTIGATE TOPOGRAPHIC MAPS
Observe and Analyze
Figure 1. Topographic Map of Model
Conclude

KEY CONCEPT

1.4 Technology is used to map Earth.

BEFORE, you learned

- Contour lines are used on topographic maps to show elevation, slope, and relief
- Contour lines follow certain rules
- Map symbols show many natural and human-made features

NOW, you will learn

- How remote-sensing images can provide detailed and accurate information about Earth
- How geographic data can be displayed in layers to build maps

VOCABULARY

remote sensing p. 30
sensor p. 31
false-color image p. 32
geographic information systems p. 33

THINK ABOUT

What can you see in this image?

Satellites can record all types of information about Earth's surface. This image shows a section of Washington, D.C. The satellite that collected the data is 680 kilometers (420 mi) above Earth. What familiar items can you see in the picture? How might images like this be useful to scientists, mapmakers, and engineers?

Remote sensing provides detailed images of Earth.

VOCABULARY
Add a word triangle for *remote sensing* to your notebook.

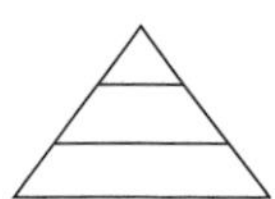

If you have ever looked at an object through a pair of binoculars, you have used remote sensing. **Remote sensing** is the use of scientific equipment to gather information about something from a distance. Remote-sensing technology can be as simple as a camera mounted on an airplane or as complex as a satellite orbiting Earth.

To get an idea of how important remote sensing is, imagine you are a mapmaker in the 1840s. You have been asked to draw a map of a state, but you have no cameras, no photographs from airplanes, and no satellites to help you. To get a good view of the land, you have to climb to the highest points and carefully draw every hill, valley, river, and landform below you. It will take you months to map the state.

Today, that same map would take far less time to make. Modern mapmakers use remote-sensing images from airplanes and satellites to develop highly detailed and accurate maps of Earth's surface.

Airplane cameras use film to record data, but satellites use sensors to build images of Earth. A **sensor** is a mechanical or electrical device that receives and responds to a signal, such as light. Satellite sensors detect far more than your eyes can see. They collect information about the different types of energy coming from Earth's surface. The satellites then send that information to computers on Earth.

This satellite image includes the Jefferson Memorial, walkways, and roads. See if you can find the memorial in the image on page 30.

The computers turn the information into images, as shown in the illustration below. Satellite data can be used to build an image of the entire planet, a single continent, or a detail of your area. For example, the image on the right shows a closeup of the Jefferson Memorial in Washington, D.C.

CHECK YOUR READING Explain how remote sensing is used to gather information about Earth.

Satellite Imaging

Objects on Earth reflect or emit different types of energy. Satellite sensors can detect and record these energies.

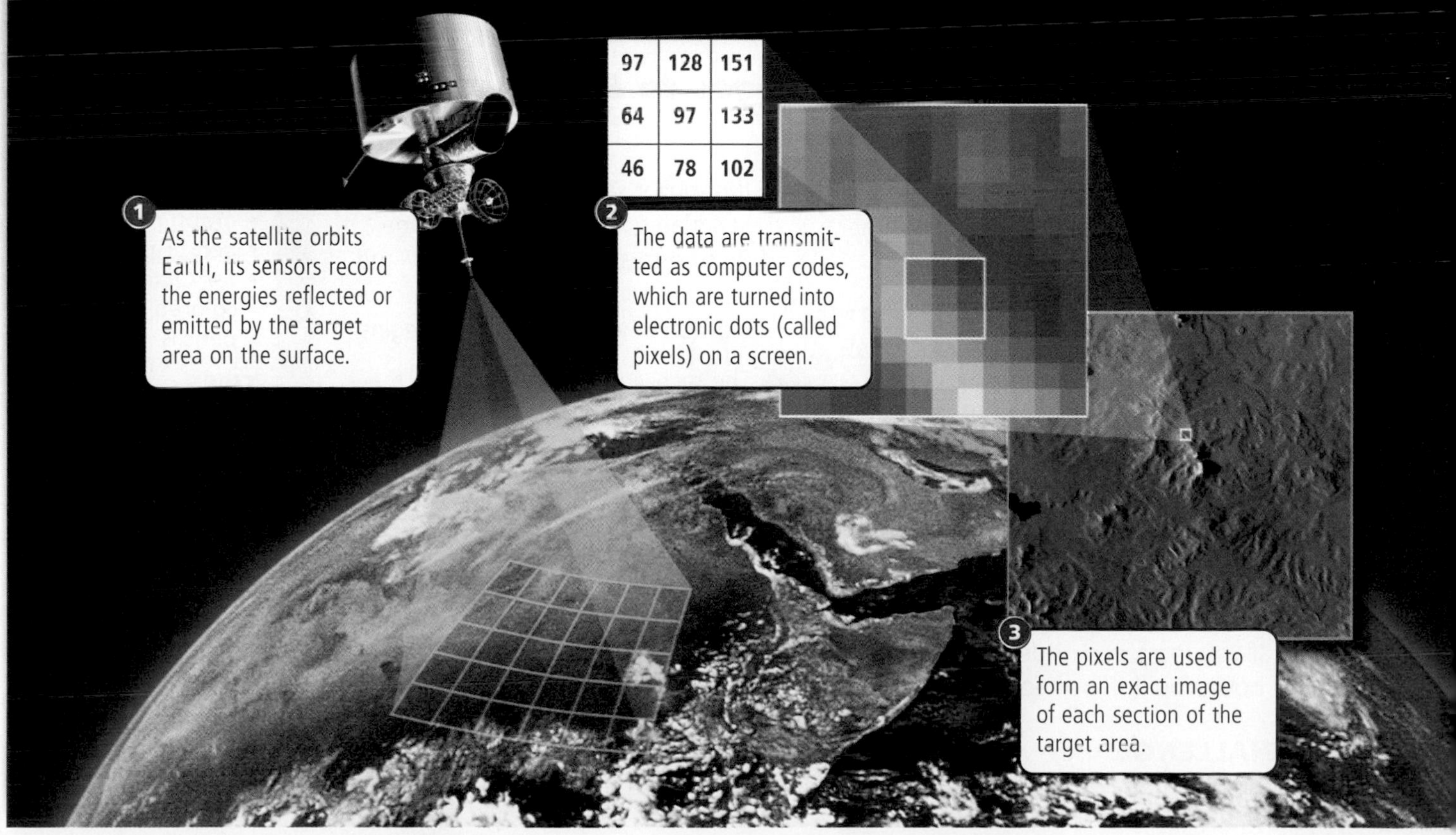

97	128	151
64	97	133
46	78	102

1. As the satellite orbits Earth, its sensors record the energies reflected or emitted by the target area on the surface.

2. The data are transmitted as computer codes, which are turned into electronic dots (called pixels) on a screen.

3. The pixels are used to form an exact image of each section of the target area.

One of the ways scientists study changes is by using false-color images. In one type of **false-color image,** Earth's natural colors are replaced with artificial ones to highlight special features. For example, fire officials used false-color images like the ones below to track the spread of a dangerous wildfire in southern Oregon.

July 21, 2002
Small fires break out.

In this false-color image, vegetation is bright green, burned areas are red, fire is bright pink, and smoke is blue.

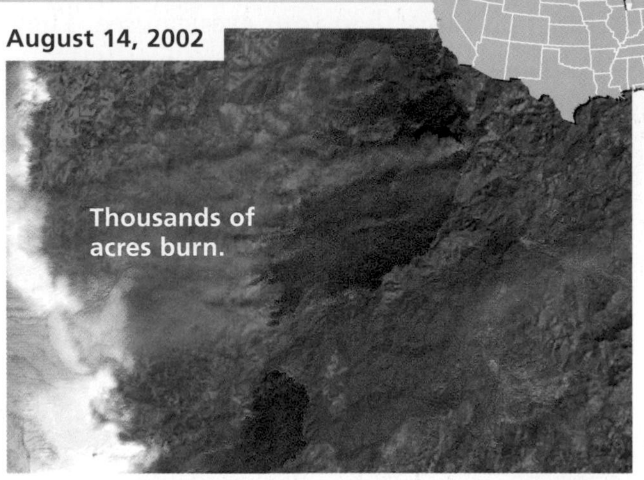

August 14, 2002
OREGON
Thousands of acres burn.

Three weeks later, as this false-color image clearly shows, the fires had spread over a large area.

INVESTIGATE Satellite Imaging

How do satellites send images to Earth?

PROCEDURE

1. Work with a partner. One of you will be the "sensor," and the other will be the "receiving station."
2. The sensor draws the initials of a famous person on a piece of graph paper. The receiving station does NOT see the drawing.
3. The sensor sends the picture to the receiving station. For blank squares, the sensor says "Zero." For filled-in squares, the sensor says "One." Be sure to start at the top row and read left to right, telling the receiving station when a new row begins.
4. The receiving station transfers the code to the graph paper. At the end, the receiver has three tries to guess whose initials were sent.

WHAT DO YOU THINK?

- What would happen if you accidentally skipped or repeated a row?
- If you increased or decreased the number and size of the squares, how would this affect the picture?

CHALLENGE Use a variety of colors to send other initials or an image. Your code must tell the receiver which color to use for each square.

SKILL FOCUS
Modeling

MATERIALS
- graph paper
- pen or pencil
- *for Challenge:* colored pens or pencils

TIME
25 minutes

MJ

Geographic information systems display data in layers.

Find out more about how GIS is used.

Any good city map will show you what is on the surface—buildings, streets, parks, and other features. But suppose you need to know about tunnels under the city. Or maybe you want to know where the most students live. An ordinary map, even one based on remote-sensing images, will not tell you what you want to know.

Instead, you would turn to geographic information systems. **Geographic information systems** (GIS) are computer systems that can store and arrange geographic data and display the data in many different types of maps. Scientists, city planners, and engineers all use GIS maps to help them make decisions. For example, suppose your city wants to build a new airport. It must be away from populated areas and near major highways. The illustration below shows how city officials might use GIS to pick the best site.

Geographic Information Systems

GIS can be used to produce maps that help people make decisions.

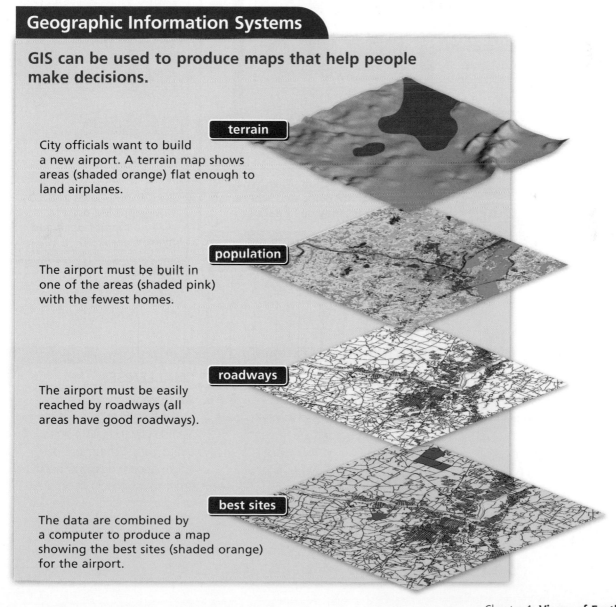

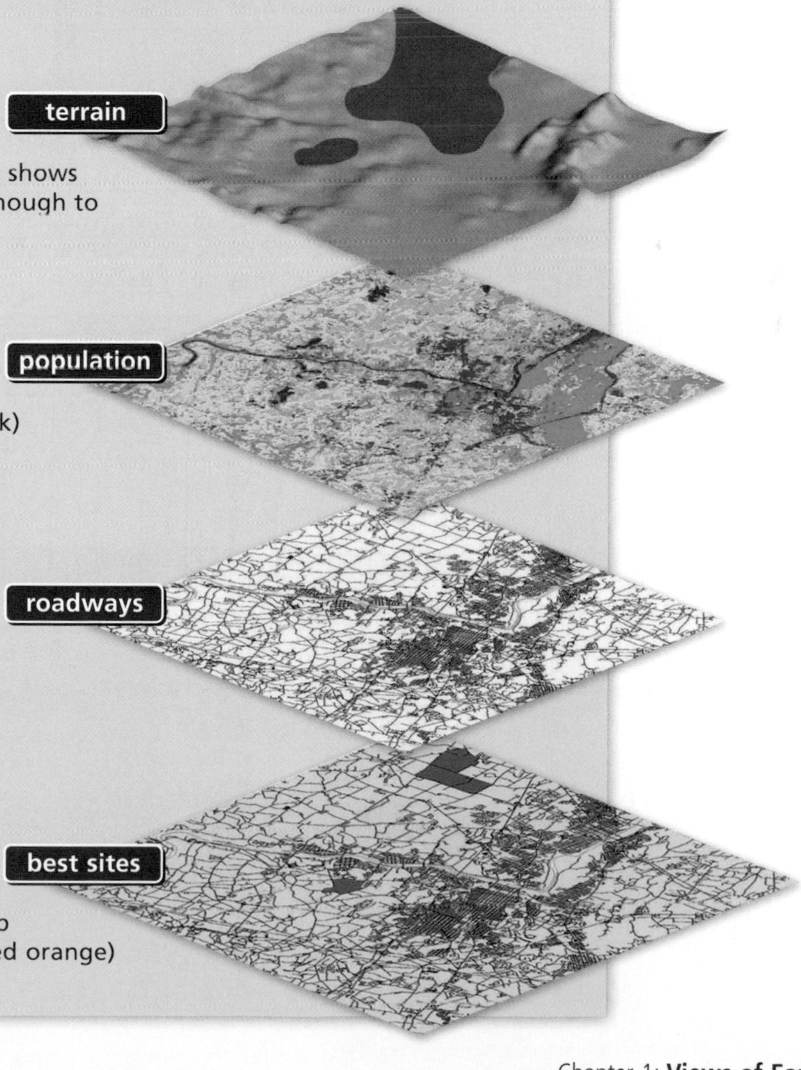

terrain

City officials want to build a new airport. A terrain map shows areas (shaded orange) flat enough to land airplanes.

population

The airport must be built in one of the areas (shaded pink) with the fewest homes.

roadways

The airport must be easily reached by roadways (all areas have good roadways).

best sites

The data are combined by a computer to produce a map showing the best sites (shaded orange) for the airport.

Any geographic information can be entered into GIS and converted into a map. These systems are especially useful in displaying information about changes in the environment.

For example, near Long Valley in California, the volcano known as Mammoth Mountain began giving off carbon dioxide, or CO_2. As the gas rose through the soil, it began killing the roots of trees nearby. Scientists measured the flow of CO_2 around Horseshoe Lake and other areas. They used computer software to build the maps shown below.

CHECK YOUR READING Summarize the ways GIS maps can be helpful to engineers, city planners, and scientists.

Mammoth Mountain

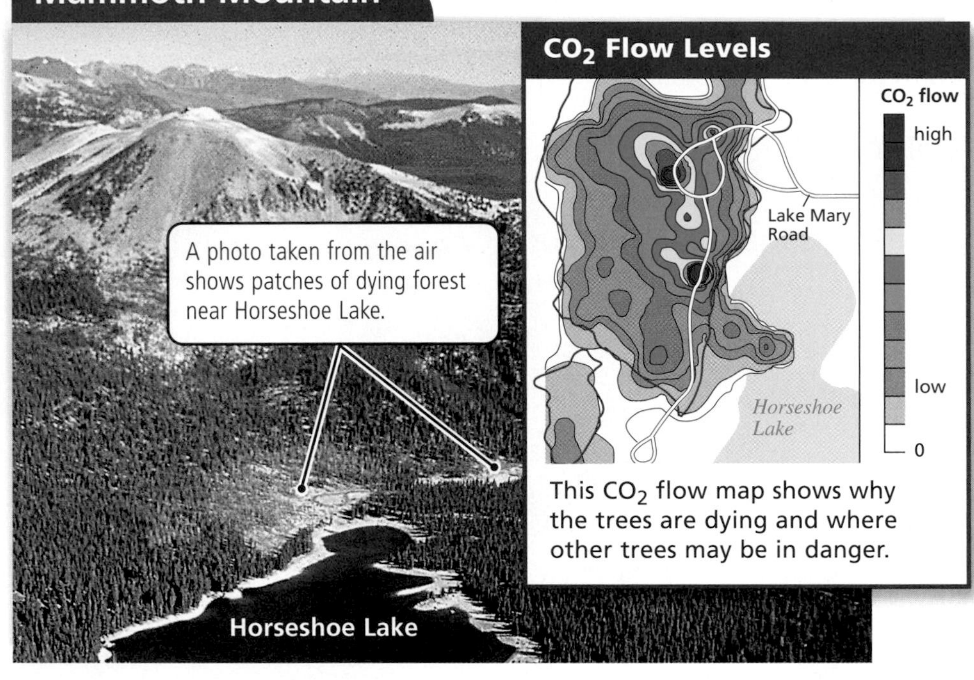

This CO_2 flow map shows why the trees are dying and where other trees may be in danger.

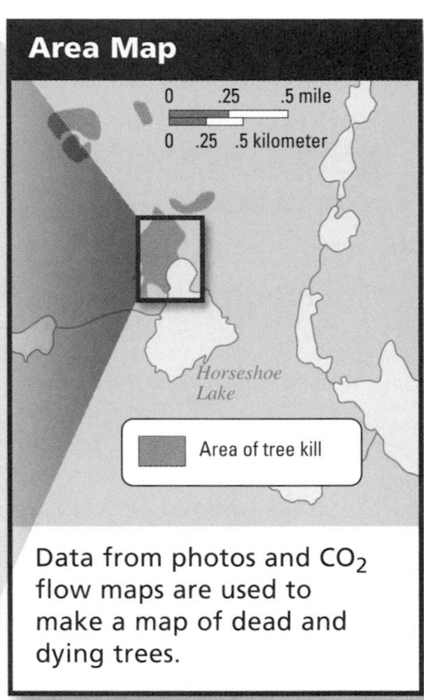

Data from photos and CO_2 flow maps are used to make a map of dead and dying trees.

1.4 Review

KEY CONCEPTS

1. How are satellites used to make images of Earth from outer space?
2. What are some of the types of information obtained by remote sensing?
3. Explain in your own words what a GIS map is.

CRITICAL THINKING

4. **Infer** Explain how satellite images might be used to predict what a natural area might look like in 50 or 100 years.
5. **Evaluate** If you wanted to compare a region before and during a flood, how could false-color images help you?

CHALLENGE

6. **Analyze** Work with a small group. Suppose you wanted to ask the city to build a skateboard park. What types of information would you need in order to propose a good site? Draw a map to display each type of information.

SKILL: INTERPRETING DATA

Which Site Is Best for an Olympic Stadium?

Imagine you live in a city that has been chosen to host the Summer Olympics. The only question is where to build the Olympic stadium—in the center of town, in the suburbs, or on the site of an old baseball park. The city government has developed maps to help them decide which is the best site. The planners know that thousands of people will come to see the games. Therefore, they reason, the stadium should be (1) easy to reach by car, (2) close to mass-transit stops, and (3) near restaurants and shops.

Analyzing Map Data

As you study the maps, keep these requirements in mind.

1. Which site(s) is/are easiest to reach by car?
2. Which site(s) is/are closest to bus and train lines?
3. Which site(s) is/are close to shopping areas?

Interpreting Data

In your **Science Notebook,** create a chart like the one below to help you interpret the data displayed on the maps. As you fill in the chart, think about which site offers the greatest benefits to all the people who will attend the Olympic Games.

	Site (A)		Site (B)		Site (C)	
	Yes	No	Yes	No	Yes	No
Near mass transit						
Near highways and roads						
Near shopping areas						

As a group Choose the best site based on your interpretation of the data. Discuss your choice with other groups to see if they agree.

CHALLENGE Once the site is chosen, the planners will start building the stadium. What types of information about the site will they need? Sketch maps displaying the information. **Hint:** The stadium will need electricity, water, and delivery of supplies.

Trains and Bus Lines

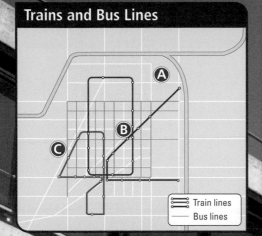

A
B
C
Train lines
Bus lines

Streets and Freeways

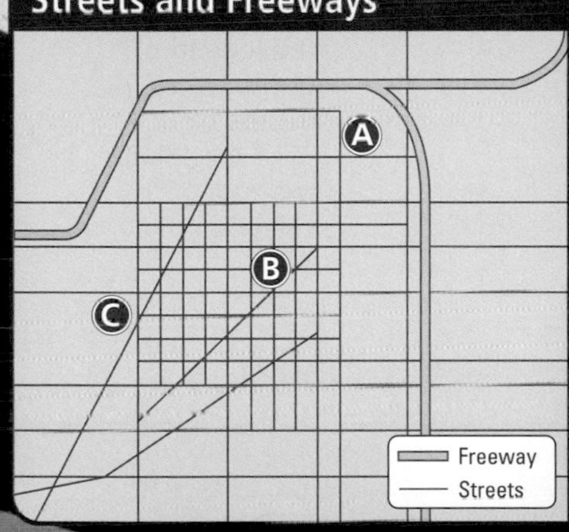

Restaurants and Shopping

Chapter Review

the BIG idea

Modern technology has changed the way we view and map Earth.

KEY CONCEPTS SUMMARY

1.1 Technology is used to explore the Earth system.

The atmosphere, hydrosphere, biosphere, and geosphere work together to form one large system called Earth.

VOCABULARY
system p. 9
atmosphere p. 10
hydrosphere p. 10
biosphere p. 11
geosphere p. 12

1.2 Maps and globes are models of Earth.

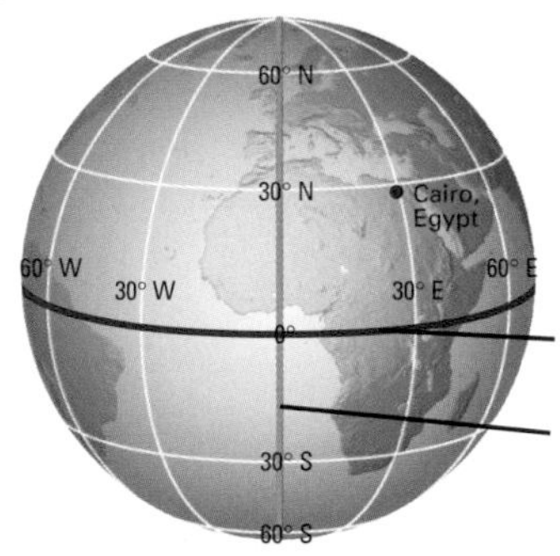

Latitude and longitude are used to locate any point on Earth.

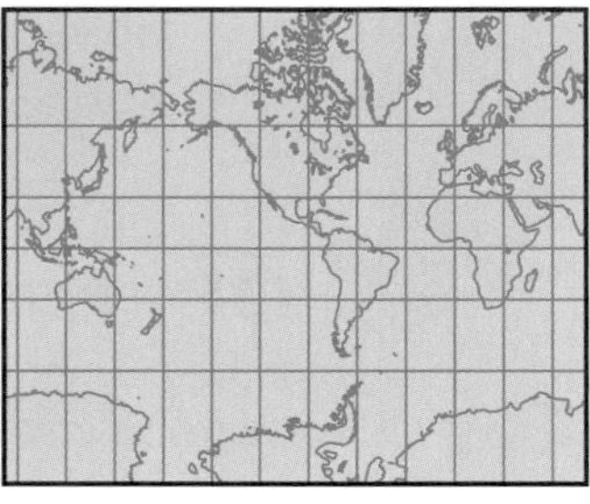

All map projections distort Earth's surface.

VOCABULARY
relief map p. 16
map scale p. 17
map legend p. 17
equator p. 18
latitude p. 18
prime meridian p. 19
longitude p. 19
projection p. 20

1.3 Topographic maps show the shape of the land.

Contour lines show elevation, slope, and relief.

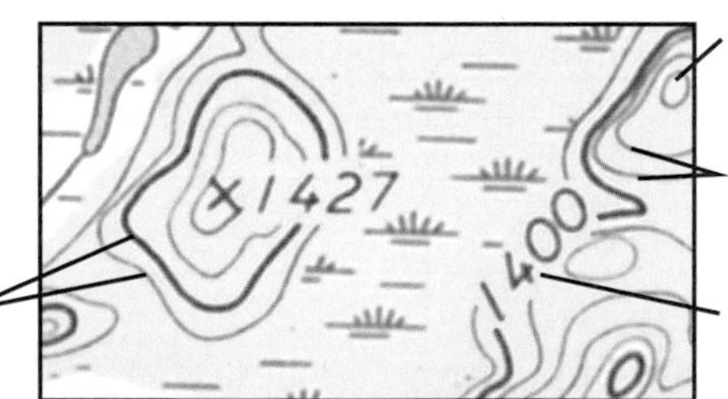

VOCABULARY
topography p. 24
contour line p. 25
elevation p. 25
slope p. 25
relief p. 25
contour interval p. 26

1.4 Technology is used to map Earth.

Remote-sensing technology gathers accurate data about Earth.

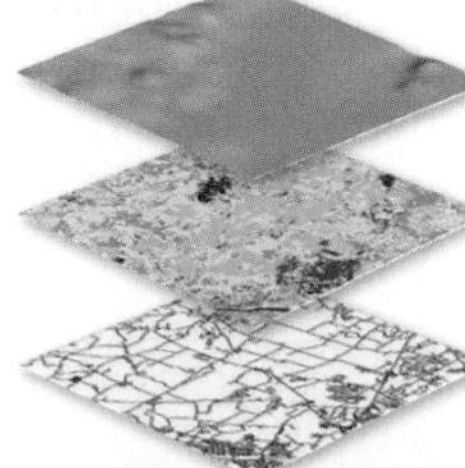

Geographic information systems are computer programs used to merge layers of information.

VOCABULARY
remote sensing p. 30
sensor p. 31
false-color image p. 32
geographic information systems p. 33

Reviewing Vocabulary

Copy and complete the chart below, using vocabulary terms from this chapter.

Term	Use	Appearance
map legend	*to explain map symbols*	*chart of symbols*
1. latitude	to show distance from the equator	
2. longitude		lines going from pole to pole
3.	to show land features	rippled and smooth areas
4. map scale	to represent distances	
5. equator		line at 0° latitude
6. prime meridian	to separate east and west hemispheres	
7.	to show height above sea level	line showing elevation
8. false-color image	to highlight information	

Reviewing Key Concepts

Multiple Choice *Choose the letter of the best answer.*

9. Which Greek prefix is matched with its correct meaning?
a. *hydro* = life **c.** *bio* = earth
b. *atmo* = gas **d.** *geo* = water

10. What portion of Earth is covered by water?
a. one-quarter **c.** three-quarters
b. one-half **d.** nine-tenths

11. The continents and ocean basins are part of Earth's
a. crust **c.** outer core
b. mantle **d.** inner core

12. Which Earth system includes humans?
a. atmosphere **c.** hydrosphere
b. biosphere **d.** geosphere

13. One way the atmosphere shapes Earth's surface is by
a. winds **c.** earthquakes
b. floods **d.** tunnels

14. How are the major parts of the Earth system related to each other?
a. They rarely can be studied together.
b. They often are in conflict.
c. They usually work independently.
d. They continually affect each other.

15. A flat map shows Earth's curved surface by means of
a. elevation **c.** relief
b. topography **d.** projection

16. People use latitude and longitude lines mostly to identify
a. map scales **c.** exact locations
b. country names **d.** distances

17. The most accurate way to show Earth's surface is a
a. globe **c.** cylindrical projection
b. conic projection **d.** planar projection

18. One example of remote sensing is the use of
a. contour lines **c.** GIS
b. projections **d.** binoculars

Short Answer *Write a few sentences to answer each question.*

19. How does the Global Positioning System work? In your answer use each of the following terms. Underline each term in your answer.

24 satellites	computer	longitude
receiver	latitude	elevation

20. How do Mercator maps distort the view of Earth's surface?

21. How do people use sensors in making maps?

Thinking Critically

Use the topographic map below to answer the next seven questions.

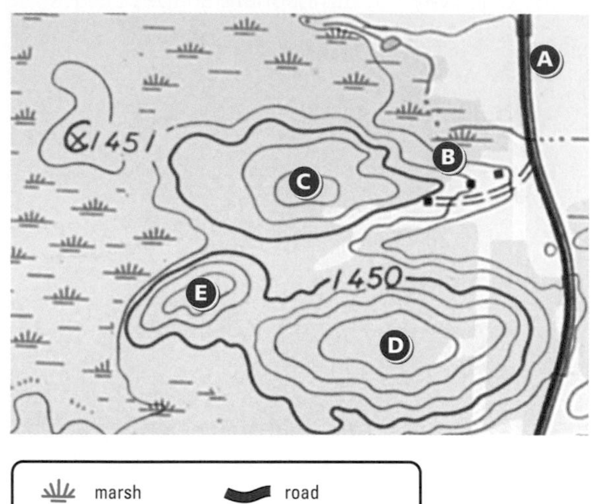

marsh | road
buildings | unpaved road

22. APPLY Imagine you are hiking through this area. Which hill—*C, D,* or *E*—has the steepest slope? How do you know?

23. ANALYZE What is the topography of the land through which the curved road *A* goes?

24. IDENTIFY CAUSE The squares at *B* represent buildings. Why do you think the buildings were placed here instead of somewhere else in the area?

25. APPLY The contour interval is 10 meters. What is the elevation of the highest point on the map?

26. SYNTHESIZE Sketch the two hills *D* and *E*. What would they look like to someone on the ground?

27. INFER Suppose someone wanted to build a road through the terrain on the far left side of the map. What are the advantages and disadvantages of such a route?

28. EVALUATE Do you think this area would be a good place to ride mountain bikes? Why or why not?

CHART INFORMATION *On a separate sheet of paper, write a word to fill each blank in the chart.*

Feature	Shown on Topographic Maps?	Belongs to Which Major System?
rivers	*yes*	*hydrosphere*
29. slope		
30. winds		
31. plants		
32. lakes		
33. relief		

the BIG idea

34. APPLY Look again at the photographs on pages 6–7. Now that you have finished the chapter, reread the question on the main photograph. What would you change in or add to your answer?

35. SYNTHESIZE Describe some of the types of information that new technology has provided about Earth.

36. DRAW CONCLUSIONS What type of technology do you think has done the most to change the way people view and map Earth? Explain your conclusion.

UNIT PROJECTS

If you are doing a unit project, make a folder for your project. Include in your folder a list of the resources you will need, the date on which the project is due, and a schedule to track your progress. Begin gathering data.

Standardized Test Practice

For practice on your state test, go to . . .
TEST PRACTICE
CLASSZONE.COM

Analyzing a Diagram

This diagram shows the four major parts of the Earth system. Use it to answer the questions below.

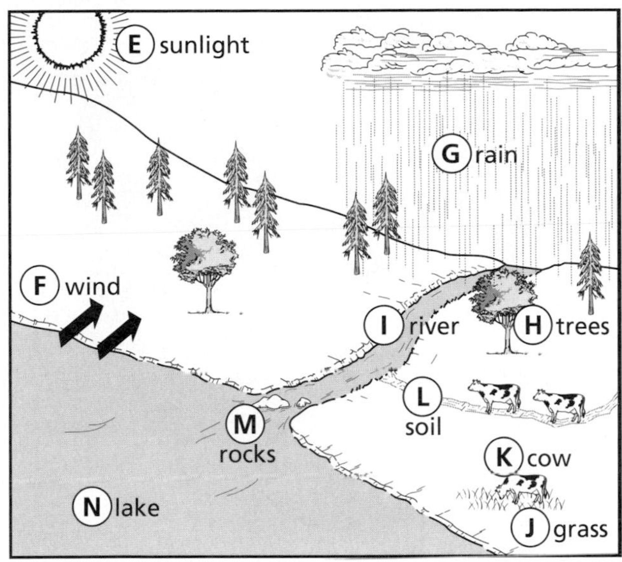

1. Where is the main source of energy for the Earth system?
   a. E
   b. F
   c. G
   d. L

2. Where is the biosphere shaping the geosphere?
   a. E
   b. F
   c. L
   d. M

3. Where is matter moving from one part of the hydrosphere to another?
   a. I to N
   b. G to H
   c. J to H
   d. N to M

4. Which items belong to the geosphere?
   a. F and G
   b. H and J
   c. I and N
   d. M and L

5. Which process is occurring at M where water is running over the rocks?
   a. The geosphere is shaping the atmosphere.
   b. The atmosphere is shaping the biosphere.
   c. The hydrosphere is shaping the geosphere.
   d. The biosphere is shaping the geosphere.

6. Where is matter moving from the atmosphere to the biosphere?
   a. E and F
   b. F and M
   c. G and H
   d. I and G

7. At K, the cow is eating grass. What kind of movement in the Earth system does this represent?
   a. from the atmosphere to the hydrosphere
   b. from the hydrosphere to the biosphere
   c. between two parts of the geosphere
   d. between two parts of the biosphere

8. Which is an example of how the hydrosphere is supported by the geosphere?
   a. I, because the river receives the rain
   b. H, because the trees are rooted in the ground
   c. M, because the river drains into the lake
   d. N, because the lake is contained by a basin

Extended Response

Answer the two questions below in detail. Include some of the terms shown in the word box. In your answers, underline each term you use.

geosphere	surface	system
atmosphere	hydrosphere	biosphere

9. Rain falls and soaks into the soil. Plants and animals use some of the water. More of the water drains into a river, then enters the ocean. Describe this process as movements among the major parts of the Earth system.

10. Describe an example of how people can shape the surface of the geosphere.

CHAPTER 2 Minerals

the BIG idea

Minerals are basic building blocks of Earth.

Key Concepts

SECTION

Minerals are all around us.
Learn about the characteristics all minerals share.

SECTION

A mineral is identified by its properties.
Learn how to identify minerals by observing and testing their properties.

SECTION

2.3 Minerals are valuable resources.
Learn how minerals form, how they are mined, and how they are used.

Internet Preview

CLASSZONE.COM

Chapter 2 online resources: Content Review, Visualization, three Resource Centers, Math Tutorial, Test Practice

Why can gold be separated from other minerals and rocks in a river?

EXPLORE the BIG idea

How Do You Turn Water into a Mineral?

Freeze some water into ice cubes. Then compare water, an ice cube, and a penny. Liquid water is not a mineral, but ice is. The surface of the penny is made of the mineral copper.

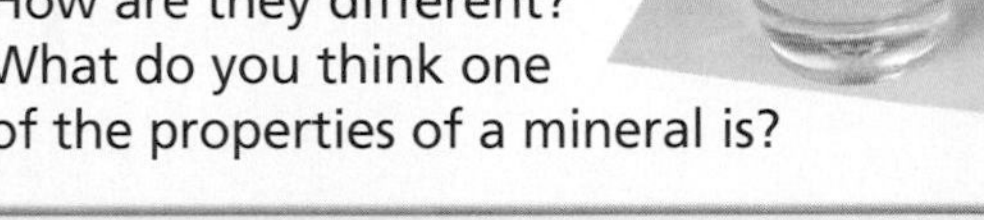

Observe and Think
How are the water, ice cube, and penny similar? How are they different? What do you think one of the properties of a mineral is?

What Makes Up Rocks?

Find three different rocks near your home or school. Examine them closely with a magnifying glass.

Observe and Think
Describe the rocks. How many materials can you see in each rock? How do you think they got there?

Internet Activity: Minerals

Go to **ClassZone.com** to find out more about minerals that are also precious metals.

Observe and Think
In addition to jewelry, how many different uses can you find for gold?

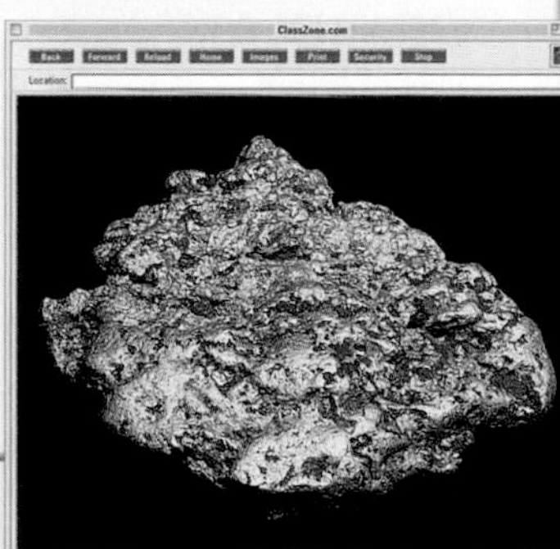

Identifying Minerals **Code: MDL014**

CHAPTER 2

Getting Ready to Learn

CONCEPT REVIEW

- Earth has four main layers: crust, mantle, outer core, and inner core.
- Matter exists in the forms of gas, liquid, and solid.
- People use maps to show many different features of Earth.

VOCABULARY REVIEW

atom *See Glossary.*

geosphere p. 12

Review concepts and vocabulary.

TAKING NOTES

SUPPORTING MAIN IDEAS

Make a chart to show each main idea and the information that supports it. Copy each blue heading. Below each heading, add supporting information, such as reasons, explanations, and examples.

VOCABULARY STRATEGY

Place each vocabulary term at the center of a **description wheel**. On the spokes write some words explaining it.

See the Note-Taking Handbook on pages R45–R51.

SCIENCE NOTEBOOK

Minerals have four characteristics.

- Minerals form naturally.
- All minerals are solids.
- Each mineral is always made of the same element or elements.
- All minerals have crystal structures.

CRYSTAL

formed by all minerals

atoms joined in a repeating 3-D pattern

KEY CONCEPT

Minerals are all around us.

BEFORE, you learned

- Earth is made of layers
- Earth's outermost rocky layer is the crust

NOW, you will learn

- What the characteristics of minerals are
- How minerals are classified into groups
- Which mineral group is most common

VOCABULARY

mineral p. 43
element p. 45
crystal p. 46

EXPLORE Minerals

What are some characteristics of a mineral?

PROCEDURE

1. Sprinkle some table salt on a sheet of colored paper. Look at a few grains of the salt through a magnifying glass. Then rub a few grains between your fingers.
2. In your notebook, describe all the qualities of the salt that you observe.
3. Examine the rock salt in the same way and describe its qualities in your notebook. How do the two differ?

WHAT DO YOU THINK?
Salt is a mineral. From your observations of salt, what do you think are some characteristics of minerals?

MATERIALS

- colored paper
- table salt
- rock salt
- magnifying glass

Minerals have four characteristics.

You use minerals all the time. Every time you turn on a microwave oven or a TV, you depend on minerals. The copper in the wires that carry electricity to the device is a mineral. Table salt, or halite (HAYL-YT), is another mineral that you use in your everyday life.

Minerals have four characteristics. A **mineral** is a substance that

- forms in nature
- is a solid
- has a definite chemical makeup
- has a crystal structure

VOCABULARY
Add a description wheel for *mineral* in your notebook.

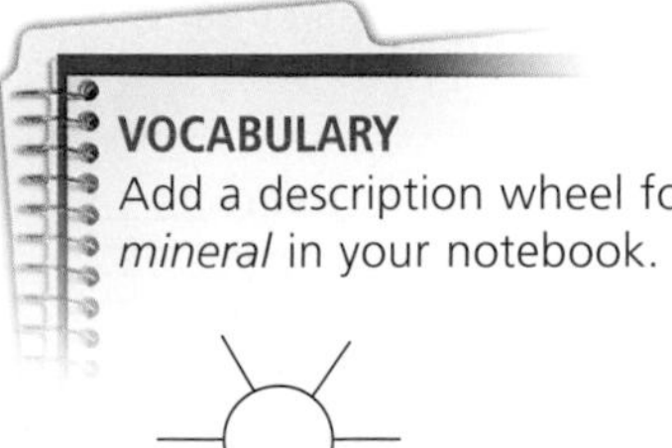

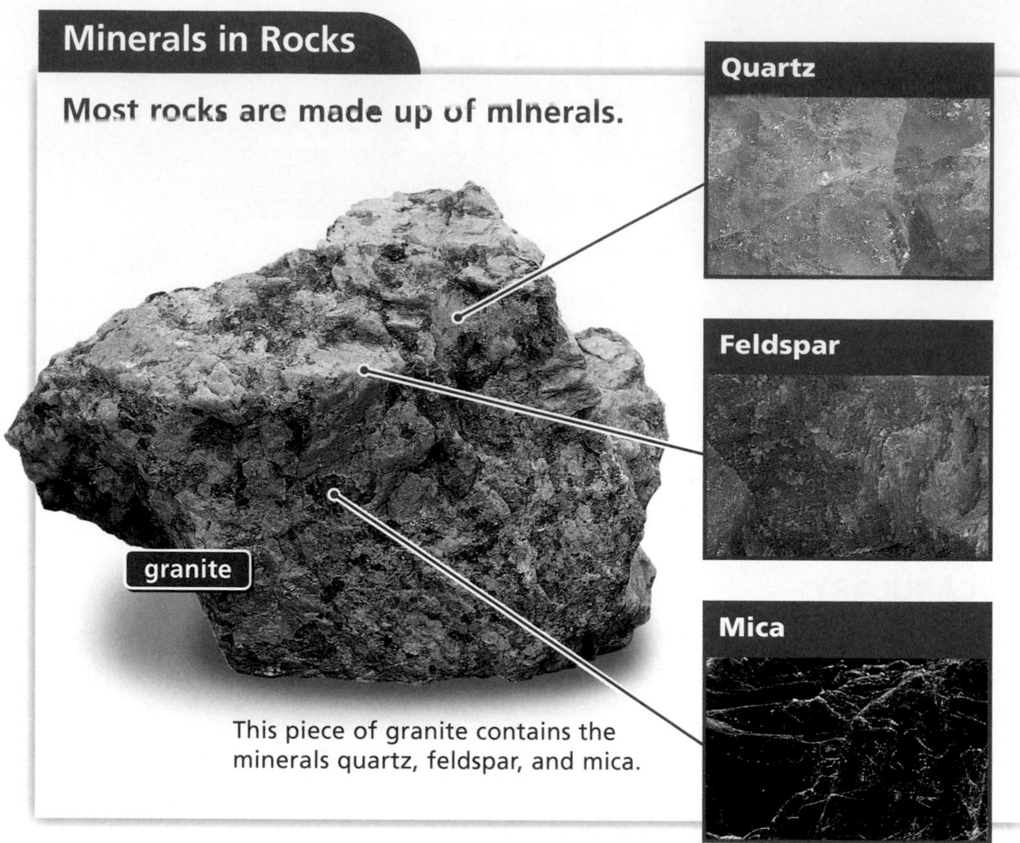

This piece of granite contains the minerals quartz, feldspar, and mica.

You might think that minerals and rocks are the same things. But a mineral must have the four characteristics listed on page 43. A rock has only two of these characteristics—it is a solid and it forms naturally. A rock usually contains two or more types of minerals.

READING TIP

Proportions show relationships between amounts. For example, a quartz crystal always has two oxygen atoms for every silicon atom.

Two samples of the same type of rock may vary greatly in the amounts of different minerals they contain. Minerals, however, are always made up of the same materials in the same proportions. A ruby is a mineral. Therefore, a ruby found in India has the same makeup as a ruby found in Australia.

CHECK YOUR READING How are minerals different from rocks?

Formed in Nature

Minerals are formed by natural processes. Every type of mineral can form in nature by processes that do not involve living organisms. As you will read, a few minerals can also be produced by organisms as part of their shells or bones.

Minerals form in many ways. The mineral halite, which is used as table salt, forms when water evaporates in a hot, shallow part of the ocean, leaving behind the salt it contained. Many types of minerals, including the ones in granite, develop when molten rock cools. Talc, a mineral that can be used to make baby powder, forms deep in Earth as high pressure and temperature cause changes in solid rock.

READING TIP

Molten rock refers to rock that has become so hot that it has melted.

Solid

A mineral is a solid—that is, it has a definite volume and a rigid shape. Volume refers to the amount of space an object takes up. For example, a golf ball has a smaller volume than a baseball, and a baseball has a smaller volume than a basketball.

A substance that is a liquid or a gas is not a mineral. However, in some cases its solid form is a mineral. For instance, liquid water is not a mineral, but ice is.

Definite Chemical Makeup

Each mineral has a definite chemical makeup: it consists of a specific combination of atoms of certain elements. An **element** is a substance that contains only one type of atom. In turn, an atom is the smallest particle an element can be divided into.

Everything you can see or touch is made up of atoms. Some substances, including the minerals gold and copper, consist of just one element. All the atoms in gold or copper are of the same type. However, most substances contain atoms of more than one element. Most minerals are compounds, substances consisting of several elements in specific proportions. Halite, for example, has one atom of sodium for every atom of chlorine.

The types of atoms that make up a mineral are part of what makes the mineral unique. The way in which the atoms are bonded, or joined together, is also important. As you will read, many properties of minerals are related to how strong or weak the bonds are.

READING TIP

You may remember *compound* from compound words—words formed by joining together smaller words: *note* + *book* = *notebook*. Likewise, a chemical compound has two or more elements joined together.

Atoms in Minerals

The mineral copper is made up only of copper atoms.

The mineral halite is made up of equal numbers of sodium and chlorine atoms.

READING VISUALS How do the diagrams show that copper consists of only one element and halite is a compound?

Crystal Structure

VISUALIZATION
CLASSZONE.COM
Explore an animation of crystal growth.

If you look closely at the particles of ice that make up frost, you will notice that they have smooth, flat surfaces. These flat surfaces form because of the arrangement of atoms in the ice, which is a mineral. Such an internal arrangement is a characteristic of minerals. It is the structure of a **crystal,** a solid in which the atoms are arranged in an orderly, repeating three-dimensional pattern.

Each mineral has its own type of crystal structure. In some cases, two minerals have the same chemical composition but different crystal structures. For example, both diamond and graphite consist of just one element—carbon. But the arrangements of the carbon atoms in these two minerals are not the same, so they have different crystal structures and very different properties. Diamonds are extremely hard and have a brilliant sparkle. Graphite is soft, gray, and dull.

In nature, a perfect crystal is rare. One can grow only when a mineral is free to form in an open space—a condition that rarely exists within Earth's crust. The photographs on page 47 show examples of nearly perfect crystals. The amount of space available for growth influences the shape and size of crystals. Most crystals have imperfect shapes because their growth was limited by other crystals forming next to them.

INVESTIGATE Crystal Shape

How do crystals differ in shape?

PROCEDURE

1. Cut sheets of paper so that they fit inside the pie plates as shown. Place one sheet in each pie plate.
2. Add the table salt to 30 mL of water in the cup. Stir the water until the salt has dissolved.
3. Pour enough salt solution into one of the pie plates to completely cover the paper with a small film of liquid. Be careful not to pour into the plate any undissolved salt that may be in the bottom of the cup.
4. Repeat steps 2 and 3 with the Epsom salts. Let the plates dry overnight.

WHAT DO YOU THINK?

- Compare and describe the shapes of the crystals.
- What do you think accounts for any differences you observe?

CHALLENGE Why are the shapes of the crystals the same as or different from the shapes in the materials you started with?

SKILL FOCUS
Observing

MATERIALS
- tablespoon
- 2 mixing cups
- 2 stirring rods
- 1 tbs table salt
- 1 tbs Epsom salts
- 60 mL water
- 2 pie plates
- 2 sheets black paper
- scissors

TIME
20 minutes for setup

Crystal Groups

Crystal groups are named by their shapes and the angles formed by imaginary lines through their centers. Crystals take many shapes, but all belong to these six groups.

Cubic
galena

Tetragonal
wulfenite

Hexagonal
beryl

Orthorhombic
topaz

Monoclinic
gypsum

Triclinic
microcline

Minerals are grouped according to composition.

SUPPORTING MAIN IDEAS
Enter this blue heading in a chart and record supporting information.

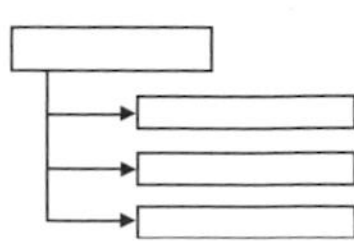

Scientists classify minerals into groups on the basis of their chemical makeups. The most common group is the silicates. All the minerals in this group contain oxygen and silicon—the two most common elements in Earth's crust—joined together.

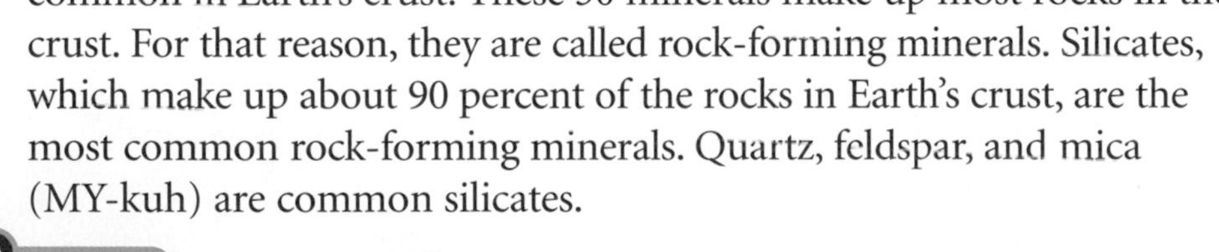

Though there are thousands of different minerals, only about 30 are common in Earth's crust. These 30 minerals make up most rocks in the crust. For that reason, they are called rock-forming minerals. Silicates, which make up about 90 percent of the rocks in Earth's crust, are the most common rock-forming minerals. Quartz, feldspar, and mica (MY-kuh) are common silicates.

Which mineral group do most rock-forming minerals belong to?

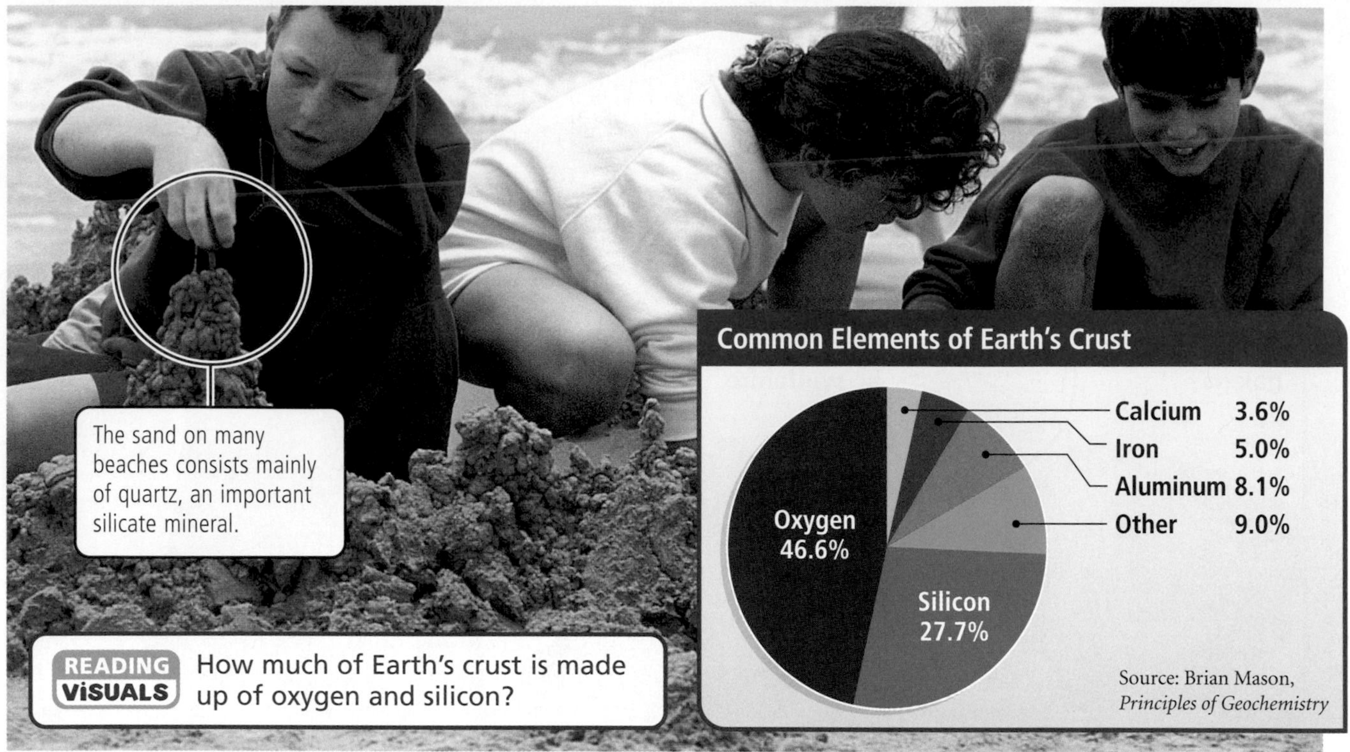

The sand on many beaches consists mainly of quartz, an important silicate mineral.

READING VISUALS How much of Earth's crust is made up of oxygen and silicon?

The second most common group of rock-forming minerals is the carbonates. All the minerals in this group contain carbon and oxygen joined together. Calcite (KAL-SYT), which is common in seashells, is a carbonate mineral.

RESOURCE CENTER
CLASSZONE.COM
Find information on minerals.

There are many other mineral groups. All are important, even though their minerals may not be as common as rock-forming minerals. For instance, the mineral group known as oxides contains the minerals from which most metals, such as tin and copper, are refined. An oxide consists of an element, usually a metal, joined to oxygen. This group includes hematite (HEE-muh-TYT), a source of iron.

CHECK YOUR READING Why is the oxide mineral group important?

2.1 Review

KEY CONCEPTS

1. What are the four characteristics of a mineral?
2. On what basis do scientists classify minerals?
3. What is the most common group of minerals? What percentage of the crust do they make up?

CRITICAL THINKING

4. **Classify** Can oil and natural gas be classified as minerals? Why or why not?
5. **Apply** When a piece of quartz is heated to a very high temperature, it melts into a liquid. Is it still a mineral? Why or why not?

CHALLENGE

6. **Interpret** You can see perfect crystals lining the inside of certain rocks when they are broken open. How do you think the crystals were able to form?

MATH in SCIENCE

MATH TUTORIAL

CLASSZONE.COM

Click on Math Tutorial for more help with percents and fractions.

SKILL: WRITING FRACTIONS AS PERCENTS

Minerals in Rocks

Like most rocks, granite is a mixture of several minerals. Each mineral makes up a certain proportion, or fraction, of the granite. You can compare mineral amounts by expressing each mineral's fraction as a percentage.

Granite

Example

To change a fraction to a percentage, you must find an equivalent fraction with 100 as the denominator. Suppose, for example, you want to change the fraction $\frac{1}{5}$ to a percentage. First, divide 100 by the denominator 5, which gives you 20. Then, multiply both the numerator and denominator by 20 to find the percentage.

$\frac{1}{5} \bullet \frac{20}{20} = \frac{20}{100}$ or 20% $\frac{1}{5}$ is 20%

The table below shows the fraction of each mineral in a granite sample.

Minerals in Granite Sample

Mineral	Fraction of Granite Sample	Percentage of Granite
Quartz	$\frac{1}{4}$	?
Feldspar	$\frac{13}{20}$	?
Mica	$\frac{3}{50}$	?
Dark minerals	$\frac{1}{25}$	?

Answer the following questions.

1. On your paper, copy the table and fill in the percentage of each mineral in the granite sample above.
2. Which minerals make up the greatest and smallest percentages of the granite?
3. In another granite sample, feldspar makes up $\frac{3}{5}$ and mica makes up $\frac{2}{25}$. What is the percentage of each mineral in the rock?

CHALLENGE The mineral hornblende is often one of the dark minerals in granite. If hornblende makes up $\frac{1}{32}$ of a granite sample, what percentage of the rock is hornblende?

KEY CONCEPT

A mineral is identified by its properties.

BEFORE, you learned

- All minerals have four characteristics
- Most minerals in Earth's crust are silicates

NOW, you will learn

- Which mineral properties are most important in identification
- How minerals are identified by their properties

VOCABULARY

streak p. 51
luster p. 52
cleavage p. 53
fracture p. 53
density p. 54
hardness p. 55

THINK ABOUT

What can you tell by looking at a mineral?

The photographs at the right show five pieces of the mineral fluorite (FLUR-YT). As you can see, the pieces are very different in color and size. Fluorite occurs in many colors, even in colorless forms. Its crystals can be well formed or poorly formed. Also, the sides of the crystals may be smooth or rough.

If you came across fluorite while hiking, would you know what it was by just looking at it? Probably not. Read on to find out how you could identify it.

A mineral's appearance helps identify it.

READING TIP

The word *characteristic* is used for a feature that is typical of a person or thing. It can be used as a noun or an adjective.

To identify a mineral, you need to observe its properties—characteristic features that identify it. You might begin by looking at the mineral's color. However, many minerals occur in more than one color, so you would need to examine other properties as well. You might also notice how the mineral reflects light, which determines how shiny or dull it is. Most minerals reflect light in characteristic ways. In this section you will read about how the properties of a mineral—including its appearance—are used to identify it.

Why do you need to look at properties other than color to identify a mineral?

Color and Streak

Some minerals can be almost any color, but most minerals have a more limited color range. For example, a particular mineral may almost always be brown to black.

Three main factors cause minerals to vary in color. First, a mineral may get its color from tiny amounts of an element that is not part of its normal chemical makeup. For example, a sample of pure quartz is clear and colorless, but tiny amounts of iron can give quartz a violet color. This violet variety of quartz is called amethyst. Second, a mineral's color can change when it is at or near Earth's surface and is in contact with the atmosphere or water. Third, mineral crystals can have defects in their crystal structures that change their color.

Some minerals have a different color when they are ground into a fine powder than when they are left whole. A mineral's **streak** is the color of the powder left behind when the mineral is scraped across a surface. Geologists use a tile of unglazed porcelain, called a streak plate, as a tool to identify minerals by their streaks. Streak is a better clue to a mineral's identity than surface color is. Look at the photographs of hematite below. Even though the mineral samples are different colors, both leave a reddish brown streak when scraped across a streak plate. All samples of the same mineral have the same streak.

READING TIP
A geologist is a scientist who studies Earth.

What is the difference between color and streak?

Streak

These samples are of the mineral hematite. They are different colors, but they have the same streak.

This hematite looks dull because it has tiny crystals that reflect light in all directions.

This hematite looks shiny because it has larger crystals.

READING VISUALS What is a clue that both samples are of the same mineral?

Luster

READING TIP

Luster comes from the Latin *lūstrāre*, "to make bright." But luster isn't always bright or shiny. Some minerals have lusters that are waxlike or dull.

A mineral's **luster** is the way in which light reflects from its surface. The two major types of luster are metallic and nonmetallic. The mineral pyrite has a metallic luster. It looks as if it were made of metal. A mineral with a nonmetallic luster can be shiny, but it does not appear to be made of metal. An example of a nonmetallic luster is the glassy luster of garnet. Compare the lusters of pyrite and garnet in the photographs below.

Pyrite has a metallic luster.

Garnet crystals in this rock have a nonmetallic luster.

Like a mineral's color, its luster may vary from sample to sample. If a mineral has been exposed to the atmosphere or to water, its surface luster can become dull. However, if the mineral is broken to reveal a fresh surface, its characteristic luster can be seen.

The way a mineral breaks helps identify it.

SUPPORTING MAIN IDEAS
Enter this blue heading in a chart and record supporting information.

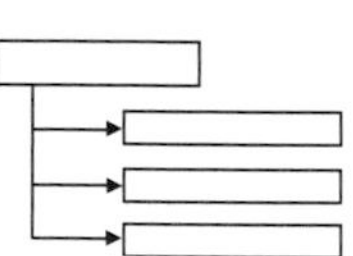

If you hit a piece of calcite with a hammer, the calcite will break into tilted blocks. You can peel off layers of mica because it splits into thin, flat sheets. Each kind of mineral always breaks in the same way, and this property can help identify a mineral. In fact, the way a mineral breaks is a better clue to its identity than are its color and luster.

Cleavage

Cleavage is a tendency to break along flat surfaces.

Calcite has cleavage.

It breaks along flat surfaces because the bonds between its atoms are less strong in some directions than in others.

Cleavage

Cleavage is the tendency of a mineral to break along flat surfaces. The way in which a mineral breaks depends on how its atoms are bonded, or joined together. In a mineral that displays cleavage, the bonds of the crystal structure are weaker in the directions in which the mineral breaks.

When geologists describe the cleavage of a mineral, they consider both the directions in which the mineral breaks and the smoothness of the broken surfaces. Mica has cleavage in one direction and breaks into sheets. The photographs on page 52 show that calcite has cleavage in three directions and breaks into tilted blocks. Because the broken surfaces of both mica and calcite are smooth, these minerals are said to have perfect cleavage.

Carbon Bonds in Graphite

strong bonds within layers

weak bonds between layers

carbon atoms

In graphite, carbon atoms are arranged in layers. Graphite has cleavage because the weak bonds between the layers break easily.

Fracture

Fracture is the tendency of a mineral to break into irregular pieces. Some minerals such as quartz break into pieces with curved surfaces, as shown below. Other minerals may break differently—perhaps into splinters or into rough or jagged pieces.

In a mineral that displays fracture, the bonds that join the atoms are fairly equal in strength in all directions. The mineral does not break along flat surfaces because there are no particular directions of weakness in its crystal structure.

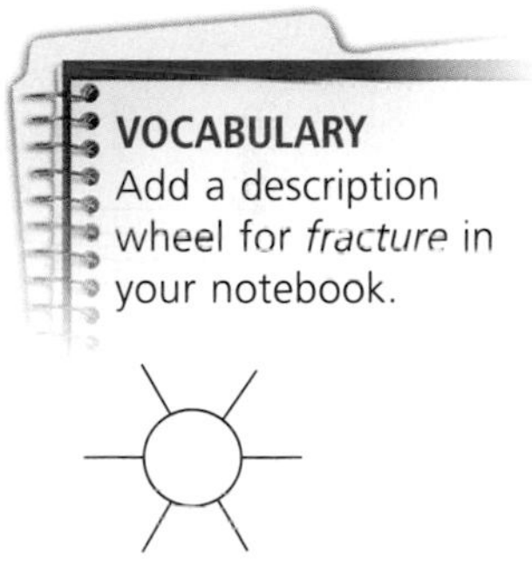

VOCABULARY
Add a description wheel for *fracture* in your notebook.

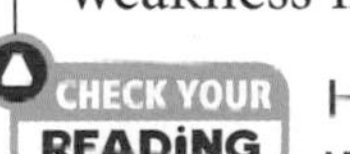

How does the strength of the bonds between atoms determine whether a mineral displays cleavage or fracture?

Fracture

Fracture is a tendency to break into irregular pieces.

Quartz does not have cleavage. It breaks by fracturing.

It breaks along irregular surfaces because the bonds between its atoms are about the same strength in every direction.

A mineral's density and hardness help identify it.

A tennis ball is not as heavy or as hard as a baseball. You would be able to tell the two apart even with your eyes closed by how heavy and hard they feel. You can identify minerals in a similar way.

Density

Even though a baseball and a tennis ball are about the same size, the baseball has more mass and so is more dense. A substance's **density** is the amount of mass in a given volume of the substance. For example, 1 cubic centimeter of the mineral pyrite has a mass of 5.1 grams, so pyrite's density is 5.1 grams per cubic centimeter.

READING TIP

The unit of density is grams per cubic centimeter and is abbreviated as g/cm^3.

Density is very helpful in identifying minerals. For example, gold and pyrite look very similar. Pyrite is often called fool's gold. However, you can tell the two minerals apart by comparing their densities. Gold is much denser than pyrite. The mass of a piece of gold is almost four times the mass of a piece of pyrite of the same size. A small amount of a very dense mineral, such as gold, can have more mass and be heavier than a larger amount of a less dense mineral, such as pyrite. A mineral's density is determined by the kinds of atoms that make up

Comparing Densities

Differences in density can be used to tell minerals apart.

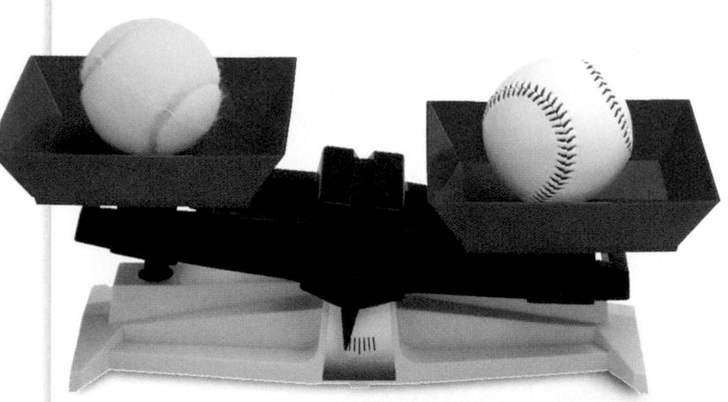

The baseball on the right has more mass, and so is denser, than a tennis ball that is about the same size.

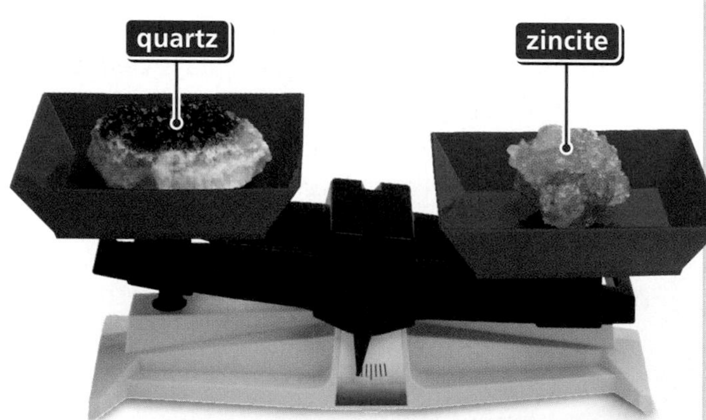

The zincite sample on the right is about twice as dense as the quartz sample.

READING VISUALS Estimate the size a piece of quartz would have to be to balance the zincite sample.

the mineral, as well as how closely the atoms are joined together. An experienced geologist can estimate the density of a mineral by lifting it. But to get an exact measurement, geologists use special scales.

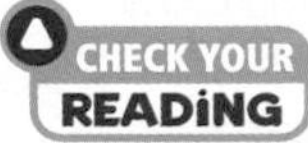
CHECK YOUR
READING
Why does a piece of gold weigh much more than a piece of pyrite that is the same size?

Hardness

One way to tell a tennis ball from a baseball without looking at them is to compare their densities. Another way is to test which one is harder. Hardness is another dependable clue to a mineral's identity.

A mineral's **hardness** is its resistance to being scratched. Like a mineral's cleavage, a mineral's hardness is determined by its crystal structure and the strength of the bonds between its atoms. Harder minerals have stronger bonds.

A scale known as the Mohs scale is often used to describe a mineral's hardness. This scale is based on the fact that a harder mineral will scratch a softer one. As you can see in the chart at the right, ten minerals are numbered in the scale, from softest to hardest. Talc is the softest mineral and has a value of 1. Diamond, the hardest of all minerals, has a value of 10.

A mineral can be scratched only by other minerals that have the same hardness or are harder. To determine the hardness of an unknown mineral, you test whether it scratches or is scratched by the minerals in the scale. For example, if you can scratch an unknown mineral with apatite but not with fluorite, the mineral's hardness is between 4 and 5 in the Mohs scale.

In place of minerals, you can use your fingernail, a copper penny, and a steel file to test an unknown mineral. To avoid damage to the minerals, you can test whether the mineral scratches these items. When using a penny to test hardness, make sure its date is 1982 or earlier. Only older pennies are made mainly of copper, which has a hardness of about 3.

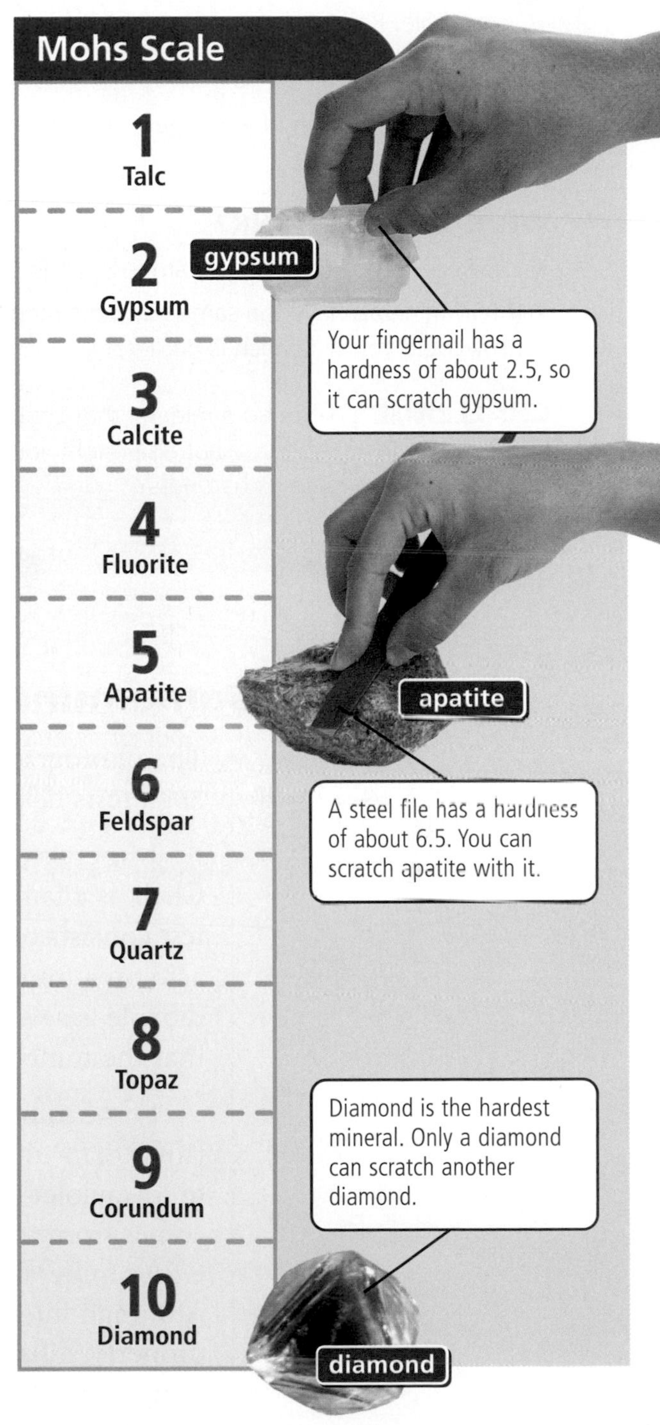
Mohs Scale
1
Talc
2
Gypsum
gypsum
3
Calcite
4
Fluorite
5
Apatite
apatite
6
Feldspar
7
Quartz
8
Topaz
9
Corundum
10
Diamond
diamond
Your fingernail has a hardness of about 2.5, so it can scratch gypsum.
A steel file has a hardness of about 6.5. You can scratch apatite with it.
Diamond is the hardest mineral. Only a diamond can scratch another diamond.

INVESTIGATE Hardness of Minerals

How hard are some common minerals?

PROCEDURE

1. Try to scratch each mineral with your fingernail, the penny, and the steel file. Record the results in a chart.
2. Assign a hardness range to each mineral.
3. In the last column of your chart, rank the minerals from hardest to softest.

WHAT DO YOU THINK?

- Use your results to assign a hardness range in the Mohs scale to each sample.
- If two minerals have the same hardness range according to your tests, how could you tell which is harder?

CHALLENGE If you had a mineral that could not be scratched by the steel file, what else might you test it with to estimate its hardness?

SKILL FOCUS
Classifying

MATERIALS
- samples of 5 minerals
- copper penny (1982 or earlier)
- steel file

TIME
20 minutes

Some minerals have special properties.

The photographs on page 57 show how geologists test some minerals. Such tests help them identify minerals that have unusual properties.

Minerals in the carbonate group, such as calcite, react with acid. Chalk is a familiar item that is made up of carbonate minerals. The test consists of putting a drop of a weak solution of hydrochloric acid on a mineral sample. If the acid reacts with the mineral, carbon dioxide gas will form and bubble out of the acid. The bubbles show that the mineral is a carbonate.

Some minerals have a property known as fluorescence (flu-REHS-uhns). Fluorescent minerals glow when they are exposed to ultraviolet (UHL-truh-VY-uh-liht) light. The word *fluorescence* comes from the name of the mineral fluorite, which has this property. Other minerals that display fluorescence include calcite and willemite. Although fluorescence is an interesting and sometimes dramatic property, it has limited value in mineral identification. Different samples of the same mineral may or may not display fluorescence, and they may glow in different colors.

CHECK YOUR READING To identify calcite, why would it be more useful to test with dilute hydrochloric acid than to check for fluorescence?

Special Properties

Fluorescence

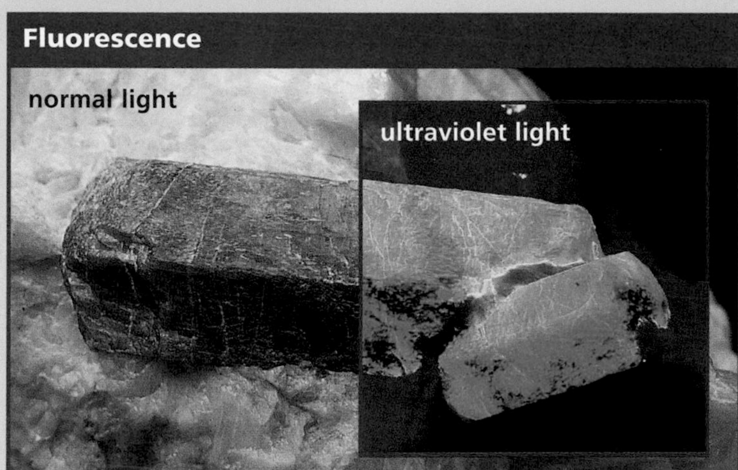

These minerals look ordinary in normal light but display red and green fluorescence under ultraviolet light.

Acid Test

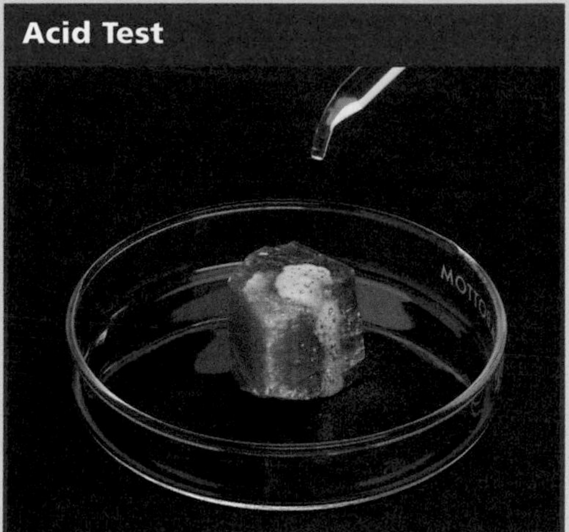

Acid in contact with carbonate minerals, such as calcite, forms bubbles.

A few minerals respond to magnets. A magnet is pulled toward these minerals. The mineral magnetite strongly attracts magnets, and some other minerals weakly attract magnets. To test a mineral, hold a magnet loosely and bring it close to the mineral. You will be able to notice if there is even a small pull of the magnet toward the mineral. Magnets are commonly used in laboratories and industries to separate magnetic minerals from other minerals.

Some rare minerals have a property known as radioactivity. They contain unstable elements that change into other elements over time. As this happens, they release energy. Geologists can measure this energy and use it to identify minerals that contain unstable elements.

2.2 Review

KEY CONCEPTS

1. Why is color not a reliable clue to the identity of a mineral?
2. What is the difference between cleavage and fracture?
3. Describe what would happen if you rubbed a mineral with a Mohs hardness value of 7 against a mineral with a value of 5.

CRITICAL THINKING

4. **Analyze** Which mineral-identification tests would be easy for a person to perform at home? Which would be difficult?
5. **Draw Conclusions** Diamond and graphite contain only carbon atoms. How can you tell which mineral's atoms are bonded more closely?

CHALLENGE

6. **Apply** The mineral topaz has perfect cleavage in one direction. It also displays fracture. Explain why a mineral such as topaz can display both cleavage and fracture.

CHAPTER INVESTIGATION

Mineral Identification

OVERVIEW AND PURPOSE In this activity, you will observe and perform tests on minerals. Then you will compare your observations to a mineral identification key.

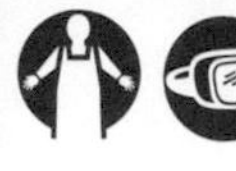   

MATERIALS

- numbered mineral samples
- hand lens
- streak plate
- copper penny
- steel file
- magnet
- dilute hydrochloric acid
- eyedropper
- Mohs scale
- Mineral Identification Key

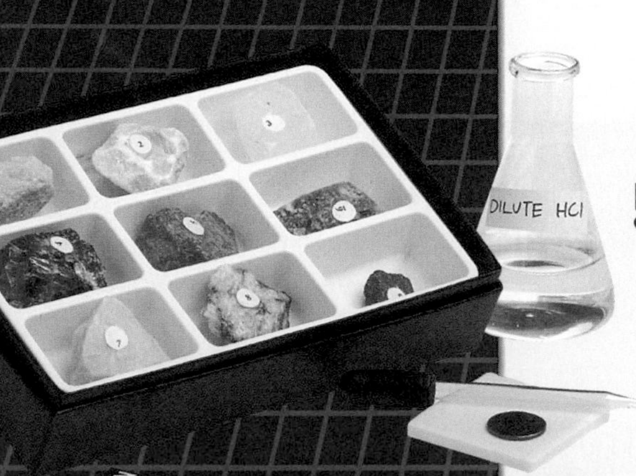

Procedure

1. Make a data table like the one shown in the notebook on the next page.

2. You will examine and identify five minerals. Get a numbered mineral sample from the mineral set. Record the number of your sample in your table.

3. First, observe the sample. Note the color and the luster of the sample. Write your observations in your table. In the row labeled "Luster," write *metallic* if the mineral appears shiny like metal. Write *nonmetallic* if the sample does not look like metal. For example, it may look glassy, pearly, or dull.

step 3

4. Observe the sample through the hand lens. Look to see any signs of how the crystals in the mineral broke. If it appears that the crystals have broken along straight lines, put a check in the row labeled "Cleavage." If it appears that the sample has fractured, put a check in the appropriate row of your table.

5. **CAUTION: Keep the streak plate on your desktop or table while you are doing the streak test. A broken streak plate can cause serious cuts.** Rub the mineral sample on the streak plate. If the sample does not leave a mark, the mineral is harder than the streak plate. Write *no* in the row labeled "Streak." If the sample does leave a mark on the streak plate, write the color of the streak in that row.

step 5

6 Test each sample for its hardness on the Mohs scale. Try to scratch the sample with each of these items in order: a fingernail, a copper penny, and a steel file. In the Mohs scale, find the hardness number of the object that first scratches the sample. Write in the table that the mineral's hardness value is between that of the hardest item that did not scratch the sample and that of the item that did scratch it.

7 Test the sample with the magnet. If the magnet is attracted to the sample, put a check in the row labeled "Magnetic."

step 7

8 Repeat steps 2 through 7 for each of the other numbered samples.

Observe and Analyze

Write It Up

1. **INTERPRET DATA** Use the Mineral Identification Key and the information in your data table to identify your samples. Write the names of the minerals in your table.
2. **COLLECT DATA** **CAUTION: Before doing the acid test, put on your safety glasses, protective gloves, and lab apron. Acids can cause burns.** If you identified one of the samples as a carbonate mineral, such as calcite, you can check your identification with the acid test. Use the eyedropper to put a few drops of dilute hydrochloric acid on the mineral. If the acid bubbles, the sample is a carbonate.

Conclude

Write It Up

1. **COMPARE AND CONTRAST** How are the minerals calcite and halite alike? Which property can you use to test whether a sample is calcite or halite?
2. **INTERPRET** Look at the data in your table. Name any minerals that you could identify on the basis of a single property.
3. **APPLY** Examine a piece of granite rock. On the basis of your examination of granite and your observations of the samples, try to determine what the light-colored, translucent mineral in the granite is and what the flaky, darker mineral is.

INVESTIGATE Further

Specific gravity is another property used to identify minerals. The specific gravity of a mineral is determined by comparing the mineral's density with the density of water.

Find the specific gravity of an unknown mineral chosen from your teacher's samples. Attach your mineral with a string to a spring scale. Record its mass and label this value *M1*. Then suspend the mineral in a beaker of water. Record the measurement of the mineral's mass in water. Label this value *M2*. To determine the mineral's specific gravity, use the following equation:

$$\frac{M1}{M1 - M2} = \text{specific gravity}$$

Do all the other steps to identify the sample. Does the specific gravity you measured match the one listed for that mineral in the identification key?

Mineral Identification

Table 1. Mineral Properties

Property	Sample Number				
	1	2	3	4	5
Color					
Luster					
Cleavage					
Fracture					
Streak					
Hardness					
Magnetic					
Acid test					
Name of mineral					

KEY CONCEPT

Minerals are valuable resources.

BEFORE, you learned

- Minerals are classified according to their compositions and crystal structures
- A mineral can be identified by its properties

NOW, you will learn

- How minerals are used in industry and art
- How minerals form
- How minerals are mined

VOCABULARY

magma p. 62
lava p. 62
ore p. 64

EXPLORE Minerals at Your Fingertips

What is an everyday use of minerals?

PROCEDURE

1. Observe the core of a wooden pencil. Even though it is called lead, it is made of a mixture of minerals—clay and graphite. A No. 4 pencil has more clay in its lead.
2. Use each pencil to draw something, noticing how each marks the page.

MATERIALS

- No. 2 wooden pencil
- No. 4 wooden pencil
- paper

WHAT DO YOU THINK?

- How is using a pencil similar to a streak test?
- When would a No. 4 pencil be more useful than a No. 2 pencil?

Minerals have many uses in industry.

Minerals are necessary to our modern way of life. Mineral deposits are sources of

- metals for cars and airplanes
- quartz and feldspar for glass
- fluorite and calcite for toothpaste
- silver compounds for photographic film
- mica and talc for paint

These examples illustrate just a few of the many ways we depend on minerals.

Give three examples of the use of minerals in familiar products.

Minerals have many uses in the arts.

RESOURCE CENTER
CLASSZONE.COM

Learn more about gemstones.

No matter what month you were born in, there is a mineral associated with it—your birthstone. The tradition of birthstones is hundreds of years old. It is one example of the value that people place on the particularly beautiful minerals known as gemstones. In fact, the ancient Egyptians used gems in necklaces and other jewelry at least 4000 years ago.

When gemstones are found, they are usually rough and irregularly shaped. Before a gemstone is used in jewelry, a gem cutter grinds it into the desired shape and polishes it. This process increases the gemstone's beauty and sparkle. The material used to shape and polish a gemstone must be at least as hard as the gemstone itself. Metals, such as gold and silver, also are used in jewelry making and other decorative arts. Both gold and silver are usually combined with copper to increase their hardness.

READING TIP

Corundum and diamond are the two hardest minerals in the Mohs scale. They are often used to grind and polish gemstones.

How are minerals prepared for use in jewelry? What other questions do you have about how minerals are used?

Uses of Minerals

Common Uses of Minerals

Mineral	Products
Quartz (source of silicon)	Optics, glass, abrasives, gems
Hematite (source of iron)	Machines, nails, cooking utensils
Gibbsite (source of aluminum)	Soda cans, shopping carts
Dolomite (source of magnesium)	Insulators, medicines
Chromite (source of chromium)	Automobile parts, stainless steel
Galena (source of lead)	Batteries, fiber optics, weights
Kaolinite (found in clay)	Ceramics, paper, cosmetics
Beryl (source of beryllium)	Aircraft frames, gems (green form is emerald)

Technology

A clear quartz crystal was sliced to make this computer chip. Minerals such as copper, silver, and gold are commonly used in electronics.

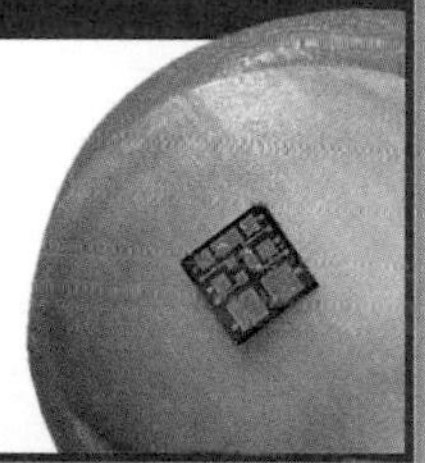

Industry

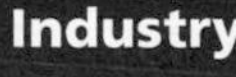

Diamonds are used as abrasives, as in this drill tip. Minerals are also used in such products as insulators and water filters.

Arts

Cinnabar is ground up to make the pigment known as vermilion. Other minerals are also used as pigments in dyes and paints. Gemstones are used in jewelry, as are platinum and gold.

Minerals form in several ways.

REMINDER

An element is a substance that contains only one type of atom. For instance, oxygen is an element. Pure oxygen contains only oxygen atoms.

Minerals form within Earth or on Earth's surface by natural processes. Minerals develop when atoms of one or more elements join together and crystals begin to grow. Recall that each type of mineral has its own chemical makeup. Therefore, what types of minerals form in an area depends in part on which elements are present there. Temperature and pressure also affect which minerals form.

Water evaporates. Water usually has many substances dissolved in it. Minerals can form when the water evaporates. For example, when salt water evaporates, the atoms that make up halite, which is used as table salt, join to form crystals. Other minerals form from evaporation too, depending on the substances dissolved in the water. The mineral gypsum often forms as water evaporates.

Hot water cools. As hot water within Earth's crust moves through rocks, it can dissolve minerals. When the water cools, the dissolved minerals separate from the water and become solid again. In some cases, minerals are moved from one place to another. Gold can dissolve in hot water that moves through the crust. As the water cools and the gold becomes solid again, it can fill cracks in rocks. In other cases, the minerals that form are different from the ones that dissolved. Lead from the mineral galena can later become part of the mineral wulfenite as atoms join together into new minerals.

Molten rock cools. Many minerals grow from magma. **Magma**—molten rock inside Earth—contains all the types of atoms that are found in minerals. As magma cools, the atoms join together to form different minerals. Minerals also form as lava cools. **Lava** is molten rock that has reached Earth's surface. Quartz is one of the many minerals that crystallize from magma and lava.

Heat and pressure cause changes. Heat and pressure within Earth cause new minerals to form as bonds between atoms break and join again. The mineral garnet can grow and replace the minerals chlorite and quartz as their atoms combine in new ways. The element carbon is present in some rocks. At high temperatures carbon forms the mineral graphite, which is used in pencils.

Organisms produce minerals. A few minerals are produced by living things. For example, ocean animals such as oysters and clams produce calcite and other carbonate minerals to form their shells. Even you produce minerals. Your body produces one of the main minerals in your bones and teeth—apatite.

How is the formation of minerals as molten rock cools similar to the formation of minerals as water evaporates?

Mineral Formation

Minerals form at Earth's surface and within Earth.

Water evaporates.

As water evaporates along a shoreline, it leaves behind substances that were dissolved in it. Here, gypsum is forming.

Hot water cools.

Gold dissolved in hot water can fill cracks in rocks as the water cools.

Molten rock cools.

Minerals such as quartz grow as molten rock cools.

Heat and pressure cause changes.

Graphite forms inside Earth when carbon is subjected to great heat.

READING VISUALS Each of the four processes shown involves heat. What is the heat source for rapid evaporation of water at Earth's surface?

Minerals and Ores Around the World

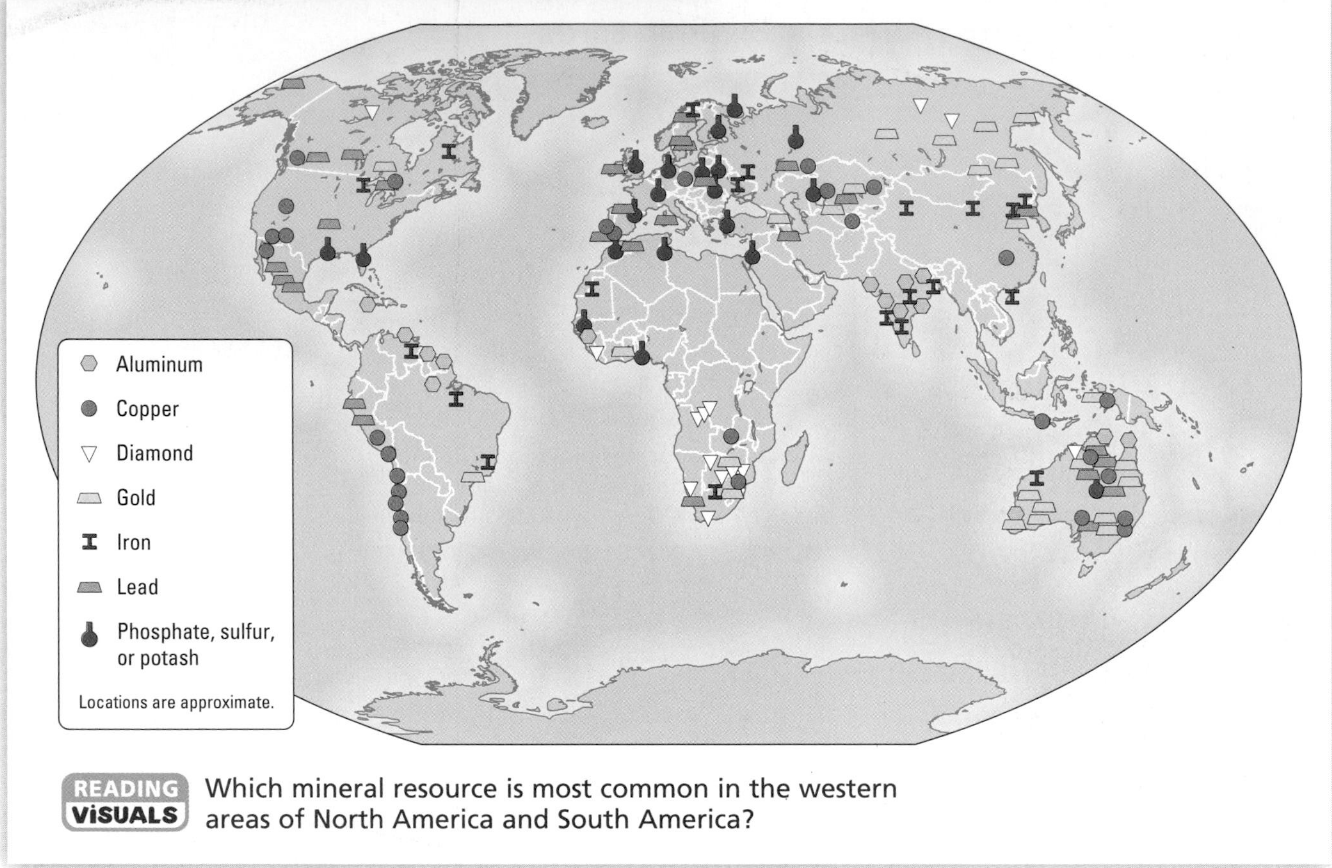

READING VISUALS Which mineral resource is most common in the western areas of North America and South America?

Many minerals are mined.

Before minerals can be used to make products, they must be removed from the ground. Some minerals are found near Earth's surface, while others lie deep underground. Some minerals are found at a wide range of depths, from the surface to deep within Earth.

READING TIP
To make a profit, mine owners must be able to sell ores for more than it cost them to dig the ores out.

Most minerals are combined with other minerals in rocks. For any mineral to be worth mining, there must be a fairly large amount of the mineral present in a rock. Rocks that contain enough of a mineral to be mined for a profit are called **ores.**

Surface Mining

Minerals at or near Earth's surface are recovered by surface mining. Some minerals, such as gold, are very dense. These minerals can build up in riverbeds as less dense minerals are carried away by the water. In a method called panning, a miner uses a pan to wash away unwanted minerals that are less dense. The gold and other dense minerals stay in the bottom of the pan and can then be further separated. In bigger riverbed mining operations, miners use machines to dig out and separate the valuable minerals.

Another method of surface mining is strip mining. Miners strip away plants, soil, and unwanted rocks from Earth's surface. Then they use special machines to dig out an ore.

Like strip mining, open-pit mining involves removing the surface layer of soil. Miners then use explosives to break up the underlying rock and recover the ore. As they dig a deep hole, or pit, to mine the ore, they build roads up the sides of the pit. Trucks carry the ore to the surface. Ores of copper and of iron are obtained by open-pit mining.

If an Olympic-sized swimming pool were filled with rock from this mine, it might contain enough copper to make a solid "beach ball" 146 cm (60 in.) in diameter.

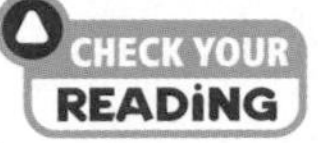

How are strip mining and open-pit mining similar? How are they different?

INVESTIGATE Mining

What are the benefits and costs of mining ores?

SKILL FOCUS
Drawing conclusions

MATERIALS
- 1 pound wild-birdseed mix with sunflower seeds
- shallow pan
- 2 small red beads
- 4 small green beads
- 8 small blue beads
- 3 medium yellow beads

TIME
25 minutes

PROCEDURE

1. Put the birdseed into a pan. Add the beads to the birdseed and mix well.
2. Search through the seeds and separate out the beads and sunflower seeds, placing each kind in a different pile. Take no more than 3 minutes.
3. Assign a value to each of the beads and seeds: red bead, \$5; green bead, \$4; blue bead, \$3; sunflower seed, \$2. Count up the value of your beads and seeds. For every yellow bead, subtract \$100, which represents the cost of restoring the land after mining.

WHAT DO YOU THINK?

- How does the difficulty of finding the red beads relate to the difficulty of finding the most valuable ores?
- How does the total value of the blue beads and the sunflower seeds compare to the total value of the red and green beads? What can you conclude about deciding which materials to mine?

CHALLENGE The sunflower seeds and the red, green, and blue beads could represent minerals that contain copper, gold, iron, and silver. Which bead or seed is most likely to represent each mineral? Explain your choices.

Deep Mining

Deep-mining methods are needed when an ore lies far below Earth's surface. These methods are used to obtain many minerals. Miners dig an opening to reach a deep ore. When the ore is inside a mountain or hill, miners can cut a level passage to reach the mineral they want. Miners dig a vertical passage to reach an ore that lies underground in a flat area or under a mountain.

From the main passage, miners blast, drill, cut, or dig the ore. If the passage is horizontal, they keep digging farther and farther into the hill or mountain. If it is vertical, they remove the ore in layers.

These gold miners are working underground near Carlin, Nevada. The world's deepest gold mine is in South Africa and extends almost 3 km (2 mi) underground.

2.3 Review

KEY CONCEPTS

1. Give two examples of the use of minerals in industry and two examples of the use of minerals in the arts.
2. What are the five ways in which minerals form?
3. What is required for rocks to be considered ores?

CRITICAL THINKING

4. **Infer** Would an ore at Earth's surface or an ore deep underground be more expensive to mine? Explain.
5. **Apply** The mineral quartz has been used as a gemstone for thousands of years. What minerals could jewelry makers use to grind and polish quartz?

CHALLENGE

6. **Analyze** Both strip mining and open-pit mining are types of surface mining. When might miners choose to use open-pit mining rather than strip mining to obtain an ore?

SCIENCE on the JOB

GEM CUTTER

Geometry for Gems

If you found a gemstone in nature, it would probably look dull and rough. You might want to take it to a gem cutter, who would use a grinding wheel to shape and polish your rough stone into a beautiful gem. You would also discover that a lot of the rough gemstone is ground away into powder.

Gem cutters use geometry to help them choose the best final shapes of gems. Geometry also helps them to shape gems with many small, flat surfaces at specific angles. These surfaces are called facets, and they make the gems sparkle.

Starred Gems

Some gems—such as certain rubies, sapphires, and forms of quartz—show a six-pointed star when cut in a rounded shape instead of facets. These gems contain tiny flaws aligned at 120-degree angles. When light hits the flaws, it scatters in a star-shaped pattern. The star ruby shown here is a good example of these beautiful gems.

Deeply Colored Gems

Some gems are shaped to show off their rich colors rather than their sparkle. These gems have fewer and larger facets. Also, many brightly colored gems contain lighter and darker areas of color. The gems are shaped so that the richest color is toward the bottom. Light entering one of these gems strikes the bottom and reflects the rich color to the viewer's eye.

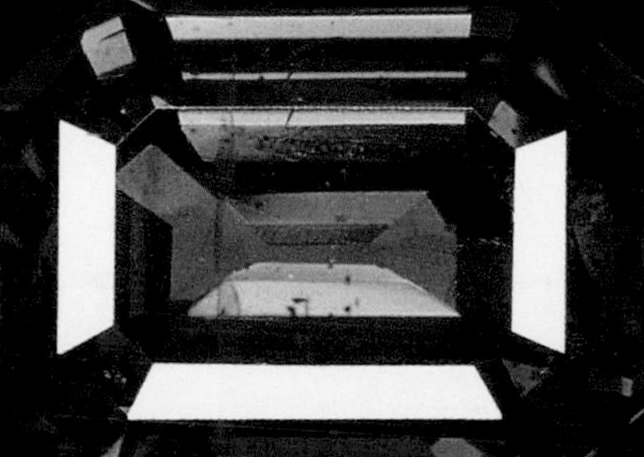

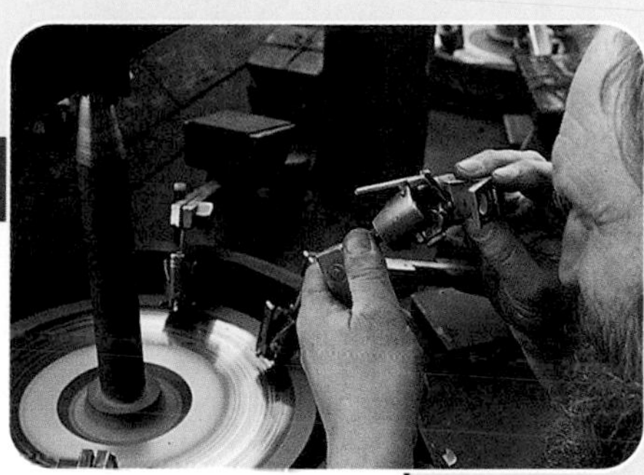

Sparkling Gems

How much a gem sparkles depends on the geometric angles at which it is cut. If the overall angle of the bottom part of a gem is too shallow **(A)** or too steep **(C)**, light will go through the gem.

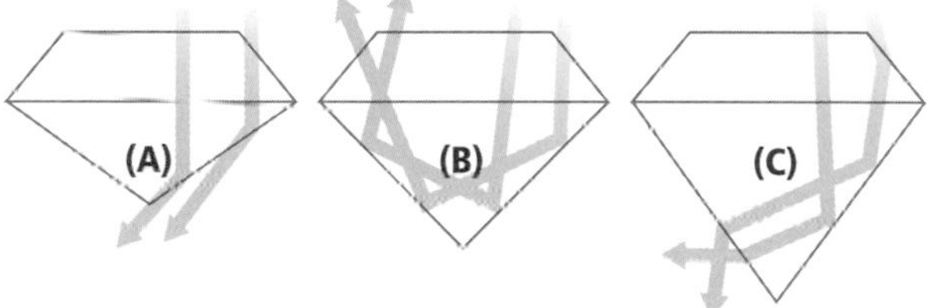

However, if the angles are correct **(B)**, light will bounce around inside the gem as it is reflected to the viewer's eye.The more facets a gem has, the more the light will bounce, and the more the gem will sparkle.

EXPLORE

1. **COMPARE** Table salt, which is the mineral halite, sparkles as light is reflected from its crystal faces. Snow, which is the mineral ice, also sparkles in sunlight. How are the crystal faces of salt and snow similar to facets? How are they different?
2. **CHALLENGE** When would it be best for a gem cutter to split an irregularly shaped crystal into two or more smaller stones before grinding them into finished gems? Remember, one larger stone is usually more valuable than two smaller ones.

2 Chapter Review

the BIG idea

Minerals are basic building blocks of Earth.

CONTENT REVIEW
CLASSZONE.COM

KEY CONCEPTS SUMMARY

2.1 Minerals are all around us.

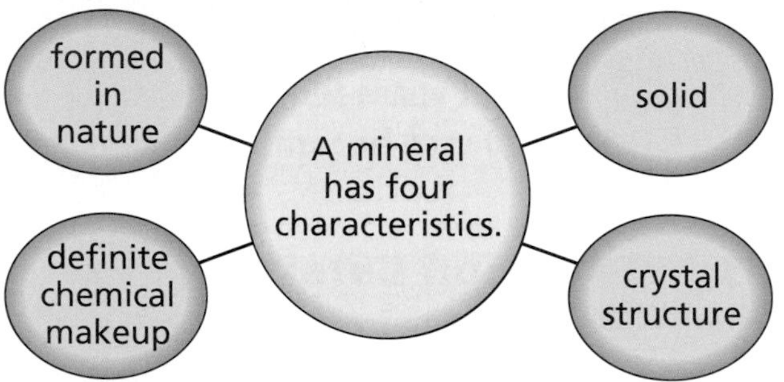
A mineral has four characteristics.
formed in nature
solid
definite chemical makeup
crystal structure

VOCABULARY
mineral p. 43
element p. 45
crystal p. 46

2.2 A mineral is identified by its properties.

Mineral Properties	wulfenite
color	orange
streak	white
luster	nonmetallic
cleavage	yes
density	6.9
hardness	3

VOCABULARY
streak p. 51
luster p. 52
cleavage p. 53
fracture p. 53
density p. 54
hardness p. 55

2.3 Minerals are valuable resources.

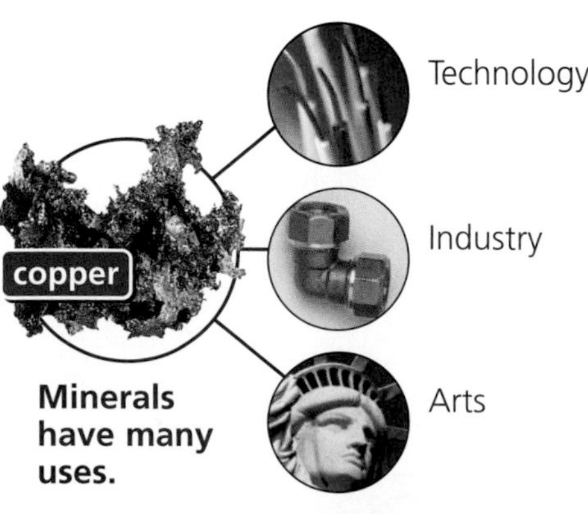
copper
Technology
Industry
Arts
Minerals have many uses.

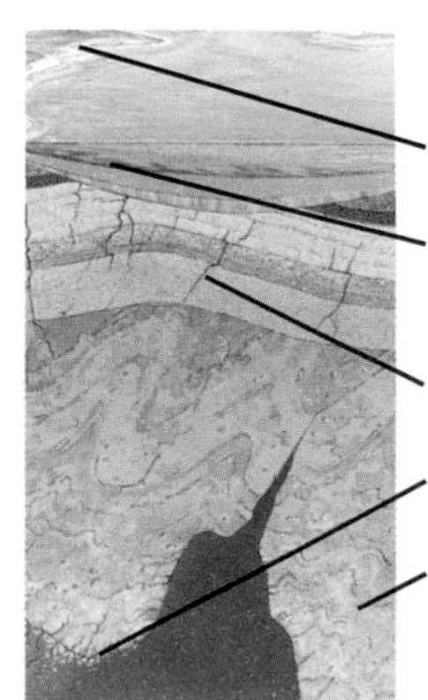
Mineral Formation
Water evaporates.
Organisms form shells or bones.
Hot water cools.
Molten rock cools.
Heat and pressure cause changes.

VOCABULARY
magma p. 62
lava p. 62
ore p. 64

Reviewing Vocabulary

On a separate sheet of paper, write a sentence describing the relationship between the two vocabulary terms.

1. mineral, crystal
2. cleavage, fracture
3. magma, lava
4. element, density
5. mineral, ore
6. element, magma

Reviewing Key Concepts

Multiple Choice *Choose the letter of the best answer.*

7. A mineral is a substance that forms
   a. from rocks
   b. in nature
   c. from one element
   d. in liquid

8. A crystal structure is characteristic of
   a. an element
   b. a rock
   c. magma
   d. a mineral

9. A mineral is made up of one or more
   a. ores
   b. rocks
   c. compounds
   d. elements

10. How is it possible for two different minerals to have the same chemical composition?
    a. They have different crystal structures.
    b. One is formed only by organisms.
    c. Only one is a rock-forming mineral.
    d. They have different appearances.

11. Most minerals in Earth's crust belong to the silicate mineral group because this group contains the
    a. rarest elements on Earth
    b. most common elements on Earth
    c. most valuable metals on Earth
    d. largest crystals on Earth

12. Which of the following is the least reliable clue to a mineral's identity?
    a. color
    b. density
    c. hardness
    d. luster

13. Many properties of a mineral are related to the
    a. number of elements of which it is made
    b. other types of minerals present as it formed
    c. strength of bonds between its atoms
    d. speed at which it formed

14. What types of minerals form in an area depends in part on
    a. which elements are present
    b. the types of rock present
    c. the density of rocks present
    d. whether crystals can form

15. Open-pit mining is used to obtain ores that lie
    a. under flat land
    b. deep in Earth's crust
    c. near the surface of Earth
    d. in riverbeds

16. Gemstones are used in
    a. building materials
    b. paper products
    c. automobile parts
    d. jewelry making

Short Answer *Write a short answer for each question.*

17. Why aren't all solids minerals? Include the term *crystal structure* in your answer.

18. Why is a mineral's streak more useful in identifying it than its color?

19. If you drop dilute hydrochloric acid on the mineral aragonite, it bubbles. What mineral group do you think aragonite belongs to? Why?

20. Describe how the strength of the bonds between atoms in a mineral determines whether the mineral displays cleavage or fracture.

Thinking Critically

Properties such as hardness and density are used to identify minerals. Use the information from the chart to answer the next five questions.

Mineral	Hardness	Density (g/cm^3)
platinum	4.5	19.0
aragonite	4	3
topaz	8	3.5
quartz	7	2.7
arsenic	3.5	5.7

21. **COMPARE** Platinum can combine with arsenic to form the mineral sperrylite. How do you think the density of sperrylite compares with the densities of platinum and arsenic?

22. **APPLY** Gems made of topaz are much more valuable than those made of quartz, even though the two minerals can look similar. Describe two methods you could use to identify quartz.

23. **APPLY** Would a miner be more likely to use the method of panning to find platinum or to find topaz? Why?

24. **INFER** Aragonite forms very attractive crystals, yet this common mineral is rarely used in jewelry. Why do you think this is?

25. **DEDUCE** About how many times heavier than a piece of quartz would you expect a piece of platinum of the same size to be? Show your work.

26. **HYPOTHESIZE** *Halite* is the mineral name for table salt. Thick layers of halite are mined near Detroit, Michigan. At one time, an ocean covered the area. Write a hypothesis that explains how the halite formed there.

27. **PREDICT** The mineral chromite is the main ore of the metal chromium. What might happen after all the chromite on Earth is mined?

28. **PREDICT** The mineral apatite is a compound in your bones and teeth. Apatite contains the elements phosphorus and calcium. How might your bones be affected if you do not have enough of these elements in your diet?

29. **DRAW CONCLUSIONS** You live on the surface of Earth's crust. The average density of the crust is about 2.8 grams per cubic centimeter. Most metal ores have densities greater than 5 grams per cubic centimeter. How common do you think metal ores are in the crust? Why?

the BIG idea

30. **ANALYZE** Minerals are basic components of planets such as Earth and Mars. Other planets in our solar system, such as Jupiter and Saturn, are called gas giants because they are composed mainly of the gases hydrogen and helium. They do not have solid surfaces. Do you think that minerals are basic components of gas giants? Why or why not?

Mars

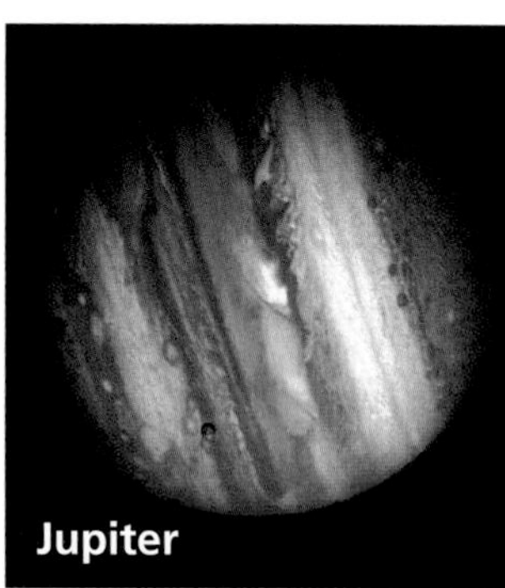
Jupiter

31. **INFER** Minerals make up much of Earth. People use minerals as sources of many materials, such as metals. Some metals are used to make machine parts or build houses. How would your life be different if minerals that contain metals were rare in Earth's crust?

UNIT PROJECTS

If you need to do an experiment for your unit project, gather the materials. Be sure to allow enough time to observe results before the project is due.

Standardized Test Practice

Analyzing a Table

This table shows characteristics of four minerals. Use it to answer the questions below.

Sample	Cleavage or Fracture	Density (g/cm^3)	Hardness (in Mohs scale)	Magnetic
E	cleavage	3.7	8.5	no
F	fracture	5.2	5.5	yes
G	fracture	2.7	7.0	no
H	cleavage	2.7	3.0	no

1. Which sample is most dense?
a. E
b. F
c. G
d. H

2. Which sample is hardest?
a. E
b. F
c. G
d. H

3. What will happen if G is rubbed against each of the other samples?
a. It will scratch only E.
b. It will scratch only F.
c. It will scratch only H.
d. It will scratch F and H.

4. Which statement accurately describes how one of the samples will affect a magnet?
a. E will attract the magnet.
b. F will attract the magnet.
c. G will be pushed away from the magnet.
d. H will be pushed away from the magnet.

5. Which sample or samples have a crystal structure?
a. E, F, G, and H
b. only F
c. E and H
d. F and G

6. Which samples are likely to break along flat surfaces?
a. E and G
b. F and G
c. G and H
d. E and H

7. An unidentified mineral sample has a density of 2.9 grams per cubic centimeter and a hardness of 6.7. Which mineral is it most like?
a. E
b. F
c. G
d. H

8. Which is true about one-cubic-centimeter pieces of these samples?
a. Each would have the same weight.
b. E would be heaviest.
c. F would be heaviest.
d. H would be heaviest.

Extended Response

Answer the two questions below in detail. Include some of the terms shown in the word box. In your answers underline each term you use.

chemical makeup	element	compound
crystal structure	Mohs scale	hardness

9. Describe the characteristics of minerals that make them different from rocks.

10. Describe the type of mineral that would work best on the tip of a drill designed to make holes in hard materials.

CHAPTER

Rocks

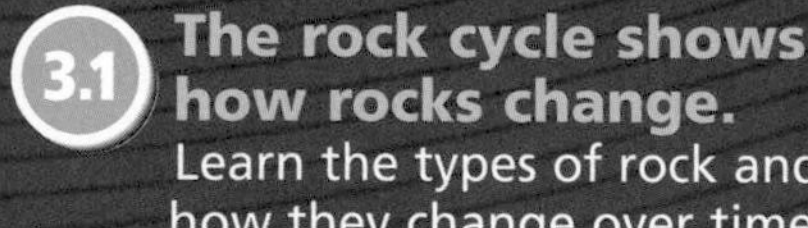

Rocks change into other rocks over time.

How long will these rocks remain as they are?

Key Concepts

SECTION

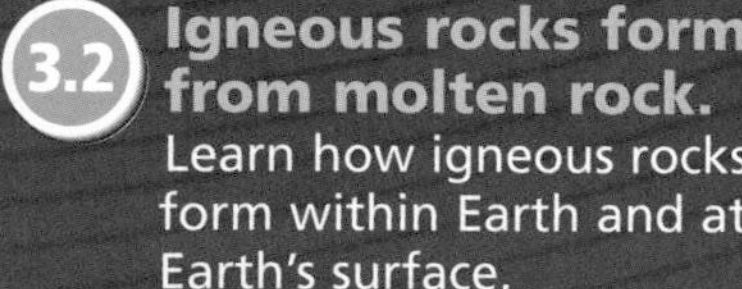

3.1 The rock cycle shows how rocks change.
Learn the types of rock and how they change over time.

SECTION

3.2 Igneous rocks form from molten rock.
Learn how igneous rocks form within Earth and at Earth's surface.

SECTION

3.3 Sedimentary rocks form from earlier rocks.
Learn how layers of loose materials develop into sedimentary rocks.

SECTION

3.4 Metamorphic rocks form as existing rocks change.
Learn how one type of rock can change into another.

Internet Preview

CLASSZONE.COM

Chapter 3 online resources: Content Review, Simulation, Visualization, four Resource Centers, Math Tutorial, Test Practice

EXPLORE the BIG idea

How Can Rocks Disappear?

Chalk is made of carbonate minerals, as is a type of rock called limestone. Put a piece of chalk in a cup. Pour vinegar over the chalk.

Observe and Think Describe what happens to the chalk. How do you think this change could happen to limestone in nature? **Hint:** Think about the amount of time it might take.

What Causes Rocks to Change?

Make two balls out of modeling clay and freeze them. Take the clay balls out of the freezer and put them on paper. Cover one ball with plastic wrap and stack books on top of it.

Observe and Think Observe how the clay balls change over time. How might rocks respond to changes in temperature, pressure, or both?

Internet Activity: Rocks

Go to **ClassZone.com** to explore how rocks form and change.

Observe and Think Give three examples of the ways in which rocks are continually changing.

The Rock Cycle **Code: MDL015**

CHAPTER 3

Getting Ready to Learn

CONCEPT REVIEW

- Every mineral has a specific chemical composition.
- A mineral's atoms are arranged in a crystal structure.
- Minerals form under a variety of conditions.

VOCABULARY REVIEW

mineral p. 43

crystal p. 46

magma p. 62

lava p. 62

CONTENT REVIEW
CLASSZONE.COM
Review concepts and vocabulary.

TAKING NOTES

MAIN IDEA WEB

Write each new blue heading in the center box. In the boxes around it, take notes about important terms and details that relate to the main idea.

SCIENCE NOTEBOOK

Rocks are not the same as minerals.

Different types of rocks contain different minerals.

Most rocks are made of minerals.

A rock may be made up of only one mineral.

A few kinds of rocks contain no minerals at all.

VOCABULARY STRATEGY

Draw a **magnet word** diagram for each new vocabulary term. Around the "magnet" write words and ideas related to the term.

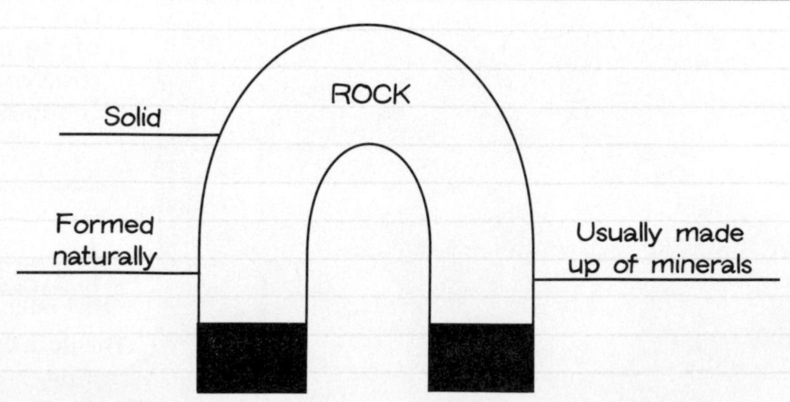

See the Note-Taking Handbook on pages R45–R51.

KEY CONCEPT

The rock cycle shows how rocks change.

BEFORE, you learned

- Minerals are basic components of Earth
- Minerals form in many different ways

NOW, you will learn

- What the three types of rocks are
- How one type of rock can change into another
- How common each rock type is in Earth's crust

VOCABULARY

rock p. 75
rock cycle p. 78
igneous rock p. 78
sedimentary rock p. 78
metamorphic rock p. 78

EXPLORE Rocks and Minerals

How do rocks differ from minerals?

PROCEDURE

1. Closely examine the rock and mineral samples. What do you notice about the forms, shapes, colors, and textures of the rock and the mineral?
2. In your notebook, make lists of the characteristics of the rock and of the mineral.

MATERIALS

- mineral sample
- rock sample
- magnifying glass

WHAT DO YOU THINK?

- What are the similarities and differences between the rock and the mineral?
- What additional observations or tests might help you determine other differences between rocks and minerals?

Most rocks are made of minerals.

If you have ever put together a jigsaw puzzle, you know that each piece is an important part of the final picture. Just as the pieces combine to form the picture, minerals combine to form most rocks. Another way to consider the relationship between minerals and rocks is to compare rocks to words. Just as letters combine to make up words, minerals combine to make up rocks. A **rock** is a naturally formed solid that is usually made up of one or more types of minerals.

The structure of rocks is different from that of minerals. A mineral is always made of the same elements in the same proportions. All minerals have an orderly crystal structure. In contrast, the proportion of different minerals in a particular kind of rock may vary. In addition, the minerals in a rock can be all jumbled together.

A few types of rocks are made up of one kind of mineral, and a few contain no minerals at all. Limestone, for example, can be composed entirely of the mineral calcite. Obsidian (ahb-SIHD-ee-uhn) is a rock that contains no minerals. It consists of natural glass, which is not a mineral because it does not have a crystal structure. Coal is another rock that is not composed of minerals. It is made up of the remains of ancient plants that have been buried and pressed into rock.

Gabbro, like most rocks, is made up of several types of minerals.

Obsidian is an unusual rock because it contains no minerals.

MAIN IDEA WEB
As you read, write each blue heading in a central box and record important details in boxes around it.

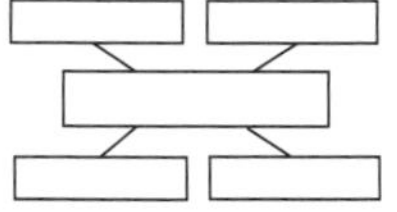

Our world is built of rocks.

Earth is built almost entirely of rock. When you look at Earth's surface, you can see soil, plants, rivers, and oceans. These surface features, however, form only a very thin covering on the planet. Between this thin layer and Earth's metallic core, Earth is made of solid and molten rock.

Because rocks are so common, it is not surprising that people use them for many different purposes, including

- the building of houses and skyscrapers
- the sources of metals, such as iron, aluminum, and copper
- the carving of statues and other works of art
- as a base for pavement for roads and highways

These huge cliffs on the coast of the Hawaiian island of Kauai show only a tiny part of the rock that makes up Earth.

People value rocks because rocks last a long time and because some are beautiful. Ancient rock structures and carvings give us a link to our distant past. Many famous monuments and sculptures are made from rocks. Granite blocks form part of the Great Wall of China. Limestone blocks make up the Great Pyramid in Egypt. The faces of four U.S. presidents are carved in the granite of Mount Rushmore.

CHECK YOUR READING Why do people use rocks for many different purposes?

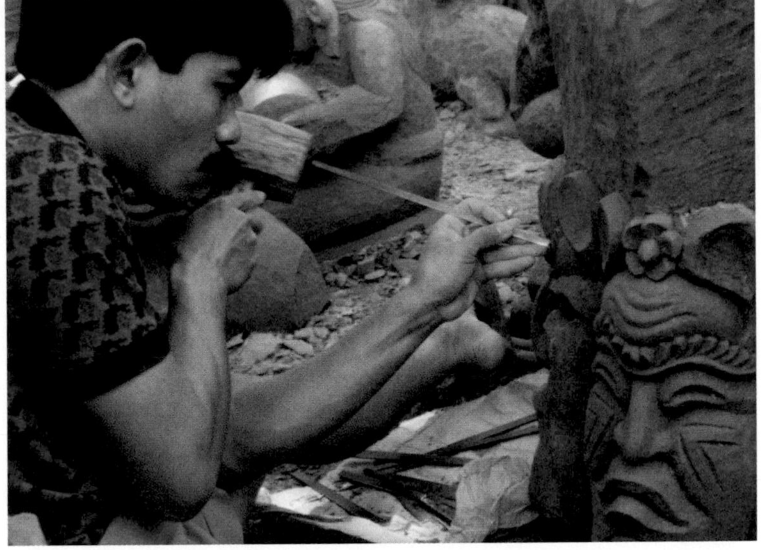

This sculptor in Indonesia, like artists throughout the world, shapes rocks into lasting works of art.

People study rocks to learn how areas have changed through time. For example, rocks show that North America, as well as most of the rest of the world, has been buried under thick layers of ice many times. You could learn about the types of rocks in your area by collecting and identifying them. You could also examine a map that shows types of rocks and where they are located. This type of map is called a geologic map. The map may be of a large area, such as your state, or a smaller area, such as your county.

INVESTIGATE Classification of Rocks

How can rocks be classified?

Geologists classify rocks by their physical characteristics. Design your own system for classifying rocks, as a scientist might.

SKILL FOCUS
Classifying

MATERIALS
6 rock samples

TIME
20 minutes

PROCEDURE

1. Examine the rock samples. Look at their physical characteristics.
2. Make a list of the differences in the physical characteristics of the rocks.
3. Use your list to decide which characteristics are most important in classifying the rocks into different types. Make a chart in which these characteristics are listed and used to classify the rocks into types.

WHAT DO YOU THINK?

- Which physical characteristic is most helpful in classifying the rocks?
- Which physical characteristic is least helpful in classifying the rocks?

CHALLENGE Is it possible to classify rocks only by the characteristics you can see?

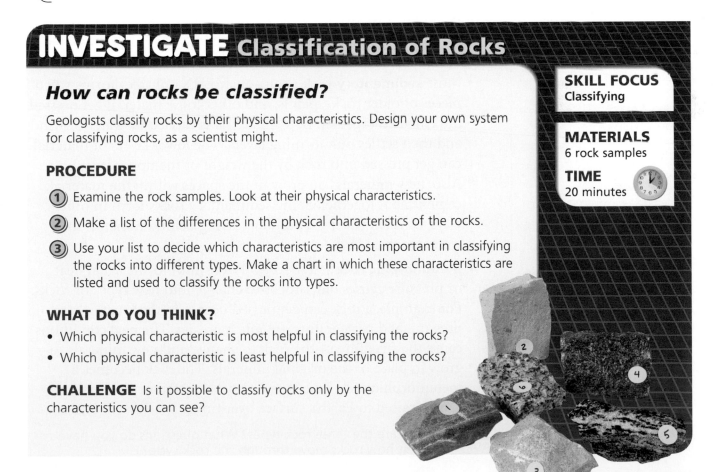

Rocks change as they move through the rock cycle.

VOCABULARY
Add a magnet word diagram for *rock cycle* to your notebook. Then add diagrams for the names of the rock types.

When you want to describe a person you can depend on, you may say that he or she is "like a rock." That's the way people think of rocks—as solid and unchanging. Nevertheless, rocks do change. But the changes usually occur over a huge span of time—thousands to millions of years. The **rock cycle** is the set of natural processes that form, change, break down, and re-form rocks.

A cycle is made up of repeating events that happen one after another. This does not mean that rocks move through the rock cycle in a particular order. As the illustration shows on page 79, a rock at any point in the cycle can change in two or three different ways. Like all cycles, the rock cycle has no beginning or ending but goes on continually.

Rock Types

The three types of rocks are classified by how they form.

- **Igneous rock** (IHG-nee-uhs) forms when molten rock cools and becomes solid. Igneous rock can form within Earth, or it can form on Earth's surface. Igneous rocks that originally formed at great depths can reach Earth's surface over time. Deep rocks may be raised closer to the surface when mountains are pushed up. At the same time, other processes can wear away the rocks that cover the deeper rocks.
- Most **sedimentary rock** (SEHD-uh-MEHN-tuh-ree) forms when pieces of older rocks, plants, and other loose material get pressed or cemented together. Loose material is carried by water or wind and then settles out, forming layers. The lower layers of material can get pressed into rock by the weight of the upper layers. Also, new minerals can grow in the spaces within the material, cementing it together. Some sedimentary rocks form in other ways, as when water evaporates, leaving behind minerals that were dissolved in it.
- **Metamorphic rock** (MEHT-uh-MAWR-fihk) forms when heat or pressure causes older rocks to change into new types of rocks. For example, a rock can get buried deeper in the crust, where pressure and temperature are much greater. The new conditions cause the structure of the rock to change and new minerals to grow in place of the original minerals. The rock becomes a metamorphic rock. Like igneous rocks, metamorphic rocks can be raised to Earth's surface over time.

READING TIP
When material dissolves in water, it breaks into many tiny parts. When the water evaporates, the parts join together and the material becomes solid again.

What are the three rock types? What questions do you have about how rocks move through the rock cycle?

The Rock Cycle

In the rock cycle, natural processes change each type of rock into other types. Rocks can take many paths through the rock cycle and change into other types in any order.

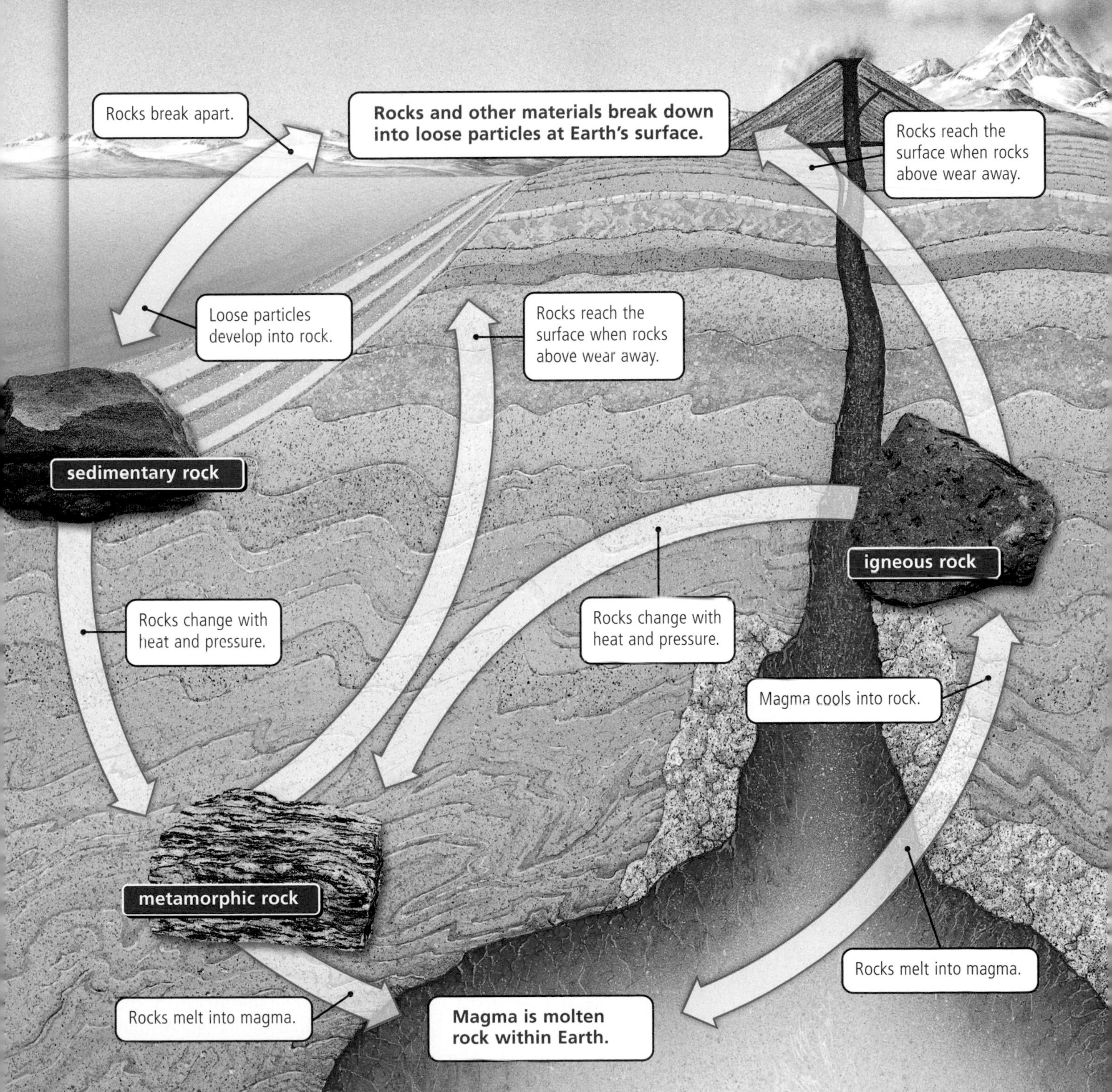

Rocks break apart.

Rocks and other materials break down into loose particles at Earth's surface.

Rocks reach the surface when rocks above wear away.

Loose particles develop into rock.

Rocks reach the surface when rocks above wear away.

sedimentary rock

igneous rock

Rocks change with heat and pressure.

Rocks change with heat and pressure.

Magma cools into rock.

metamorphic rock

Rocks melt into magma.

Rocks melt into magma.

Magma is molten rock within Earth.

READING VISUALS What are three different ways an igneous rock can change as it moves to another stage of the rock cycle?

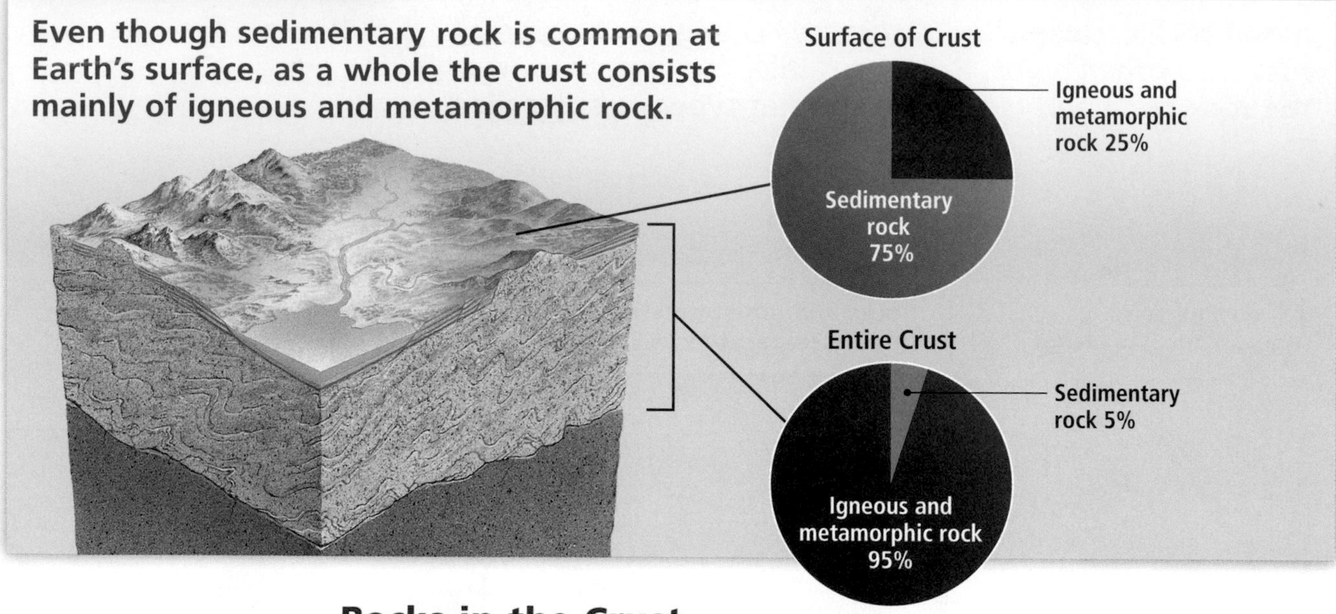

Rocks in the Crust

Igneous, sedimentary, and metamorphic rocks are all found in Earth's crust. But these rock types are not evenly distributed. Most of Earth's crust—95 percent of it—consists of igneous rock and metamorphic rock. Sedimentary rock, which forms a thin covering on Earth's surface, makes up only 5 percent of the crust.

The distribution of rock types is a reflection of the rock cycle. Sedimentary rocks are most common at the surface because they are formed by processes that occur at the surface. Most igneous rocks and metamorphic rocks are formed by processes that occur deeper within Earth.

Would you expect to find sedimentary rock deep in Earth's crust? Why or why not?

KEY CONCEPTS

1. How are rocks and minerals different?
2. What are the three types of rock?
3. Which rock types are most common within Earth's crust? Which type is most common at Earth's surface?

CRITICAL THINKING

4. **Analyze** Why is the set of natural processes by which rocks change into other types of rocks called a cycle?
5. **Infer** Which type of rock would you expect to be common on the floor of a large, deep lake? Why?

CHALLENGE

6. **Synthesize** Draw a diagram showing how an igneous rock could change into a metamorphic rock and how the metamorphic rock could change into a sedimentary rock.

EXTREME SCIENCE

Rocks from Space

Earth makes its own rocks. But some rocks come from space and land on Earth's surface. About 30,000 rocks with masses greater than 100 grams (3.5 oz) fall to Earth's surface every year. That's a rate of more than 80 rocks per day!

- A rock from space that reaches Earth's surface after passing through its atmosphere is called a meteorite.
- Most meteorites go unnoticed when they strike Earth. Either they fall in areas where there are few people, or they fall into the ocean.
- The largest rock from space ever found on Earth is called the Hoba meteorite. It weighs 60 tons! It landed in what is now Namibia, Africa, about 80,000 years ago.

This rock is a piece of the meteorite that formed Barringer Crater.

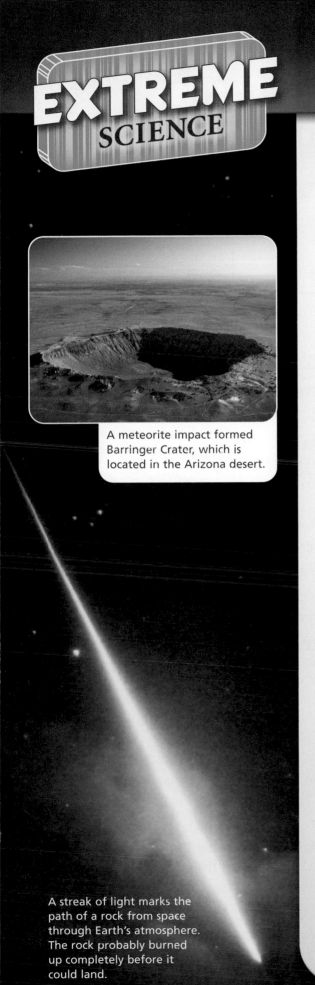

A meteorite impact formed Barringer Crater, which is located in the Arizona desert.

Meteorite Hunters Search Ice

Meteorite hunters search the icy wastes of Antarctica for these rocks. Do more meteorites fall there? No. But they are easy to see against the ice. The cold also helps preserve them in their original condition. In addition, the movements of the ice gather meteorites together in certain locations.

Meteorites Blast Earth

Large meteorites are very rare. This is fortunate, because they hit with great power. About 50,000 years ago, a meteorite that was about 45 meters (150 ft) in diameter slammed into what is now Arizona and blasted a crater 1.2 kilometers (0.75 mi) wide. Craters from ancient impacts may be hard to recognize because the land has been reshaped by geological processes. Evidence can still be found, though. The energy of an impact is so high that some minerals, such as quartz, are permanently altered.

A streak of light marks the path of a rock from space through Earth's atmosphere. The rock probably burned up completely before it could land.

EXPLORE

1. **PREDICT** Oceans cover about 71 percent of Earth's surface. Calculate how many meteorites with masses greater than 100 grams are likely to fall into the ocean each year. How many are likely to fall on land?
2. **CHALLENGE** Use information from the Resource Center to describe how a meteorite impact could have helped cause the dinosaurs to become extinct.

RESOURCE CENTER
CLASSZONE.COM
Learn more about meteorites and meteorite impacts.

KEY CONCEPT

Igneous rocks form from molten rock.

BEFORE, you learned

- Earth's interior is very hot
- Most minerals in Earth's crust are silicates

NOW, you will learn

- Why igneous rocks formed at Earth's surface are different from those formed within Earth
- Why silica content is important in classifying igneous rocks
- Why igneous rocks can make long-lasting landforms

VOCABULARY

intrusive igneous rock p. 83

extrusive igneous rock p. 83

THINK ABOUT

Why do two rocks made of the same minerals look very different?

Look at a sample of granite and a sample of rhyolite (RY-uh-LYT). These two igneous rocks contain the same minerals, so their chemical compositions are very similar. Yet granite and rhyolite look very different. What do you think might cause this difference?

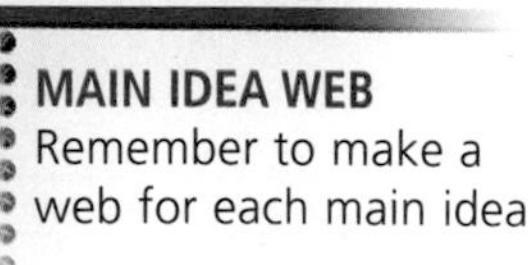

MAIN IDEA WEB

Remember to make a web for each main idea.

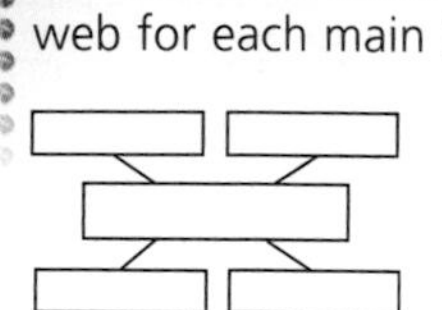

Magma and lava form different types of igneous rocks.

Igneous rocks form from molten rock, but where does molten rock come from? The temperature inside Earth increases with depth. That is, the farther down you go, the hotter it gets. Deep within Earth, temperatures are hot enough—750°C to 1250°C (about 1400°F to 2300°F)—to melt rock. This molten rock is called magma. Molten rock that reaches Earth's surface is called lava.

An igneous rock is classified on the basis of its mineral composition and the size of its mineral crystals. A rock formed from magma can have the same composition as a rock formed from lava. The rocks, though, will have different names, because the sizes of their crystals will be very different. You will read why later in this section.

People's decisions about how to use igneous rocks are based in part on the rocks' crystal sizes. For example, rocks with large mineral crystals are often used as building stones because they are attractive.

Origin of Igneous Rocks

Depending on where they form, igneous rocks are classified as intrusive (ihn-TROO-sihv) or extrusive (ihk-STROO-sihv). An **intrusive igneous rock** is one that forms when magma cools within Earth. An **extrusive igneous rock** is one that forms when lava cools on Earth's surface.

Granite is a common intrusive rock in continents. If magma with the same composition reaches the surface, it forms extrusive rocks such as rhyolite and pumice (PUHM-ihs). Basalt (buh-SAWLT) is an extrusive igneous rock that forms the ocean floor. Gabbro is an intrusive rock that has the same composition as basalt.

VOCABULARY
Add magnet word diagrams for *intrusive igneous rock* and *extrusive igneous rock* to your notebook.

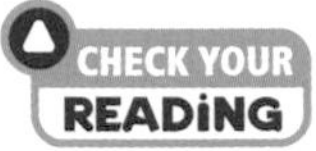

How are gabbro and basalt similar? How are they different?

You can see extrusive igneous rocks at Earth's surface. But intrusive igneous rocks form within Earth. How do they reach the surface? Forces inside Earth can push rocks up, as when mountains form. Also, water and wind break apart and carry away surface rocks. Then deeper rocks are uncovered at the surface.

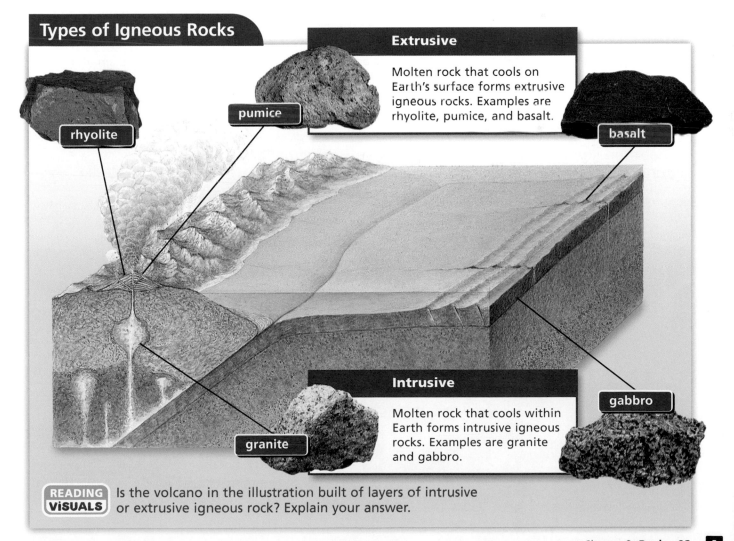

Types of Igneous Rocks

Extrusive

Molten rock that cools on Earth's surface forms extrusive igneous rocks. Examples are rhyolite, pumice, and basalt.

rhyolite
pumice
basalt

Intrusive

Molten rock that cools within Earth forms intrusive igneous rocks. Examples are granite and gabbro.

granite
gabbro

READING VISUALS Is the volcano in the illustration built of layers of intrusive or extrusive igneous rock? Explain your answer.

Textures of Igneous Rocks

Explore an animation showing how crystals form as molten rock cools.

The texture of an igneous rock—that is, the size of its mineral crystals—depends on how quickly magma or lava cooled to form it. In an icemaker, crystals form as water freezes into ice. In a similar way, mineral crystals form as molten rock freezes into solid rock.

The magma that forms intrusive igneous rocks stays below the surface of Earth. Large crystals can form in intrusive rocks because

- the interior of Earth is very hot
- the high temperatures allow magma to cool slowly
- slow cooling allows time for large mineral crystals to form

The lava that forms extrusive igneous rocks reaches Earth's surface. Very small crystals form in extrusive rocks because

- the surface of Earth is cooler than Earth's interior
- the lower temperatures cause the lava to cool quickly
- there is no time for large mineral crystals to form

Some igneous rocks contain crystals of very different sizes. These rocks formed from magma that started cooling within Earth and then erupted onto the surface. The large crystals grew as the magma cooled slowly. The small crystals grew as the lava cooled quickly.

How does an igneous rock that has both large and small mineral crystals form?

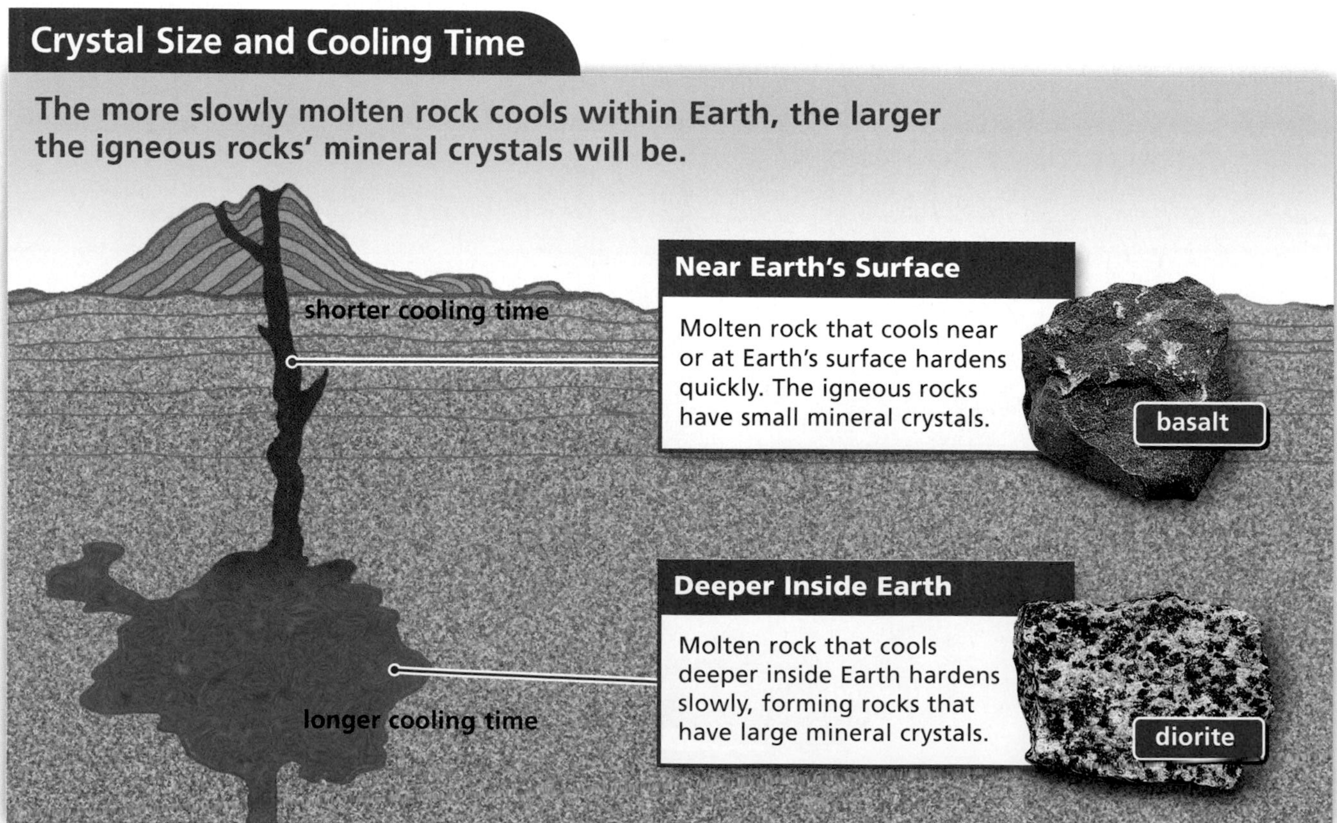

Crystal Size and Cooling Time
The more slowly molten rock cools within Earth, the larger the igneous rocks' mineral crystals will be.
shorter cooling time
longer cooling time
Near Earth's Surface
Molten rock that cools near or at Earth's surface hardens quickly. The igneous rocks have small mineral crystals.
basalt
Deeper Inside Earth
Molten rock that cools deeper inside Earth hardens slowly, forming rocks that have large mineral crystals.
diorite

INVESTIGATE Crystal Size

How does cooling time affect crystal size?

SKILL FOCUS
Analyzing

MATERIALS
Mineral Crystal Diagrams datasheet

TIME
20 Minutes

PROCEDURE

1. Look at the Mineral Crystal Diagrams datasheet.
2. Describe your observations of the crystals in each of the igneous-rock diagrams A–C on the lines provided.
3. Describe what is shown in each of graphs 1–3 on the lines provided.
4. Match each igneous-rock diagram with its corresponding graph.
5. On the back of the paper, explain why you matched each crystal diagram with a particular graph.

WHAT DO YOU THINK?

- Which diagram shows an intrusive igneous rock, such as gabbro?
- Where do you think the rock shown in diagram B formed? Explain your answer.

CHALLENGE Write a hypothesis to explain why the rock shown in diagram C might be found at a shallow depth in Earth's crust.

Composition of Igneous Rocks

Texture is not enough to identify an igneous rock. Think about substances that have similar textures, such as sugar and salt. A spoonful of sugar and a spoonful of salt both consist of small white grains. However, sugar and salt are different materials—that is, they have different compositions. Likewise, different igneous rocks might have similar textures. To identify them, you must also consider their compositions.

Most igneous rocks are mainly made up of silicate minerals, which you read about in the last chapter. The silicate mineral group is the most common group in Earth's crust. Silicate minerals contain varying amounts of silica, a compound of silicon and oxygen. After identifying the texture of an igneous rock, geologists classify the rock on the basis of how rich it is in silica.

Special equipment must be used to determine a rock's exact composition, but you can estimate the level of silica in an igneous rock by looking at its color. Igneous rocks with high levels of silica, such as granite and rhyolite, are typically light in color. Those with low levels of silica, such as gabbro and basalt, are dark in color.

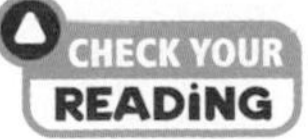

Would you expect a light gray igneous rock to be rich or poor in silica? Why?

Find out more about igneous rocks.

Igneous rocks make long-lasting landforms.

In northwestern New Mexico, a great peak rises out of a flat, barren desert. The Navajo call the peak Tsé Bit'a'í (tseh biht-ah-ih), meaning "rock with wings." In English, it's called Ship Rock, because it looks something like a sailing ship. Ship Rock is an example of the kinds of landforms that are made of igneous rocks. A landform is a natural feature on Earth's land surface.

Intrusive Rock Formations

Ship Rock actually formed about one kilometer below the surface of Earth 30 million years ago. It is all that remains of magma that once fed a volcano. The magma cooled slowly and formed intrusive igneous rock.

As magma pushes up toward Earth's surface, it makes channels and other formations underground. Formations of intrusive igneous rock can be harder and more lasting than other types of rock. Notice in the illustration below how igneous rock has been left at the surface as other, weaker types of rock have been worn away.

Intrusive Rock Formation

Wind and water wear away surrounding, weaker rock to reveal intrusive rock formations, such as Ship Rock.

Ancient Land Surface

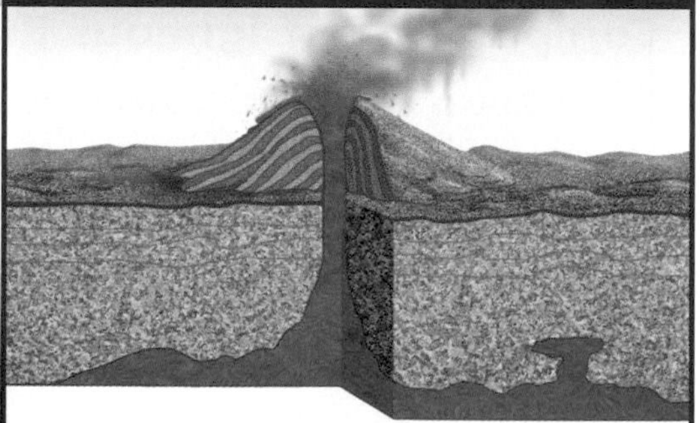

Magma that remains below the surface will later become intrusive igneous rock.

Present-Day Land Surface

Surface rock has worn away to reveal some of the intrusive rock.

READING VISUALS Where in the bottom illustration is more intrusive rock likely to be uncovered next?

Extrusive Rock Formations

When magma makes its way to Earth's surface through a volcano or crack, the lava may erupt in different ways. Some lava can build huge plateaus when it erupts from long cracks in Earth's surface. Lava that is low in silica, such as basalt lava, flows easily and spreads out in thin sheets over great distances. The Columbia Plateau in Oregon and Washington is made of basalt. When lava that is low in silica erupts at a single point, it can build up a huge volcano with gently sloping sides. The Hawaiian Islands are a chain of volcanoes that are built of basalt lava. The volcanoes started erupting on the sea floor and over a very long time grew tall enough to rise above the surface of the ocean as islands.

READING TIP

Notice what properties of basalt lava allow it to build large plateaus.

Basalt lava can flow long distances. Here it is spreading over a road in Hawaii.

Lava that contains a greater amount of silica does not flow easily. Silica-rich lava tends to build cone-shaped volcanoes with steep sides. Volcanoes fed by silica-rich magma tend to erupt explosively. Because the magma is thick and sticky, pressure can build up in volcanoes until they explode. An example is Mount St. Helens in the state of Washington. Its 1980 eruption reduced the volcano's height by 400 meters (about 1300 ft). Lava flows are adding new extrusive igneous rock. At the current rate it will take more than 200 years for the volcano to reach its pre-1980 height.

CHECK YOUR READING Why does silica-rich lava tend to build steep volcanoes instead of spreading out?

3.2 Review

KEY CONCEPTS

1. What is the main difference between intrusive and extrusive igneous rocks?
2. What are the two major properties used to classify igneous rocks?
3. Why can intrusive igneous rocks be left behind when surrounding rocks are worn away?

CRITICAL THINKING

4. **Draw Conclusions** If granite within Earth melts and then erupts at the surface, what type of extrusive rock is likely to form?
5. **Analyze** Would you expect extrusive rocks produced by an explosive volcano to be light or dark in color? Why?

CHALLENGE

6. **Synthesize** Why are the names *intrusive* and *extrusive* appropriate for the two types of igneous rocks?

MATH TUTORIAL
CLASSZONE.COM
Click on Math Tutorial for more help with estimating areas.

SKILL: ESTIMATING AREA

Resurfacing Earth

Lava flows from volcanoes are common on the island of Hawaii. The map below shows lava flows from the Kilauea volcano. The flow shown in blue destroyed more than 180 homes and covered the region in a layer of lava up to 25 meters thick.

Kilauea Lava Flows

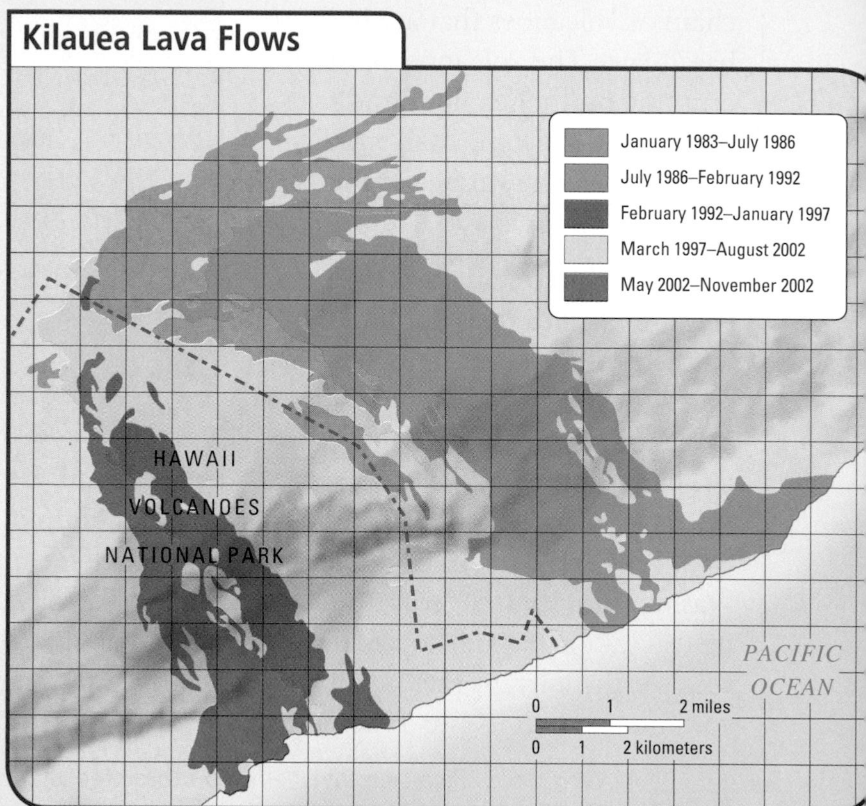

Use the map to answer the following questions.

1. How many squares does the lava flow shown in yellow cover? First, count the complete grid squares covered by the lava flow shown in yellow. Next, think of partially covered grid squares as fractions, and add them together to get whole squares. Finally, add the number of these squares to the number of complete squares.
2. What is the area of the flow in square kilometers?
3. Use the same method to estimate the areas of the flows shown in purple and blue.

CHALLENGE To estimate the area covered by all the lava flows shown on the map, would it be better to estimate the area of each flow separately and then add the results together? Or would it be better to estimate the total area of the flows in one step? Explain your reasoning.

KEY CONCEPT

Sedimentary rocks form from earlier rocks.

BEFORE, you learned

- Most rocks are made of minerals
- Some ocean organisms build their shells from minerals
- Dissolved minerals re-form as water evaporates

NOW, you will learn

- What kinds of materials make up sedimentary rocks
- What the processes that form sedimentary rocks are
- How sedimentary rocks record past conditions

VOCABULARY

sediment p. 89

EXPLORE Particle Layers

What happens as rock particles settle in water?

PROCEDURE

1. Pour 2 cups of water into the jar.
2. Add the gravel and sand to the water.
3. Shake the jar for a few seconds and then set it down on a counter. Observe and record what happens to the materials in the water.

MATERIALS

- jar
- measuring cup
- water
- 1/3 cup gravel
- 1/3 cup sand

WHAT DO YOU THINK?

- What determines how the materials settle to the bottom of the jar?
- In a lake, how would a mixture of different-sized rock particles settle to the bottom?

Some rocks form from rock particles.

If the sand grains on a beach become naturally cemented together, they form a sedimentary rock called sandstone. Most sedimentary rock forms as sandstone does—from loose material that gets pressed together or cemented into rock. Sedimentary rock forms in other ways, too.

Sedimentary rock takes its name from the word *sediment*, which means "something that settles." **Sediments** are materials that settle out of water or air. In addition to loose pieces of rocks and minerals, pieces of plant and animal remains can also make up sediments. Sedimentary rocks develop from layers of sediments that build up on land or underwater.

VOCABULARY
Add a magnet word diagram for *sediment* to your notebook.

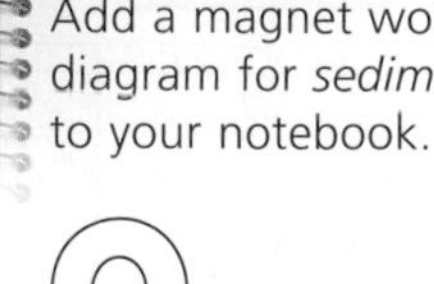

What types of material can make up sediments?

Forming and Transporting Rock Particles

A sandy ocean beach, a gravel bar in a river, and a muddy lake bottom all consist mainly of rock particles. These particles were broken away from rocks by the action of water or wind or a combination of both. Such particles may vary in size from boulders to sand to tiny bits of clay.

Just as water washes mud off your hands as it runs over them, rainwater washes away rock particles as it flows downhill. The water carries these rock particles to streams and rivers, which eventually empty into lakes or oceans. Strong winds also pick up sand and rock dust and carry them to distant places.

Find information on sedimentary rocks.

As winds or water currents slow down, rock particles settle on the land or at the bottom of rivers, lakes, and oceans. The sediments form layers as larger particles settle first, followed by smaller ones.

Forming Loose Sediments into Rocks

If you have ever watched workers building a road, you know that they first put down layers of gravel and other materials. Then they press the layers together, using a huge roller. In a similar way, layers of sediments

Sorting Sediments by Size

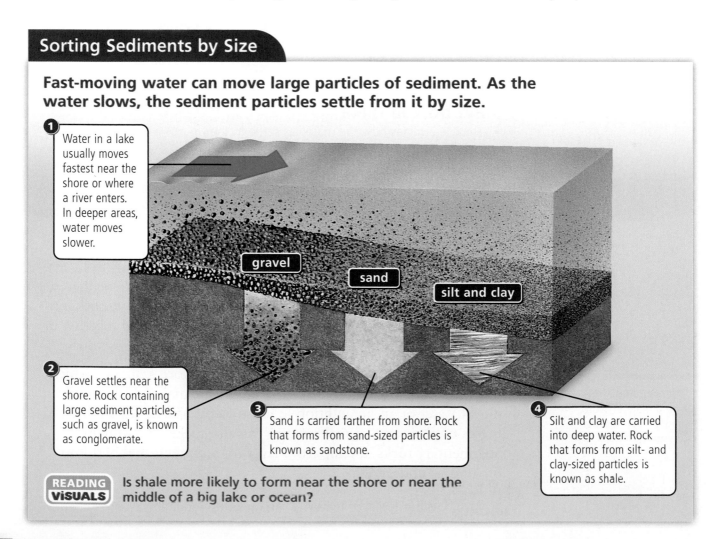

Fast-moving water can move large particles of sediment. As the water slows, the sediment particles settle from it by size.

1. Water in a lake usually moves fastest near the shore or where a river enters. In deeper areas, water moves slower.

gravel

sand

silt and clay

2. Gravel settles near the shore. Rock containing large sediment particles, such as gravel, is known as conglomerate.
3. Sand is carried farther from shore. Rock that forms from sand-sized particles is known as sandstone.
4. Silt and clay are carried into deep water. Rock that forms from silt- and clay-sized particles is known as shale.

READING VISUALS Is shale more likely to form near the shore or near the middle of a big lake or ocean?

composed of rock particles may get pressed together to form rock. One layer gets buried by another, and then another. The overlying layers apply pressure to, or press down on, the sediments underneath.

Small particles of sediment, such as silt and clay, may be formed into rock by pressure alone. In other sedimentary rocks the particles are held together by minerals that have crystallized between them, acting as cement. Over a long time, these processes transform loose sediments into sedimentary rocks.

What are two processes that can change sediments into rocks?

Some rocks form from plants or shells.

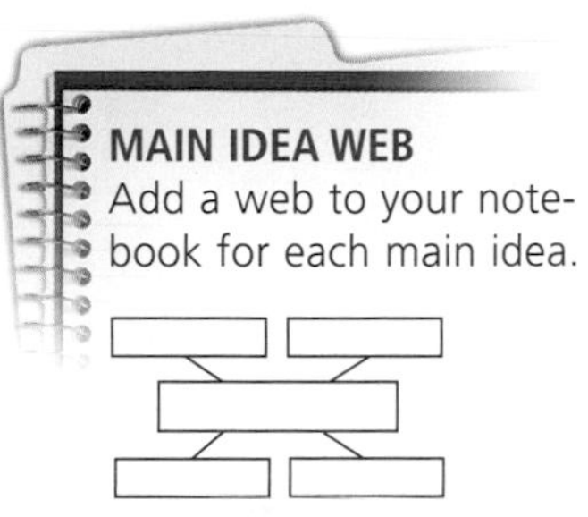

MAIN IDEA WEB
Add a web to your notebook for each main idea.

Processes similar to the ones that produce sedimentary rocks from rock particles also produce rocks from shells or plant remains. These remains are fossils. A fossil is the remains or trace of an organism from long ago.

Coal

If you look at a piece of coal through a magnifying glass, you may be able to make out the shapes of bits of wood or leaves. That is because coal is made up of remains of plants—dead wood, bark, leaves, stems, and roots. Coal is an unusual sedimentary rock because it forms from plants instead of earlier rocks.

The coal people use today started forming millions of years ago in swamps. As plants died, their remains fell upon the remains of earlier plants. Then layers of other sediments buried the layers of plant remains. The weight of the sediments above pressed the plant material into coal.

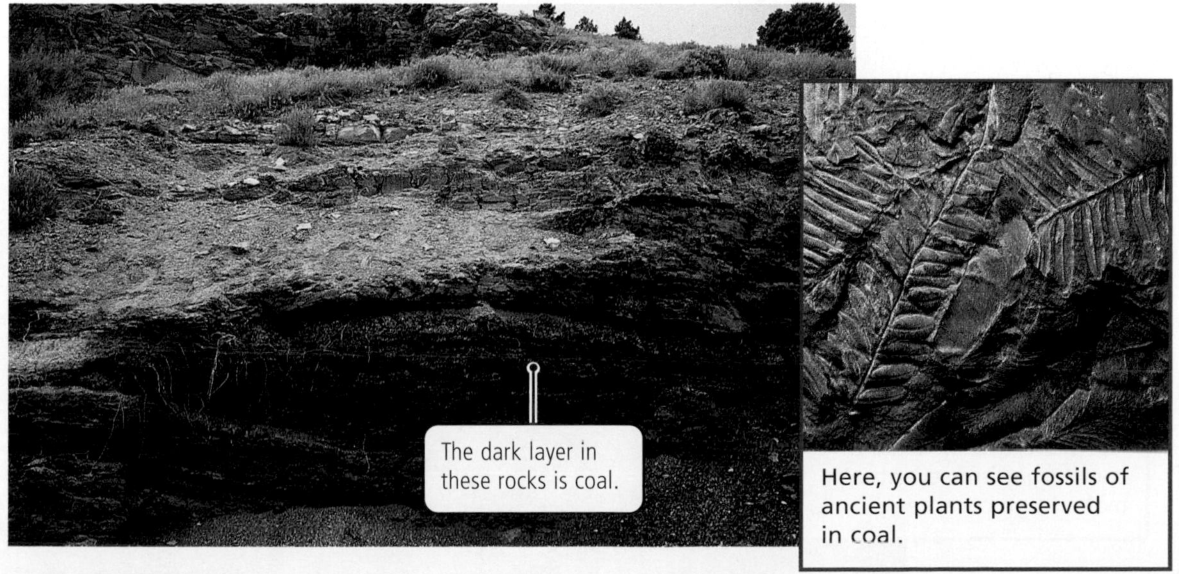

The dark layer in these rocks is coal.

Here, you can see fossils of ancient plants preserved in coal.

Limestone

Limestone is made up of carbonate minerals, such as calcite. The shells and skeletons of ocean organisms are formed of these minerals. When the organisms die, the shells and skeletons settle on the ocean floor as layers of sediment. Over time, the layers become buried, pressed together, and cemented to form limestone. The photographs below show how loose shells can become limestone.

These shells were made by ocean organisms.

The shells get cemented together into limestone as some of their minerals dissolve and re-form.

Individual shells become harder to see as minerals in the limestone continue to dissolve and re-form.

Over time, what was once loose sediment becomes limestone with no recognizable shells.

Notice that limestone made up of cemented shells and the limestone in coral reefs were both formed by ocean organisms.

The famous white cliffs of Dover, England, consist of a type of limestone called chalk. The limestone began to form millions of years ago, when the land was under the ocean. The rock developed from shells of tiny organisms that float in the ocean. Most limestone comes from shells and skeletons of ocean organisms. The materials the organisms use to build their shells and skeletons are present in ocean water because they were dissolved from earlier rocks. Like almost all sedimentary rock, limestone forms from material that came from older rocks.

Coral reefs also consist of limestone that comes from organisms. However, in the case of reefs, the limestone is produced directly as coral organisms build their skeletons one on top of another. In the formation of coral, the rock does not go through a loose-sediment stage.

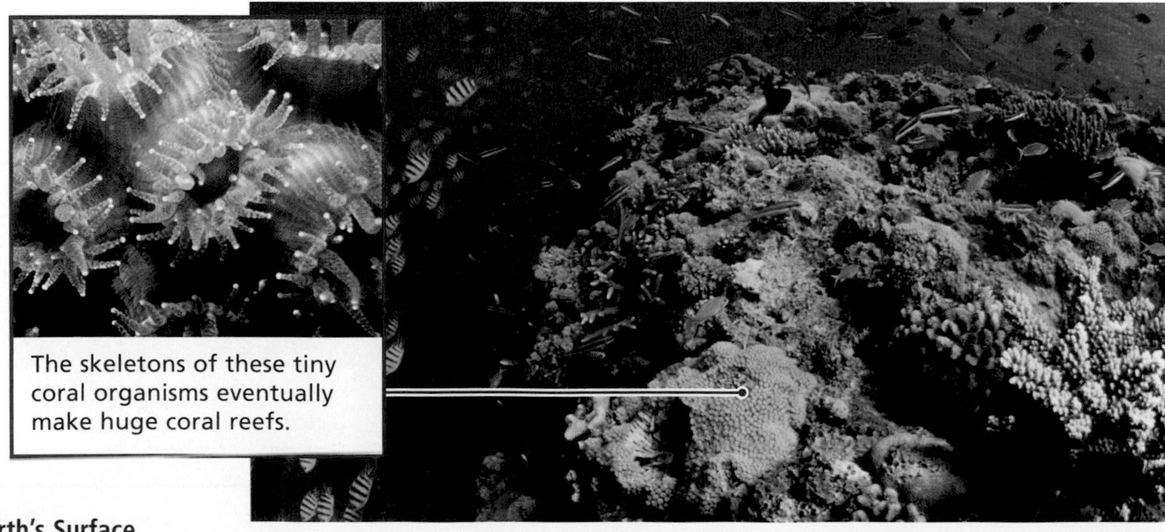

The skeletons of these tiny coral organisms eventually make huge coral reefs.

Some rocks form when dissolved minerals re-form from water.

If you have grown crystals in a container, you know that some substances can dissolve in water and then re-form as the water evaporates. The same process happens in nature. Some sedimentary rocks are made up of minerals that crystallized as water dried up.

Water is shaping this limestone cavern. Water dissolves and transports minerals, then leaves the minerals behind as it evaporates.

The water in oceans, lakes, rivers, and streams contains minerals that came from rocks. Some of these minerals are in solid form. As rainwater washes over rocks, it picks up pieces of minerals and rock particles and carries them into streams and rivers, where many of them settle to the bottom. However, some of the minerals dissolve in the water and are carried along with it.

Water often flows through cracks in rock that is near Earth's surface. As water moves through limestone, some of the rock dissolves. A large open space, or cave, can be left in the rock. As the water flows and drips through the cave, some of it evaporates. The new limestone that forms can take many odd and beautiful shapes.

Sometimes minerals crystallize along the edges of lakes and oceans where the climate is dry and a lot of water evaporates quickly. Over time, the minerals build up and form layers of sedimentary rock. Rock salt and gypsum form in this way. Under the city of Detroit, for example, is a large bed of rock salt that developed when part of an ancient ocean dried up.

How are the origins of rock salt and some limestone similar?

These limestone towers in Mono Lake, California, formed underwater. They are now above the surface because the lake level has dropped.

INVESTIGATE Rock Layers

How do sedimentary rocks form in layers?

PROCEDURE

1. Prepare the plaster of Paris by mixing it with the water.
2. Mix 2 tablespoons of the gravel with 2 tablespoons of the plaster of Paris and pour the mixture into the paper cup.
3. Mix the sand with 2 tablespoons of the plaster of Paris and the food coloring. Add the mixture to the paper cup, on top of the gravel mixture.
4. Mix the rest of the gravel with the rest of the plaster of Paris. Add the mixture to the paper cup, on top of the sand mixture.
5. After the mixtures harden for about 5 minutes, tear apart the paper cup and observe the layers.

WHAT DO YOU THINK?

- How is the procedure you used to make your model similar to the way sedimentary rock forms?
- Describe how similar layers of real rock could form.

CHALLENGE How would you create a model to show the formation of fossil-rich limestone?

SKILL FOCUS
Modeling

MATERIALS
- 1 paper cup
- 3 mixing cups
- 6 tbs plaster of Paris
- 3 tbs water
- 4 tbs gravel
- 2 tbs sand
- 3 drops food coloring

TIME
20 minutes

Sedimentary rocks show the action of wind and water.

READING TIP
Notice that sedimentary rocks are laid down in layers. As conditions in an area change, so do the characteristics of the layers.

Sedimentary rocks are laid down in layers, with the oldest layers on the bottom. A geologist studying layers of sedimentary rocks can tell something about what conditions were like in the past. For instance, fossils of fish or shells in a layer of rock show that the area was covered by a lake or an ocean long ago.

Fossils are not the only way to tell something about what past conditions were like. The sediments themselves contain a great deal of information. For example, a layer of sedimentary rock may contain sediment particles of different sizes. The largest particles are at the very bottom of the layer. Particles higher in the layer become increasingly smaller. A layer like this shows that the water carrying the sediment was slowing down. The largest particles dropped out when the water was moving quickly. Then smaller and smaller particles dropped out

Crossbeds

The tilted layers in these sandstone rocks are called crossbeds. The layers were once moving sand dunes.

Ripples

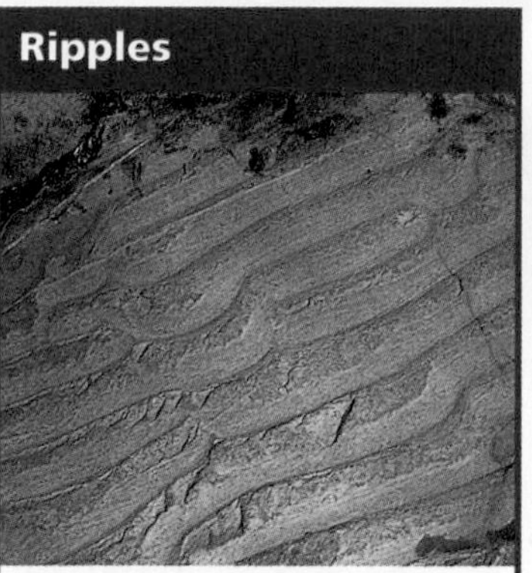

The surface of this sandstone preserves ancient sand ripples.

Mud Cracks

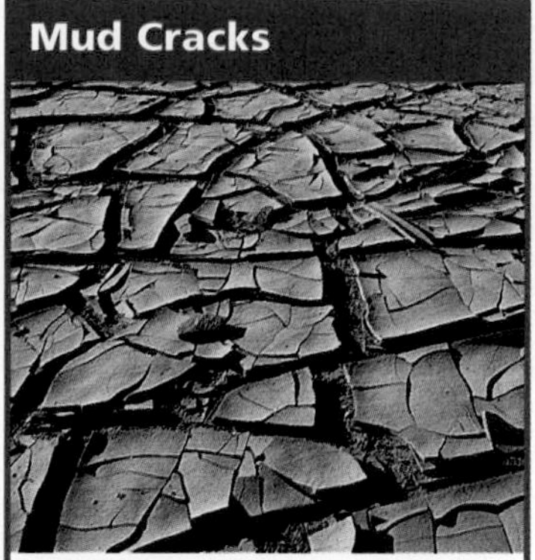

As wet silt and clay dry out, cracks develop on the surface of the sediment.

as the water slowed. This type of layer is often created by a flood, when a large amount of water is at first moving quickly.

Sedimentary rocks can give information about the directions in which long-ago wind or water currents were traveling when sediments settled from them. Sand can be laid down in tilted layers on the slopes of sand dunes or sandbars. Sand can also form ripples as water or wind moves over its surface. If the sand has been buried and cemented into sandstone, a geologist can examine it and tell the direction in which the water or wind was moving.

Some rocks made of clay or silt have cracks that developed when the mud from which they formed dried out. Mud cracks show that the rocks formed in areas where wet periods were followed by dry periods.

What could a geologist learn by finding rocks that have ripples or mud cracks?

3.3 Review

KEY CONCEPTS

1. What types of material can make up sediments?
2. Describe the three processes by which sedimentary rocks form.
3. Describe how a sedimentary rock can show how fast water was flowing when its sediments were laid down.

CRITICAL THINKING

4. **Infer** Why is coal called a fossil fuel?
5. **Analyze** How could the speed of flowing water change to lay down alternating layers of sand and mud?

CHALLENGE

6. **Synthesize** How is it possible for a single sedimentary rock to contain rock particles, animal shells, and minerals that crystallized from water?

KEY CONCEPT

3.4 Metamorphic rocks form as existing rocks change.

BEFORE, you learned

- Igneous rocks form as molten rock cools
- Sedimentary rocks form from earlier rocks

NOW, you will learn

- How a rock can change into another type of rock
- How new minerals can grow in existing rocks

VOCABULARY

metamorphism p. 96
recrystallization p. 97
foliation p. 100

THINK ABOUT

How does a rock change into another kind of rock?

Examine a sample of shale and a sample of schist (shihst). Shale, a sedimentary rock, can change into schist. Think about how this change could occur without the shale's melting or breaking apart. Make a prediction about what process changes shale into schist.

Heat and pressure change rocks.

When you cook popcorn, you use heat to increase the pressure within small, hard kernels until they explode into a fluffy snack. Cooking popcorn is just one example of the many ways in which heat and pressure can change the form of things—even things like rocks.

The process in which an existing rock is changed by heat or pressure—or both—is called **metamorphism** (MEHT-uh-MAWR-FIHZ-uhm). The original sedimentary or igneous rock is called the parent rock. The resulting rock is a metamorphic rock. Even a metamorphic rock can be a parent rock for another type of metamorphic rock.

READING TIP

Rocks change into other rocks by the process of metamorphism. A similar word, *metamorphosis,* refers to what happens when a caterpillar changes into a butterfly.

Many of the metamorphic rocks people use were once sedimentary rocks. Limestone is the parent rock of marble, which is used by builders and artists. Shale can be the parent rock of schist, which can be a source of the gemstone garnet. Some schists are a source of the mineral graphite, which is used in pencils.

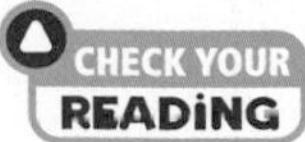

CHECK YOUR READING Give an example of a way people use metamorphic rocks.

During metamorphism, rocks undergo many changes. One type of change occurs when pressure causes a rock's minerals to flatten out in one direction. Other changes can occur in a rock's minerals, but the rock remains solid. Rocks do not melt when they undergo metamorphism. If the temperature gets high enough to melt the rock, the end result is an igneous rock, not a metamorphic rock.

Heat and pressure can break the bonds that join atoms in minerals. Then the atoms can join together differently as new bonds form. This process is called **recrystallization.** It has two main results. First, individual mineral crystals can grow larger as more atoms join their crystal structures. Second, atoms can combine in different ways, and new minerals can form in place of older ones. For example, shale is a sedimentary rock that is formed from silt and clay. During recrystallization, garnet can form from these materials.

How Rocks Change

Because pressure and temperature increase with depth, rocks change when they are buried deeper in the crust.

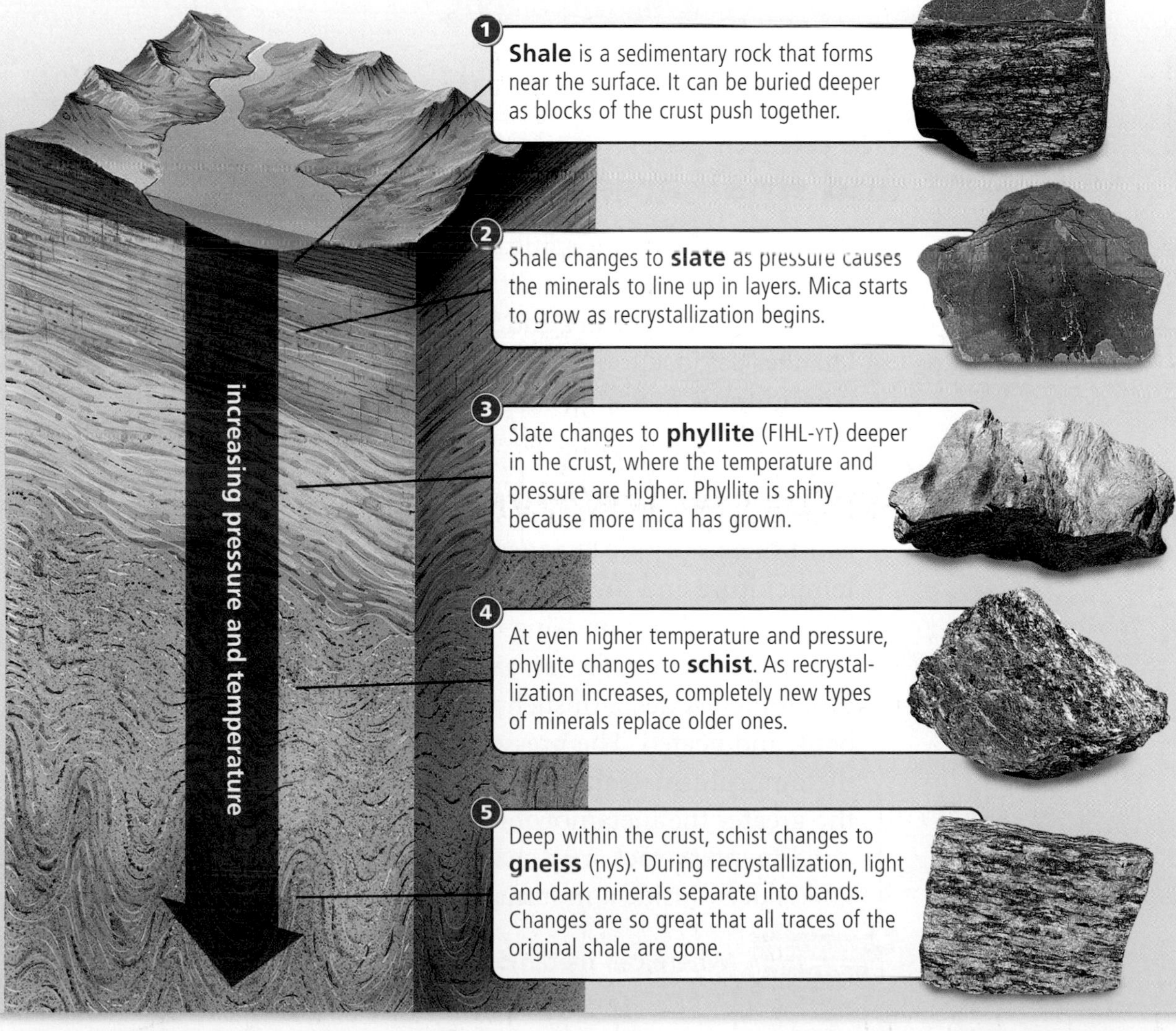

increasing pressure and temperature

1. **Shale** is a sedimentary rock that forms near the surface. It can be buried deeper as blocks of the crust push together.
2. Shale changes to **slate** as pressure causes the minerals to line up in layers. Mica starts to grow as recrystallization begins.
3. Slate changes to **phyllite** (FIHL-YT) deeper in the crust, where the temperature and pressure are higher. Phyllite is shiny because more mica has grown.
4. At even higher temperature and pressure, phyllite changes to **schist**. As recrystallization increases, completely new types of minerals replace older ones.
5. Deep within the crust, schist changes to **gneiss** (nys). During recrystallization, light and dark minerals separate into bands. Changes are so great that all traces of the original shale are gone.

INVESTIGATE Metamorphic Changes

How can pressure and temperature change a solid?

PROCEDURE

1. Use a vegetable peeler to make a handful of wax shavings of three different colors. Mix the shavings.
2. Use your hands to warm the shavings, and then squeeze them into a wafer.

WHAT DO YOU THINK?

- Describe what happened to the wax shavings.
- How do the changes you observed resemble metamorphic changes in rocks?

CHALLENGE What changes that occur in metamorphic rocks were you unable to model in this experiment?

SKILL FOCUS
Modeling

MATERIALS
- 3 candles of different colors
- vegetable peeler

TIME
10 minutes

Metamorphic changes occur over large and small areas.

The types of metamorphic changes that occur depend on the types of parent rocks and the conditions of temperature and pressure. When both high temperature and high pressure are present, metamorphic changes can occur over very large areas. When only one of these conditions is present, changes tend to occur over smaller areas.

Change over Large Areas

Most metamorphic changes occur over large areas in which both temperature and pressure are high. An example is a region where large blocks of rock are pressing together and pushing up mountain ranges. This process can affect an area hundreds of kilometers wide and tens of kilometers deep. In such an area, rocks are buried, pressed together, bent, and heated. The pressure and heat cause the rocks to undergo metamorphism. Generally, the deeper below the surface the rocks are, the greater the metamorphic changes that occur in them. For example, a sedimentary rock may change to slate near the surface but become gneiss deep inside a mountain.

Where can metamorphic changes occur over large areas?

Change over Small Areas

Some metamorphic changes occur over small areas. For example, magma can push into rocks underground, or surface rock can be covered by a lava flow. The magma or lava heats the rock it is in contact with, causing recrystallization. These changes are mainly due to high temperature, not pressure. The rocks get roasted but not squeezed. The thickness of rock changed by the heat can range from less than one meter to several hundred meters, depending on the amount and temperature of the molten rock.

Small areas of metamorphic rock can also be formed by high pressure alone. At or near Earth's surface, rocks move and grind past one another during earthquakes. Rocks that grind together in this way can be subjected to high pressures that cause metamorphic changes.

Find information on metamorphic rocks.

Metamorphic Changes

Changes can occur over hundreds of kilometers or over just a few centimeters.

Changes over Large Areas

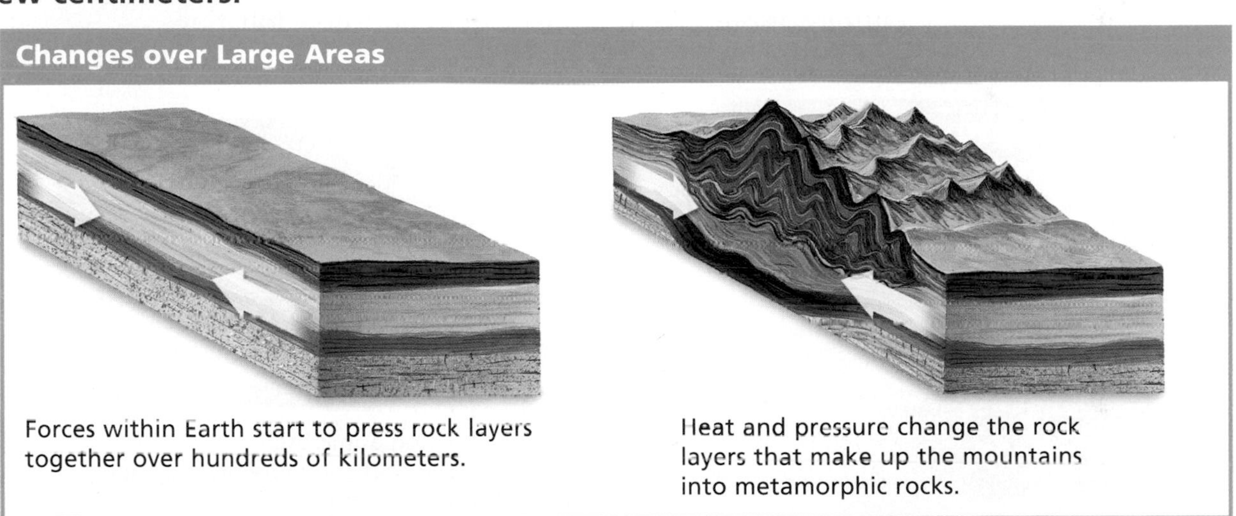

Forces within Earth start to press rock layers together over hundreds of kilometers.

Heat and pressure change the rock layers that make up the mountains into metamorphic rocks.

Changes over Small Areas

Magma can push into rock layers and cause changes over areas ranging from a few centimeters to tens of meters.

The magma is hot enough to bake the surrounding rocks into metamorphic rocks.

READING VISUALS Compare how heat and pressure cause changes over the large and small areas shown above.

Most metamorphic rocks develop bands of minerals.

VOCABULARY
Add a magnet word diagram for *foliation* to your notebook.

Some buildings have floors covered with tiles of the metamorphic rock slate. This rock is especially useful for tiles because it displays foliation, a common property of metamorphic rocks. **Foliation** is an arrangement of minerals in flat or wavy parallel bands. Slate can be split into thin sheets along the boundaries between its flat bands of minerals.

You may be familiar with the word *foliage.* Both *foliage* and *foliation* come from the Latin word *folium,* meaning "leaf." Foliated rocks either split easily into leaflike sheets or have bands of minerals that are lined up and easy to see.

Foliated Rocks

Foliation develops when rocks are under pressure. Foliation is common in rocks produced by metamorphic changes that affect large areas. However, as you will see, a metamorphic rock that consists almost entirely of one type of mineral does not show foliation.

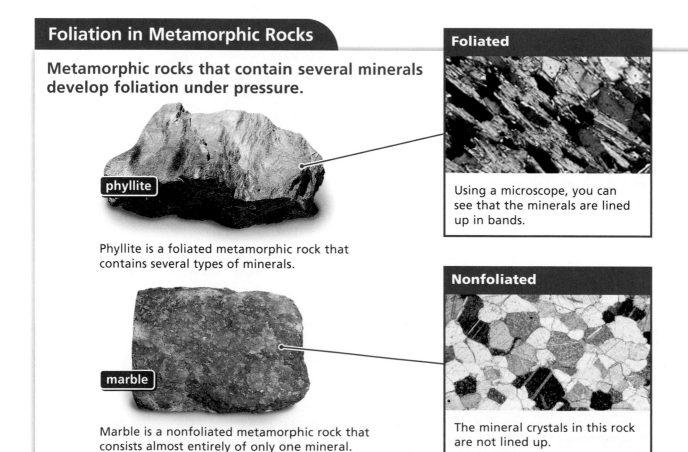

Foliation in Metamorphic Rocks

Metamorphic rocks that contain several minerals develop foliation under pressure.

Phyllite is a foliated metamorphic rock that contains several types of minerals.

Foliated

Using a microscope, you can see that the minerals are lined up in bands.

Marble is a nonfoliated metamorphic rock that consists almost entirely of only one mineral.

Nonfoliated

The mineral crystals in this rock are not lined up.

READING VISUALS Compare the pictures of the minerals in the foliated rock and the nonfoliated rock. What is different about their arrangements?

Foliation develops when minerals flatten out or line up in bands. At low levels of metamorphism, the bands are extremely thin, as in slate. With higher pressure and temperature, the mineral mica can grow and make the rock look shiny, as is common in phyllite and schist. At even higher levels of metamorphism, the minerals in the rock tend to separate into light and dark bands, like those in gneiss.

How do rocks change as foliation develops?

Nonfoliated Rocks

Metamorphic rocks that do not show foliation are called nonfoliated rocks. One reason a metamorphic rock may not display foliation is that it is made up mainly of one type of mineral, so that different minerals cannot separate and line up in layers. One common nonfoliated metamorphic rock is marble, which develops from limestone. Marble is used as a decorative stone. It is good for carving and sculpting. Because marble is nonfoliated, it does not split into layers as an artist is working with it. Another example of a nonfoliated rock is quartzite. It forms from sandstone that is made up almost entirely of pieces of quartz.

Another reason that a metamorphic rock may lack foliation is that it has not been subjected to high pressure. Hornfels is a metamorphic rock that can form when a rock is subjected to high temperatures. Hornfels, which often forms when magma or lava touches other rock, is nonfoliated.

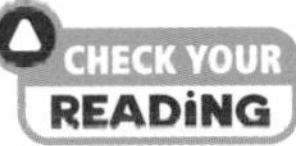

What are two reasons a metamorphic rock might not show foliation?

KEY CONCEPTS

1. What conditions can cause a sedimentary or igneous rock to change into a metamorphic rock?
2. How do new minerals grow within existing rocks?
3. Why do bands of minerals develop in most metamorphic rocks?

CRITICAL THINKING

4. **Draw Conclusions** Would gneiss be more likely to form at shallow depths or at great depths where mountains are being pushed up? Why?
5. **Infer** Would you expect to find foliated or nonfoliated metamorphic rocks next to a lava flow? Why?

CHALLENGE

6. **Synthesize** What features of sedimentary rocks are unlikely to be found in metamorphic rocks? What features of metamorphic rocks do not occur in sedimentary rocks?

CHAPTER INVESTIGATION

Rock Classification

OVERVIEW AND PURPOSE In this activity you will examine rock samples and refer to a rock classification key. You will classify each sample as igneous, sedimentary, or metamorphic.

Procedure

1. Make a data table like the one shown on the **Science Notebook** page.

2. Get a numbered rock sample. Record its number in your data table.

3. Observe the sample as a whole. Then closely examine it with the hand lens. Record in your table all visible properties of the sample. For example, include properties such as mineral or sediment size, layering, or banding.

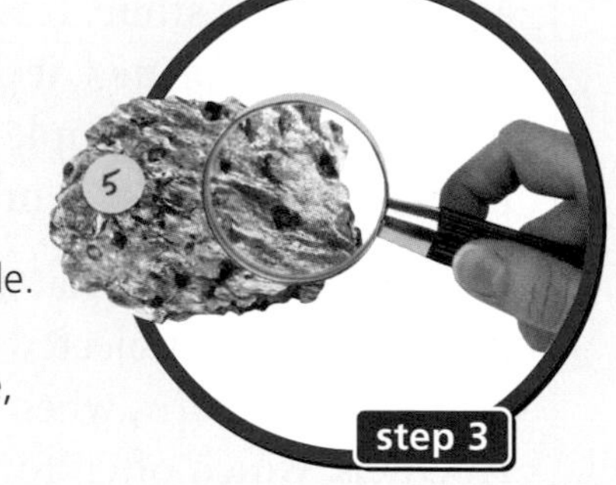

4. Look at the Rock Classification Key. Each item in the key consists of paired statements. Start with item 1 of the key. Choose the statement that best describes the rock you are examining. Look at the end of the statement and then go to the item number indicated.

MATERIALS
- magnifying glass
- 6–8 rock samples
- Rock Classification Key

Name ______ Period ______ Date ______

CHAPTER 3 | CHAPTER INVESTIGATION DATASHEET
Rock Classification Key

Match each rock diagram with the graph that shows how quickly it cooled.

1. Look at the composition of your rock. Is the rock made up of visible particles (for example, mineral crystals or sand)?
a) Some or all of the particles are visible. [go to step 3]
b) The rock does not contain any visible particles. [go to step 2]

2. Look at the texture of your rock. Is the rock glassy, porous (sponge-like), or completely solid?
a) The rock is glassy or porous. [the rock is igneous]
b) The rock is completely solid. [go to step 6]

3. Determine the type of particles that make up the rock.
a) The rock has visible mineral crystals. [go to step 4]
b) The rock is made up of individual particles (such as sand or pebbles) that are cemented together. [the rock is sedimentary]

4. Determine if the mineral crystals of the rock tend to line up or form bands.
a) The mineral crystals are not lined up in any particular direction. [go to step 8]
b) The mineral crystals tend to line up or to form bands. [the rock is metamorphic]

5. Determine if the rock is made up of layers or if it tends to break into layers.
a) The rock has no layers and does not break into layers. [the rock is igneous]
b) The rock has layers or tends to break into layers. [go to step 7]

6. Determine how shiny the rock is.
a) The rock is not shiny. [the rock is sedimentary]
b) The rock is somewhat to quite shiny. [the rock is metamorphic]

7. Determine if the rock is made up of one or more types of mineral crystals.
a) All the crystals appear to be of the same mineral. [the rock is metamorphic]
b) The crystals are of two or more types of minerals. [the rock is igneous]

CHAPTER 3 Earth's Surface

5. Examine the rock sample again and choose the statement that best describes the rock.

6. Continue to work through the key until your choices lead you to a classification that fits your rock. Repeat steps 2–5 for each of the numbered samples.

Observe and Analyze

1. **INTERPRET** Referring to the Rock Classification Key and the observations you recorded, write the type of each rock in your data table.
2. **IDENTIFY LIMITS** What problems, if any, did you experience in applying the key? Which samples did not seem to fit easily into a category? How could you improve the key?

Conclude

1. **COMPARE AND CONTRAST** How are igneous and metamorphic rocks similar? How can you tell them apart?
2. **ANALYZE** Examine a sample of sedimentary rock in which visible particles are cemented together. In addition to sight, what other sense could help you classify this sample?
3. **APPLY** What have you learned from this investigation that would help you make a classification key that someone else could follow? How might you make a key to classify the recordings in a music collection? Write two pairs of numbered statements that would start the classification process.

INVESTIGATE Further

CHALLENGE Make a rock classification key to distinguish between rocks from Earth and rocks from the Moon. Here are some facts to consider. The surface of the Moon was once covered by a thick layer of magma. The Moon has no running water and almost no atmosphere. Minerals on Earth often contain tiny amounts of water. Minerals on the Moon almost never contain any water. The Moon does not have processes that can cause a rock to change into another type of rock.

An astronaut photographed this rock on the Moon. The rock sits in a valley that formed 4 billion years ago. The rock may not have changed or moved since that time.

Rock Classification

Observe and Analyze

Table 1. Rock Sample Properties

Sample Number	Description of Visible Properties	Rock Type

Conclude

3 Chapter Review

the BIG idea

Rocks change into other rocks over time.

KEY CONCEPTS SUMMARY

3.1 The rock cycle shows how rocks change.

Processes at Earth's surface and heat within Earth cause rocks to change into other types of rocks.

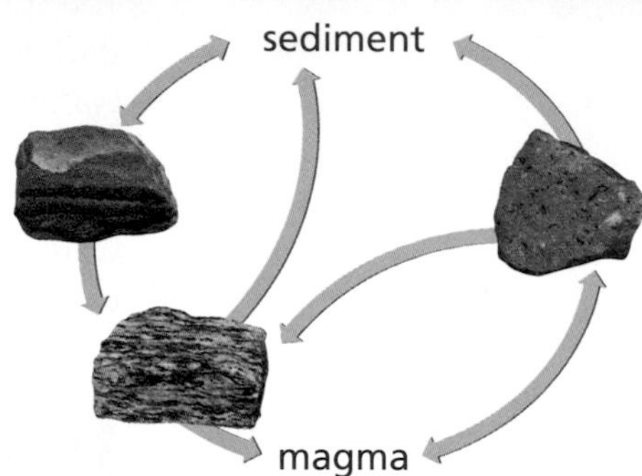

VOCABULARY
rock p. 75
rock cycle p. 78
igneous rock p. 78
sedimentary rock p. 78
metamorphic rock p. 78

3.2 Igneous rocks form from molten rock.

As molten rock cools, minerals crystallize and form igneous rocks.

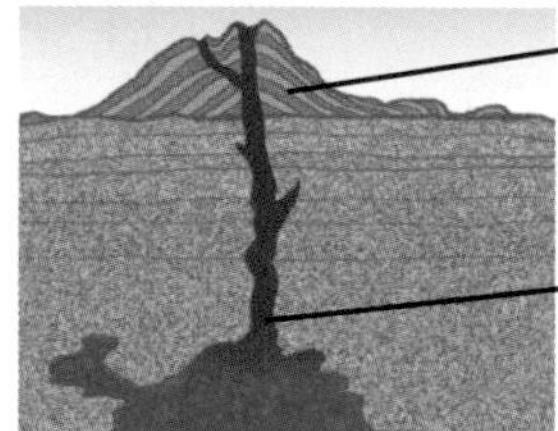

Extrusive igneous rocks cool quickly at Earth's surface.
Intrusive igneous rocks cool slowly within Earth.

VOCABULARY
intrusive igneous rock p. 83
extrusive igneous rock p. 83

3.3 Sedimentary rocks form from earlier rocks.

Layers of sedimentary rocks form as
- sediments are pressed or cemented together
- dissolved minerals re-form as water evaporates

VOCABULARY
sediment p. 89

3.4 Metamorphic rocks form as existing rocks change.

Metamorphic rocks form as the structures of the parent rocks change and as their minerals recrystallize.

heat and pressure

VOCABULARY
metamorphism p. 96
recrystallization p. 97
foliation p. 100

Reviewing Vocabulary

Copy and complete the chart below. There may be more than one correct response.

Rock Type	Forms From	Example / Identifying characteristic
intrusive igneous rock	magma	1.
		large mineral crystals
extrusive igneous rock	2.	basalt
		3.
sedimentary rock	4.	conglomerate
		contains large pieces of earlier rocks
sedimentary rock	ancient plant remains	5.
		may contain plant fossils
sedimentary rock	6.	limestone
		7.
foliated metamorphic rock	parent rock that has several types of minerals	8.
		minerals are lined up
nonfoliated metamorphic rock	9.	10.
		11.

Reviewing Key Concepts

Multiple Choice *Choose the letter of the best answer.*

12. The three groups of rock are sedimentary, metamorphic, and

a. limestone **c.** igneous
b. granite **d.** coal

13. The rock cycle shows how rocks continually

a. increase in size
b. increase in number
c. become more complex
d. change over time

14. Which kind of rock forms when molten rock cools?

a. metamorphic **c.** igneous
b. sedimentary **d.** extrusive

15. An existing rock can change into another type of rock when it is subjected to great

a. pressure **c.** flooding
b. winds **d.** foliation

16. Which kind of rock forms by recrystallization?

a. intrusive igneous
b. extrusive igneous
c. sedimentary
d. metamorphic

17. Geologists classify an igneous rock on the basis of its crystal size and the amount of ______ its minerals contain.

a. carbon **c.** sediment
b. silica **d.** foliation

18. Pieces of rock can settle from water and get cemented into

a. metamorphic rock
b. sedimentary rock
c. igneous rock
d. extrusive rock

19. Rock salt is an example of a sedimentary rock that develops from dissolved minerals as

a. water evaporates
b. magma cools
c. sediments break down
d. sand settles in water

Short Answer *Write a short answer to each question.*

20. What is the difference between a rock and a mineral?

21. Compare the distribution of rock types at Earth's surface to their distribution in the entire crust. How are any differences related to processes occurring in the rock cycle?

22. How is the texture of an igneous rock related to the rate at which it cooled?

TIMELINES in Science

HISTORY OF THE EARTH SYSTEM

Systems of air, water, rocks, and living organisms have developed on Earth during the planet's 4.6 billion years of history. More and more scientists have become curious about how these parts of Earth work together. Today, scientists think of these individual systems as part of one large Earth system.

The timeline shows a few events in the history of the Earth system. Scientists have developed special tools and procedures to study this history. The boxes below the timeline show how technology has led to new knowledge about the Earth system and how that knowledge has been applied.

4.6 BYA

Earth Forms in New Solar System

The Sun and nine planets, one of which is Earth, form out of a cloud of gas and dust. Earth forms and grows larger as particles collide with it. While Earth is still young, a slightly smaller object smashes into it and sends huge amounts of material flying into space. Some of this material forms a new object—the Moon.

EVENTS

5 BYA

Billion Years Ago

APPLICATIONS AND TECHNOLOGY

TECHNOLOGY

Measuring Age of Solar System

In 1956, Clair C. Patterson published his estimate that the solar system was 4.55 billion years old. Previously, scientists had learned how to use radioactive elements present in rocks to measure their ages. Patterson used this technology to determine the ages of meteorites that were formed along with the solar system and later fell to Earth. Since 1956, scientists have studied more samples and used new technologies. These studies have generally confirmed Patterson's estimate.

This iron meteorite fell in Siberia in 1947. Data from such meteorites are clues to how and when the solar system formed.

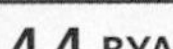

4.4 BYA

Earth Gains Atmosphere, Ocean

Earth's atmosphere forms as volcanoes release gases, including water vapor. Though some gases escape into space, Earth's gravity holds most of them close to the planet. The atmosphere contains no free oxygen. As Earth starts to cool, the water vapor becomes water droplets and falls as rain. Oceans begin to form.

3.5 BYA

Organisms Affect Earth System

Tiny organisms use energy from sunlight to make their food, giving off oxygen as a waste product. The oxygen combines with other gases and with minerals. It may be another billion years before free oxygen starts to build up in the atmosphere.

1.8 BYA

First Supercontinent Forms

All of Earth's continents come together to form one huge supercontinent. The continents and ocean basins are still moving and changing. This supercontinent will break apart in the future. New supercontinents will form and break apart as time goes on.

4 BYA 3 BYA 2 BYA 1 BYA

APPLICATION

Measuring Ozone Levels

In 1924, scientists developed the first instrument to measure ozone, the Dobson spectrophotometer. Ozone is a molecule that consists of three oxygen atoms. In the 1970s, scientists realized that levels of ozone in the upper atmosphere were falling. Countries have taken action to preserve the ozone layer, which protects organisms—including humans—from dangerous ultraviolet radiation. Today, computers process ozone data as they are collected and make them quickly available to researchers around the world.

A Dobson spectrophotometer measures the total amount of ozone in the atmosphere above it.

480 MYA

Plants Appear on Land

The earliest plants appear. These plants, perhaps similar to mosses, join the lichens that already live on land. Through photosynthesis, plants and lichens decrease the amount of carbon dioxide in the air and increase the amount of oxygen. These changes may lead to the eventual development of large, complex animals.

600 MYA

New Animals Appear

The first multi-celled animals appear in the ocean. Some types of these animals are fastened to the sea floor and get food from particles in water flowing past them. Worms are the most complex type of animals to appear so far.

200 MYA

Atlantic Ocean Forms

Earth's continents, which have been combined into the supercontinent Pangaea, start to separate. As what are now the continents of North America and Africa spread apart, the Atlantic Ocean forms.

800 MYA | **600 MYA** | **400 MYA** | **200 MYA**

Million Years Ago

TECHNOLOGY

Ocean-Floor Core Samples

In the 1960s, scientists began drilling holes into the sea floor to collect long cores, or columns, of sediment and rock. The cores give clues about Earth's climate, geology, and forms of life for millions of years.

The research ship *JOIDES Resolution* has a drilling rig built into it. Equipment attached to the rig is lowered to the sea floor to collect core samples.

12,000 years ago

Earth Emerges from Ice—Again

Earth's temperature warms slightly. Kilometers-thick ice sheets that formed during the latest of Earth's many ice ages start to melt. Forests and grasslands expand. Sea level rises about 100 meters (330 ft), and the ocean floods the edges of the continents.

1972

New View of Earth

Harrison "Jack" Schmitt, an astronaut traveling 24,000 kilometers (15,000 mi) above Earth, takes a photograph. It is the first to show Earth fully lit by the Sun, and the image is sometimes called the Blue Marble. It helps people see the planet as one system.

RESOURCE CENTER
CLASSZONE.COM

Learn more about the Earth system.

100 MYA **Today**

INTO THE FUTURE

In almost every area of life, from music to food to sports, the world has become more connected. Science is no exception. In the past century, scientists have begun to monitor the ozone layer. They have realized that the processes that cause continents to change positions also cause earthquakes and volcanic eruptions to occur.

Changes in technology are likely to help scientists increase their understanding of the Earth system. For example, instruments on artificial satellites measure changes in clouds, ocean life, and land temperatures. These types of data help scientists understand how changes in one part of Earth affect other parts.

APPLICATION

International Space Station

The International Space Station has laboratories in which scientists study Earth, the solar system, and the universe. Also, scientists are doing research to better understand the effects of very low gravity on people. This work is part of an effort to develop the life-support systems needed for people to remain in space a long time. Eventually it might aid in the further exploration of space by humans.

ACTIVITIES

Taking a Core Sample

Add layers of damp sand of different colors to a paper cup. Switch cups with a partner. Press a clear straw through the sand, put your finger over the top of the straw, and pull the straw out. Determine the order in which your partner added the sand layers. How would you know if there was a layer of sand that did not go across the entire cup?

Writing About Science

Imagine you are living in microgravity like the astronauts on the International Space Station. Write a detailed description of two hours of your day.

CHAPTER 4 Weathering and Soil Formation

the BIG idea

Natural forces break rocks apart and form soil, which supports life.

Key Concepts

SECTION

4.1 Mechanical and chemical forces break down rocks.
Learn about the natural forces that break down rocks.

SECTION

4.2 Weathering and organic processes form soil.
Learn about the formation and properties of soil.

SECTION

4.3 Human activities affect soil.
Learn how land use affects soil and how soil can be protected and conserved.

How is rock related to soil?

Internet Preview

CLASSZONE.COM

Chapter 4 online resources: Content Review, two Visualizations, two Resource Centers, Math Tutorial, Test Practice

Ice Power

Fill a plastic container to the top with water and seal the lid tightly. Place it in the freezer overnight. Check on your container the next morning.

Observe and Think
What happened to the container? Why?

Getting the Dirt on Soil

Remove the top and bottom of a tin can. Be careful of sharp edges. Measure and mark 2 cm from one end of the can. Insert the can 2 cm into the ground, up to the mark. Fill the can with water and time how long it takes for the can to drain. Repeat the procedure in a different location.

Observe and Think
What do you think affects how long it takes for soil to absorb water?

Internet Activity: Soil Formation

Go to **ClassZone.com** to watch how soil forms. Learn how materials break down and contribute to soil buildup over time.

Observe and Think
What do rocks and soil have in common? What do organic matter and soil have in common?

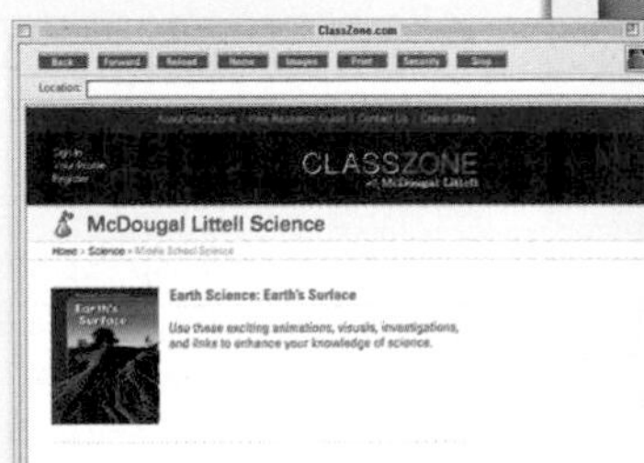

Soil Conservation **Code: MDL016**

CHAPTER 4

Getting Ready to Learn

CONCEPT REVIEW

- The atmosphere, hydrosphere, biosphere, and geosphere interact to shape Earth's surface.
- Natural processes form, change, break down, and re-form rocks.

VOCABULARY REVIEW

cleavage p. 53
fracture p. 53
rock p. 75
rock cycle p. 78
sediment p. 89

CONTENT REVIEW
CLASSZONE.COM
Review concepts and vocabulary.

TAKING NOTES

COMBINATION NOTES

To take notes about a new concept, first make an informal outline of the information. Then make a sketch of the concept and label it so that you can study it later.

CHOOSE YOUR OWN STRATEGY

Take notes about new vocabulary terms, using one or more of the strategies from earlier chapters—**magnet word, word triangle,** or **description wheel.** Feel free to mix and match the strategies, or use an entirely different vocabulary strategy.

See the Note-Taking Handbook on pages R45–R51.

SCIENCE NOTEBOOK

NOTES

Causes of Mechanical Weathering
- Ice
- Pressure Release
- Plant Roots
- Moving Water

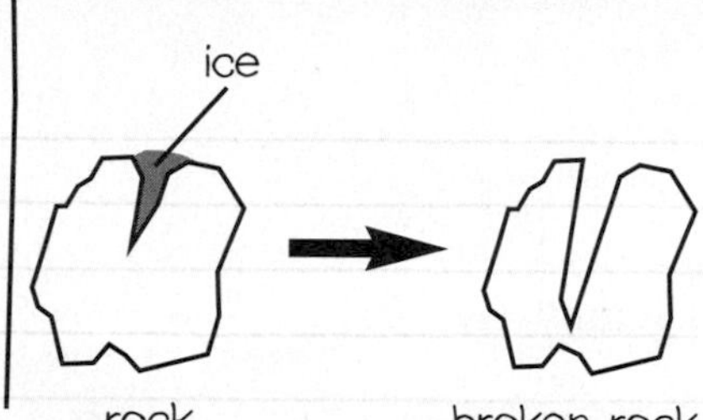

Description Wheel

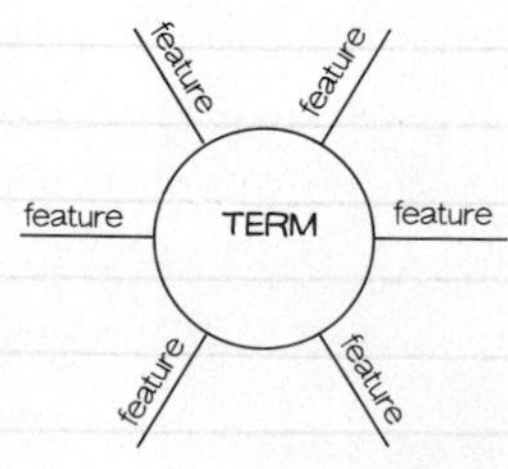

Word Triangle

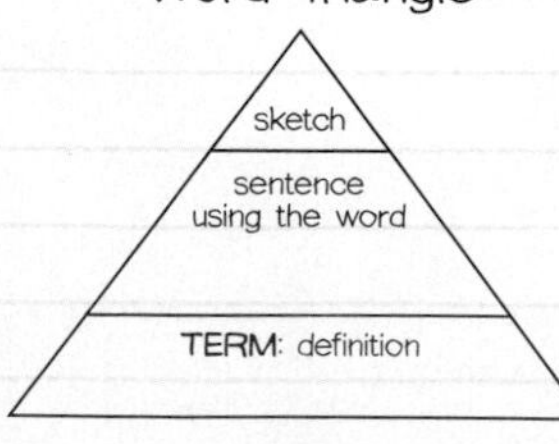

Magnet Word

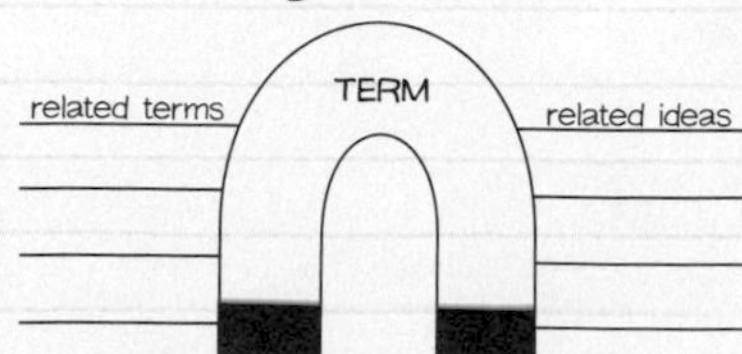

KEY CONCEPT

Mechanical and chemical forces break down rocks.

BEFORE, you learned
- Minerals make up most rocks
- Different minerals have different properties
- Rocks are broken down to form sediments

NOW, you will learn
- How mechanical weathering breaks down rocks
- How chemical weathering changes rocks
- What factors affect the rate at which weathering occurs

VOCABULARY

weathering p. 115
mechanical weathering p. 116
exfoliation p. 116
abrasion p. 116
chemical weathering p. 118

EXPLORE Mechanical Weathering

What causes rocks to break down?

PROCEDURE

1. Place a handful of rocks on a piece of dark-colored construction paper. Observe the rocks and take notes on their appearance.
2. Place the rocks in a coffee can. Put the lid on the can and shake the can forcefully for 2 minutes, holding the lid tightly shut.
3. Pour the rocks onto the construction paper. Observe them and take notes on any changes in their appearance.

MATERIALS
- coffee can with lid
- rocks
- dark-colored construction paper

WHAT DO YOU THINK?
- What happened to the rocks and why?
- What forces in nature might affect rocks in similar ways?

Weathering breaks rocks into smaller pieces.

Think about the tiniest rock you have ever found. How did it get so small? It didn't start out that way! Over time, natural forces break rocks into smaller and smaller pieces. If you have ever seen a concrete sidewalk or driveway that has been cracked by tree roots, you have seen this process. The same thing can happen to rocks.

VOCABULARY
Remember to add *weathering* to your notebook, using the vocabulary strategy of your choice.

Weathering is the process by which natural forces break down rocks. In this section you will read about two kinds of weathering. One kind occurs when a rock is physically broken apart—like the cracked sidewalk. Another kind occurs when a chemical reaction changes the makeup of a rock.

Mechanical weathering produces physical changes in rocks.

RESOURCE CENTER
CLASSZONE.COM
Learn more about weathering.

If you smash a walnut with a hammer, you will break it into a lot of small pieces, but you will not change what it is. Even though the pieces of the walnut are no longer connected together, they are still composed of the same materials. **Mechanical weathering**—the breaking up of rocks by physical forces—works in much the same way. In this natural process, physical forces split rocks apart but do not change their composition—what they are made of. Ice wedging, pressure release, plant root growth, and abrasion can all cause mechanical weathering.

READING TiP
The word *expand* means "to increase in size or volume."

1 **Ice Wedging** When water freezes, it expands. When water freezes in the cracks and pores of rocks, the force of its expansion is strong enough to split the rocks apart. This process, which is called ice wedging, can break up huge boulders. Ice wedging is common in places where temperatures rise above and fall below the freezing point for water, which is 0°C (32°F).

2 **Pressure Release** Rock deep within Earth is under great pressure from surrounding rocks. Over time, Earth's forces can push the rock up to the surface, or the overlying rocks and sediment can wear away. In either case, the pressure inside the rock is still high, but the pressure on the surface of the rock is released. This release of pressure causes the rock to expand. As the rock expands, cracks form in it, leading to exfoliation. **Exfoliation** (ehks-FOH-lee-AY-shuhn) is a process in which layers or sheets of rock gradually break off. This process is sometimes called onion-skin weathering, because the rock surface breaks off in thin layers similar to the layers of an onion.

3 **Plant Root Growth** Trees, bushes, and other plants may take root in cracks in rocks. As the roots of these plants grow, they wedge open the cracks. The rock—even if it is large—can be split completely apart.

4 **Abrasion** Water can wear down rocks on riverbeds and along shorelines by abrasion. **Abrasion** (uh-BRAY-zhuhn) is the process of wearing down by friction, the rubbing of one object or surface against another. The force of moving water alone can wear away particles of rock. Water also causes rocks to tumble downstream. The tumbling rocks wear down as they grind against the riverbed and against each other. Ocean waves beating against a rocky shore also wear down rocks by abrasion.

How does moving water weather rocks?

Mechanical Weathering

Ice wedging, pressure release, plant root growth, and abrasion can all break apart rocks.

1 Ice Wedging

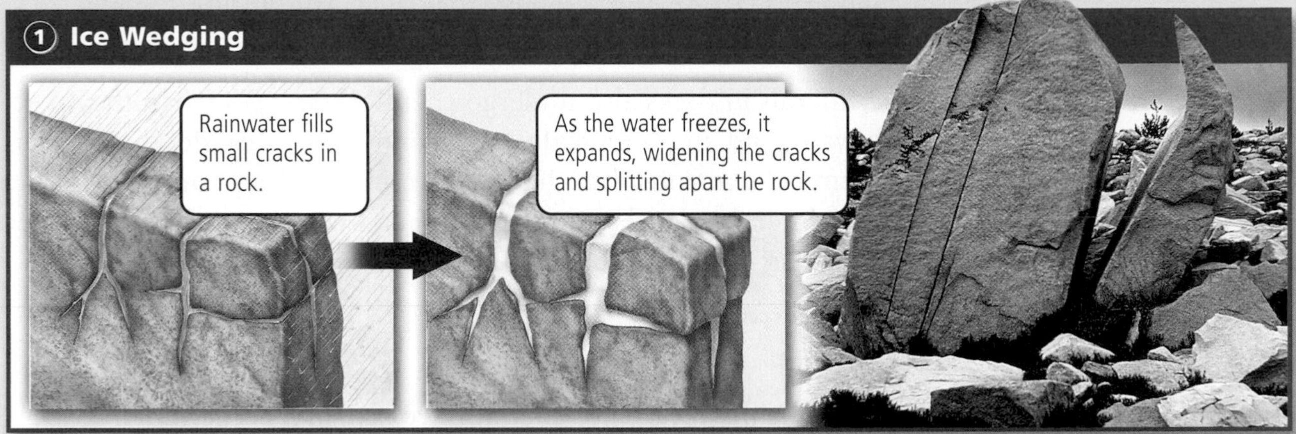

Rainwater fills small cracks in a rock.
As the water freezes, it expands, widening the cracks and splitting apart the rock.

2 Pressure Release

Earth's forces can push rock that formed deep underground up to the surface.

The release of pressure causes the rock to expand and crack.

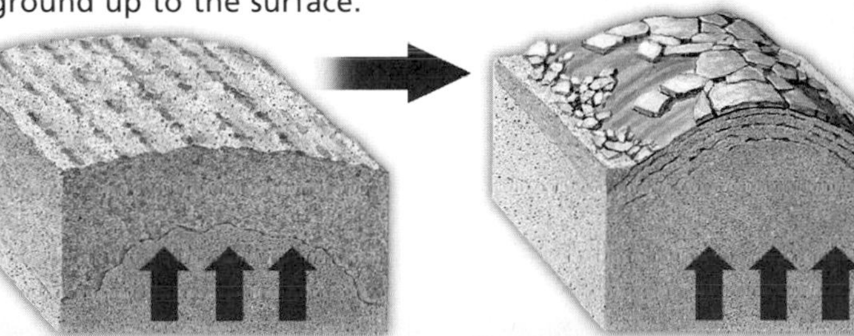

3 Plant Root Growth

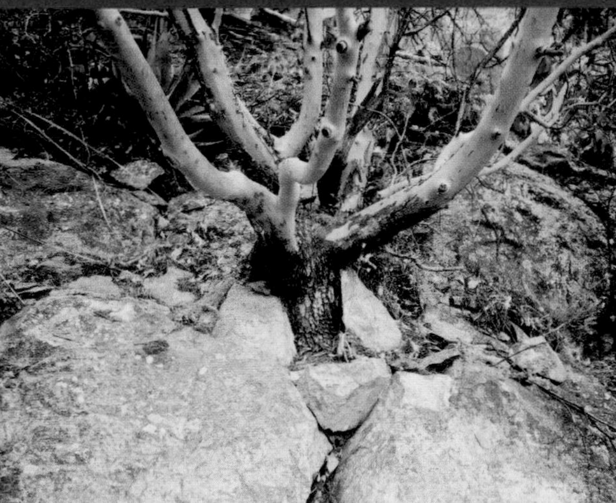

When plants grow in cracks in a rock, their roots can widen the cracks and force the rock apart.

4 Abrasion

Flowing water can move rocks, causing them to rub together and wear down into rounded shapes.

READING VISUALS What evidence of mechanical weathering can you see in each photograph above?

Chemical weathering changes the mineral composition of rocks.

Watch chemical weathering in action.

If you have seen an old rusty nail, you have witnessed the result of a chemical reaction and a chemical change. The steel in the nail contains iron. Oxygen in air and water react with the iron to form rust.

Minerals in rocks also undergo chemical changes when they react with water and air. **Chemical weathering** is the breakdown of rocks by chemical reactions that change the rocks' makeup, or composition. When minerals in rocks come into contact with air and water, some dissolve and others react and are changed into different minerals.

Dissolving

Water is the main cause of chemical weathering. Some minerals completely dissolve in ordinary water. The mineral halite, which is the same compound as table salt, dissolves in ordinary water. Many more minerals dissolve in water that is slightly acidic—like lemonade. In the atmosphere, small amounts of carbon dioxide dissolve in rainwater. The water and carbon dioxide react to form a weak acid. After falling to Earth, the rainwater moves through the soil, picking up additional

INVESTIGATE Chemical Weathering

What is necessary for rust to form?

PROCEDURE

1. Place a piece of steel wool in a cup filled to the top with water. Place a second piece of steel wool in a cup with a small amount of water. The water should touch but not cover the steel wool. Place a third piece in a cup with no water.
2. Allow the three cups to sit overnight. Observe the appearance of the steel wool in each container the next day.

WHAT DO YOU THINK?

- What happened to the steel wool in each cup?
- Judging by the appearance of the pieces of steel wool, what do you think is necessary for rusting to occur?

CHALLENGE Tear the steel wool that rusted most apart and compare the appearances of the inside and the outside. Why might the inside and the outside look different?

SKILL FOCUS
Identifying variables

MATERIALS
- steel wool
- 3 cups
- water

TIME
15 minutes

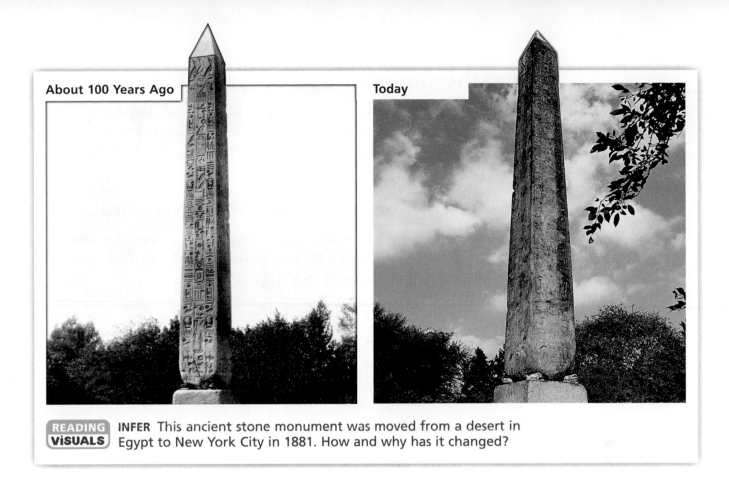

About 100 Years Ago

Today

READING VISUALS **INFER** This ancient stone monument was moved from a desert in Egypt to New York City in 1881. How and why has it changed?

carbon dioxide from decaying plants. The slightly acidic water breaks down minerals in rocks. In the process, the rocks may also break apart into smaller pieces.

Air pollution can make rainwater even more acidic than it is naturally. Power plants and automobiles produce gases such as sulfur dioxide and nitric oxide, which react with water vapor in the atmosphere to form acid rain. Acid rain causes rocks to weather much faster than they would naturally. The photographs above show how acid rain can damage a granite column in just a hundred years.

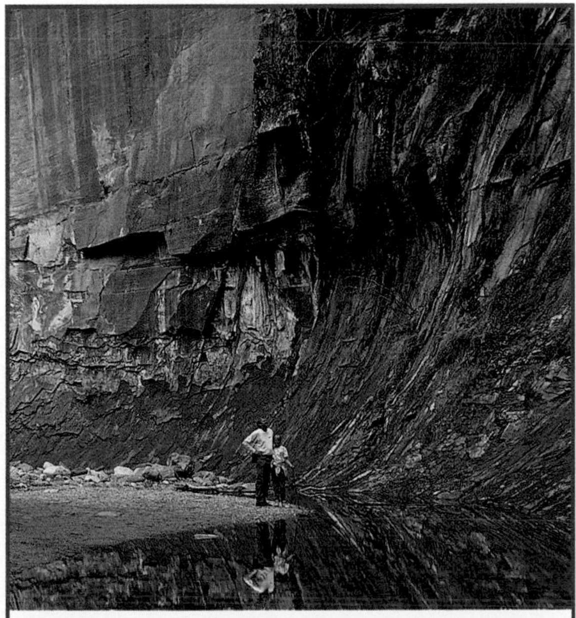

The rocks in Oak Creek Canyon are reddish because iron in the rocks reacted with water and air to produce iron oxides.

Rusting

The oxygen in the air is also involved in chemical weathering. Many common minerals contain iron. When these minerals dissolve in water, oxygen in the air and the water combines with the iron to produce iron oxides, or rust. The iron oxides form a coating that colors the weathered rocks like those you see in the photograph of Oak Creek Canyon in Arizona.

How is air involved in chemical weathering?

Weathering occurs at different rates.

COMBINATION NOTES
Record in your notes three factors that affect the rate at which rock weathers.

Most weathering occurs over long periods of time—hundreds, thousands, or even millions of years. It can take hundreds or thousands of years for a very hard rock to wear down only a few millimeters—a few times the thickness of your fingernail. But the rate of weathering is not the same for all rocks. Factors such as surface area, rock composition, and location influence the rate of weathering.

Surface Area The more of a rock's surface that is exposed to air and water, the faster the rock will break down. A greater surface area allows chemical weathering to affect more of a rock.

1 Over time, mechanical weathering breaks a rock into smaller pieces.

2 As a result, more of the rock's surface is exposed to chemical weathering.

Rock Composition Different kinds of rock break down at different rates. Granite, for example, breaks down much more slowly than limestone. Both of these rocks are often used for tombstones and statues.

Climate Water is needed for chemical weathering to occur, and heat speeds up chemical weathering. As a result, chemical weathering occurs faster in hot, wet regions than it does in cold, dry regions. However, mechanical weathering caused by freezing and thawing occurs more in cold regions than in hot regions.

4.1 Review

KEY CONCEPTS

1. What is weathering?
2. What are four causes of mechanical weathering?
3. How do water and air help cause chemical weathering?
4. Describe three factors that affect the rate at which weathering occurs.

CRITICAL THINKING

5. **Infer** How does mechanical weathering affect the rate of chemical weathering?
6. **Predict** Would weathering affect a marble sculpture inside a museum? Explain your answer.

CHALLENGE

7. **Infer** The word *weather* is most commonly used to refer to the state of the atmosphere at a certain time. Why do you think the same word is used to refer to the breakdown of rocks?

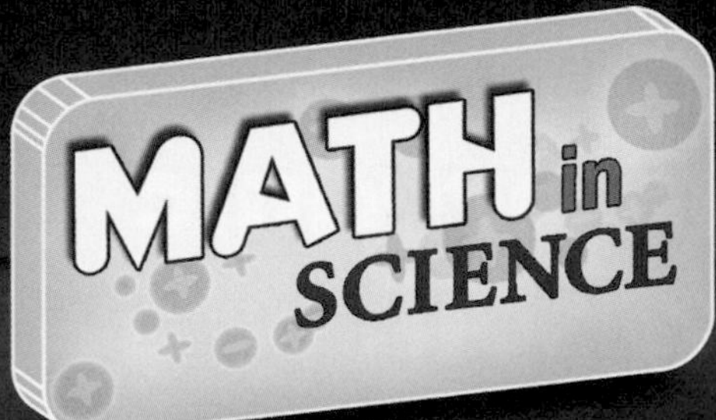

SKILL: FINDING THE SURFACE AREA OF A RECTANGULAR PRISM

Rock Weathering

How quickly a rock weathers depends, in part, on its surface area. The greater the surface area, the more quickly the rock weathers. Do you think a rock will weather more quickly if you break it in half? You can find out by using a rectangular prism to represent the rock.

MATH TUTORIAL

CLASSZONE.COM

Click on Math Tutorial for more help with finding the surface areas of rectangular prisms.

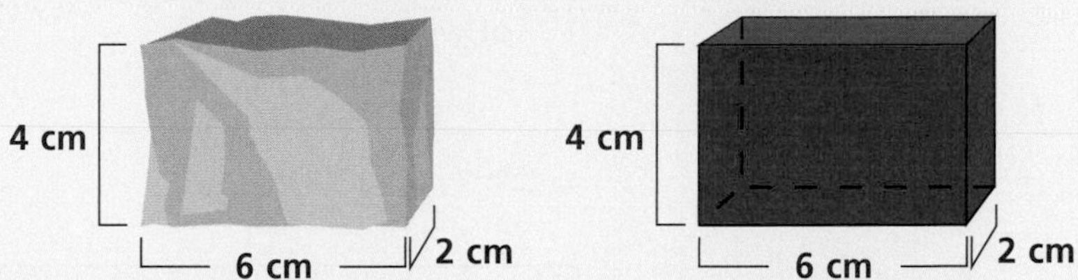

Weathering has broken apart these rocks in the Isles of Scilly, England.

Example

To find the surface area of the prism, add the areas of its faces.

(1) Find the area of each face.

Area of top (or bottom) face: $6 \text{ cm} \times 2 \text{ cm} = 12 \text{ cm}^2$

Area of front (or back) face: $6 \text{ cm} \times 4 \text{ cm} = 24 \text{ cm}^2$

Area of right (or left) face: $4 \text{ cm} \times 2 \text{ cm} = 8 \text{ cm}^2$

(2) Add the areas of all six faces to find the surface area.

$$\text{Surface area} = 12 \text{ cm}^2 + 12 \text{ cm}^2 + 24 \text{ cm}^2 + 24 \text{ cm}^2 + 8 \text{ cm}^2 + 8 \text{ cm}^2 = 88 \text{ cm}^2$$

ANSWER The surface area of the prism is 88 cm^2.

For the rock broken in half, you can use two smaller rectangular prisms to represent the two halves.

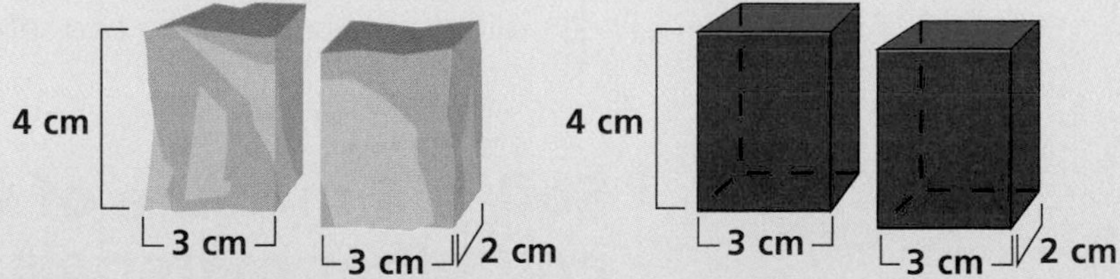

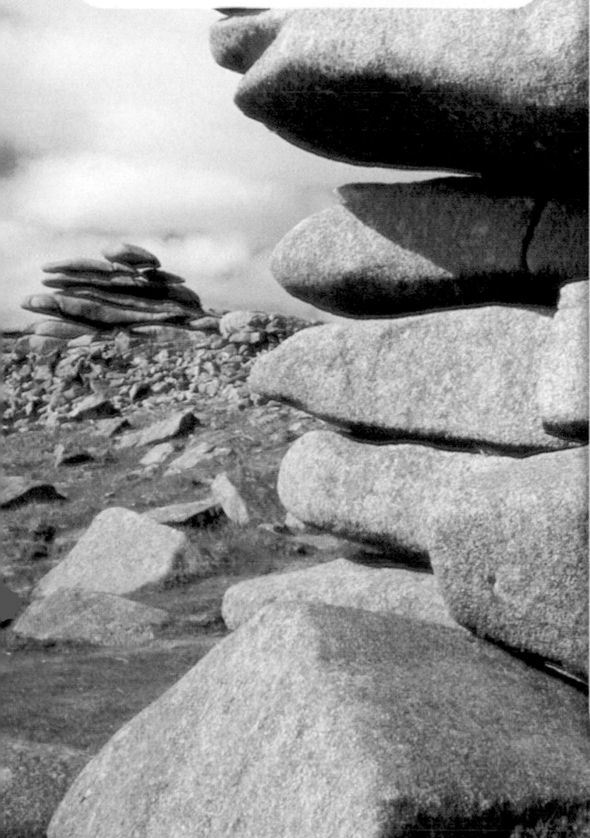

Answer the following questions.

1. What is the surface area of each of the smaller rectangular prisms?

2. How does the total surface area of the two smaller prisms compare with the surface area of the larger prism?

3. Will the rock weather more quickly in one piece or broken in half?

CHALLENGE If the two smaller prisms both broke in half, what would be the total surface area of the resulting four prisms?

KEY CONCEPT

Weathering and organic processes form soil.

BEFORE, you learned

- Weathering processes break down rocks
- Climate influences the rate of weathering

NOW, you will learn

- What soil consists of
- How climate and landforms affect a soil's characteristics
- How the activities of organisms affect a soil's characteristics
- How the properties of soil differ

VOCABULARY

humus p. 123
soil horizon p. 124
soil profile p. 124

EXPLORE Soil Composition

What makes soils different?

PROCEDURE

1. Spread some potting soil on a piece of white paper. Spread another type of soil on another piece of white paper.
2. Examine the two soil samples with a hand lens. Use the tweezers to look for small pieces of rock or sand, humus, and clay. Humus is brown or black, and clay is lighter in color. Record your observations.

WHAT DO YOU THINK?

- How do the two soil samples differ? How are they alike?
- What might account for the differences between the two soils?

MATERIALS

- potting soil
- local soil sample
- white paper (2 pieces)
- hand lens
- tweezers

Soil is a mixture of weathered rock particles and other materials.

Soil may not be the first thing you think of when you wake up in the morning, but it is a very important part of your everyday life. You have spent your whole life eating food grown in soil, standing on soil, and living in buildings built on soil. Soil is under your feet right now—or at least there used to be soil there before the building you are in was constructed. In this section you will learn more about the world of soil beneath your feet.

Why is soil important?

Soil Composition

Soil is a mixture of four materials: weathered rock particles, organic matter, water, and air. Weathered rock particles are the main ingredient of soil. Soils differ, depending on what types of rock the rock particles came from—for example, granite or limestone.

Water and air each make up about 20 to 30 percent of a soil's volume. Organic matter makes up about 5 percent. The word *organic* (awr-GAN-ihk) means "coming from living organisms." Organic matter in soil comes from the remains and waste products of plants, animals, and other living organisms. For example, leaves that fall to a forest floor decay and become part of the soil. The decayed organic matter in soil is called **humus** (HYOO-muhs).

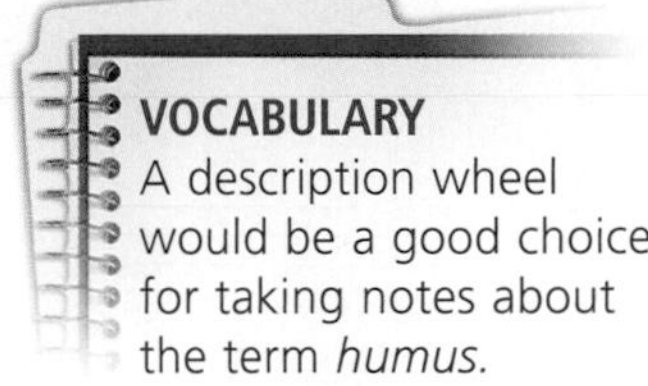

VOCABULARY
A description wheel would be a good choice for taking notes about the term *humus*.

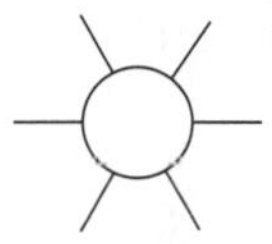

All soils are not the same. Different soils are made up of different ingredients and different amounts of each ingredient. In the photographs below, the black soil contains much more decayed plant material than the red soil. The black soil also contains more water. The kind of soil that forms in an area depends on a number of factors, including

- the kind of rock in the area
- the area's climate, or overall weather pattern over time
- the landforms in the area, such as mountains and valleys
- the plant cover in the area
- the animals and other organisms in the area
- time

The composition of a soil determines what you can grow in it, what you can build on it, and what happens to the rainwater that falls on it.

READING VISUALS COMPARE AND CONTRAST These two soils look different because they contain different ingredients. How would you describe their differences?

Soil Horizons

This soil profile in Hagerstown, Maryland, shows distinct A, B, and C horizons.

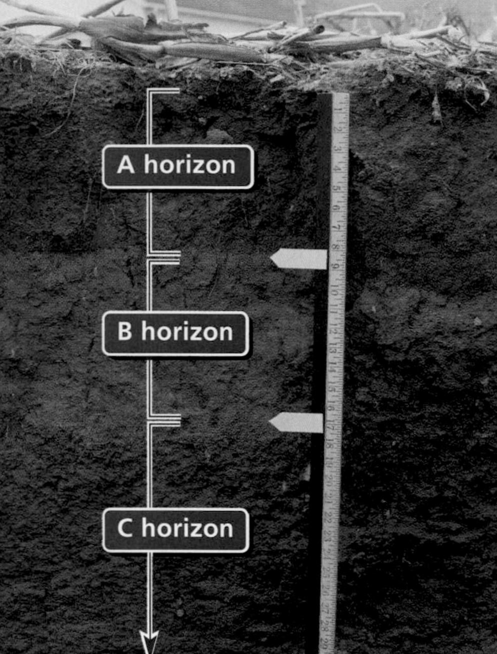

If you dig a deep hole in the ground, you might notice that the deeper soil looks different. As you dig down, you will find larger rock particles that are less weathered. There is also less organic matter in deeper soil.

Soil develops in a series of horizontal layers called soil horizons. A **soil horizon** is a layer of soil with properties that differ from those of the layer above or below it. Geologists label the main horizons A, B, and C. In some places there may also be a layer of dead leaves and other organic matter at the surface of the ground.

- **The A horizon** is the upper layer of soil and is commonly called topsoil. It contains the most organic matter of the three horizons. Because of the humus the A horizon contains, it is often dark in color.
- **The B horizon** lies just below the A horizon. It has little organic matter and is usually brownish or reddish in color. It contains clay and minerals that have washed down from the A horizon.
- **The C horizon** is the deepest layer of soil. It consists of the largest and least-weathered rock particles. Its color is typically light yellowish brown.

The soil horizons in a specific location make up what geologists call a **soil profile.** Different locations can have very different soil profiles. The A horizon, for example, may be very thick in some places and very thin in others. In some areas, one or more horizons may even be missing from the profile. For example, a soil that has had only a short time to develop might be missing the B horizon.

What are soil horizons?

Climate and landforms affect soil.

COMBINATION NOTES
Record in your notes four categories of soil that form in different climate regions.

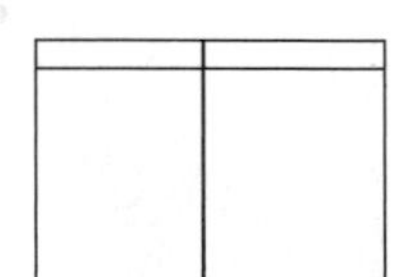

Different kinds of soils form in different climates. The soil that forms in a hot, wet climate is different from the soil of a cold, dry climate. Climate also influences the characteristics and thickness of the soil that develops from weathered rock. Tropical, desert, temperate, and arctic soils are four types of soil that form in different climate regions.

The shape of the land also affects the development of soil. For example, mountain soils may be very different from the soils in nearby valleys. The cold climate on a mountain results in slow soil formation, and the top layer of soil continually washes down off the slopes. As a result, mountain slopes have soils with thin A horizons that cannot support large plants. The soil that washes down the slopes builds up in the surrounding valleys, so the valleys may have soils with thick A horizons that can support many plants.

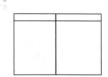

World Soil Types

Different types of soils form in different climates.

Tropical Soils

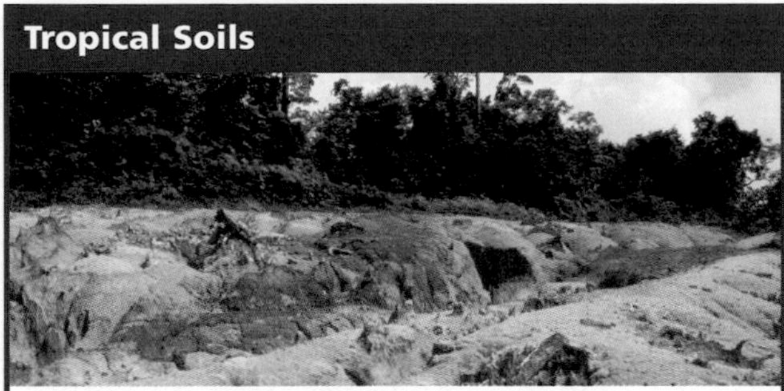

Tropical soils form in warm, rainy regions. Heavy rains wash away minerals, leaving only a thin surface layer of humus. Tropical soils are not suitable for growing most crops.

Desert Soils

Desert soils form in dry regions. These soils are shallow and contain little organic matter. Because of the low rainfall, chemical weathering and soil formation occur very slowly in desert regions.

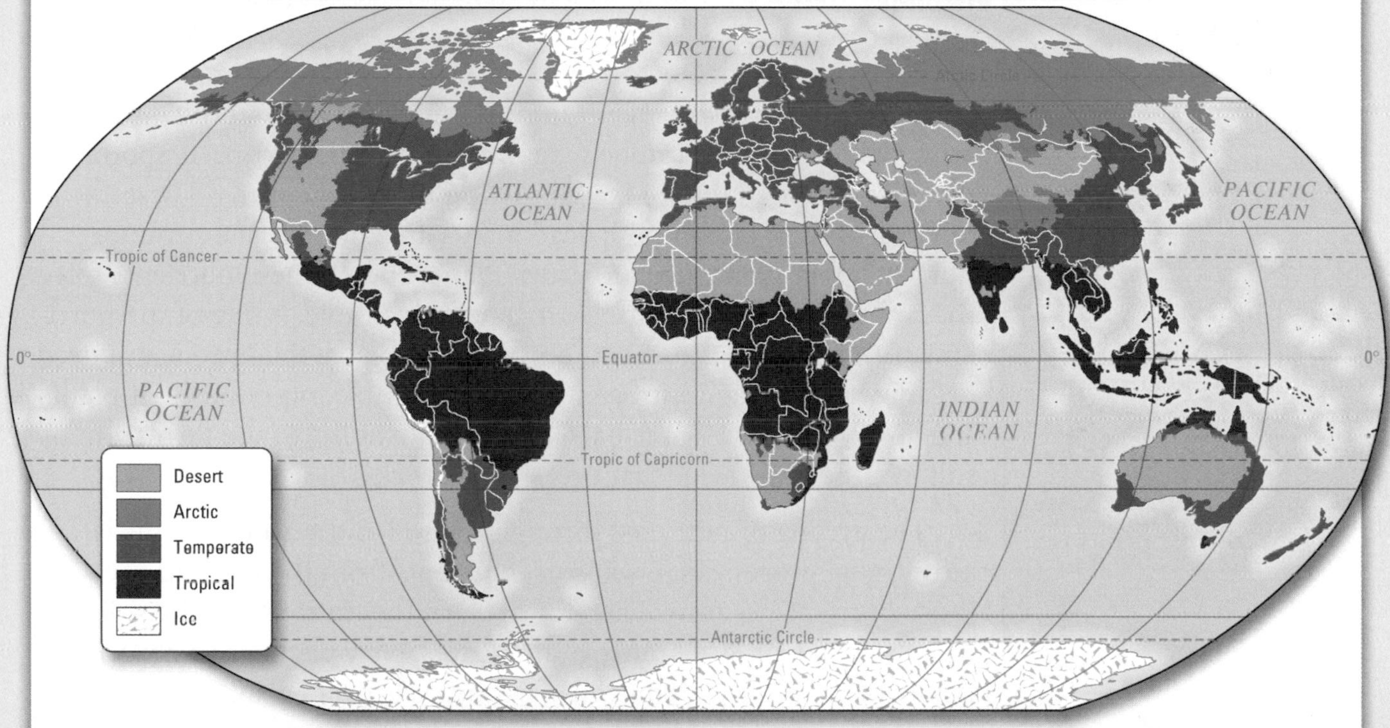

Temperate Soils

Temperate soils form in regions with moderate rainfall and temperatures. Some temperate soils are dark-colored, rich in organic matter and minerals, and good for growing crops.

Arctic Soils

Arctic soils form in cold, dry regions where chemical weathering is slow. They typically do not have well-developed horizons. Arctic soils contain a lot of rock fragments.

The activities of organisms affect soil.

COMBINATION NOTES
Record in your notes three types of organisms that affect soil characteristics.

Under the ground beneath your feet is a whole world of life forms that are going about their daily activities. The living organisms in a soil have a huge impact on the soil's characteristics. In fact, without them, the soil would not be able to support the wide variety of plants that people depend on to live. The organisms that affect the characteristics of soils include plants, microorganisms (MY-kroh-AWR-guh-NIHZ-uhmz), and animals.

Plants, such as trees and grasses, provide most of the organic matter that gets broken down to form humus. Trees add to the organic matter in soil as they lose their branches and leaves. Trees and other plants also contribute to humus when they die and decompose, or break down.

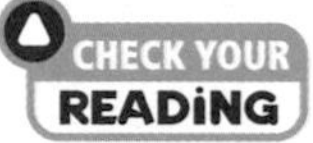
How are plants and humus related?

READING TIP
A decomposer is an organism that decomposes, or breaks down, dead plants and animals.

Microorganisms include decomposers such as bacteria and fungi (FUHN-jy). The prefix *micro-* means "very small." Microorganisms are so small that they can be seen only with a microscope. A spoonful of soil may contain more than a million microorganisms! These microorganisms decompose dead plants and animals and produce nutrients that plants need to grow. Plants absorb these nutrients from the soil through their roots. Nitrogen, for example, is one of the nutrients plants need to grow. Microorganisms change the nitrogen in dead organic matter—and nitrogen in the air—into compounds that plants can absorb and use. Some bacteria also contribute to the formation of soil by producing acids that break down rocks.

The cycling of nutrients through the soil and through plants is a continual process. Plants absorb nutrients from the soil and use those nutrients to grow. Then they return the nutrients to the soil when they die or lose branches and leaves. New plants then absorb the nutrients from the soil and start the cycle over again.

Animals such as earthworms, ants, termites, mice, gophers, moles, and prairie dogs all make their homes in the soil. All of these animals loosen and mix the soil as they tunnel through it. They create spaces in the soil, thereby adding to its air content and improving its ability to absorb and drain water. Burrowing animals also bring partly weathered rock particles to the surface of the ground, where they become exposed to more weathering. Just like plants, animals return nutrients to the soil when their bodies decompose after death.

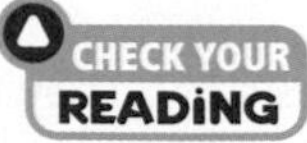
How do animals affect soil? Name at least three ways.

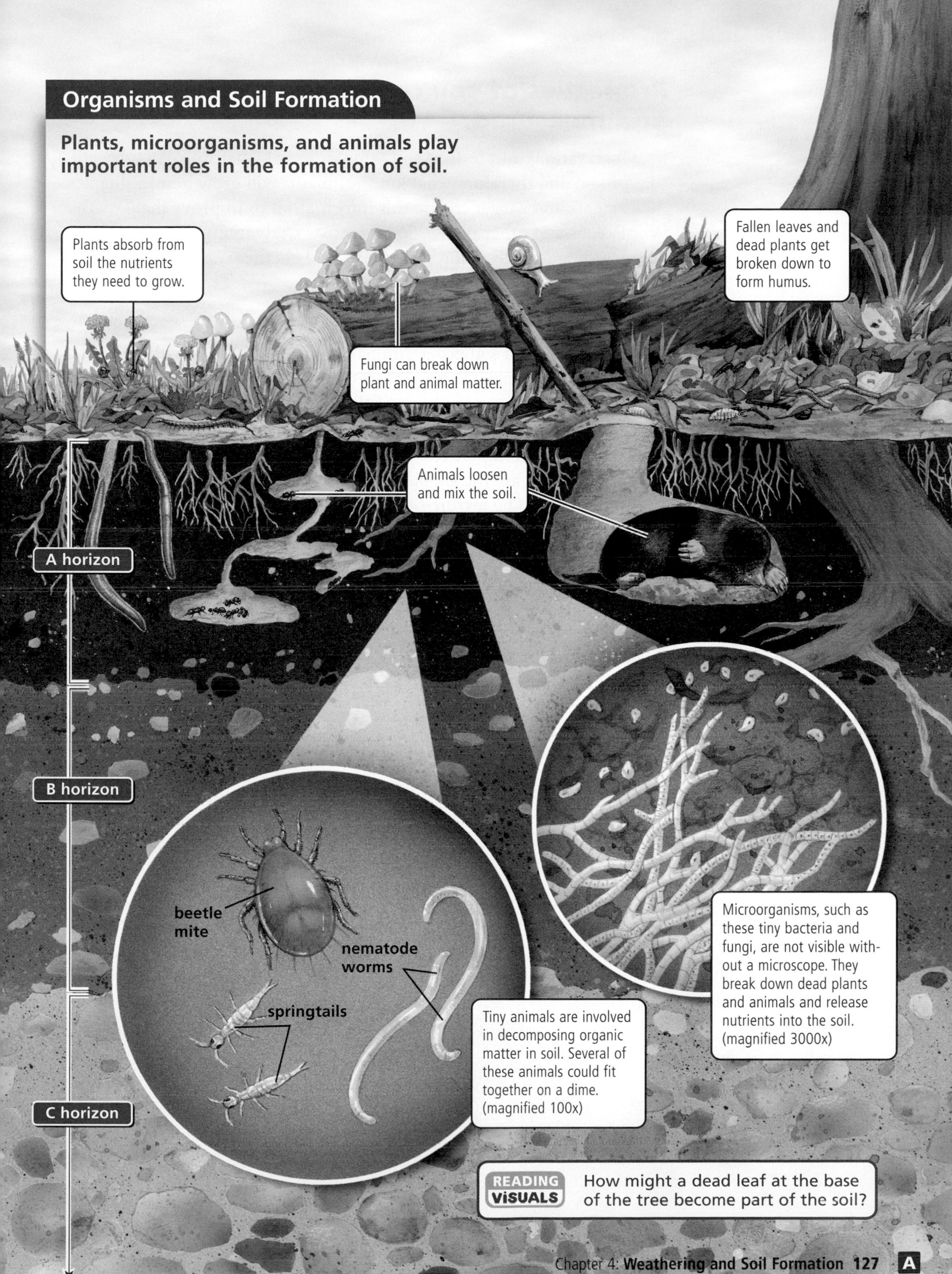
Organisms and Soil Formation
Plants, microorganisms, and animals play important roles in the formation of soil.
Plants absorb from soil the nutrients they need to grow.
Fungi can break down plant and animal matter.
Fallen leaves and dead plants get broken down to form humus.
Animals loosen and mix the soil.
A horizon
B horizon
C horizon
beetle mite
nematode worms
springtails
Tiny animals are involved in decomposing organic matter in soil. Several of these animals could fit together on a dime. (magnified 100x)
Microorganisms, such as these tiny bacteria and fungi, are not visible without a microscope. They break down dead plants and animals and release nutrients into the soil. (magnified 3000x)
READING VISUALS
How might a dead leaf at the base of the tree become part of the soil?

Properties of soil can be observed and measured.

Observations and tests of soil samples reveal what nutrients the soils contain and therefore what kinds of plants will grow best in them. Farmers and gardeners use this information to improve the growth of crops and other plants. Soil scientists study many soil properties, including texture, color, pore space, and chemistry.

Texture

The texture of a soil is determined by the size of the weathered rock particles it contains. Soil scientists classify the rock particles in soils into three categories, on the basis of size: sand, silt, and clay. Sand particles are the largest and can be seen without a microscope. Silt particles are smaller than sand particles—too small to be seen without a microscope. Clay particles are the smallest. Most soils contain a mixture of sand, silt, and clay. The texture of a soil influences how easily air and water move through the soil.

Soil Texture

The texture of a soil is determined by the amounts of sand, silt, and clay it contains.

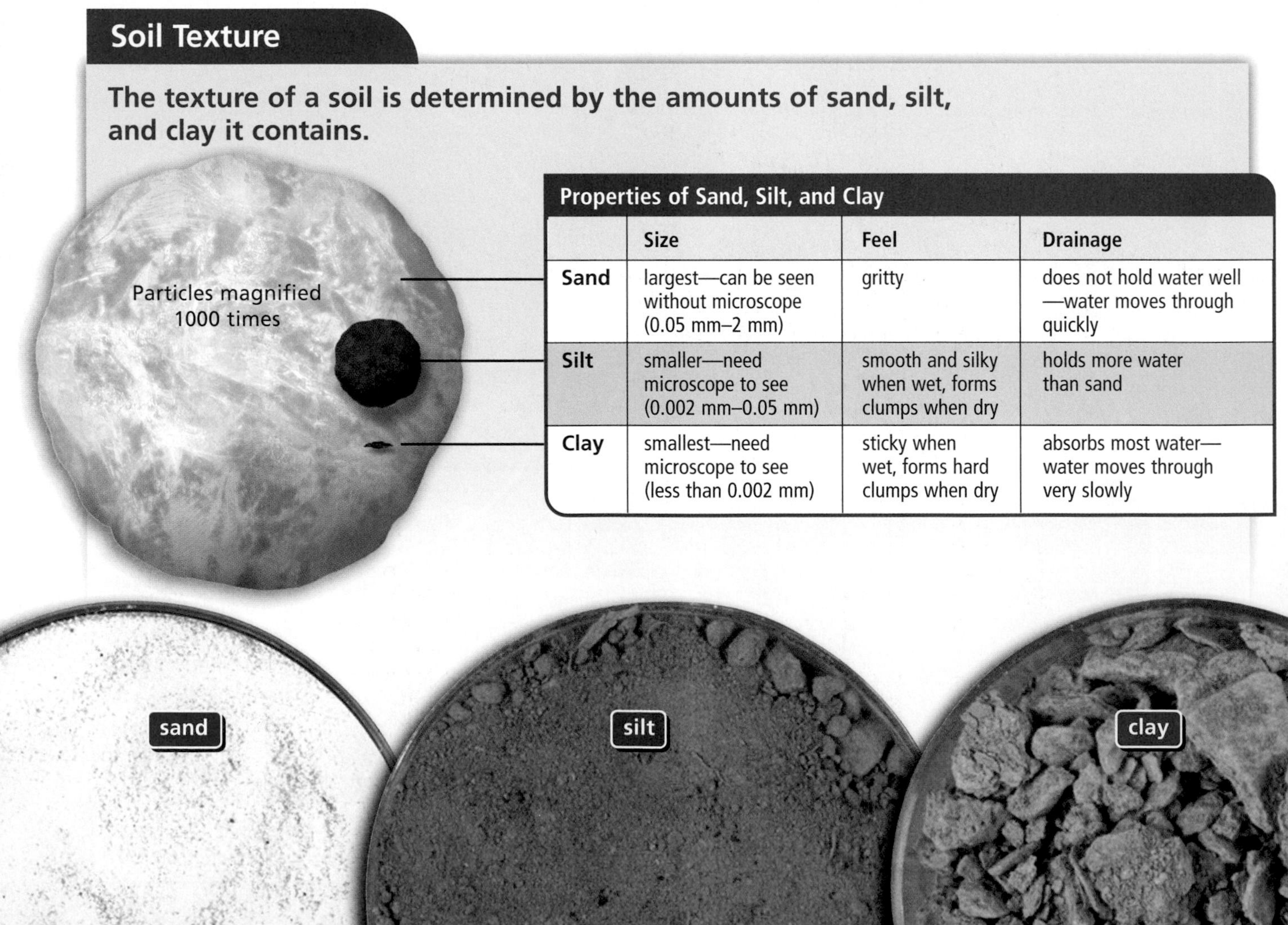

Properties of Sand, Silt, and Clay

	Size	Feel	Drainage
Sand	largest—can be seen without microscope (0.05 mm–2 mm)	gritty	does not hold water well —water moves through quickly
Silt	smaller—need microscope to see (0.002 mm–0.05 mm)	smooth and silky when wet, forms clumps when dry	holds more water than sand
Clay	smallest—need microscope to see (less than 0.002 mm)	sticky when wet, forms hard clumps when dry	absorbs most water—water moves through very slowly

Color

The color of a soil is a clue to its other properties. Soil colors include red, brown, yellow, green, black, and even white. Most soil colors come from iron compounds and humus. Iron gives soil a reddish color. Soils with a high humus content are usually black or brown. Besides indicating the content of a soil, color may also be a clue to how well water moves through the soil—that is, how well the soil drains. Bright-colored soils, for instance, drain well.

Investigate soil.

Pore Space

Pore space refers to the spaces between soil particles. Water and air move through the pore spaces in a soil. Plant roots need both water and air to grow. Soils range from about 25 to 60 percent pore space. An ideal soil for growing plants has 50 percent of its volume as pore space, with half of the pore space occupied by air and half by water.

Chemistry

Plants absorb the nutrients they need from the water in soil. These nutrients may come from the minerals or the organic matter in the soil. To be available to plant roots, the nutrients must be dissolved in water. How well nutrients dissolve in the water in soil depends on the water's pH, which is a measure of acidity. Farmers may apply lime to make soil less acidic. To make soil more acidic, an acid may be applied.

How does soil acidity affect whether the nutrients in soil are available to plants?

This gardener is adding lime to the soil to make it less acidic.

4.2 Review

KEY CONCEPTS

1. What are the main ingredients of soil?
2. How do climate and landforms affect soils' characteristics?
3. How do the activities of organisms affect the characteristics of soil?
4. Describe four properties of soil.

CRITICAL THINKING

5. **Compare and Contrast** How would a soil containing a lot of sand differ from a soil with a lot of clay?
6. **Infer** Which would you expect to be more fertile, the soil on hilly land or the soil on a plain? Why?

CHALLENGE

7. **Synthesize** What kinds of roots might you expect to find on plants that grow in arctic soils? Why?

CHAPTER INVESTIGATION

Testing Soil

OVERVIEW AND PURPOSE Soil is necessary for life. Whether a soil is suitable for farming or construction, and whether it absorbs water when it rains, depends on the particular properties of that soil. In this investigation you will

- test a soil sample to measure several soil properties
- identify the properties of your soil sample

MATERIALS

- dried soil sample
- 250 mL graduated cylinder
- 1 qt jar, with lid
- water
- 2 L plastic bottle
- scissors
- window screening
- rubber band
- pH test strips
- clock with second hand
- *for Challenge:* Texture Flow Chart

Procedure

PORE-SPACE TEST

1. Measure 200 mL of the dried soil sample in a graduated cylinder. Pour it into the jar.
2. Rinse the graduated cylinder, then fill it with 200 mL of water. Slowly pour the water into the jar until the soil is so soaked that any additional water would pool on top.
3. Record the amount of water remaining in the graduated cylinder. Then determine by subtraction the amount you added to the soil sample. Make a soil properties chart in your **Science Notebook** and record this number in it.
4. Discard the wet soil according to your teacher's instructions, and rinse the jar.

pH TEST AND DRAINAGE TEST

5. Cut off the top of a plastic bottle and use a rubber band to attach a piece of window screening over its mouth. Place the bottle top, mouth down, into the jar.
6. Use the graduated cylinder to measure 200 mL of soil, and pour the soil into the inverted bottle top.
7. Rinse the graduated cylinder, and fill it with 100 mL of water. Test the water's pH, using a pH test strip. Record the result in the "before" space in your soil properties chart.
8. Pour the water into the soil. Measure the amount of time it takes for the first drips to fall into the jar. Record the result in your soil properties chart.

top of plastic bottle

jar

window screening

9 Once the water stops dripping, remove the bottle top. Use a new pH strip to measure the pH of the water in the jar. Record this measurement in the "after" space in your soil properties chart and note any differences in the appearance of the water before and after its filtering through the soil.

10 Discard the wet soil according to your teacher's instructions, and rinse the jar.

PARTICLE-TYPE TEST

11 Add water to the jar until it is two-thirds full. Pour in soil until the water level rises to the top of the jar, then replace the lid. Shake the jar, and set it to rest undisturbed on a countertop overnight.

12 The next day, observe the different soil layers. The sample should have separated into sand (on the bottom), silt (in the middle), and clay (on the top). Measure the height of each layer, as well as the overall height of the three layers. Record your measurements in your soil properties chart.

13 Use the following formula to calculate the percentage of each kind of particle in the sample:

$$\frac{\text{height of layer}}{\text{total height of all layers}} \times 100$$

Record your results and all calculations in your soil properties chart.

Observe and Analyze

Write It Up

1. **RECORD** Complete your soil properties chart.
2. **IDENTIFY** How did steps 1–3 test your soil sample's pore space?
3. **IDENTIFY** How did steps 5–9 test your soil sample's drainage rate?

Conclude

1. **EVALUATE** In step 3 you measured the amount of space between the soil particles in your sample. In step 8 you measured how quickly water passed through your sample. Are these two properties related? Explain your answer.
2. **EVALUATE** Would packing down or loosening up your soil sample change any of the properties you tested? Explain your answer.
3. **INTERPRET** What happened to the pH of the water that passed through the soil? Why do you think that happened?
4. **ANALYZE** Look at the percentages of sand, silt, and clay in your sample. How do the percentages help to explain the properties you observed and measured?

INVESTIGATE Further

CHALLENGE Soil texture depends on the size of the weathered rock particles the soil contains. Use the Texture Flow Chart to determine the texture of your soil sample.

Testing Soil

Observe and Analyze

Table 1. Soil Properties Chart

Property	Result	Notes and Calculations
Pore space	_ mL water added	
pH	before: pH = _ after: pH = _	
Drainage	_ seconds	
Particle type	height of sand = _ cm height of silt = _ cm height of clay = _ cm total height = _ cm	

Conclude

KEY CONCEPT

Human activities affect soil.

BEFORE, you learned

- Soils consist mainly of weathered rock and organic matter
- Soils vary, depending on climate
- Organisms affect the characteristics of soil
- Soil properties can be measured

NOW, you will learn

- Why soil is a necessary resource
- How people's use of land affects soil
- How people can conserve soil

VOCABULARY

desertification p. 133

THINK ABOUT

How does land use affect soil?

Look outside for evidence of ways that people have affected the soil. Make a list of all the things that you can see or think of. Use your list to make a two-column table with the headings "Activity" and "Effects."

Soil is a necessary resource.

Soil helps sustain life on Earth—including your life. You already know that soil supports the growth of plants, which in turn supply food for animals. Therefore, soil provides you with nearly all the food you eat. But that's not all. Many other items you use, such as cotton clothing and medicines, come from plants. Lumber in your home comes from trees. Even the oxygen you breathe comes from plants.

Besides supporting the growth of plants, soil plays other life-sustaining roles. Soil helps purify, or clean, water as it drains through the ground and into rivers, lakes, and oceans. Decomposers in soil also help recycle nutrients by breaking down the remains of plants and animals, releasing nutrients that living plants use to grow. In addition, soil provides a home for a variety of living things, from tiny one-celled organisms to small mammals.

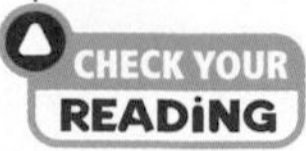

Why is soil a necessary resource?

Land-use practices can harm soil.

The way people use land can affect the levels of nutrients and pollution in soil. Any activity that exposes soil to wind and rain can lead to soil loss. Farming, construction and development, and mining are among the main activities that impact soil resources.

Farming

Farming is very important to society because almost all of the world's food is grown on farms. Over the 10,000 years humans have been farming, people have continually improved their farming methods. However, farming has some harmful effects and can lead to soil loss.

COMBINATION NOTES
Remember to take notes about how farming affects soil.

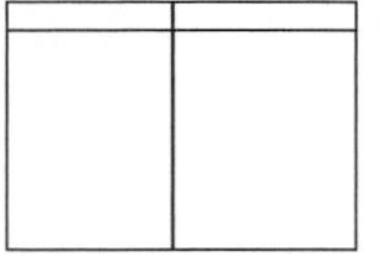

Farmers often add nutrients to soil in the form of organic or artificial fertilizers to make their crops grow better. However, some fertilizers can make it difficult for microorganisms in the soil to produce nutrients naturally. Fertilizers also add to water pollution when rainwater draining from fields carries the excess nutrients to rivers, lakes, and oceans.

Over time, many farming practices lead to the loss of soil. All over the world, farmers clear trees and other plants and plow up the soil to plant crops. Without its natural plant cover, the soil is more exposed to rain and wind and is therefore more likely to get washed or blown away. American farmers lose about five metric tons of soil for each metric ton of grain they produce. In many other parts of the world, the losses are even higher.

Another problem is overgrazing. Overgrazing occurs when farm animals eat large amounts of the land cover. Overgrazing destroys natural vegetation and causes the soil to wash or blow away more easily. In many dry regions of the world, overgrazing and the clearing of land for farming have led to desertification. **Desertification** (dih-ZUR-tuh-fih-KAY-shuhn) is the expansion of desert conditions in areas where the natural plant cover has been destroyed.

Exposed soil can be blown away by wind or washed away by rain.

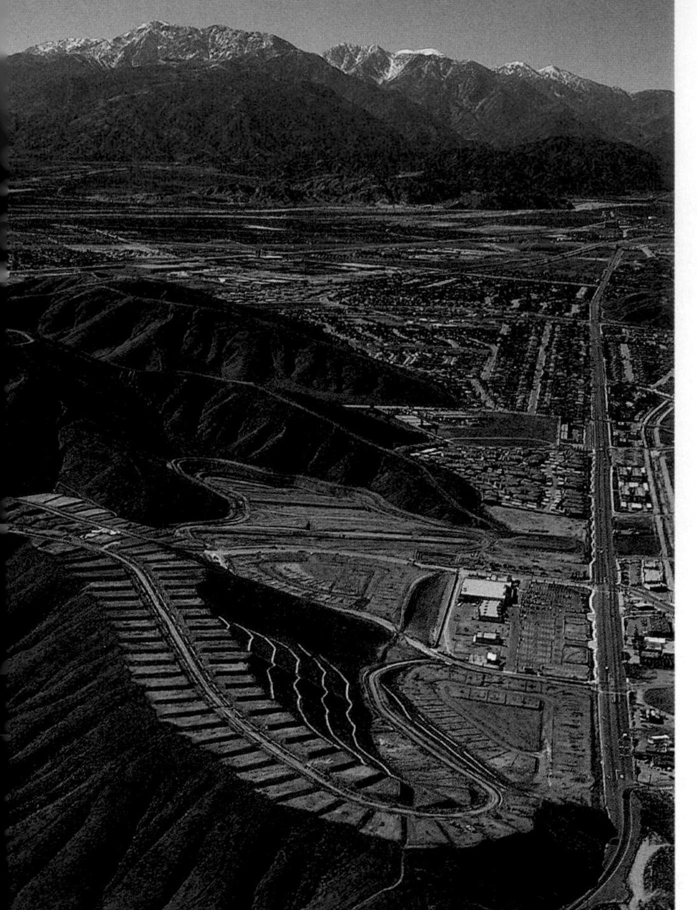

The top of this hill in San Bernardino County, California, was cleared for a housing development. A house will be built on each flat plot of land.

Construction and Development

To make roads, houses, shopping malls, and other buildings, people need to dig up the soil. Some of the soil at construction sites washes or blows away because its protective plant cover has been removed. The soil that is washed or blown away ends up in nearby low-lying areas, in rivers and streams, or in downstream lakes or reservoirs. This soil can cause problems by making rivers and lakes muddy and harming the organisms that live in them. The buildup of soil on riverbeds raises the level of the rivers and may cause flooding. The soil can also fill up lakes and reservoirs.

Mining

Some methods of mining cause soil loss. For example, the digging of strip mines and open-pit mines involves the removal of plants and soil from the surface of the ground.

By exposing rocks and minerals to the air and to rainwater, these forms of mining speed up the rate of chemical weathering. In mining operations that expose sulfide minerals, the increased chemical weathering causes a type of pollution known as acid drainage. Abandoned mines can fill with rainwater. Sulfide minerals react with the air and the water to produce sulfuric acid. Then the acid water drains from the mines, polluting the soil in surrounding areas.

CHECK YOUR READING How do some methods of mining affect the soil?

To make this open-pit mine in Cananea, Mexico, plants and soil were removed from the surface of the ground.

Soil can be protected and conserved.

Soil conservation is very important, because soil can be difficult or impossible to replace once it has been lost. Soil takes a very long time to form. A soil with well-developed horizons may take hundreds of thousands of years to form! Most soil conservation methods are designed to hold soil in place and keep it fertile. Below are descriptions of a few of the many soil conservation methods that are used by farmers around the world.

Crop rotation is the practice of planting different crops on the same field in different years or growing seasons. Grain crops, such as wheat, use up a lot of the nitrogen—a necessary plant nutrient—in the soil. The roots of bean crops, such as soybeans, contain bacteria that restore nitrogen to the soil. By rotating these crops, farmers can help maintain soil fertility.

Conservation tillage includes several methods of reducing the number of times fields are tilled, or plowed, in a year. The less soil is disturbed by plowing, the less likely it is to be washed or blown away. In one method of conservation tillage, fields are not plowed at all. The remains of harvested crops are simply left on the fields to cover and protect the soil. New seeds are planted in narrow bands of soil.

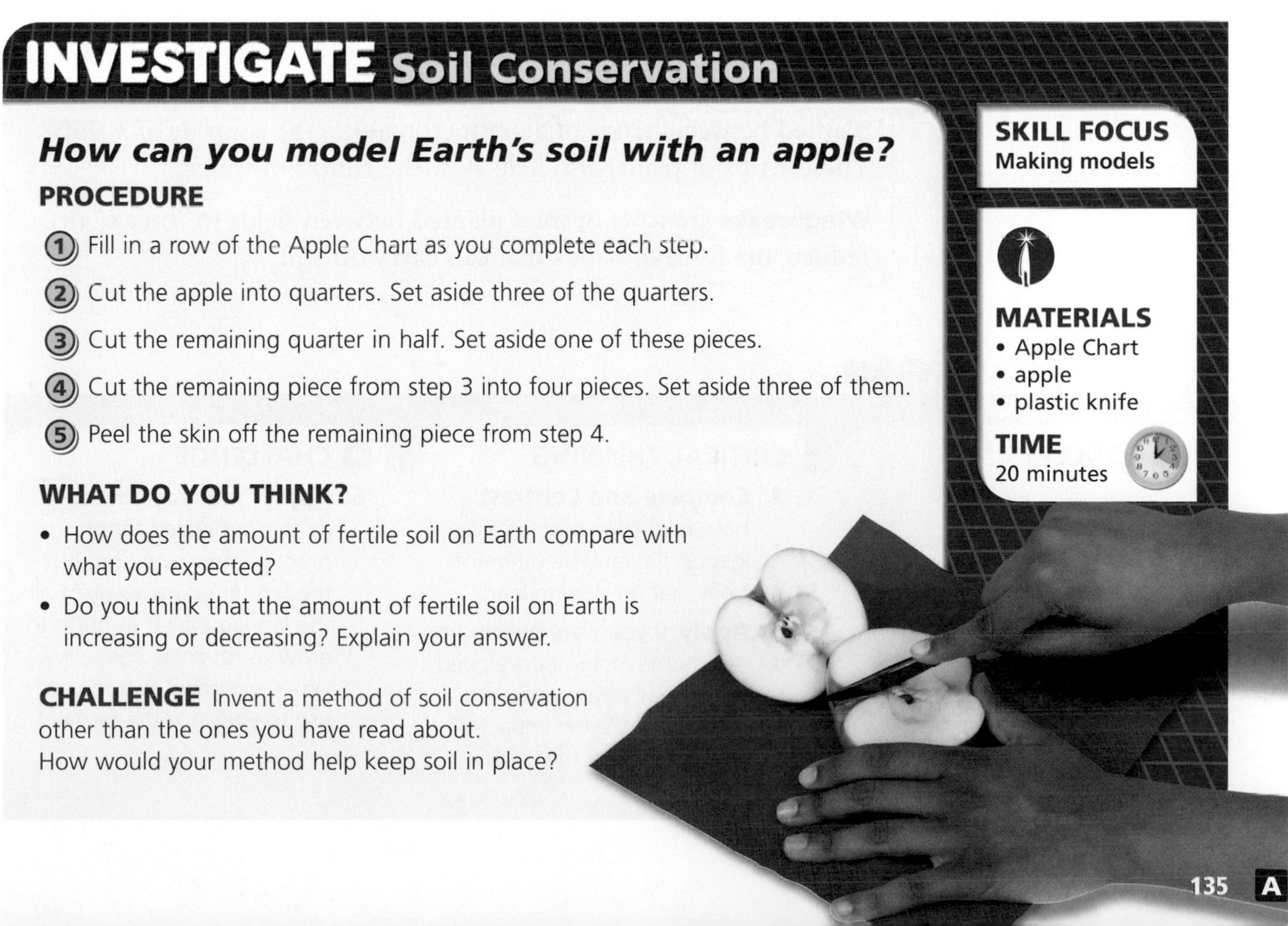

INVESTIGATE Soil Conservation

How can you model Earth's soil with an apple?

PROCEDURE

1. Fill in a row of the Apple Chart as you complete each step.
2. Cut the apple into quarters. Set aside three of the quarters.
3. Cut the remaining quarter in half. Set aside one of these pieces.
4. Cut the remaining piece from step 3 into four pieces. Set aside three of them.
5. Peel the skin off the remaining piece from step 4.

WHAT DO YOU THINK?

- How does the amount of fertile soil on Earth compare with what you expected?
- Do you think that the amount of fertile soil on Earth is increasing or decreasing? Explain your answer.

CHALLENGE Invent a method of soil conservation other than the ones you have read about. How would your method help keep soil in place?

SKILL FOCUS
Making models

MATERIALS
- Apple Chart
- apple
- plastic knife

TIME
20 minutes

Terracing

Contour Plowing

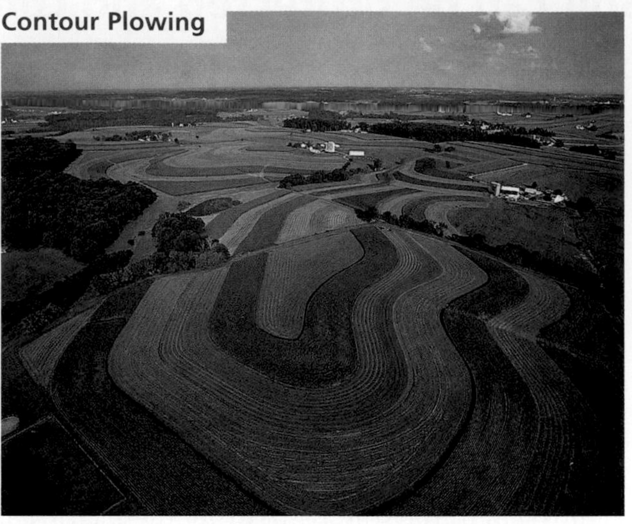

READING VISUALS **COMPARE** Both terracing and contour plowing are soil conservation methods used on sloping land. How does each method help conserve soil?

Terraces are flat, steplike areas built on a hillside to hold rainwater and prevent it from running downhill. Crops are planted on the flat tops of the terraces.

Contour plowing is the practice of plowing along the curves, or contours, of a slope. Contour plowing helps channel rainwater so that it does not run straight downhill, carrying away soil with it. A soil conservation method called strip-cropping is often combined with contour plowing. Strips of grasses, shrubs, or other plants are planted between bands of a grain crop along the contour of a slope. These strips of plants also help slow the runoff of water.

Windbreaks are rows of trees planted between fields to "break," or reduce, the force of winds that can carry off soil.

4.3 Review

KEY CONCEPTS

1. Why is soil a necessary resource?
2. How do land-use practices in farming, construction and development, and mining affect soil?
3. Describe at least three methods of soil conservation.

CRITICAL THINKING

4. **Compare and Contrast** How might the problem of soil loss on flat land be different from that on sloping land?
5. **Apply** If you were building a new home in an undeveloped area, what steps would you take to reduce the impact of construction on the soil?

CHALLENGE

6. **Apply** You have advised an inexperienced farmer to practice strip-cropping, but the farmer wants to plant all the land in wheat in order to grow as much as possible. What argument would you use to convince the farmer?

SCIENCE on the JOB

LANDSCAPE ARCHITECT

Soil, Water, and Architecture

Landscape architects design the landscapes around buildings and in parks. For example, they decide where to build sidewalks and where to place benches. Since flowing water can wash away soil, they try to control how water moves. They select plants, modify the slope of the land, and install drainage systems that will control the water. The plan below was used to build the park shown in the photographs.

Existing Plants

Large oak trees were already growing on the land. The trees were left in place to provide shade and help protect the soil.

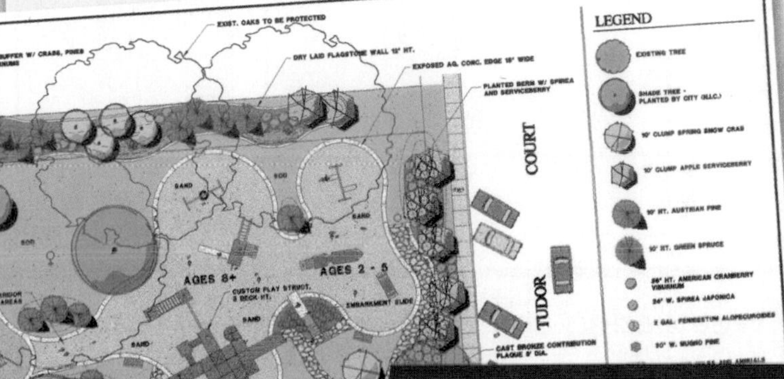

Retaining Wall

The landscape architect added mounds of soil planted with bushes to help divide the inside of the park from the roads around it. Stone walls hold the soil of the mounds in place. Without the walls, the soil would wash down onto the walkways.

Plan for New Park

A landscape architect used a computer program to draw this plan for a park. The program is designed to make the plan look as if it were drawn by hand.

EXPLORE

1. ANALYZE Examine the soil, drainage, plants, and other elements of the landscape of a park or the area around a building. Describe any areas where soil may wash away.

2. CHALLENGE Design a landscape surrounding a new school, stadium, or other building. Draw a sketch and add notes to explain your choices of locations for trees, sidewalks, and other features.

4 Chapter Review

the BIG idea

Natural forces break rocks apart and form soil, which supports life.

KEY CONCEPTS SUMMARY

4.1 Mechanical and chemical forces break down rocks.

Over time, **mechanical weathering** breaks a rock into smaller pieces.

Chemical weathering affects exposed rock surfaces.

VOCABULARY
weathering p. 115
mechanical weathering p. 116
exfoliation p. 116
abrasion p. 116
chemical weathering p. 118

4.2 Weathering and organic processes form soil.

Soil has measurable properties, such as color, texture, pore space, and chemistry.

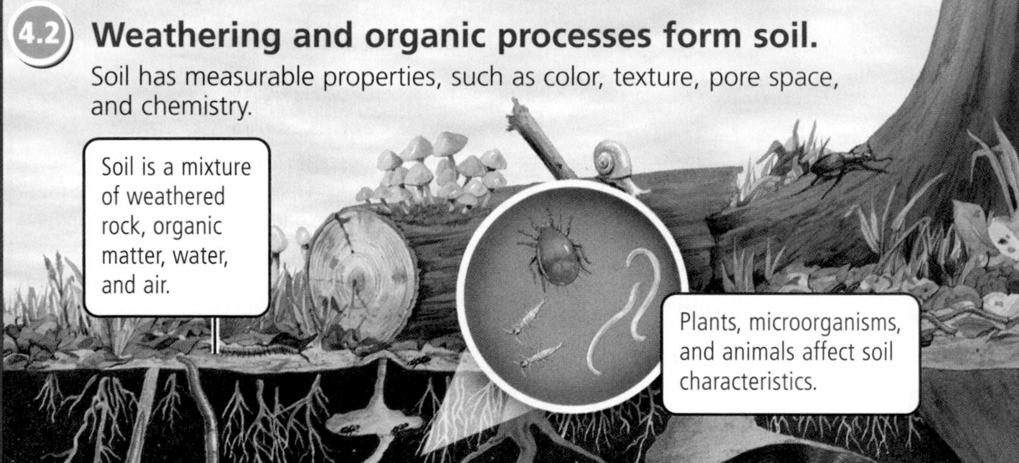

Soil is a mixture of weathered rock, organic matter, water, and air.
Plants, microorganisms, and animals affect soil characteristics.

VOCABULARY
humus p. 123
soil horizon p. 124
soil profile p. 124

4.3 Human activities affect soil.

Soil is essential to life and takes a long time to form. It is difficult or impossible to replace soil that has been lost.

Soil Loss

Farming, construction and development, and mining are three human activities that affect soil.

Soil Conservation

Soil conservation practices help keep soil from blowing or washing away.

VOCABULARY
desertification p. 133

Reviewing Vocabulary

Copy the three-column chart below. Complete the chart for each term. The first one has been done for you.

Term	Definition	Example
EXAMPLE chemical weathering	the breakdown of rocks by chemical reactions that change the rocks' mineral composition	Iron reacts with air and water to form iron oxides or rust.
1. mechanical weathering		
2. abrasion		
3. exfoliation		
4. desertification		

Reviewing Key Concepts

Multiple Choice *Choose the letter of the best answer.*

5. The force of expanding water in the cracks and pores of a rock is an example of
- **a.** chemical weathering
- **b.** mechanical weathering
- **c.** oxidation
- **d.** desertification

6. The breakdown of a rock by acidic water is an example of
- **a.** chemical weathering
- **b.** mechanical weathering
- **c.** oxidation
- **d.** desertification

7. Soil is a mixture of what four materials?
- **a.** granite, limestone, nitrogen, and air
- **b.** plant roots, iron oxides, water, and air
- **c.** rock particles, plant roots, humus, and nitrogen
- **d.** rock particles, humus, water, and air

8. What is the main component of soil?
- **a.** humus
- **b.** water
- **c.** air
- **d.** rock particles

9. What is humus?
- **a.** the decomposed rock particles in soil
- **b.** the decomposed organic matter in soil
- **c.** the material that makes up the B horizon
- **d.** the material that makes up the C horizon

10. Three factors that affect the rate of weathering are
- **a.** microorganisms, plants, and animals
- **b.** weather, landforms, and rainfall
- **c.** surface area, rock composition, and climate
- **d.** texture, color, and pore space

11. Microorganisms affect the quality of soil by
- **a.** decomposing organic matter
- **b.** creating tunnels
- **c.** absorbing water
- **d.** increasing mechanical weathering

12. The movement of air and water through a soil is influenced most by the soil's
- **a.** color and chemistry
- **b.** texture and pore space
- **c.** pH and nitrogen content
- **d.** microorganisms

13. Contour plowing, strip-cropping, and terracing are conservation methods designed to reduce the
- **a.** runoff of water
- **b.** activity of microorganisms
- **c.** acidity of soil
- **d.** pore space of soil

Short Answer *Write a few sentences to answer each question.*

14. How do farming, construction and development, and mining affect soil?

15. How do ice wedging, pressure release, plant root growth, and abrasion cause mechanical weathering?

16. How do air and water cause chemical weathering?

Thinking Critically

Use the photograph to answer the next three questions.

17. **APPLY** Make a sketch of the soil profile above, labeling the A, B, and C horizons.

18. **OBSERVE** What does the color of the top layer indicate about this soil?

19. **APPLY** Which part of the profile is most affected by chemical and mechanical weathering? Why?

20. **APPLY** Suppose that you own gently sloping farmland. Describe the methods that you would use to hold the soil in place and maintain its fertility.

21. **SYNTHESIZE** Describe the composition, color, texture, and amount of pore space of a soil that would be good for growing crops.

22. **COMPARE AND CONTRAST** How does mechanical weathering differ from chemical weathering? How are the two processes similar?

23. **PREDICT** What effect will the continued growth of the world's population likely have on soil resources?

24. **ANALYZE** Soil loss is a problem all over the world. Where might lost soil end up?

25. **ANALYZE** Can lost soil be replaced? Explain.

26. **ANALYZE** Copy the concept map below and fill it in with the following terms and phrases.

acidic water	chemical weathering
damaged statue	exfoliation
mechanical weathering	moving water
oxygen and water	pressure release
rounded rocks	rust

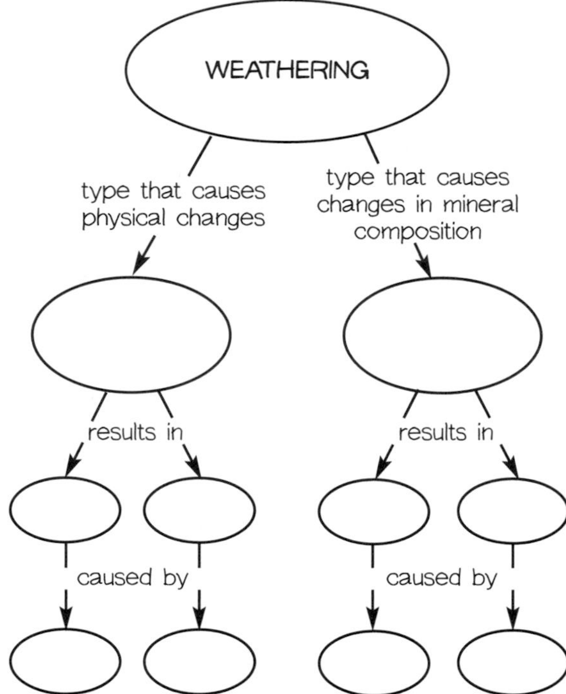

27. **ANALYZE** Add to the concept map to show the three factors that affect the rate of weathering.

the BIG idea

28. **MODEL** Draw a diagram that shows an example of a natural force breaking rocks apart to form soil that supports life.

29. **SYNTHESIZE** A cycle is a series of events or actions that repeats regularly. Describe a cycle that involves soil and living things.

UNIT PROJECTS

If you need to create graphs or other visuals for your project, be sure you have grid paper, poster board, markers, or other supplies.

Analyzing a Table

The table indicates some of the characteristics of four soil samples. Use the table to answer the questions below.

Sample	Color	Ability to Hold Water	Percentage of Pore Space	Percentage of Humus
1	black	average	50%	9%
2	yellowish brown	low	70%	3%
3	reddish brown	average	60%	3%
4	very red	average to low	65%	2%

1. Soils that contain a lot of sand do not hold water very well. Which sample probably contains the most sand?

a. 1
b. 2
c. 3
d. 4

2. Iron gives soil a reddish color. Which sample probably contains the most iron?

a. 1
b. 2
c. 3
d. 4

3. Crops grow best in soils with about half of their volume consisting of pore space. Which soil has an ideal amount of pore space for growing crops?

a. 1
b. 2
c. 3
d. 4

4. What soil color might indicate a high level of organic matter?

a. black
b. yellow
c. red-brown
d. red

5. Imagine you have an additional soil sample. The sample is dark brown, has an average ability to hold water, and has 55% pore space. What percentage of humus would this soil most likely contain?

a. 1%
b. 2%
c. 3%
d. 8%

Extended Response

Answer the two questions below in detail. Include some of the terms shown in the word box. In your answers, underline each term you use.

abrasion	moving water
chemical weathering	plant roots
ice	rusting
mechanical weathering	

6. Jolene is comparing a rock from a riverbed and a rock from deep underground. One is very smooth. The other has very sharp edges. Explain which rock was probably found in each location.

7. In a museum, Hank sees two iron knives that were made in the early 1800s. One has spent 200 years on the top of a fortress wall. The other one has been stored in the museum for 200 years. Why might the two knives look different?

CHAPTER

Erosion and Deposition

the BIG idea

Water, wind, and ice shape Earth's surface.

Key Concepts

SECTION

Forces wear down and build up Earth's surface.
Learn how natural forces shape and change the land.

SECTION

Moving water shapes land.
Learn about the effects of water moving over land and underground.

SECTION

Waves and wind shape land.
Discover how waves and wind affect land.

SECTION

Glaciers carve land and move sediments.
Learn about the effect of ice moving over land.

Internet Preview

CLASSZONE.COM

Chapter 5 online resources: Content Review, two Visualizations, three Resource Centers, Math Tutorial, Test Practice

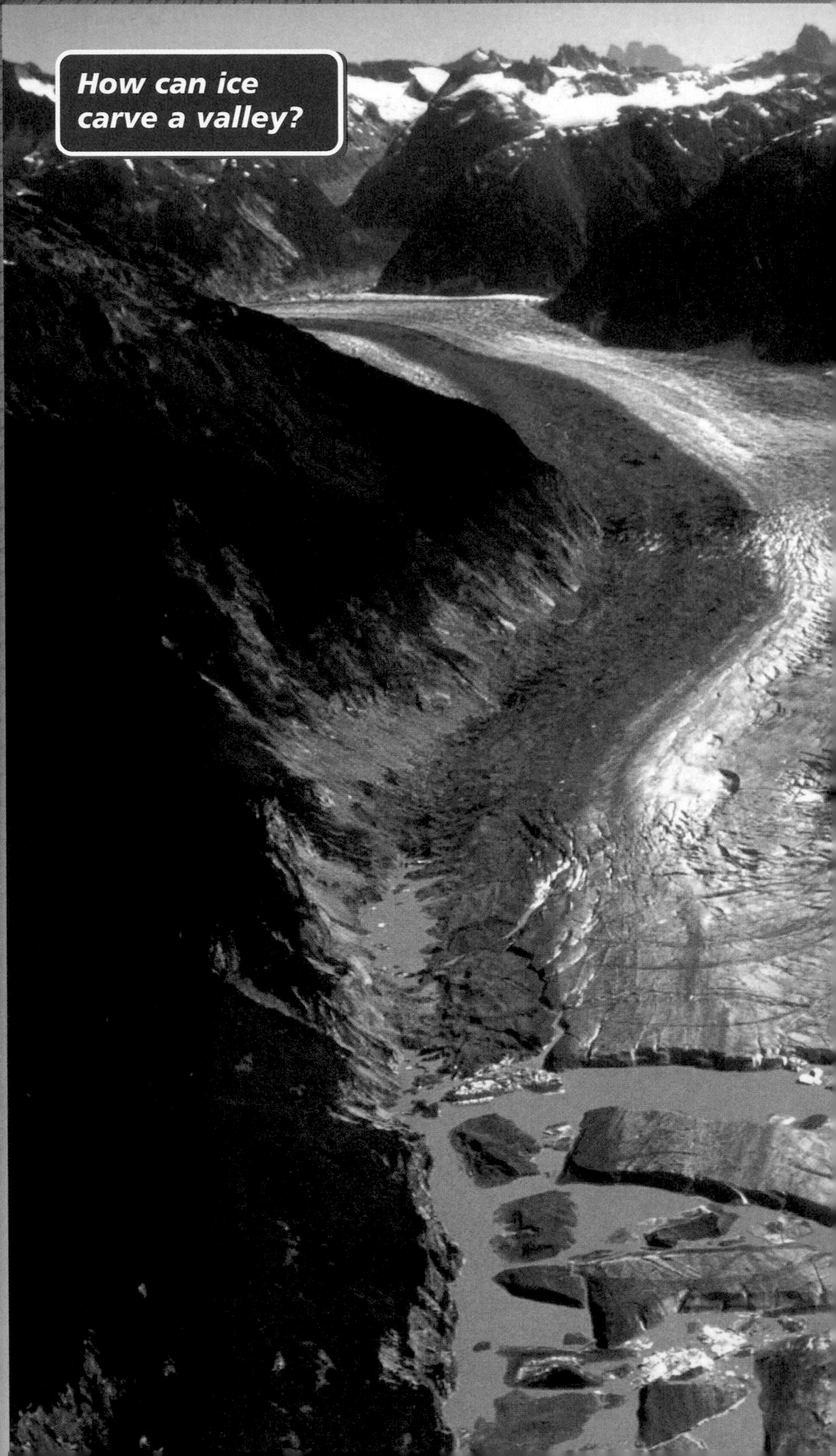

How can ice carve a valley?

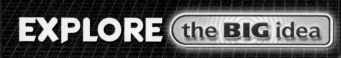

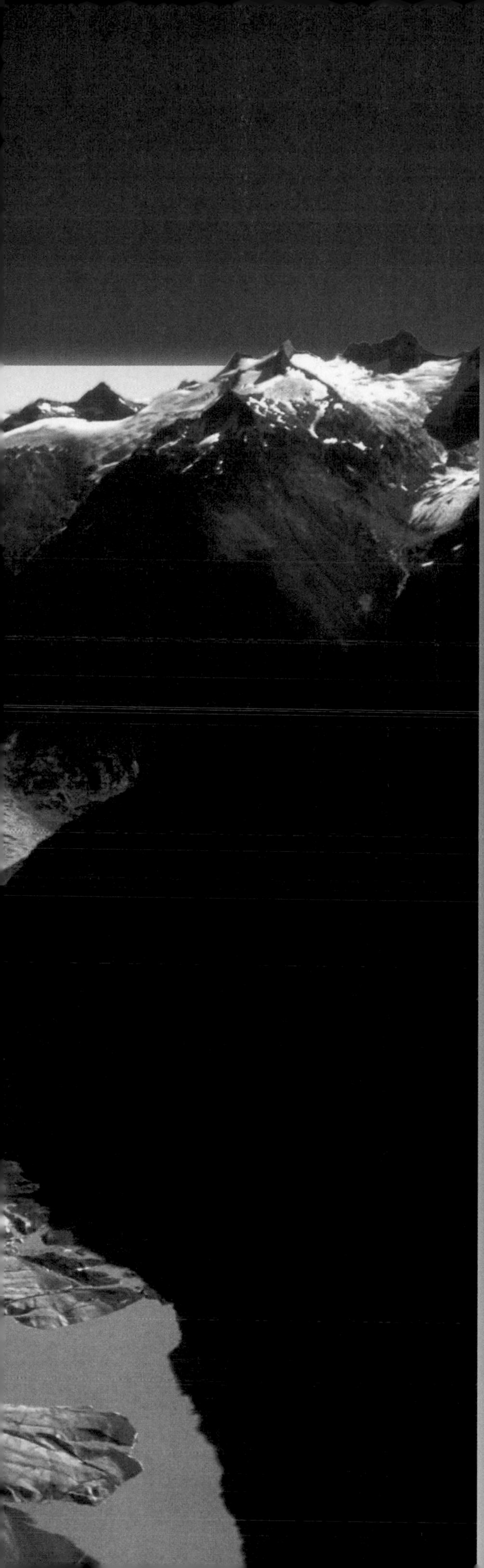

EXPLORE the BIG idea

Where Has Water Been?

Think about what water does when it falls and flows on the ground. Go outside your school or home and look at the ground and pavement carefully. Look in dry places for evidence of where water has been.

Observe and Think What evidence did you find? How does it show that water was in a place that is now dry?

How Do Waves Shape Land?

Pile a mixture of sand and gravel on one side of a pie tin to make a "beach." Slowly add water away from the beach until the tin is about one-third full. Use your hand to make waves in the tin and observe what happens.

Observe and Think
What happened to the beach? How did the waves affect the sand and gravel?

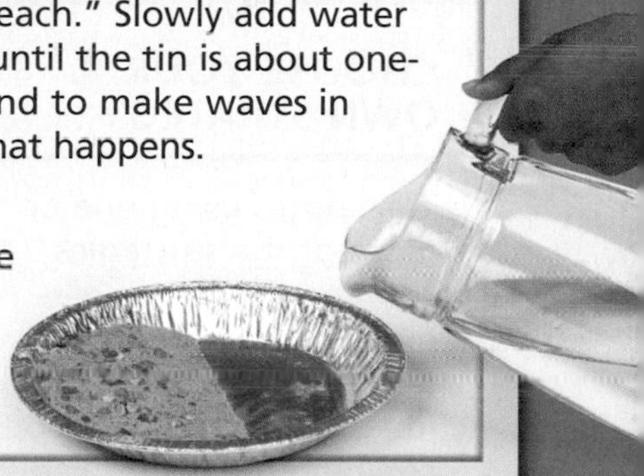

Internet Activity: Wind Erosion

Go to **ClassZone.com** to learn about one type of wind erosion. See how wind can form an arch in rock.

Observe and Think
How long do you think it would take for wind to form an arch?

Wind Erosion **Code: MDL017**

CHAPTER 5

Getting Ready to Learn

CONCEPT REVIEW

- Weathering breaks down rocks.
- Water and ice are agents of weathering.
- Soil contains weathered rock and organic material.

VOCABULARY REVIEW

sediment p. 89

weathering p. 115

abrasion p. 116

CONTENT REVIEW

CLASSZONE.COM

Review concepts and vocabulary.

TAKING NOTES

CHOOSE YOUR OWN STRATEGY

Take notes using one or more of the strategies from earlier chapters—**main idea and detail notes, supporting main ideas, main idea web,** or **combination notes.** Feel free to mix and match the strategies, or use an entirely different note-taking strategy.

VOCABULARY STRATEGY

Write each new vocabulary term in the center of a **four square** diagram. Write notes in the squares around each term. Include a definition, some characteristics, and some examples of the term. If possible, write some things that are not examples of the term.

See the Note-Taking Handbook on pages R45–R51.

SCIENCE NOTEBOOK

Supporting Main Ideas

Main Idea Web

Main Idea and Detail Notes

Definition	Characteristics
process in which weathered particles are picked up and moved	gravity is important part; wind and ice are agents
EROSION	
Examples	**Nonexamples**
mass wasting, mudflow, slump, creep	longshore current, humus

KEY CONCEPT

Forces wear down and build up Earth's surface.

BEFORE, you learned

- Weathering breaks rocks apart
- Weathering forms soil

NOW, you will learn

- How erosion moves and deposits rock and soil
- How gravity causes movement of large amounts of rock and soil

VOCABULARY

erosion p. 145
deposition p. 145
mass wasting p. 147

THINK ABOUT

How did natural forces shape this landform?

This valley in Iceland was formed by the action of water. How long might it have taken to form? Where did the material that once filled the valley go?

Natural forces move and deposit sediments.

The valley in the photograph was formed by the movement of water. The water flowed over the land and carried away weathered rock and soil, shaping a valley where the water flows. In this section you will learn about the processes that shape landscapes.

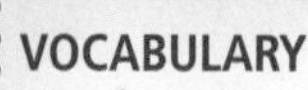

VOCABULARY
Use four square diagrams to take notes about the terms *erosion* and *deposition*.

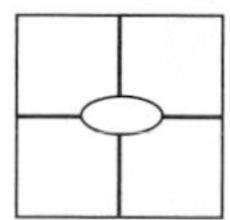

The process in which weathered particles are picked up and moved from one place to another is called **erosion** (ih-ROH-zhuhn). Erosion has a constant impact on Earth's surface. Over millions of years, it wears down mountains by removing byproducts of weathering and depositing them elsewhere. The part of the erosion process in which sediment is placed in a new location, or deposited, is called **deposition** (DEHP-uh-ZIHSH-uhn).

The force of gravity is an important part of erosion and deposition. Gravity causes water to move downward, carrying and depositing sediment as it flows. Gravity can pull huge masses of ice slowly down mountain valleys. And gravity causes dust carried by the wind to fall to Earth.

Erosion of weathered rock by the movement of water, wind, and ice occurs in three major ways:

- **Water** Rainwater and water from melting snow flow down sloping land, carrying rock and soil particles. The water makes its way to a river, which then carries the sediment along. The sediment gets deposited on the river's bottom, banks, or floodplain, or near its mouth. Waves in oceans and lakes also carry sediment and deposit it to form beaches and other features.
- **Wind** Strong winds lift tiny particles of dust and carry them long distances. When the wind dies down, the particles drop to the ground. Wind can also push larger particles of sand along the ground.
- **Ice** As ice moves slowly downhill, it transports rock and soil particles that are embedded in it.

What are the three major ways in which erosion moves sediment?

INVESTIGATE Erosion

How does the effect of rainwater on sloping land differ from its effect on flat land?

DESIGN YOUR OWN EXPERIMENT

SKILL FOCUS
Designing experiments

MATERIALS
- soil
- 2 large trays
- pitcher of water

TIME
25 minutes

Streams are one of the main agents of erosion on Earth. Design an experiment to show the effect that rainwater has on sloping land.

PROCEDURE

1. Figure out how to use the soil, water, and trays to test the effects of rainwater on sloping land and on flat land.
2. Write up your procedure.
3. Carry out your experiment.

WHAT DO YOU THINK?

- What were the results of your experiment? Did it work? Why or why not?
- What were the variables in your experiment?
- What does your experiment demonstrate about erosion and running water?

CHALLENGE How would you design an experiment to demonstrate the relationship between floods and erosion?

Gravity can move large amounts of rock and soil.

Along the California coast many homes are built atop beautiful cliffs, backed by mountains and looking out to the sea. These homes may seem like great places to live. They are, however, in a risky location.

The California coast region and other mountainous areas have many landslides. A landslide is one type of **mass wasting**—the downhill movements of masses of rock and soil.

VOCABULARY
Be sure to make a four square diagram for *mass wasting* in your notebook.

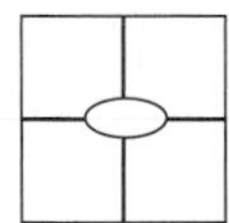

In mass wasting, gravity pulls material downward. A triggering event, such as heavy rain or an earthquake, might loosen the rock and soil. As the material becomes looser, it gives way to the pull of gravity and moves downward.

Mass wasting can occur suddenly or gradually. It can involve tons of rock sliding down a steep mountain slope or moving little by little down a gentle hillside. One way to classify an occurrence of mass wasting is by the type of material that is moved and the speed of the movement. A sudden, fast movement of rock and soil is called a landslide. Movements of rock are described as slides or falls. Movement of mud or soil is described as a mudflow.

Mass Wasting of Rock

Mass wasting of rock includes rockfalls and rockslides:

- In a rockfall, individual blocks of rock drop suddenly and fall freely down a cliff or steep mountainside. Weathering can break a block of rock from a cliff or mountainside. The expansion of water that freezes in a crack, for example, can loosen a block of rock.
- In a rockslide, a large mass of rock slides as a unit down a slope. A rockslide can reach a speed of a hundred kilometers per hour. Rockslides can be triggered by earthquakes.

Mass wasting of rock often takes place in high mountains. In some places, rocks can fall or slide onto roads. You might also see evidence of rockfalls and rockslides at the base of steep cliffs, where piles of rock slope outward.

Rockslides, such as this one in California, can drop huge amounts of rock onto highways.

Mudflows in 1999 in Venezuela happened very quickly and took as many as 30,000 lives.

Mudflow

Sometimes a mountain slope collapses. Then a mixture of rock, soil, and plants—called debris (duh-BREE)—falls or slides down. Like mass wasting of rock, mass movements of debris are common in high mountains with steep slopes.

Learn more about mudflows.

A major type of mass wasting of debris is a mudflow. A mudflow consists of debris with a large amount of water. Mudflows often happen in mountain canyons and valleys after heavy rains. The soil becomes so heavy with water that the slope can no longer hold it in place. The mixture of soil, water, and debris flows downward, picking up sediment as it rushes down. When it reaches a valley, it spreads in a thin sheet over the land.

Mudflows also occur on active volcanoes. In 1985, a huge mudflow destroyed the town of Armero, Colombia, and killed more than 20,000 people. When a volcano erupted there, the heat caused ice and snow near the top of the volcano to melt, releasing a large amount of water that mixed with ash from the volcano. The mixture of ash and water rushed down the volcano and picked up debris. It formed gigantic mudflows that poured into all the surrounding valleys.

Mount St. Helens, a volcanic mountain in the state of Washington, is a place where large mudflows have occurred. During an eruption in 1980, some mudflows from the volcano traveled more than 90 kilometers (56 mi) from the mountain.

What causes a mudflow to occur?

In this example of slump, at Mesa Verde National Park in Colorado, a huge mass of rock and soil moved downward.

Slumps and Creep

Slumps and creep are two other main types of mass wasting on hilly land. These forms of mass wasting can be much less dramatic than rockslides or mudflows. But they are the types of mass movement that you are most likely to see evidence of.

A slump is a slide of loose debris that moves as a single unit. Slumps can occur along roads and highways where construction has made slopes unstable. They can cover sections of highway with debris. Like other types of mass movement, slumps can be triggered by heavy rain.

The slowest form of mass movement of soil or debris is creep. The soil or debris moves at a rate of about 1 to 10 millimeters a year—a rate too slow to actually be seen. But evidence of creep can be seen on hillsides that have old fences or telephone poles. The fences or poles may lean downward, or some may be out of line. They have been moved by the creeping soil. The soil closer to the surface moves faster than the soil farther down, which causes the fences or poles to lean.

1 Originally, the fence posts stand vertically in the ground.

2 Over many years, the soil holding the posts slowly shifts downhill, and the posts lean.

Even the slight slope of this land in Alberta, Canada, caused these posts to tilt because of creep.

Creep can affect buildings as well. The weight of a heavy mass of soil moving slowly downhill can be great enough to crack a building's walls. Creep affects all hillsides covered with soil, but its rate varies. The wetter the soil, the faster it will creep downhill.

5.1 Review

KEY CONCEPTS

1. How does erosion change landscapes?
2. Describe why weathering is important in erosion.
3. How can gravity move large amounts of rock and soil?

CRITICAL THINKING

4. **Compare and Contrast** What is the main difference between erosion and mass wasting?
5. **Infer** What force and what cause can contribute to both erosion and mass wasting?

CHALLENGE

6. **Rank** Which of the four locations would be the best and worst places to build a house? Rank the four locations and explain your reasoning.

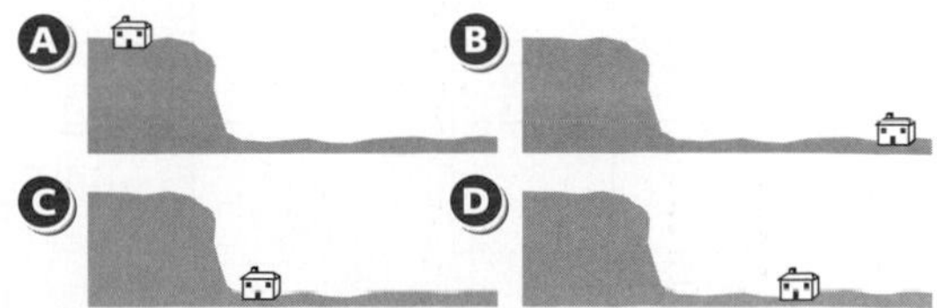

KEY CONCEPT

Moving water shapes land.

BEFORE, you learned

- Erosion is the movement of rock and soil
- Gravity causes mass movements of rock and soil

NOW, you will learn

- How moving water shapes Earth's surface
- How water moving underground forms caves and other features

VOCABULARY

drainage basin p. 151
divide p. 151
floodplain p. 152
alluvial fan p. 153
delta p. 153
sinkhole p. 155

EXPLORE Divides

How do divides work?

PROCEDURE

1. Fold the sheet of paper in thirds and tape it as shown to make a "ridge."
2. Drop the paper clips one at a time directly on top of the ridge from a height of about 30 cm. Observe what happens and record your observations.

WHAT DO YOU THINK?
How might the paper clips be similar to water falling on a ridge?

MATERIALS

- sheet of paper
- tape
- paper clips

Streams shape Earth's surface.

If you look at a river or stream, you may be able to notice something about the land around it. The land is higher than the river. If a river is running through a steep valley, you can easily see that the river is the low point. But even in very flat places, the land is sloping down to the river, which is itself running downhill in a low path through the land.

Running water is the major force shaping the landscape over most of Earth. From the broad, flat land around the lower Mississippi River to the steep mountain valleys of the Himalayas, water running downhill changes the land. Running water shapes a variety of landforms by moving sediment in the processes of erosion and deposition. In this section, you will learn how water flows on land in systems of streams and rivers and how water shapes and changes landscapes. You also will learn that water can even carve out new features underground.

NOTE-TAKING STRATEGY
A main idea and detail notes chart would be a good strategy to use for taking notes about streams and Earth's surface.

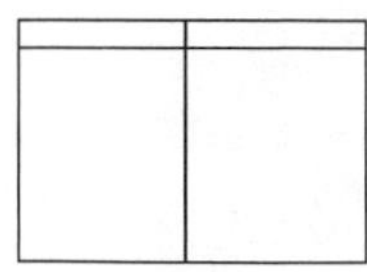

Drainage Basins and Divides

When water falls or ice melts on a slope, some of the water soaks into the ground and some of it flows down the slope in thin sheets. But within a short distance this water becomes part of a channel that forms a stream. A stream is any body of water—large or small—that flows down a slope along a channel.

Streams flow into one another to form complex drainage systems, with small streams flowing into larger ones. The area of land in which water drains into a stream system is called a **drainage basin.** In most drainage basins, the water eventually drains into a lake or an ocean. For example, in the Mississippi River drainage basin, water flows into the Mississippi, and then drains into the Gulf of Mexico, which is part of the ocean.

Drainage basins are separated by ridges called divides, which are like continuous lines of high land. A **divide** is a ridge from which water drains to one side or the other. Divides can run along high mountains. On flatter ground, a divide can simply be the the highest line of land and can be hard to see.

Divides are the borders of drainage basins. A basin can be just a few kilometers wide or can drain water from a large portion of a continent. The Continental Divide runs from Alaska to Mexico. Most water that falls west of the Continental Divide ends up draining into the Pacific Ocean. Most water that falls east of it drains into the Gulf of Mexico and Atlantic Ocean.

Divides and Drainage Basins

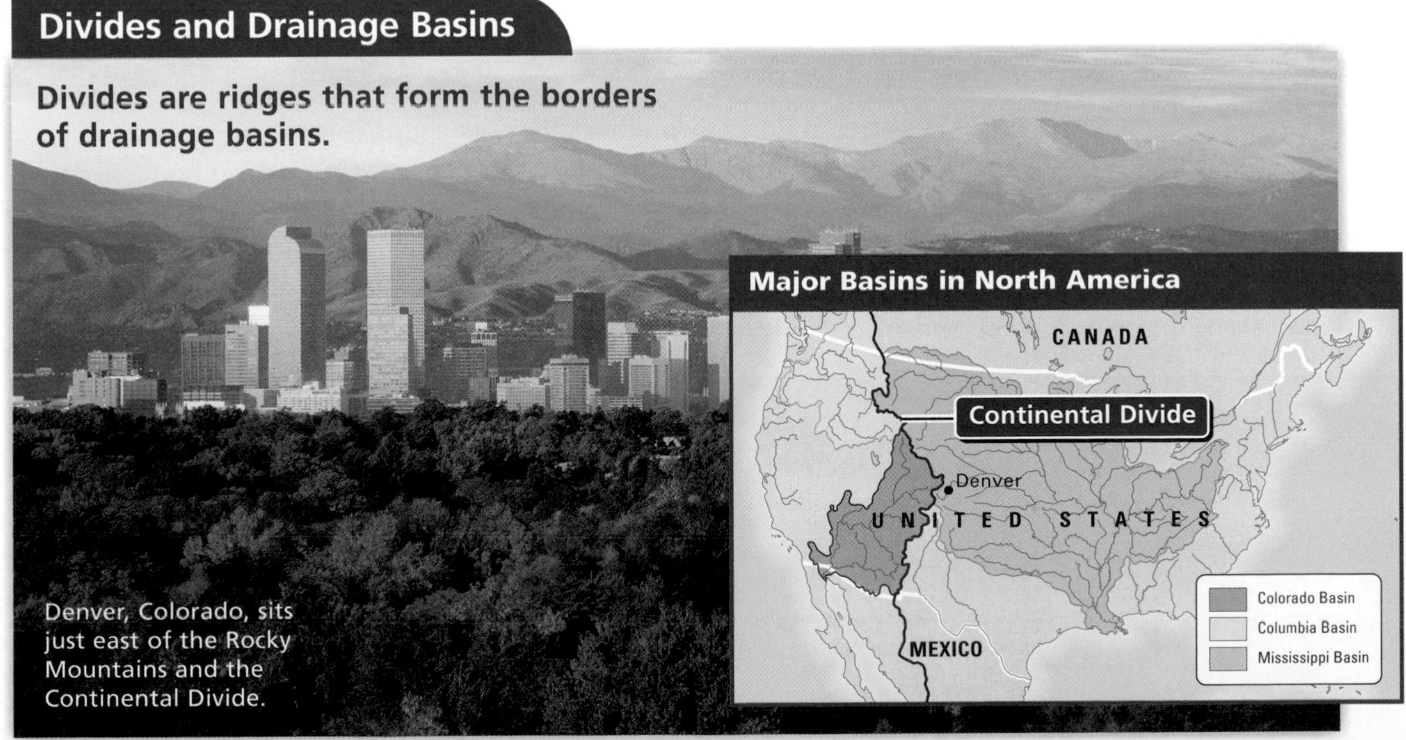

Denver, Colorado, sits just east of the Rocky Mountains and the Continental Divide.

Downtown Davenport, Iowa, sits in the floodplain of the Mississippi River and was covered with water when the river flooded in 1993.

Valleys and Floodplains

As streams flow and carry sediment from the surface of the land, they form valleys. In high mountains, streams often cut V-shaped valleys that are narrow and steep walled. In lower areas, streams may form broad valleys that include floodplains. A **floodplain** is an area of land on either side of a stream that is underwater when the stream floods. The floodplain of a large river may be many kilometers wide.

When a stream floods, it deposits much of the sediment that it carries onto its floodplain. This sediment can make the floodplain very fertile—or able to support a lot of plant growth. In the United States, the floodplains of the Mississippi River are some of the best places for growing crops.

Find out more about rivers and erosion.

Why is fertile land often found on flat land around rivers?

Stream Channels

As a stream flows through a valley, its channel may run straight in some parts and curve around in other parts. Curves and bends that form a twisting, looping pattern in a stream channel are called meanders (mee-AN-duhrz). The moving water erodes the outside banks and deposits sediment along the inside banks. Over many years, meanders shift position.

The meanders of this river and oxbow lakes formed as the river deposited sediment and changed course.

During a flood, the stream may cut a new channel that bypasses a meander. The cut-off meander forms a crescent-shaped lake, which is called an oxbow lake. This term comes from the name of a U-shaped piece of wood that fits under the neck of an ox and is attached to its yoke.

Alluvial Fans and Deltas

Besides shaping valleys and forming oxbow lakes, streams also create landforms called alluvial fans and deltas. Both of these landforms are formed by the deposition of sediment.

An **alluvial fan** (uh-LOO-vee-uhl) is a fan-shaped deposit of sediment at the base of a mountain. It forms where a stream leaves a steep valley and enters a flatter plain. The stream slows down and spreads out on the flatter ground. As it slows down, it can carry less sediment. The slower-moving water drops some of its sediment, leaving it at the base of the slope.

This alluvial fan was formed by a stream flowing into the Jago River in Alaska.

A **delta** is an area of land formed by the buildup of sediment at the end, or mouth, of a river. When a river enters the ocean, the river's water slows down, and the river drops much of its sediment. This sediment gradually builds up to form a plain. Like alluvial fans, deltas tend to be fan-shaped. Over a very long time, a river may build up its delta far out into the sea. A large river, such as the Mississippi, can build up a huge delta. Like many other large rivers on Earth, the Mississippi has been building up its delta out into the sea for many thousands of years.

From Divide to Delta

On their path to the ocean, streams and rivers slow down and flatten out.

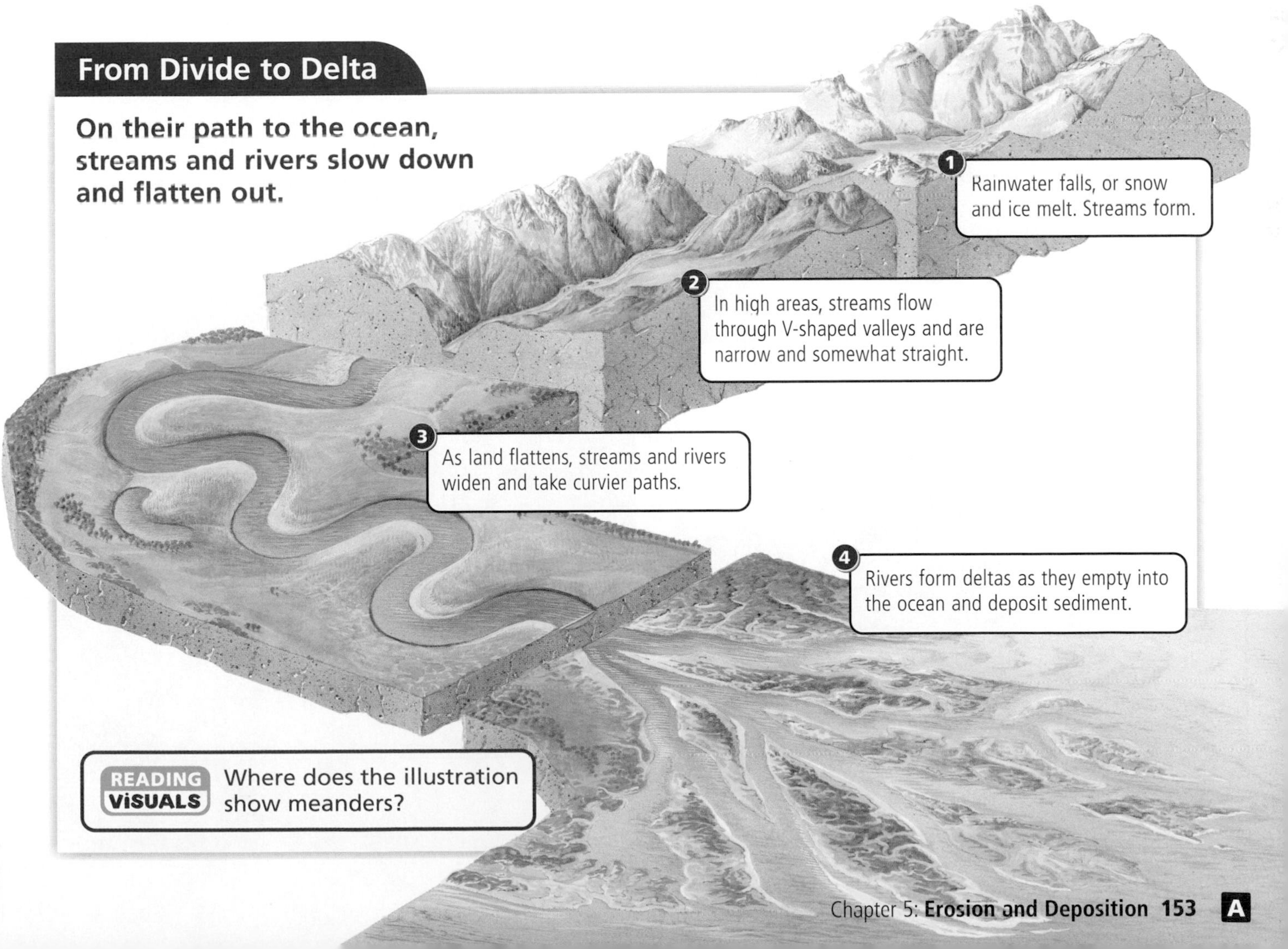

1. Rainwater falls, or snow and ice melt. Streams form.
2. In high areas, streams flow through V-shaped valleys and are narrow and somewhat straight.
3. As land flattens, streams and rivers widen and take curvier paths.
4. Rivers form deltas as they empty into the ocean and deposit sediment.

READING VISUALS Where does the illustration show meanders?

Water moving underground forms caverns.

Not all rainwater runs off the land and flows into surface streams. Some of it evaporates, some is absorbed by plants, and some soaks into the ground and becomes groundwater. At a certain depth below the surface, the spaces in soil and rock become completely filled with water. The top of this water-filled region is called the water table. The water below the water table is called groundwater.

The water table is at different distances below the surface in different places. Its level also can change over time in the same location, depending on changes in rainfall. Below the water table, groundwater flows slowly through underground beds of rock and soil, where it causes erosion to take place.

Observe the process of cave formation.

You have read that chemicals in water and air can break down rock. As you read in Chapter 4, rainwater is slightly acidic. This acidic water can dissolve certain rocks, such as limestone. In some areas, where the underground rock consists of limestone, the groundwater can dissolve some of the limestone and carry it away. Over time, this

Cavern Formation

Caves form as water underground dissolves limestone, leaving open spaces.

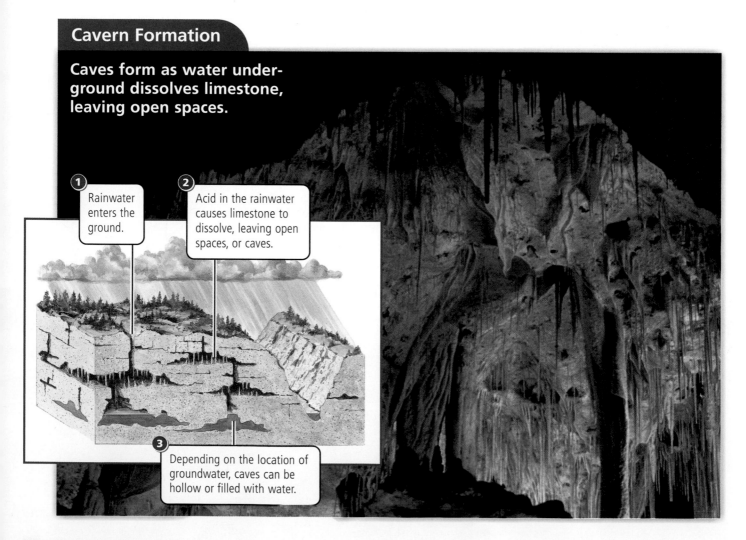

1. Rainwater enters the ground.
2. Acid in the rainwater causes limestone to dissolve, leaving open spaces, or caves.
3. Depending on the location of groundwater, caves can be hollow or filled with water.

This sinkhole took down a large part of a parking lot in Atlanta, Georgia.

process produces open spaces, or caves. Large caves are called caverns. If the water table drops, a cavern may fill with air.

Some caverns have huge networks of rooms and passageways. Mammoth Cave in Kentucky, for example, is part of a cavern system that has more than 560 kilometers (about 350 mi) of explored passageways. Within the cavern are lakes and streams.

A surface feature that often occurs in areas with caverns is a sinkhole. A **sinkhole** is a basin that forms when the roof of a cave becomes so thin that it suddenly falls in. Sometimes it falls in because water that supported the roof has drained away. Landscapes with many sinkholes can be found in southern Indiana, south central Kentucky, and central Tennessee. In Florida, the collapse of shallow underground caverns has produced large sinkholes that have destroyed whole city blocks.

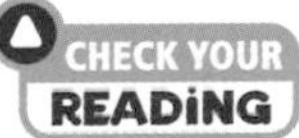

Why do caverns form in areas with limestone?

KEY CONCEPTS

1. What is the difference between a drainage basin and a divide?
2. How do streams change as they flow from mountains down to plains?
3. How do caverns form?

CRITICAL THINKING

4. **Sequence** Draw a cartoon with three panels showing how a sinkhole forms.
5. **Compare and Contrast** Make a Venn diagram to compare and contrast alluvial fans and deltas.

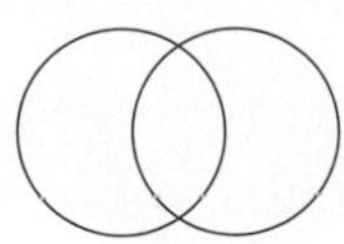

CHALLENGE

6. **Apply** During a flood, a river drops the largest pieces of its sediment on the floodplain close to its normal channel. Explain why. (**Hint:** Think about the speed of the water.)

CHAPTER INVESTIGATION

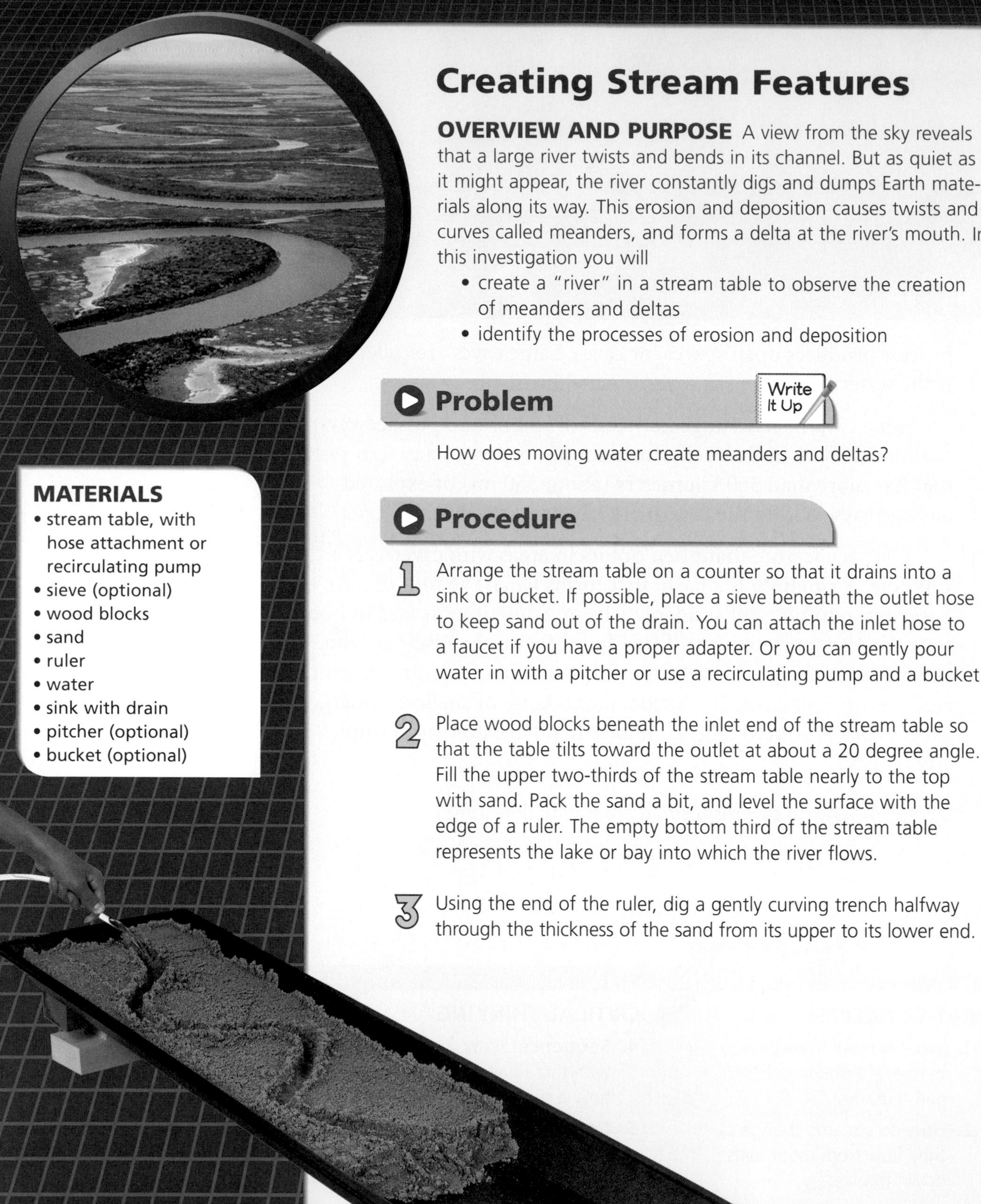

Creating Stream Features

OVERVIEW AND PURPOSE A view from the sky reveals that a large river twists and bends in its channel. But as quiet as it might appear, the river constantly digs and dumps Earth materials along its way. This erosion and deposition causes twists and curves called meanders, and forms a delta at the river's mouth. In this investigation you will

- create a "river" in a stream table to observe the creation of meanders and deltas
- identify the processes of erosion and deposition

Problem

Write It Up

How does moving water create meanders and deltas?

MATERIALS
- stream table, with hose attachment or recirculating pump
- sieve (optional)
- wood blocks
- sand
- ruler
- water
- sink with drain
- pitcher (optional)
- bucket (optional)

Procedure

1. Arrange the stream table on a counter so that it drains into a sink or bucket. If possible, place a sieve beneath the outlet hose to keep sand out of the drain. You can attach the inlet hose to a faucet if you have a proper adapter. Or you can gently pour water in with a pitcher or use a recirculating pump and a bucket.

2. Place wood blocks beneath the inlet end of the stream table so that the table tilts toward the outlet at about a 20 degree angle. Fill the upper two-thirds of the stream table nearly to the top with sand. Pack the sand a bit, and level the surface with the edge of a ruler. The empty bottom third of the stream table represents the lake or bay into which the river flows.

3. Using the end of the ruler, dig a gently curving trench halfway through the thickness of the sand from its upper to its lower end.

4 Direct a gentle flow of tap water into the upper end of the trench. Increase the flow slightly when the water begins to move through the trench. You may have to try this several times before you find the proper rate of flow to soak the sand and fill the stream channel. Avoid adding so much water that it pools at the top before moving into the channel. You can also change the stream table's tilt.

5 Once you are successful in creating a river, observe its shape and any movement of the sand. Continue until the top part of the sand is completely washed away and your river falls apart. Scrape the sand back into place with the ruler and repeat the procedure until you thoroughly understand the stream and sand movements.

Observe and Analyze

Write It Up

1. **RECORD** Diagram your stream-table setup, and make a series of drawings showing changes in your river over time. Be sure to label the river's features, as well as areas of erosion and deposition. Be sure to diagram the behavior of the sand at the river's mouth.
2. **RECORD** Write a record of the development of your river from start to finish. Include details such as the degree of tilt you used, your method of introducing water into the stream table, and features you observed forming.

Conclude

Write It Up

1. **EVALUATE** How do you explain the buildup of sand at the mouth of your river? Use the words *speed, erosion,* and *deposition* in your answer. Did the slope of the stream change over time?
2. **INTERPRET** Where in your stream table did you observe erosion occurring? Deposition? What features did each process form?
3. **INFER** What might have occurred if you had increased the amount or speed of the water flowing into your river?
4. **IDENTIFY LIMITS** In what ways was your setup a simplified version of what would actually occur on Earth? Describe the ways in which an actual stream would be more complex.
5. **APPLY** Drawing on what you observed in this investigation, make two statements that relate the age of a stream to (1) the extent of its meanders and (2) to the size of its delta or alluvial fan.

INVESTIGATE Further

CHALLENGE Revise this activity to test a problem statement about a specific stream feature. You could choose to vary the stream's slope, speed, or volume to test the changes' effects on meanders and deltas, for example. Or you could vary the sediment size and observe the movements of each size. Write a hypothesis and design an experimental procedure. Identify the independent and dependent variables.

Creating stream features

Observe and Analyze

1. Before adding water

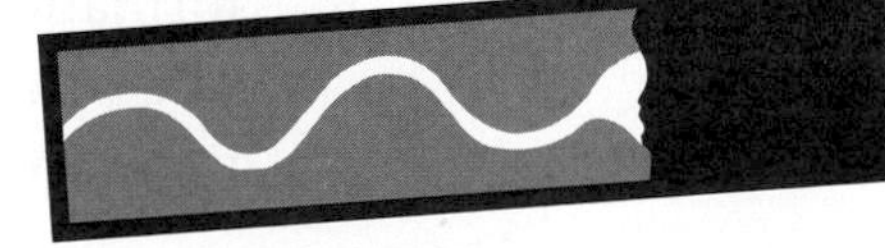

2. After one minute

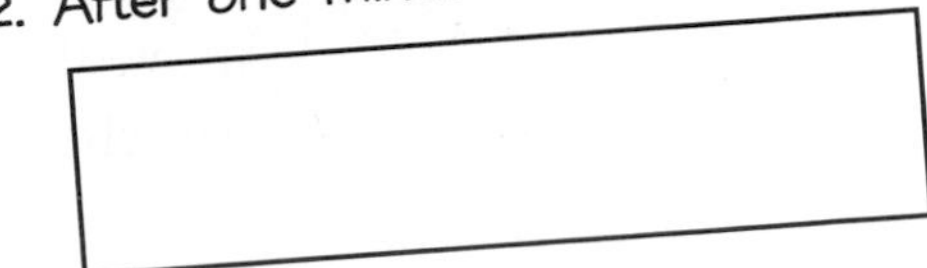

KEY CONCEPT

Waves and wind shape land.

BEFORE, you learned

- Stream systems shape Earth's surface
- Groundwater creates caverns and sinkholes

NOW, you will learn

- How waves and currents shape shorelines
- How wind shapes land

VOCABULARY

longshore drift p. 159
longshore current p. 159
sandbar p. 160
barrier island p. 160
dune p. 161
loess p. 162

THINK ABOUT

How did these pillars of rock form?

The rock formations in this photograph stand along the shoreline near the small town of Port Campbell, Australia. What natural force created these isolated stone pillars? What evidence of this force can you see in the photograph?

NOTE-TAKING STRATEGY
Remember to organize your notes in a chart or web as you read.

Waves and currents shape shorelines.

The stone pillars, or sea stacks, in the photograph above are a major tourist attraction in Port Campbell National Park. They were formed by the movement of water. The constant action of waves breaking against the cliffs slowly wore them away, leaving behind pillarlike formations. Waves continue to wear down the pillars and cliffs at the rate of about two centimeters (one inch) a year. In the years to come, the waves will likely wear away the stone pillars completely.

The force of waves, powered by wind, can wear away rock and move thousands of tons of sand on beaches. The force of wind itself can change the look of the land. Moving air can pick up sand particles and move them around to build up dunes. Wind can also carry huge amounts of fine sediment thousands of kilometers.

In this section, you'll read more about how waves and wind shape shorelines and a variety of other landforms.

Shorelines

Some shorelines, like the one near Port Campbell, Australia, are made up of steep, rock cliffs. As waves crash against the rock, they wear away the bottom of the cliffs. Eventually, parts of the cliffs above break away and fall into the water, where they are worn down and carried away by the water.

While high, rocky coasts get worn away, low coastlines often get built up. As you read earlier, when a stream flows into an ocean or a lake, it deposits its sediment near its mouth. This sediment mixes with the sediment formed by waves beating against the coast. Waves and currents move this sediment along the shore, building up beaches. Two terms are used to describe the movement of sediment and water along a shore: *longshore drift* and *longshore current.*

- **Longshore drift** is the zigzag movement of sand along a beach. Waves formed by wind blowing across the water far from shore may hit a shoreline at an angle. These angled waves carry sand up onto the shore, and then gravity pulls the water and sand directly back into the water. The sand gradually moves down the beach. The illustration below shows longshore drift.
- A **longshore current** is movement of water along a shore as waves strike the shore at an angle. The direction of the longshore current can change from day to day as the direction of the waves striking the shore changes.

Longshore drift moves large amounts of sand along beaches. It can cause a beach to shrink at one location and grow at another.

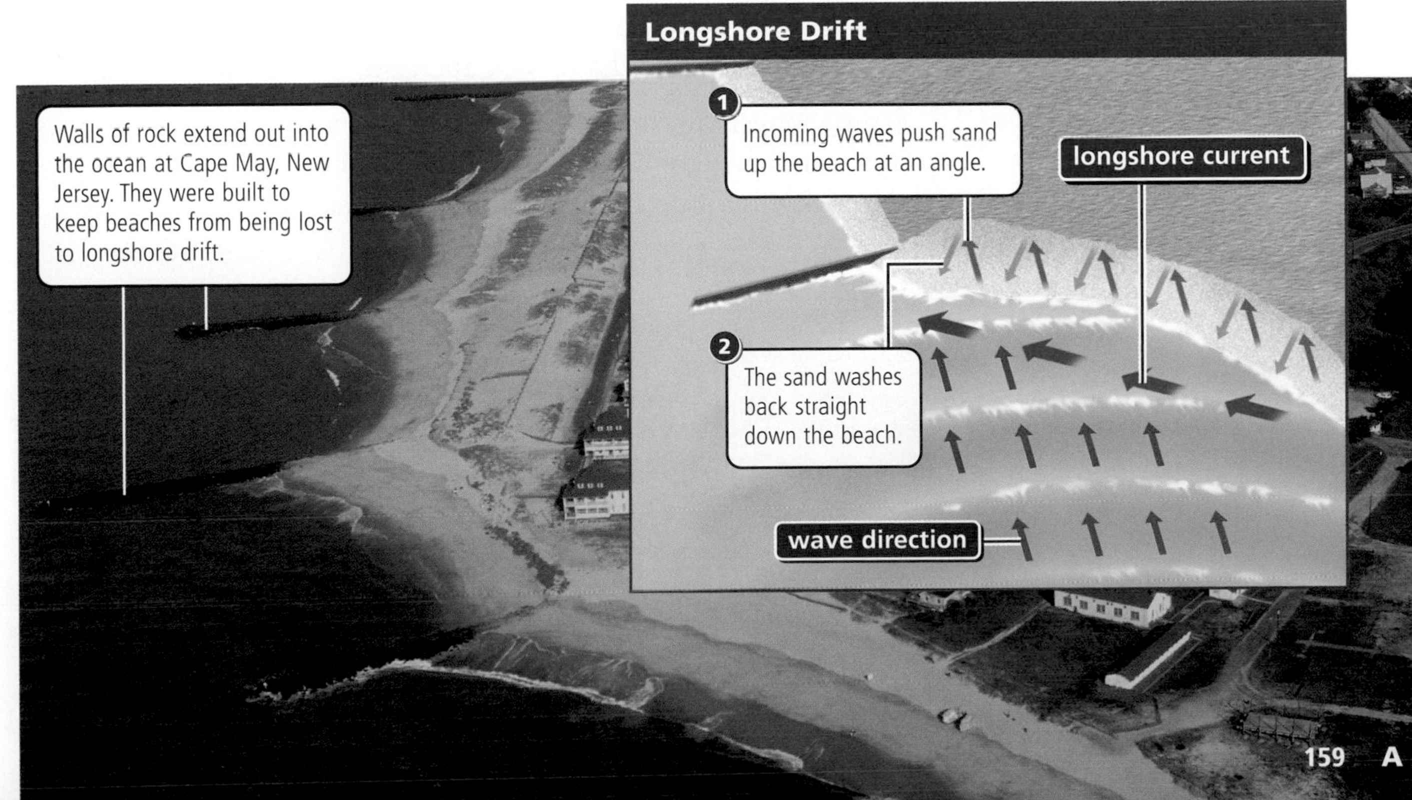

Longshore Drift
1 Incoming waves push sand up the beach at an angle.
longshore current
2 The sand washes back straight down the beach.
wave direction

Walls of rock extend out into the ocean at Cape May, New Jersey. They were built to keep beaches from being lost to longshore drift.

INVESTIGATE Longshore Drift

How does sand move along a beach?

SKILL FOCUS
Observing

MATERIALS
- 2 or 3 books
- coin

TIME
15 minutes

PROCEDURE

1. Prop up a book as shown.
2. Hold a coin with your finger against the bottom right corner of the book.
3. Gently flick the coin up the slope of the book at an angle. The coin should slide back down the book and fall off the bottom. If necessary, readjust the angle of the book and the strength with which you are flicking the coin.
4. Repeat step 3 several times. Observe the path the coin takes. Record your observations. Include a diagram that shows the general path the coin takes as it slides up and down the book.

WHAT DO YOU THINK?

- What path did the coin take on its way up? On its way down?
- In this model of longshore drift, what represents the beach, what represents the sand, and what represents a wave?

CHALLENGE In this model, in which direction will the longshore current move? How could you change the model to change the direction of the current?

Sandbars and Barrier Islands

As they transport sand, ocean waves and currents shape a variety of coastal landforms. Longshore currents, for example, often deposit sand along shorelines. The sand builds up to form sandbars. A **sandbar** is a ridge of sand built up by the action of waves and currents. A sandbar that has built up above the water's surface and is joined to the land at one end is called a spit. The tip of Cape Cod, Massachusetts, is a spit.

Strong longshore currents that mostly move in one direction may produce sandbars that build up over time into barrier islands. A **barrier island** is a long, narrow island that develops parallel to a coast.

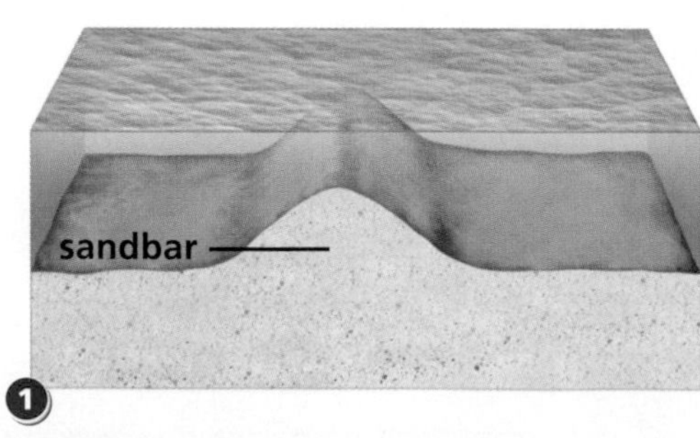

1. Waves and currents move and build up sand deposits to form a sandbar under the water surface.

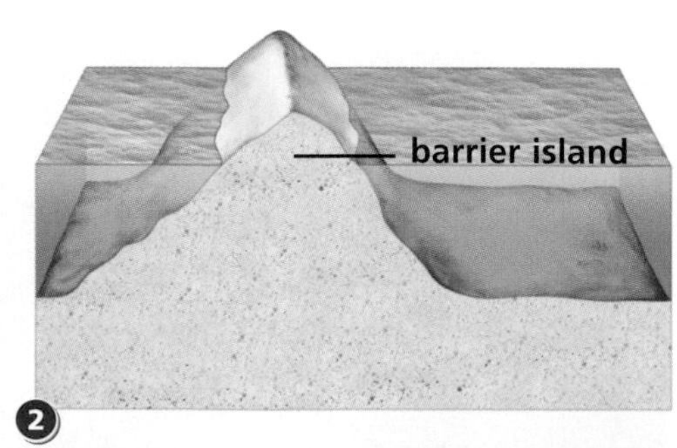

2. As more sand is deposited, the sandbar rises above the surface to become a barrier island.

This lighthouse on a barrier island in North Carolina had to be moved because of beach erosion. The photograph shows the lighthouse before it was moved.

A barrier island gets its name from the fact that it forms a barrier between the ocean waves and the shore of the mainland. As a barrier island builds up, grasses, bushes, and trees begin to grow on it.

Barrier islands are common along gently sloping coasts around the world. They occur along the coasts of New Jersey and North Carolina and along the coastline of the Gulf of Mexico. Padre Island in Texas is a barrier island about 180 kilometers (110 mi) in length.

Barrier islands constantly change shape. Hurricanes or other storms can speed up the change. During large storms, waves can surge across the land, carrying away huge amounts of sediment and depositing it elsewhere. Houses on beaches can be destroyed in storms.

How and where do barrier islands form?

Wind shapes land.

At Indiana Dunes National Lakeshore, not far from the skyscrapers of Chicago, you can tumble or slide down huge sand dunes. First-time visitors to the Indiana dunes find it hard to believe that sand formations like these can be found so far from a desert or an ocean. What created this long stretch of dune land along the southern shore of Lake Michigan? The answer: wind. A **dune** is a mound of sand built up by wind.

Like water, wind has the power to transport and deposit sediment. Although wind is a less powerful force of erosion than moving water, it can still shape landforms, especially in dry regions and in areas that have few or no plants to hold soil in place. Wind can build up dunes, deposit layers of dust, or make a land surface as hard as pavement.

Wind makes sand particles build up and tumble down, causing a dune to migrate, or move.

These hills of sand are at the Great Sand Dunes National Monument in Colorado.

Dune Formation

Even a light breeze can carry dust. A moderate wind can roll and slide grains of sand along a beach or desert, creating ripples. Only a strong wind, however, can actually pick up and carry sand particles. When the wind dies down or hits something—such as a cliff or a hill—it drops the sand. Over time, the deposits of sand build up to create dunes.

Some dunes start out as ripples that grow larger. Others form as wind-carried sand settles around a rock, log, or other obstacle. In climates with enough rainfall, plants begin to grow on dunes a short distance from beaches.

Dunes form only where there are strong winds and a constant supply of loose sand. They can be found on the inland side of beaches of oceans and large lakes, on the sandy floodplains of large rivers, and in sandy deserts.

Dunes can form in a variety of sizes and shapes. They can reach heights of up to 300 meters (about 1000 ft). Some dunes are curved; others are long, straight ridges; still others are mound-shaped hills. A dune usually has a gentle slope on the side that faces the wind and a steeper slope on the side sheltered from the wind.

Loess

Besides forming dunes, wind also changes the soil over large regions of Earth by depositing dust. A strong windstorm can move millions of tons of dust. As the wind dies down, the dust drops to the ground. Deposits of fine wind-blown sediment are called **loess** (LOH-uhs).

In some regions, deposits of loess have built up over thousands and even millions of years. Loess is a valuable resource because it forms good soil for growing crops.

This loess deposit in Iowa built up over many thousands of years.

Loess covers about 10 percent of the land surface of Earth. China has especially large deposits of loess, covering hundreds of thousands of square kilometers. Some of the deposits are more than 300 meters (about 1000 ft) thick. Such thick deposits take a long time to develop. Some of the loess deposits in China are 2 million years old. Winds blowing over the deserts and dry regions of central Asia carried the dust that formed these deposits.

Parts of east central Europe and the Mississippi Valley in the United States also contain significant loess deposits. In the central United States, loess deposits are between 8 and 30 meters (25 and 100 ft) thick.

Desert Pavement

Not only does wind shape land surfaces by depositing dust; it also shapes land surfaces by removing dust. When wind blows away all the smallest particles from a mixture of sand, silt, and gravel, it leaves behind just a layer of stones and gravel. This stony surface is called desert pavement because it looks like a cobblestone pavement. The coarse gravel and rocks are too large to be picked up by wind.

Desert pavement is made up of particles too large to be picked up by wind.

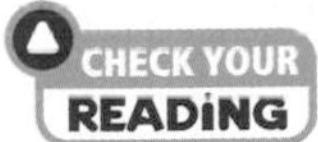

CHECK YOUR READING How are both loess and desert pavement formed by wind?

5.3 Review

KEY CONCEPTS

1. What kinds of landforms do longshore drift and longshore currents produce?
2. How do dunes form?
3. How does loess form, and why is it important?

CRITICAL THINKING

4. **Identify Cause and Effect** Is longshore drift the cause or effect of a longshore current? Explain.
5. **Predict** What effect would a barrier island have on the shoreline of the mainland?

CHALLENGE

6. **Hypothesize** The south and east shores of Lake Michigan have large areas of sand dunes, but the north and west shores do not. Write a hypothesis that explains why. You might want to use a map and draw the shape of Lake Michigan to explain.

CONNECTING SCIENCES

EARTH SCIENCE AND LIFE SCIENCE

Life on Dunes

Sand dunes are a difficult environment for most organisms. For example, few plants can gather enough nutrition from sand to grow quickly. However, any plant that grows slowly is likely to be buried by the shifting sand. Plants and animals that thrive on dunes generally have unusual traits that help them survive in dune conditions.

The leaves of American beach grass contain silica, the main component of sand. The leaves are therefore very tough. Why is this important on a dune?

American Beach Grass

Among the first plants to grow on new coastal dunes is American beach grass. It grows faster as sand begins to bury it, and it can grow up to 1 meter (more than 3 ft) per year. Its large root system—reaching down as much as 3 meters (about 10 ft)—helps it gather food and water. The roots also help hold sand in place. As the grass's roots make the dunes stable, other plants can begin to grow there.

Sand Food

One of the most unusual plants in desert dunes is called sand food. It is one of the few plants that cannot convert sunlight into energy it can use. Instead, its long underground stem grabs onto the root of another plant and sucks food from it. Most of the plant is the stem. Sand food plants may be more than 2 meters (almost 7 ft) long.

Fowler's Toad

Fowler's toad is one of the animals that can live in coastal dunes. During the day, sunlight can make the top layer of the sand very hot and dry. These toads dig down into the sand, where they are safe, cool, and moist. They are most active at night.

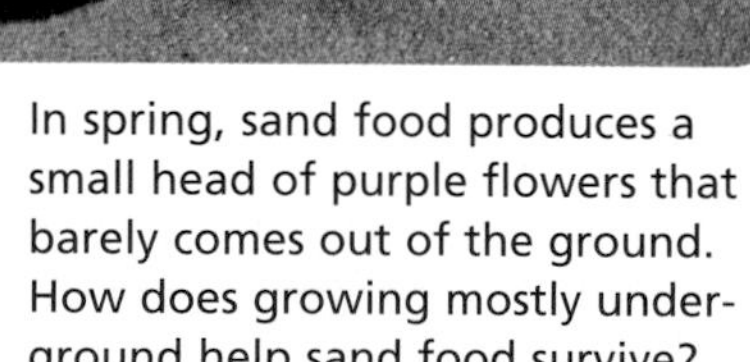

In spring, sand food produces a small head of purple flowers that barely comes out of the ground. How does growing mostly underground help sand food survive?

Fowler's toads have a brownish or greenish color that makes them hard to see against a sandy background. How would this help protect them from animals that want to eat them?

EXPLORE

1. **GENERALIZE** Dune plants often have long roots. Propose an explanation for this.
2. **CHALLENGE** Use library or Internet resources to learn about another plant or animal that lives on dunes. Describe how it has adapted to the conditions in which it lives.

KEY CONCEPT

Glaciers carve land and move sediments.

BEFORE, you learned

- Running water shapes landscapes
- Wind changes landforms

NOW, you will learn

- How moving ice erodes land
- How moving ice deposits sediment and changes landforms

VOCABULARY

glacier p. 165
till p. 168
moraine p. 168
kettle lake p. 169

EXPLORE Glaciers

How do glaciers affect land?

PROCEDURE

1. Flatten the clay on top of a paper towel.
2. Drag the ice cube across the clay as shown. Record your observations.
3. Leave the ice cube to melt on top of the clay.

MATERIALS

- modeling clay
- paper towel
- ice cube containing sand and gravel

WHAT DO YOU THINK?

- What happened when you dragged the ice cube across the clay?
- What happened to the sand and gravel in the ice cube as it melted?

Glaciers are moving bodies of ice.

VOCABULARY
Remember to add a four square diagram for *glacier* to your notebook.

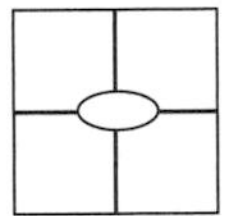

You might not think of ice as something that moves. But think about what happens to an ice cube on a table. The cube begins to melt, makes a small puddle, and may slide a little. The water under the cube makes the table surface slippery, which allows the ice cube to slide.

A similar process happens on a much larger scale with glaciers. A **glacier** is a large mass of ice that moves over land. A glacier forms in a cold region when more snow falls than melts each year. As the snow builds up, its weight presses the snow on the bottom into ice. On a mountain, the weight of a heavy mass of ice causes it to flow downward, usually slowly. On flatter land, the ice spreads out as a sheet. As glaciers form, move, and melt away, they shape landscapes.

Extent of Glaciers

Glaciers can exist only in places where it is cold enough for water to stay frozen year round. Glaciers are found in mountain ranges all over the world and in land regions near the north and south poles.

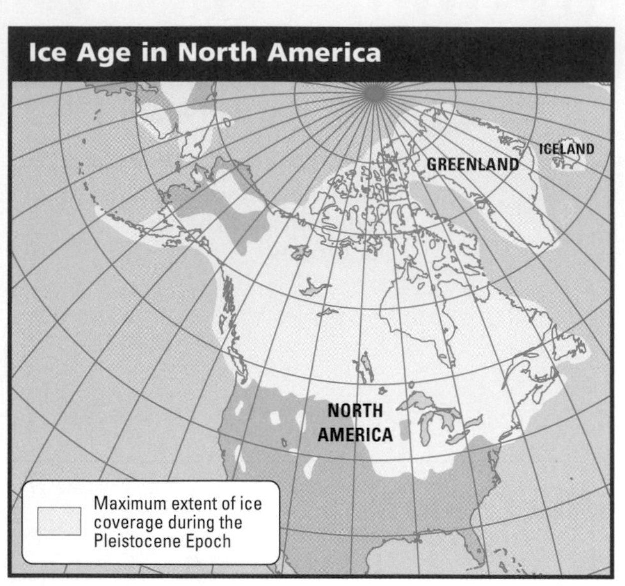

Today, glaciers cover about 10 percent of Earth's land surface. However, the amount of land surface covered by glaciers has varied greatly over Earth's history. Glaciers have expanded during long cold periods called ice ages and have disappeared during long warm periods. About 30,000 years ago—during the last major ice age—glaciers extended across the northern parts of North America and Eurasia. They covered nearly 30 percent of the present land surface of Earth.

There are two major types of glaciers: alpine glaciers and continental glaciers.

Learn more about the movement and effects of glaciers.

Alpine Glaciers

Alpine glaciers, also called valley glaciers, form in mountains and flow down through valleys. As these glaciers move, they cause erosion, breaking up rock and carrying and pushing away the resulting sediment. Over time, an alpine glacier can change a V-shaped mountain valley into a U-shaped valley with a wider, flatter bottom.

Some glaciers extend all the way down into the lower land at the bases of mountains. At an alpine glacier's lower end, where temperatures are warmer, melting can occur. The melting glacier drops sediment, and streams flowing from the glacier carry some of the sediment away. If an alpine glacier flows into the ocean, big blocks may break off and become icebergs.

Continental Glaciers

Continental glaciers, also called ice sheets, are much larger than alpine glaciers. They can cover entire continents, including all but the highest mountain peaks. An ice sheet covered most of Canada and the northern United States during the last ice age. This ice sheet melted and shrank about 10,000 years ago.

Today, ice sheets cover most of Greenland and Antarctica. Each of these glaciers is shaped like a wide dome over the land. The ice on Antarctica is as much as 4500 meters (15,000 ft) thick.

What are the two major types of glaciers and where do they form?

Types of Glaciers and Movement

A glacier is a large mass of ice that moves over land.

Alpine Glaciers

A glacier, such as this one in Alaska, changes the landscape as it moves down a mountain valley.

Continental Glaciers

Huge sheets of ice cover the continent of Antarctica and other land regions.

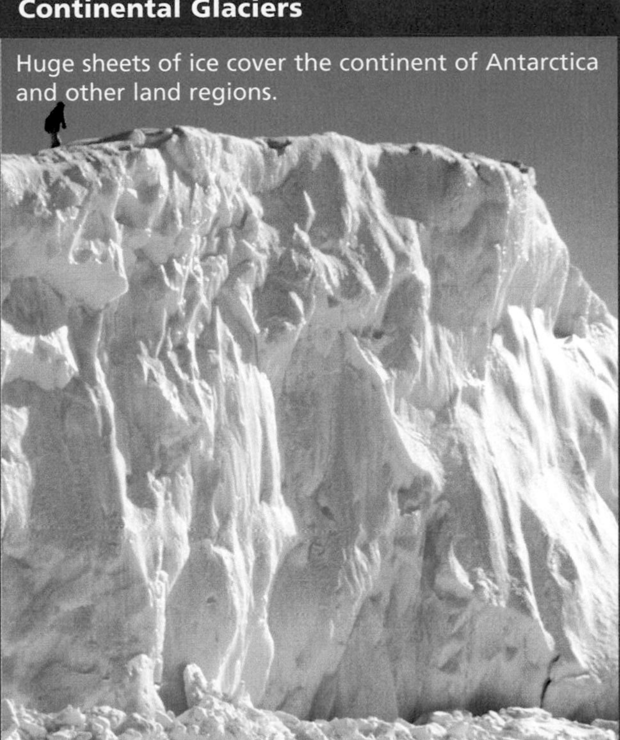

Glacier Movement

Gravity causes the ice in a glacier to move downhill. Two different processes cause glaciers to move: flowing and sliding.

Flowing The ice near the surface of a glacier is brittle, and cracks often form in it. However, deep inside a glacier, ice does not break as easily because it is under great pressure from the weight of the ice above it. Instead of breaking, ice inside a glacier flows like toothpaste being squeezed in its tube.

As a glacier moves, it breaks up rock and pushes and carries sediment.

Sliding The weight of a glacier and heat from Earth cause ice at the bottom of a glacier to melt. A layer of water forms under the glacier. The glacier slides along on this layer of water just as an ice cube might slide on a countertop.

READING VISUALS In the illustration, why are cracks shown near the surface of the glacier and not at the bottom?

A moving glacier left visible abrasion lines on this rock.

Glaciers deposit large amounts of sediment.

As glaciers have melted and retreated, they have shaped the landscapes of many places on Earth. As a glacier moves or expands, it transports a vast amount of sediment—a mix of boulders, small rocks, sand, and clay. It acts like a plow, pushing rock and soil and plucking out big blocks of rock. As a glacier moves over rock, it scratches and scrapes the rock in a process called abrasion. Abrasion leaves visible grooves on rock surfaces.

Moraines

When glaciers expand and advance and then melt and retreat, they affect both the land underneath them and the land around them. A glacier pushes huge amounts of sediment to its sides and front. When the glacier retreats, the deposits of sediment remain as visible evidence that ice once moved through. The sediment left directly on the ground surface by a retreating glacier is called **till.**

A deposit of till left behind by a retreating glacier is called a **moraine** (muh-RAYN). The ridges of till deposited at the sides of a glacier are called lateral moraines. The till that marks the farthest advance of a glacier forms a deposit called an end moraine. Moraines formed by continental glaciers, such as those in North America during the ice age, can be huge—many kilometers long.

The blanket of till that a glacier deposits along its bottom is called a ground moraine. Rock deposits from glaciers can often be identified as till because the till rocks are different, in type or age, from the rock that was present before the glacier formed.

Draw a sketch of a glacier and label where lateral, end, and ground moraines would form.

A glacier scooped out this valley in California and left behind lateral moraines.

Lakes

Besides ridges, hills, and blankets of till, melting glaciers also leave behind depressions of various sizes that can become lakes. Landscapes shaped by glaciers are often dotted with small kettle lakes as well as larger lakes. A **kettle lake** is a bowl-shaped depression that was formed by a block of ice from a glacier and then became filled with water.

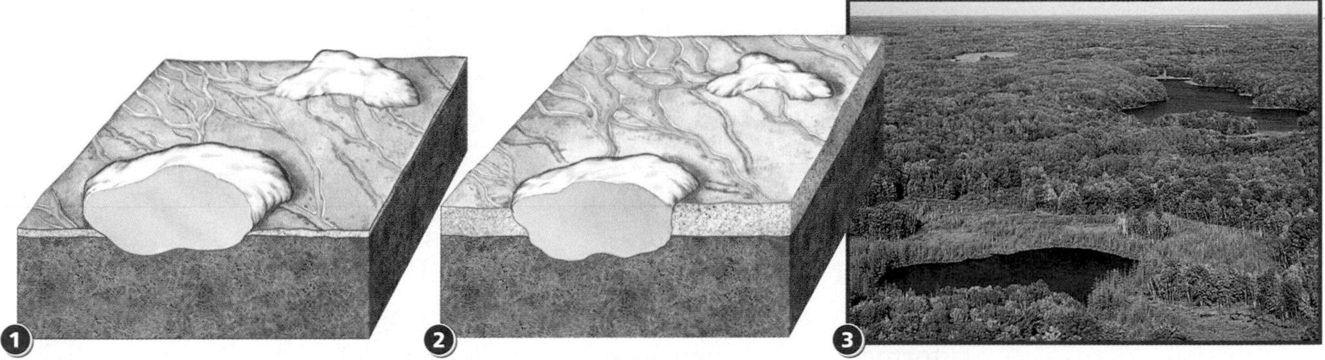

1. As a glacier moves away, it leaves huge blocks of ice.
2. Over time, sediment builds up around the ice.
3. The ice melts, leaving behind bowls that become kettle lakes. These lakes are in Wisconsin.

The last ice sheet in North America formed many kettle lakes in some regions. Kettle lakes are common in Michigan, Wisconsin, and Minnesota.

INVESTIGATE Kettle Lake Formation

How do kettle lakes form?

DESIGN YOUR OWN

Kettle lakes form when sediment builds up around blocks of ice left behind by a retreating glacier. Use what you know about kettle lake formation to design a model of the process.

PROCEDURE

1. Use the tray, the ice cubes, and the other materials to model how sediment builds up around ice blocks.
2. Write a description of the process you used to make your model.

WHAT DO YOU THINK?

- Describe how your model worked. What did you do first? What happened next?
- Did your model accurately represent the formation of kettle lakes? Did it work? Why or why not?
- What were the limitations of your model? Are there any aspects of kettle lake formation that are not represented? If so, what are they?

SKILL FOCUS
Designing models

MATERIALS
- shallow tray
- ice cubes
- modeling clay
- sand
- gravel
- water

TIME
30 minutes

Great Lakes Formation

1 14,000 Years Ago

The ice sheet covering a land of river valleys began to retreat.

2 7000 Years Ago

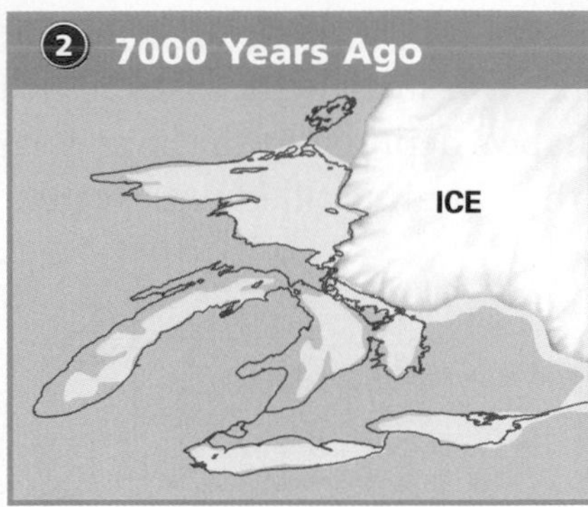

Water filled the bowls carved out by the ice.

3 Today

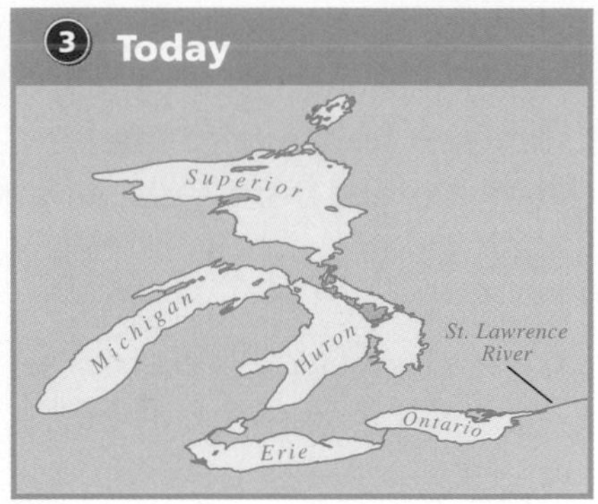

The Great Lakes contain 20 percent of the world's fresh lake water.

Many large lakes are the result of ice ages. In some places, lakes formed after glaciers in valleys melted and left behind moraines that dammed the valleys. Many of these lakes are long and narrow, like the Finger Lakes in New York, which are named for their slender shape.

The Great Lakes were formed thousands of years ago as an ice sheet moved over the land and then melted. A million years ago, the region of the Great Lakes had many river valleys. The ice sheet gouged out large depressions in the land and left piles of rock and debris that blocked water from draining out. In some areas, where the deepest Great Lakes are now, the enormous weight of the glacier actually caused the land to sink as much as one kilometer.

The ice sheet started to melt about 14,000 years ago. By about 7000 years ago, it had melted past what would become Lake Erie and Lake Ontario, the lakes farthest to the east.

What are two ways the ice sheet formed the Great Lakes?

KEY CONCEPTS

1. Describe the two processes that cause glaciers to move.
2. What are the two major types of glaciers, and where are they found?
3. Describe the land features left behind by glaciers that have melted and shrunk.

CRITICAL THINKING

4. **Compare and Contrast** Identify two ways in which the erosion effects of glaciers differ from those of rivers.
5. **Predict** How would glaciers be affected by changes in climate, such as global warming and global cooling?

CHALLENGE

6. **Infer** Regions near the equator are generally the warmest on Earth. However, in one small area of Africa, there are glaciers close to the equator. Form a hypothesis to explain why these glaciers exist.

MATH TUTORIAL

CLASSZONE.COM

Click on Math Tutorial for more help with making line graphs.

SKILL: CREATING A LINE GRAPH

Snow Line Elevation and Latitude

Glaciers form above the snow line, the lowest elevation at which there is permanent snow in the summer. The snow line elevation depends on temperature and precipitation. In the hot tropics the snow line is high in the mountains, while at the poles it is near sea level. The table shows the snow line elevations at different locations on Earth. The latitude of each location indicates how far the location is from the equator; the latitude of the equator is 0 degrees, and the latitude of the North Pole is 90 degrees.

Location	Latitude (degrees north)	Snow Line Elevation (meters)
North Pole	90	0
Juneau, Alaska	58	1050
Glacier National Park	49	2600
Sierra Nevada	37	3725
Himalayas (East Nepal)	28	5103
Ecuador	0	4788

Follow the steps below to make a line graph of the data.

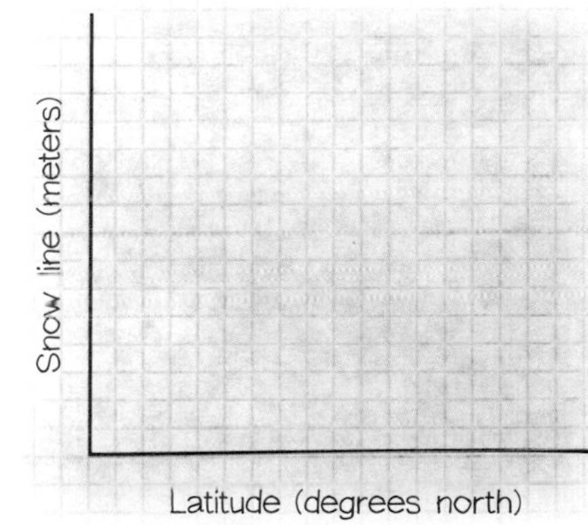

(1) On a sheet of graph paper, draw and label axes. Put latitude on the horizontal axis and snow line elevation on the vertical axis.

(2) Choose and mark a scale for each axis.

(3) Graph each point.

(4) Draw line segments to connect the points.

Use your graph to answer the following questions.

1. Mount Kenya is very close to the equator. Estimate the snow line elevation on Mount Kenya.
2. Mount Rainier is at 47 degrees north latitude and is 4389 meters tall. Can there be glaciers on Mount Rainier? If so, estimate the elevation above which the glaciers form.
3. Mount Washington in New Hampshire is at 45 degrees north latitude and is 1917 meters tall. Can there be glaciers on Mount Washington? If so, estimate their lowest elevation.

CHALLENGE Temperatures are hotter at the equator than at 28 degrees north latitude. Why is the snow line lower at the equator in Ecuador? (**Hint:** The answer involves precipitation.)

5 Chapter Review

the BIG idea

Water, wind, and ice shape Earth's surface.

5.1 Forces wear down and build up Earth's surface.

Water, wind, and ice move sediment in the process called **erosion**. The placement of sediment in a new location is **deposition**, part of the erosion process.

VOCABULARY
erosion p. 145
deposition p. 145
mass wasting p. 147

5.2 Moving water shapes land.

Water drains from land in **drainage basins,** which are separated by **divides.** As water flows over land and underground, it moves sediment and changes land features.

VOCABULARY
drainage basin p. 151
divide p. 151
floodplain p. 152
alluvial fan p. 153
delta p. 153
sinkhole p. 155

5.3 Waves and wind shape land.

The action of water moves sand and builds up new landforms, such as sandbars and barrier islands. Wind forms dunes.

VOCABULARY
longshore drift p. 159
longshore current p. 159
sandbar p. 160
barrier island p. 160
dune p. 161
loess p. 162

5.4 Glaciers carve land and move sediments.

Glaciers are large bodies of ice that change landscapes as they move.

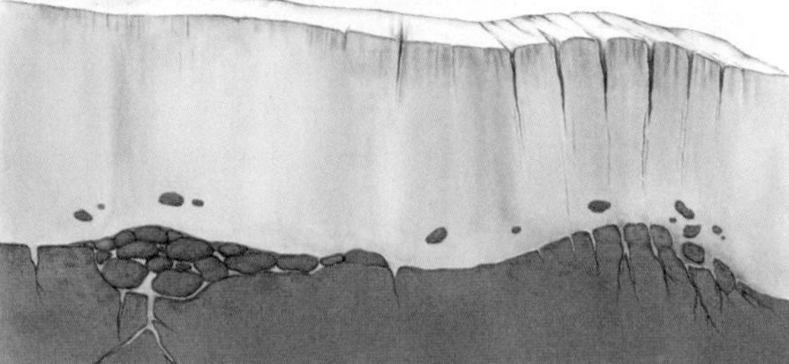

VOCABULARY
glacier p. 165
till p. 168
moraine p. 168
kettle lake p. 169

Reviewing Vocabulary

Copy and complete the chart below. Explain how each landscape feature is formed.

Feature	How It Forms
EXAMPLE delta	A river deposits sediment as it enters the ocean.
1. alluvial fan	
2. sinkhole	
3. sandbar	
4. barrier island	
5. dune	
6. loess	
7. moraine	
8. kettle lake	

Reviewing Key Concepts

Multiple Choice *Choose the letter of the best answer.*

9. The first stage in the erosion process is
- **a.** deposition
- **b.** mass wasting
- **c.** drainage
- **d.** weathering

10. The main natural force responsible for mass movements of rocks and debris is
- **a.** rainwater
- **b.** wind
- **c.** gravity
- **d.** fire

11. A sinkhole is formed by the collapse of
- **a.** an alluvial fan
- **b.** a cavern
- **c.** a moraine
- **d.** a kettle lake

12. Rivers transport sediment to
- **a.** drainage basins
- **b.** oceans and lakes
- **c.** the water table
- **d.** moraines

13. Drainage basins are separated by a
- **a.** moraine
- **b.** divide
- **c.** tributary
- **d.** barrier island

14. In high mountains, a valley carved by a stream has the shape of a
- **a.** U
- **b.** crescent
- **c.** plate
- **d.** V

15. An oxbow lake is formed by the cutting off of a
- **a.** meander
- **b.** drainage basin
- **c.** sinkhole
- **d.** glacier

16. Sandbars, spits, and barrier islands can all be built up by
- **a.** glaciers
- **b.** ocean waves
- **c.** wind
- **d.** mass wasting

17. A dune is a sand mound built up primarily by
- **a.** gravity
- **b.** running water
- **c.** glaciers
- **d.** wind

18. Strong winds can transport large quantities of
- **a.** gravel
- **b.** wet sand
- **c.** dry sand
- **d.** clay

19. A mountain valley carved by a glacier has the shape of a
- **a.** U
- **b.** crescent
- **c.** bowl
- **d.** V

Short Answer *Answer each of the following questions in a sentence or two.*

20. How is deposition part of the erosion process?

21. How can rainwater in the Rocky Mountains end up in the ocean?

22. What is the effect of a longshore current on a beach?

23. Why is a mass movement of mud called a flow?

24. What visual evidence is a sign of creep?

25. What is the connection between icebergs and glaciers?

Thinking Critically

This photograph shows two glaciers joining to form one (A). Make a sketch of the glaciers to answer the next three questions.

26. **APPLY** Place an arrow to show in which direction the main glacier (A) is moving.

27. **ANALYZE** Mark the places where you think till would be found.

28. **APPLY** Mark the location of a lateral moraine.

29. **ANALYZE** Why does the main glacier not have an end moraine?

30. **COMPARE AND CONTRAST** Compare the main glacier valley in the photograph with the valley at the far right (B). How are the valleys different? Explain why they might be different.

31. **APPLY** In exploring an area of land, what clues would you look for to determine whether glaciers were once there?

32. **COMPARE AND CONTRAST** How is a deposit of till from a glacier similar to a river delta? How is it different?

33. **EVALUATE** If you were growing crops on a field near a slow-moving, curvy river, what would an advantage of the field's location be? What might be a disadvantage?

34. **COMPARE AND CONTRAST** How are mudflows and mass wasting of rock similar? How are they different? Include references to speed and types of material in your answer.

35. **INFER** If the wind usually blows from west to east over a large area of land, and the wind usually slows down over the eastern half of the area, where would you be likely to find loess in the area? Explain your answer.

36. **APPLY** If you were considering a location for a house and were concerned about creep, what two factors about the land would you consider?

37. **SYNTHESIZE** Describe how the processes of erosion and deposition are involved in the formation of kettle lakes.

the BIG idea

38. **SYNTHESIZE** Describe how snow falling onto the Continental Divide in the Rocky Mountains can be part of the process of erosion and deposition. Include the words *divide, glacier, stream,* and *ocean* in your answer.

39. **PROVIDE EXAMPLES** Choose three examples of erosion processes—one each from Sections 5.2, 5.3, and 5.4. Explain how gravity is involved in each of these processes.

UNIT PROJECTS

Evaluate all the data, results, and information in your project folder. Prepare to present your project. Be ready to answer questions posed by your classmates about your results.

Standardized Test Practice

For practice on your state test, go to . . . TEST PRACTICE CLASSZONE.COM

Analyzing a Diagram

Use the diagram to answer the questions below.

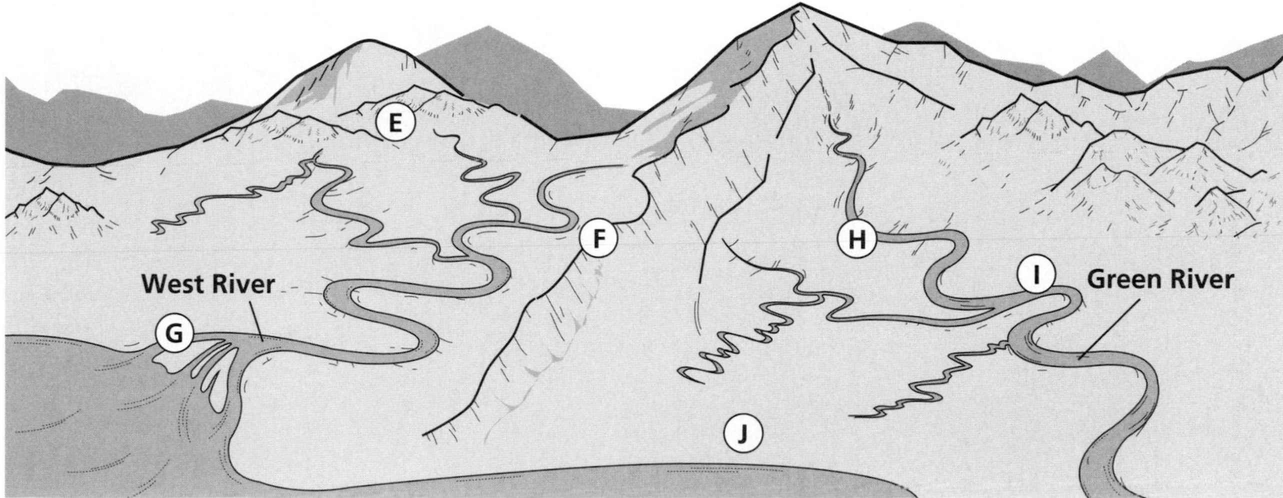

1. Where would a glacier be most likely to form?
   - **a.** E
   - **b.** F
   - **c.** G
   - **d.** H

2. Where is a divide?
   - **a.** E
   - **b.** F
   - **c.** H
   - **d.** I

3. Where is a delta?
   - **a.** E
   - **b.** F
   - **c.** G
   - **d.** J

4. Which process could move sediment from point E to point G?
   - **a.** weathering
   - **b.** erosion
   - **c.** deposition
   - **d.** drifting

5. Which word best describes the building up of sediment at point G?
   - **a.** weathering
   - **b.** erosion
   - **c.** deposition
   - **d.** drifting

6. Why might the water in the Green River move faster at point H than at point I?
   - **a.** The river at point H is warmer.
   - **b.** The river at point H is smaller.
   - **c.** The slope at point H is steeper.
   - **d.** More rain falls at point H.

Extended Response

Answer the two questions below in detail. Include some of the terms shown in the word box. In your answers, underline each term you use.

ocean waves	currents	barrier island
grass	glaciers	kettle lakes

7. Each year, Clark and his family visit the ocean. Clark notices that a sandbar near the coast is slightly larger each year. Predict what will happen if this trend continues.

8. Annika often goes fishing at one of several small, round lakes that are within 20 miles of her house in Minnesota. How might these lakes have formed?

Student Resource Handbooks

Scientific Thinking Handbook R2

Lab Handbook R10

Math Handbook R36

Note-Taking Handbook R45

Making Observations

An **observation** is an act of noting and recording an event, characteristic, behavior, or anything else detected with an instrument or with the senses.

Observations allow you to make informed hypotheses and to gather data for experiments. Careful observations often lead to ideas for new experiments. There are two categories of observations:

- **Quantitative observations** can be expressed in numbers and include records of time, temperature, mass, distance, and volume.
- **Qualitative observations** include descriptions of sights, sounds, smells, and textures.

EXAMPLE

A student dissolved 30 grams of Epsom salts in water, poured the solution into a dish, and let the dish sit out uncovered overnight. The next day, she made the following observations of the Epsom salt crystals that grew in the dish.

To determine the mass, the student found the mass of the dish before and after growing the crystals and then used subtraction to find the difference.

The student measured several crystals and calculated the mean length. (To learn how to calculate the mean of a data set, see page R36.)

Table 1. Observations of Epsom Salt Crystals

Quantitative Observations	Qualitative Observations
• mass = 30 g • mean crystal length = 0.5 cm • longest crystal length = 2 cm	• Crystals are clear. • Crystals are long, thin, and rectangular. • White crust has formed around edge of dish. Epsom salt crystals

Photographs or sketches are useful for recording qualitative observations.

MORE ABOUT OBSERVING

- Make quantitative observations whenever possible. That way, others will know exactly what you observed and be able to compare their results with yours.
- It is always a good idea to make qualitative observations too. You never know when you might observe something unexpected.

Predicting and Hypothesizing

A **prediction** is an expectation of what will be observed or what will happen. A **hypothesis** is a tentative explanation for an observation or scientific problem that can be tested by further investigation.

EXAMPLE

Suppose you have made two paper airplanes and you wonder why one of them tends to glide farther than the other one.

1. Start by asking a question.
2. Make an educated guess. After examination, you notice that the wings of the airplane that flies farther are slightly larger than the wings of the other airplane.
3. Write a prediction based upon your educated guess, in the form of an "If . . . , then . . ." statement. Write the independent variable after the word *if,* and the dependent variable after the word *then.*
4. To make a hypothesis, explain why you think what you predicted will occur. Write the explanation after the word *because.*

1. Why does one of the paper airplanes glide farther than the other?
2. The size of an airplane's wings may affect how far the airplane will glide.
3. Prediction: If I make a paper airplane with larger wings, then the airplane will glide farther.

To read about independent and dependent variables, see page R30.

4. Hypothesis: If I make a paper airplane with larger wings, then the airplane will glide farther, because the additional surface area of the wing will produce more lift.

Notice that the part of the hypothesis after *because* adds an explanation of why the airplane will glide farther.

MORE ABOUT HYPOTHESES

- The results of an experiment cannot prove that a hypothesis is correct. Rather, the results either support or do not support the hypothesis.
- Valuable information is gained even when your hypothesis is not supported by your results. For example, it would be an important discovery to find that wing size is not related to how far an airplane glides.
- In science, a hypothesis is supported only after many scientists have conducted many experiments and produced consistent results.

Inferring

An **inference** is a logical conclusion drawn from the available evidence and prior knowledge. Inferences are often made from observations.

SCIENTIFIC THINKING HANDBOOK

EXAMPLE

A student observing a set of acorns noticed something unexpected about one of them. He noticed a white, soft-bodied insect eating its way out of the acorn.

The student recorded these observations.

Observations

- There is a hole in the acorn, about 0.5 cm in diameter, where the insect crawled out.
- There is a second hole, which is about the size of a pinhole, on the other side of the acorn.
- The inside of the acorn is hollow.

Here are some inferences that can be made on the basis of the observations.

Inferences

- The insect formed from the material inside the acorn, grew to its present size, and ate its way out of the acorn.
- The insect crawled through the smaller hole, ate the inside of the acorn, grew to its present size, and ate its way out of the acorn.
- An egg was laid in the acorn through the smaller hole. The egg hatched into a larva that ate the inside of the acorn, grew to its present size, and ate its way out of the acorn.

When you make inferences, be sure to look at all of the evidence available and combine it with what you already know.

MORE ABOUT INFERENCES

Inferences depend both on observations and on the knowledge of the people making the inferences. Ancient people who did not know that organisms are produced only by similar organisms might have made an inference like the first one. A student today might look at the same observations and make the second inference. A third student might have knowledge about this particular insect and know that it is never small enough to fit through the smaller hole, leading her to the third inference.

Identifying Cause and Effect

In a **cause-and-effect relationship,** one event or characteristic is the result of another. Usually an effect follows its cause in time.

There are many examples of cause-and-effect relationships in everyday life.

Cause	Effect
Turn off a light.	Room gets dark.
Drop a glass.	Glass breaks.
Blow a whistle.	Sound is heard.

Scientists must be careful not to infer a cause-and-effect relationship just because one event happens after another event. When one event occurs after another, you cannot infer a cause-and-effect relationship on the basis of that information alone. You also cannot conclude that one event caused another if there are alternative ways to explain the second event. A scientist must demonstrate through experimentation or continued observation that an event was truly caused by another event.

EXAMPLE

Make an Observation

Suppose you have a few plants growing outside. When the weather starts getting colder, you bring one of the plants indoors. You notice that the plant you brought indoors is growing faster than the others are growing. You cannot conclude from your observation that the change in temperature was the cause of the increased plant growth, because there are alternative explanations for the observation. Some possible explanations are given below.

- The humidity indoors caused the plant to grow faster.
- The level of sunlight indoors caused the plant to grow faster.
- The indoor plant's being noticed more often and watered more often than the outdoor plants caused it to grow faster.
- The plant that was brought indoors was healthier than the other plants to begin with.

To determine which of these factors, if any, caused the indoor plant to grow faster than the outdoor plants, you would need to design and conduct an experiment.

See pages R28–R35 for information about designing experiments.

Recognizing Bias

Television, newspapers, and the Internet are full of experts claiming to have scientific evidence to back up their claims. How do you know whether the claims are really backed up by good science?

Bias is a slanted point of view, or personal prejudice. The goal of scientists is to be as objective as possible and to base their findings on facts instead of opinions. However, bias often affects the conclusions of researchers, and it is important to learn to recognize bias.

When scientific results are reported, you should consider the source of the information as well as the information itself. It is important to critically analyze the information that you see and read.

SOURCES OF BIAS

There are several ways in which a report of scientific information may be biased. Here are some questions that you can ask yourself:

1. **Who is sponsoring the research?**

   Sometimes, the results of an investigation are biased because an organization paying for the research is looking for a specific answer. This type of bias can affect how data are gathered and interpreted.

2. **Is the research sample large enough?**

   Sometimes research does not include enough data. The larger the sample size, the more likely that the results are accurate, assuming a truly random sample.

3. **In a survey, who is answering the questions?**

   The results of a survey or poll can be biased. The people taking part in the survey may have been specifically chosen because of how they would answer. They may have the same ideas or lifestyles. A survey or poll should make use of a random sample of people.

4. **Are the people who take part in a survey biased?**

   People who take part in surveys sometimes try to answer the questions the way they think the researcher wants them to answer. Also, in surveys or polls that ask for personal information, people may be unwilling to answer questions truthfully.

SCIENTIFIC BIAS

It is also important to realize that scientists have their own biases because of the types of research they do and because of their scientific viewpoints. Two scientists may look at the same set of data and come to completely different conclusions because of these biases. However, such disagreements are not necessarily bad. In fact, a critical analysis of disagreements is often responsible for moving science forward.

Identifying Faulty Reasoning

Faulty reasoning is wrong or incorrect thinking. It leads to mistakes and to wrong conclusions. Scientists are careful not to draw unreasonable conclusions from experimental data. Without such caution, the results of scientific investigations may be misleading.

EXAMPLE

Scientists try to make generalizations based on their data to explain as much about nature as possible. If only a small sample of data is looked at, however, a conclusion may be faulty. Suppose a scientist has studied the effects of the El Niño and La Niña weather patterns on flood damage in California from 1989 to 1995. The scientist organized the data in the bar graph below.

Flood and Storm Damage in California

Estimated damage (millions of dollars): 0, 500, 1000, 1500, 2000

Starting year of season (July 1–June 30): 1989, 1992, 1995

Weak–moderate El Niño

Strong El Niño

SOURCE: *Governor's Office of Emergency Services, California*

The scientist drew the following conclusions:

1. The La Niña weather pattern has no effect on flooding in California.
2. When neither weather pattern occurs, there is almost no flood damage.
3. A weak or moderate El Niño produces a small or moderate amount of flooding.
4. A strong El Niño produces a lot of flooding.

For the six-year period of the scientist's investigation, these conclusions may seem to be reasonable. However, a six-year study of weather patterns may be too small of a sample for the conclusions to be supported. Consider the following graph, which shows information that was gathered from 1949 to 1997.

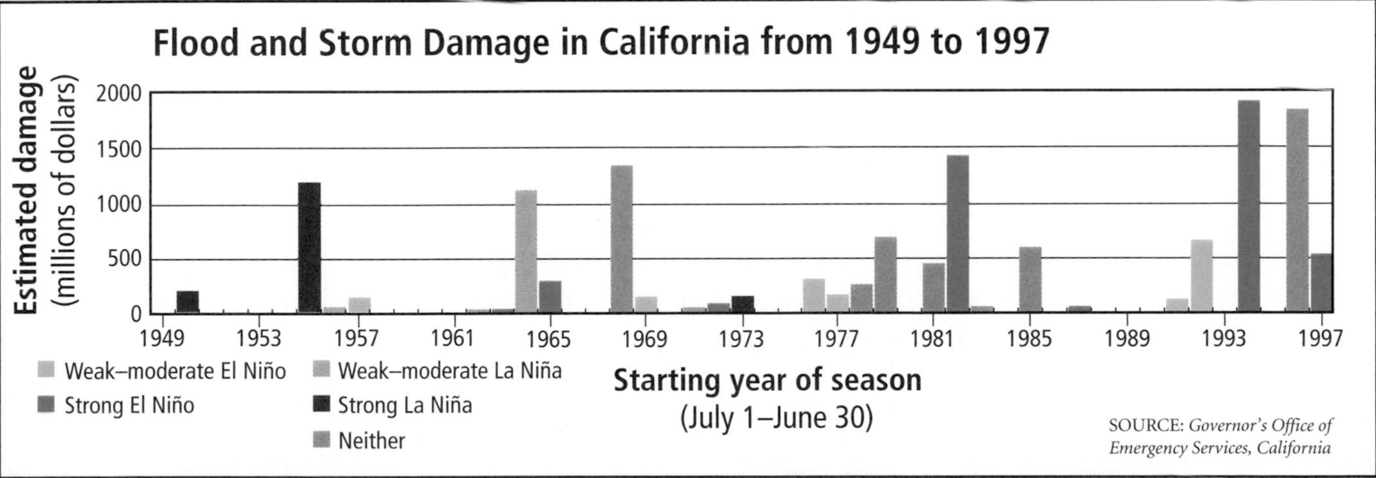

The only one of the conclusions that all of this information supports is number 3: a weak or moderate El Niño produces a small or moderate amount of flooding. By collecting more data, scientists can be more certain of their conclusions and can avoid faulty reasoning.

Analyzing Statements

To **analyze** a statement is to examine its parts carefully. Scientific findings are often reported through media such as television or the Internet. A report that is made public often focuses on only a small part of research. As a result, it is important to question the sources of information.

Evaluate Media Claims

To **evaluate** a statement is to judge it on the basis of criteria you've established. Sometimes evaluating means deciding whether a statement is true.

Reports of scientific research and findings in the media may be misleading or incomplete. When you are exposed to this information, you should ask yourself some questions so that you can make informed judgments about the information.

1. **Does the information come from a credible source?**

   Suppose you learn about a new product and it is stated that scientific evidence proves that the product works. A report from a respected news source may be more believable than an advertisement paid for by the product's manufacturer.

2. **How much evidence supports the claim?**

   Often, it may seem that there is new evidence every day of something in the world that either causes or cures an illness. However, information that is the result of several years of work by several different scientists is more credible than an advertisement that does not even cite the subjects of the experiment.

3. **How much information is being presented?**

   Science cannot solve all questions, and scientific experiments often have flaws. A report that discusses problems in a scientific study may be more believable than a report that addresses only positive experimental findings.

4. **Is scientific evidence being presented by a specific source?**

   Sometimes scientific findings are reported by people who are called experts or leaders in a scientific field. But if their names are not given or their scientific credentials are not reported, their statements may be less credible than those of recognized experts.

Differentiate Between Fact and Opinion

Sometimes information is presented as a fact when it may be an opinion. When scientific conclusions are reported, it is important to recognize whether they are based on solid evidence. Again, you may find it helpful to ask yourself some questions.

1. **What is the difference between a fact and an opinion?**

   A **fact** is a piece of information that can be strictly defined and proved true. An **opinion** is a statement that expresses a belief, value, or feeling. An opinion cannot be proved true or false. For example, a person's age is a fact, but if someone is asked how old they feel, it is impossible to prove the person's answer to be true or false.

2. **Can opinions be measured?**

   Yes, opinions can be measured. In fact, surveys often ask for people's opinions on a topic. But there is no way to know whether or not an opinion is the truth.

HOW TO DIFFERENTIATE FACT FROM OPINION

Opinions
Notice words or phrases that express beliefs or feelings. The words *unfortunately* and *careless* show that opinions are being expressed.

Opinion
Look for statements that speculate about events. These statements are opinions, because they cannot be proved.

Human Activities and the Environment

Unfortunately, human use of fossil fuels is one of the most significant developments of the past few centuries. Humans rely on fossil fuels, a nonrenewable energy resource, for more than 90 percent of their energy needs.

This careless misuse of our planet's resources has resulted in pollution, global warming, and the destruction of fragile ecosystems. For example, oil pipelines carry more than one million barrels of oil each day across tundra regions. Transporting oil across such areas can only result in oil spills that poison the land for decades.

Facts
Statements that contain statistics tend to be facts. Writers often use facts to support their opinions.

Safety Rules

Before you work in the laboratory, read these safety rules twice. Ask your teacher to explain any rules that you do not completely understand. Refer to these rules later on if you have questions about safety in the science classroom.

Directions

- Read all directions and make sure that you understand them before starting an investigation or lab activity. If you do not understand how to do a procedure or how to use a piece of equipment, ask your teacher.
- Do not begin any investigation or touch any equipment until your teacher has told you to start.
- Never experiment on your own. If you want to try a procedure that the directions do not call for, ask your teacher for permission first.
- If you are hurt or injured in any way, tell your teacher immediately.

Dress Code

goggles

apron

gloves

- Wear goggles when
  — using glassware, sharp objects, or chemicals
  — heating an object
  — working with anything that can easily fly up into the air and hurt someone's eye
- Tie back long hair or hair that hangs in front of your eyes.
- Remove any article of clothing—such as a loose sweater or a scarf—that hangs down and may touch a flame, chemical, or piece of equipment.
- Observe all safety icons calling for the wearing of eye protection, gloves, and aprons.

Heating and Fire Safety

fire safety

heating safety

- Keep your work area neat, clean, and free of extra materials.
- Never reach over a flame or heat source.
- Point objects being heated away from you and others.
- Never heat a substance or an object in a closed container.
- Never touch an object that has been heated. If you are unsure whether something is hot, treat it as though it is. Use oven mitts, clamps, tongs, or a test-tube holder.
- Know where the fire extinguisher and fire blanket are kept in your classroom.
- Do not throw hot substances into the trash. Wait for them to cool or use the container your teacher puts out for disposal.

Electrical Safety

electrical safety

- Never use lamps or other electrical equipment with frayed cords.
- Make sure no cord is lying on the floor where someone can trip over it.
- Do not let a cord hang over the side of a counter or table so that the equipment can easily be pulled or knocked to the floor.
- Never let cords hang into sinks or other places where water can be found.
- Never try to fix electrical problems. Inform your teacher of any problems immediately.
- Unplug an electrical cord by pulling on the plug, not the cord.

Chemical Safety

chemical safety

poison

fumes

- If you spill a chemical or get one on your skin or in your eyes, tell your teacher right away.
- Never touch, taste, or sniff any chemicals in the lab. If you need to determine odor, waft. Wafting consists of holding the chemical in its container 15 centimeters (6 in.) away from your nose, and using your fingers to bring fumes from the container to your nose.
- Keep lids on all chemicals you are not using.
- Never put unused chemicals back into the original containers. Throw away extra chemicals where your teacher tells you to.
- Pour chemicals over a sink or your work area, not over the floor.
- If you get a chemical in your eye, use the eyewash right away.
- Always wash your hands after handling chemicals, plants, or soil.

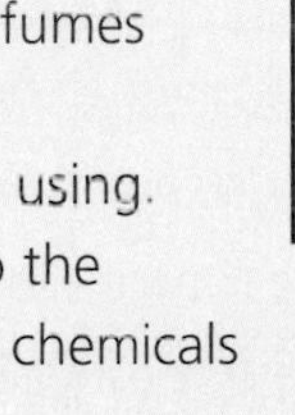

Wafting

Glassware and Sharp-Object Safety

sharp objects

- If you break glassware, tell your teacher right away.
- Do not use broken or chipped glassware. Give these to your teacher.
- Use knives and other cutting instruments carefully. Always wear eye protection and cut away from you.

Animal Safety

- Never hurt an animal.
- Touch animals only when necessary. Follow your teacher's instructions for handling animals.
- Always wash your hands after working with animals.

Cleanup

disposal

- Follow your teacher's instructions for throwing away or putting away supplies.
- Clean your work area and pick up anything that has dropped to the floor.
- Wash your hands.

Using Lab Equipment

Different experiments require different types of equipment. But even though experiments differ, the ways in which the equipment is used are the same.

Beakers

- Use beakers for holding and pouring liquids.
- Do not use a beaker to measure the volume of a liquid. Use a graduated cylinder instead. (See page R16.)
- Use a beaker that holds about twice as much liquid as you need. For example, if you need 100 milliliters of water, you should use a 200- or 250-milliliter beaker.

Test Tubes

- Use test tubes to hold small amounts of substances.
- Do not use a test tube to measure the volume of a liquid.
- Use a test tube when heating a substance over a flame. Aim the mouth of the tube away from yourself and other people.
- Liquids easily spill or splash from test tubes, so it is important to use only small amounts of liquids.

Test-Tube Holder

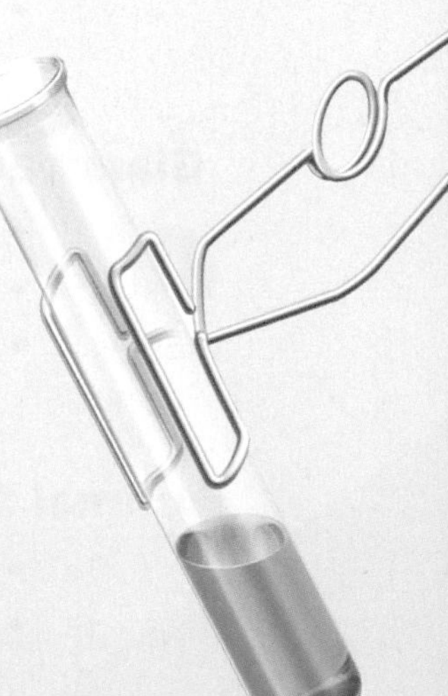

- Use a test-tube holder when heating a substance in a test tube.
- Use a test-tube holder if the substance in a test tube is dangerous to touch.
- Make sure the test-tube holder tightly grips the test tube so that the test tube will not slide out of the holder.
- Make sure that the test-tube holder is above the surface of the substance in the test tube so that you can observe the substance.

LAB HANDBOOK

Test-Tube Rack

- Use a test-tube rack to organize test tubes before, during, and after an experiment.
- Use a test-tube rack to keep test tubes upright so that they do not fall over and spill their contents.
- Use a test-tube rack that is the correct size for the test tubes that you are using. If the rack is too small, a test tube may become stuck. If the rack is too large, a test tube may lean over, and some of its contents may spill or splash.

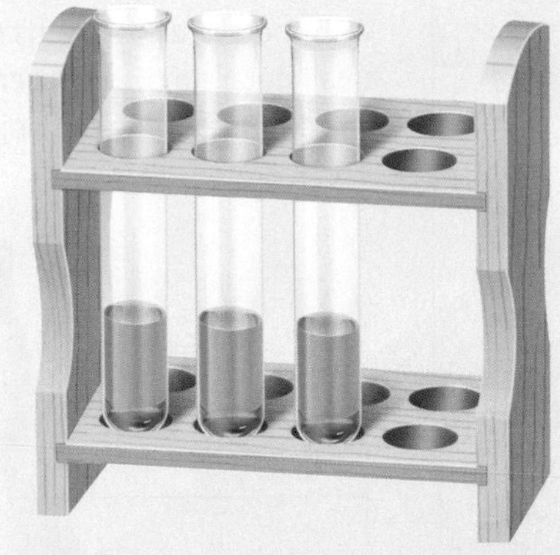

Forceps

- Use forceps when you need to pick up or hold a very small object that should not be touched with your hands.
- Do not use forceps to hold anything over a flame, because forceps are not long enough to keep your hand safely away from the flame. Plastic forceps will melt, and metal forceps will conduct heat and burn your hand.

Hot Plate

- Use a hot plate when a substance needs to be kept warmer than room temperature for a long period of time.
- Use a hot plate instead of a Bunsen burner or a candle when you need to carefully control temperature.
- Do not use a hot plate when a substance needs to be burned in an experiment.
- Always use "hot hands" safety mitts or oven mitts when handling anything that has been heated on a hot plate.

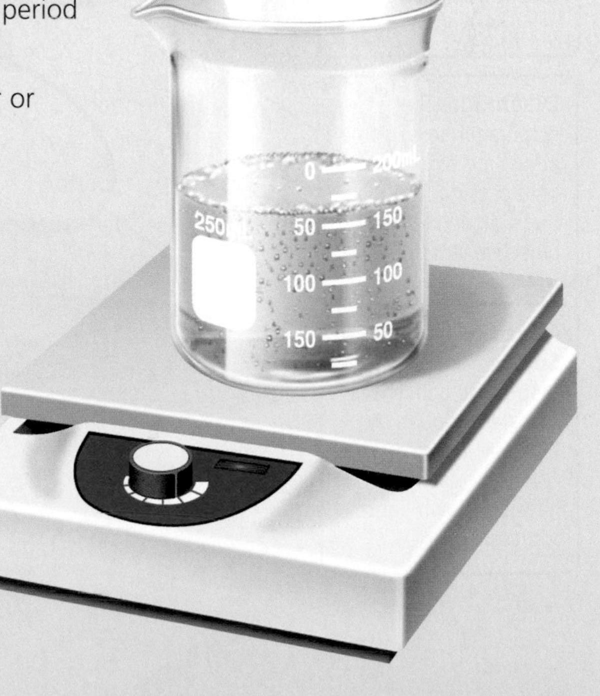

Microscope

Scientists use microscopes to see very small objects that cannot easily be seen with the eye alone. A microscope magnifies the image of an object so that small details may be observed. A microscope that you may use can magnify an object 400 times—the object will appear 400 times larger than its actual size.

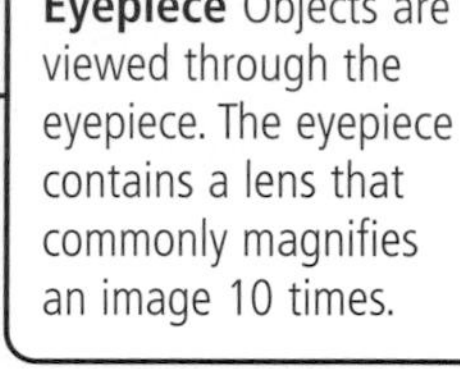

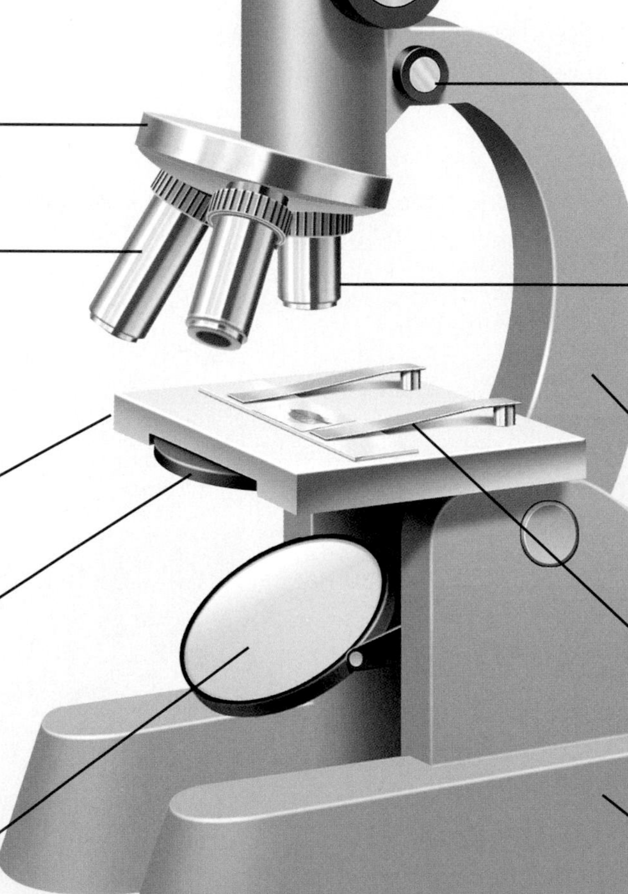
Eyepiece Objects are viewed through the eyepiece. The eyepiece contains a lens that commonly magnifies an image 10 times.
Body The body separates the lens in the eyepiece from the objective lenses below.
Coarse Adjustment This knob is used to focus the image of an object when it is viewed through the low-power lens.
Nosepiece The nosepiece holds the objective lenses above the stage and rotates so that all lenses may be used.
Fine Adjustment This knob is used to focus the image of an object when it is viewed through the high-power lens.
High-Power Objective Lens This is the largest lens on the nosepiece. It magnifies an image approximately 40 times.
Low-Power Objective Lens This is the smallest lens on the nosepiece. It magnifies an image approximately 10 times.
Stage The stage supports the object being viewed.
Arm The arm supports the body above the stage. Always carry a microscope by the arm and base.
Diaphragm The diaphragm is used to adjust the amount of light passing through the slide and into an objective lens.
Stage Clip The stage clip holds a slide in place on the stage.
Mirror or Light Source Some microscopes use light that is reflected through the stage by a mirror. Other microscopes have their own light sources.
Base The base supports the microscope.

VIEWING AN OBJECT

1. Use the coarse adjustment knob to raise the body tube.
2. Adjust the diaphragm so that you can see a bright circle of light through the eyepiece.
3. Place the object or slide on the stage. Be sure that it is centered over the hole in the stage.
4. Turn the nosepiece to click the low-power lens into place.
5. Using the coarse adjustment knob, slowly lower the lens and focus on the specimen being viewed. Be sure not to touch the slide or object with the lens.
6. When switching from the low-power lens to the high-power lens, first raise the body tube with the coarse adjustment knob so that the high-power lens will not hit the slide.
7. Turn the nosepiece to click the high-power lens into place.
8. Use the fine adjustment knob to focus on the specimen being viewed. Again, be sure not to touch the slide or object with the lens.

MAKING A SLIDE, OR WET MOUNT

Place the specimen in the center of a clean slide.

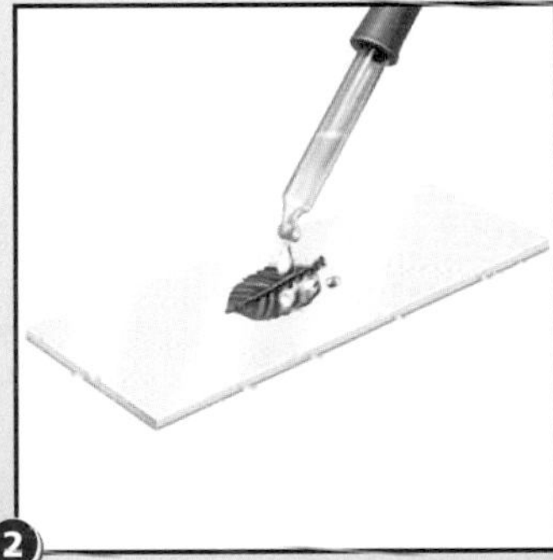

Place a drop of water on the specimen.

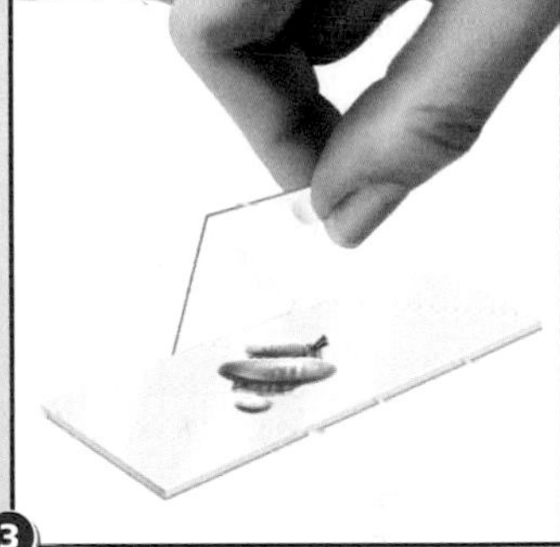

Place a cover slip on the slide. Put one edge of the cover slip into the drop of water and slowly lower it over the specimen.

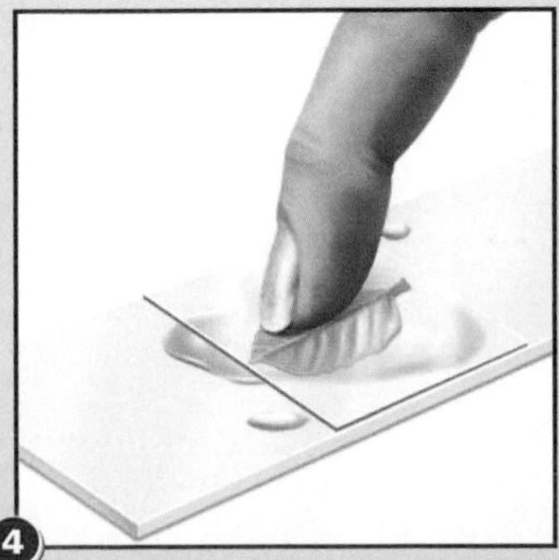

Remove any air bubbles from under the cover slip by gently tapping the cover slip.

Dry any excess water before placing the slide on the microscope stage for viewing.

LAB HANDBOOK

Spring Scale (Force Meter)

- Use a spring scale to measure a force pulling on the scale.
- Use a spring scale to measure the force of gravity exerted on an object by Earth.
- To measure a force accurately, a spring scale must be zeroed before it is used. The scale is zeroed when no weight is attached and the indicator is positioned at zero.
- Do not attach a weight that is either too heavy or too light to a spring scale. A weight that is too heavy could break the scale or exert too great a force for the scale to measure. A weight that is too light may not exert enough force to be measured accurately.

Graduated Cylinder

- Use a graduated cylinder to measure the volume of a liquid.
- Be sure that the graduated cylinder is on a flat surface so that your measurement will be accurate.
- When reading the scale on a graduated cylinder, be sure to have your eyes at the level of the surface of the liquid.
- The surface of the liquid will be curved in the graduated cylinder. Read the volume of the liquid at the bottom of the curve, or meniscus (muh-NIHS-kuhs).
- You can use a graduated cylinder to find the volume of a solid object by measuring the increase in a liquid's level after you add the object to the cylinder.

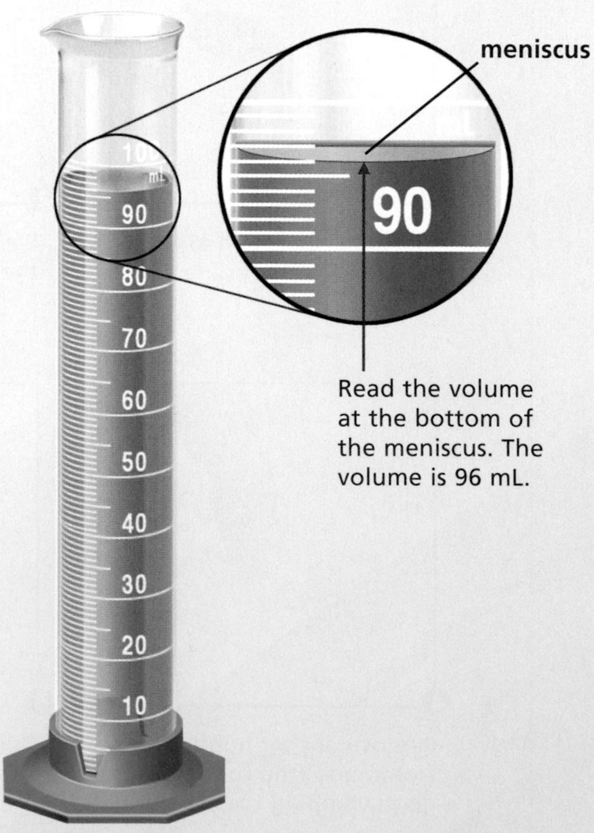

Read the volume at the bottom of the meniscus. The volume is 96 mL.

Metric Rulers

- Use metric rulers or meter sticks to measure objects' lengths.
- Do not measure an object from the end of a metric ruler or meter stick, because the end is often imperfect. Instead, measure from the 1-centimeter mark, but remember to subtract a centimeter from the apparent measurement.
- Estimate any lengths that extend between marked units. For example, if a meter stick shows centimeters but not millimeters, you can estimate the length that an object extends between centimeter marks to measure it to the nearest millimeter.
- **Controlling Variables** If you are taking repeated measurements, always measure from the same point each time. For example, if you're measuring how high two different balls bounce when dropped from the same height, measure both bounces at the same point on the balls—either the top or the bottom. Do not measure at the top of one ball and the bottom of the other.

EXAMPLE

How to Measure a Leaf

1. Lay a ruler flat on top of the leaf so that the 1-centimeter mark lines up with one end. Make sure the ruler and the leaf do not move between the time you line them up and the time you take the measurement.
2. Look straight down on the ruler so that you can see exactly how the marks line up with the other end of the leaf.
3. Estimate the length by which the leaf extends beyond a marking. For example, the leaf below extends about halfway between the 4.2-centimeter and 4.3-centimeter marks, so the apparent measurement is about 4.25 centimeters.
4. Remember to subtract 1 centimeter from your apparent measurement, since you started at the 1-centimeter mark on the ruler and not at the end. The leaf is about 3.25 centimeters long (4.25 cm – 1 cm = 3.25 cm).

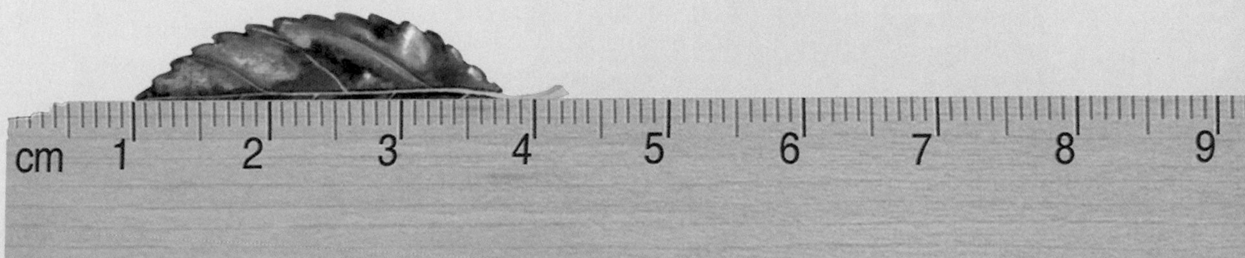

Triple-Beam Balance

This balance has a pan and three beams with sliding masses, called riders. At one end of the beams is a pointer that indicates whether the mass on the pan is equal to the masses shown on the beams.

1. Make sure the balance is zeroed before measuring the mass of an object. The balance is zeroed if the pointer is at zero when nothing is on the pan and the riders are at their zero points. Use the adjustment knob at the base of the balance to zero it.
2. Place the object to be measured on the pan.
3. Move the riders one notch at a time away from the pan. Begin with the largest rider. If moving the largest rider one notch brings the pointer below zero, begin measuring the mass of the object with the next smaller rider.
4. Change the positions of the riders until they balance the mass on the pan and the pointer is at zero. Then add the readings from the three beams to determine the mass of the object.

300 g	position of largest rider
90 g	position of middle rider
+ 3 g	position of smallest rider
393 g	mass of beaker

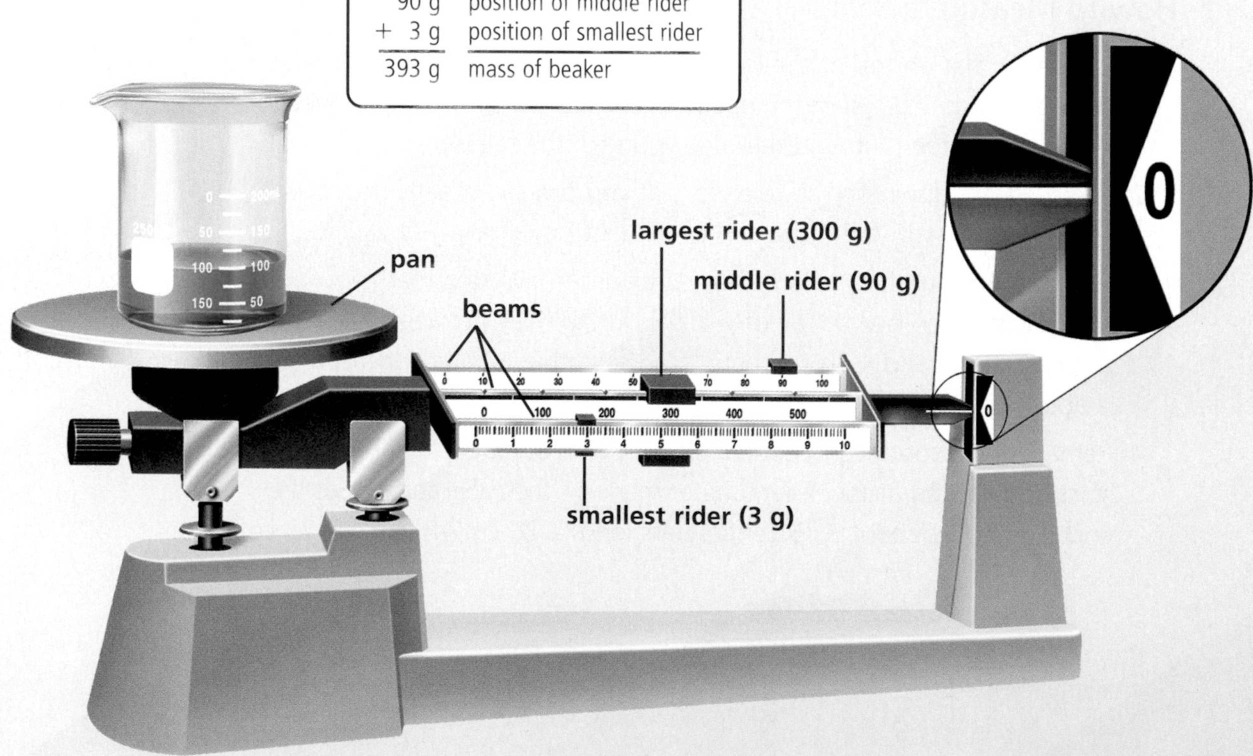

Double-Pan Balance

This type of balance has two pans. Between the pans is a pointer that indicates whether the masses on the pans are equal.

1. Make sure the balance is zeroed before measuring the mass of an object. The balance is zeroed if the pointer is at zero when there is nothing on either of the pans. Many double-pan balances have sliding knobs that can be used to zero them.
2. Place the object to be measured on one of the pans.
3. Begin adding standard masses to the other pan. Begin with the largest standard mass. If this adds too much mass to the balance, begin measuring the mass of the object with the next smaller standard mass.
4. Add standard masses until the masses on both pans are balanced and the pointer is at zero. Then add the standard masses together to determine the mass of the object being measured.

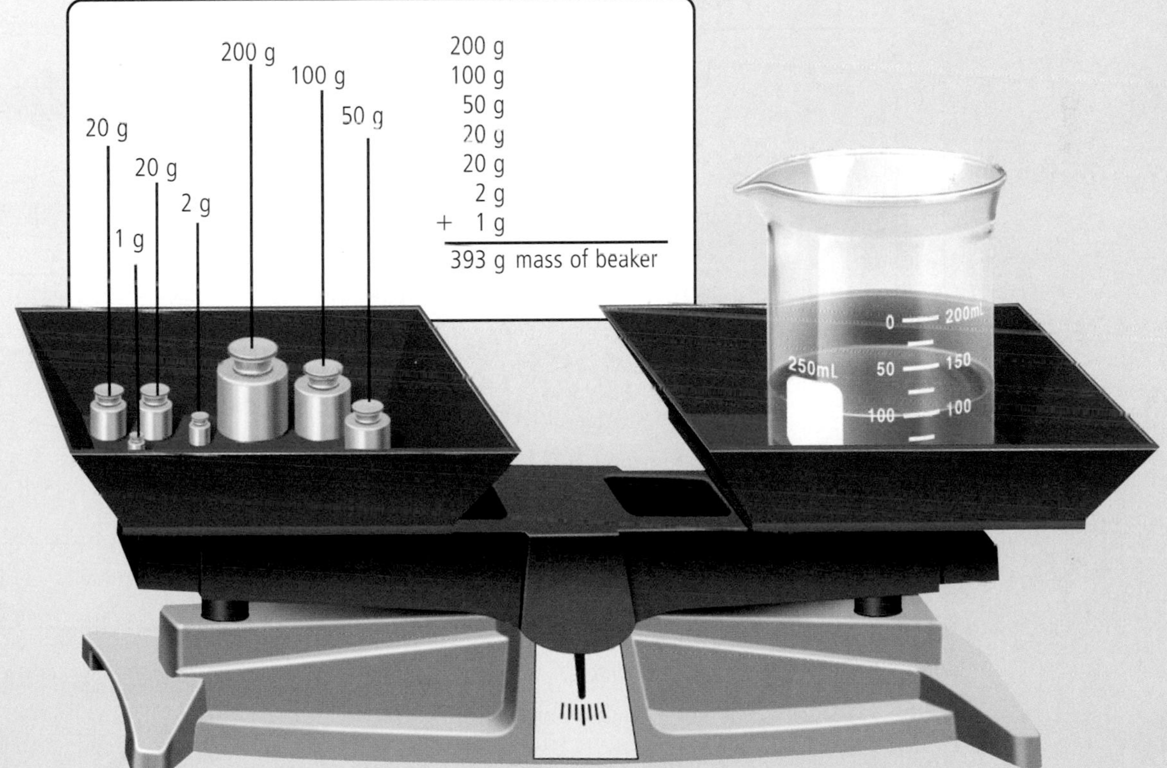

Never place chemicals or liquids directly on a pan. Instead, use the following procedure:

1. Determine the mass of an empty container, such as a beaker.
2. Pour the substance into the container, and measure the total mass of the substance and the container.
3. Subtract the mass of the empty container from the total mass to find the mass of the substance.

The Metric System and SI Units

Scientists use International System (SI) units for measurements of distance, volume, mass, and temperature. The International System is based on multiples of ten and the metric system of measurement.

Basic SI Units		
Property	**Name**	**Symbol**
length	meter	m
volume	liter	L
mass	kilogram	kg
temperature	kelvin	K

SI Prefixes		
Prefix	**Symbol**	**Multiple of 10**
kilo-	k	1000
hecto-	h	100
deca-	da	10
deci-	d	0.1 $(\frac{1}{10})$
centi-	c	0.01 $(\frac{1}{100})$
milli-	m	0.001 $(\frac{1}{1000})$

Changing Metric Units

You can change from one unit to another in the metric system by multiplying or dividing by a power of 10.

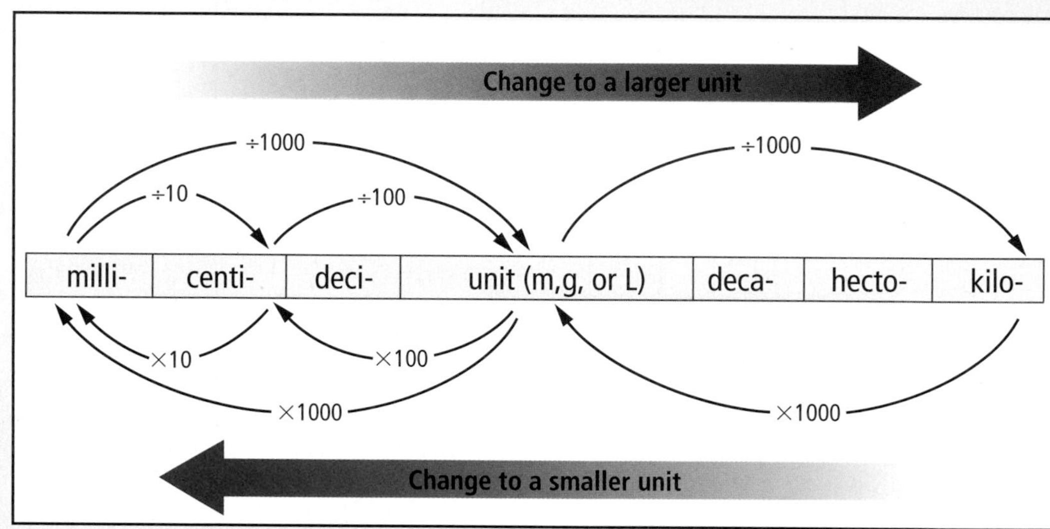

Example

Change 0.64 liters to milliliters.

(1) Decide whether to multiply or divide.

(2) Select the power of 10.

ANSWER 0.64 L = 640 mL

Change to a smaller unit by multiplying.

mL ← × 1000 — L

0.64 × 1000 = **640.**

Example

Change 23.6 grams to kilograms.

(1) Decide whether to multiply or divide.

(2) Select the power of 10.

ANSWER 23.6 g = 0.0236 kg

Change to a larger unit by dividing.

g — ÷ 1000 → kg

23.6 ÷ 1000 = **0.0236**

LAB HANDBOOK

Temperature Conversions

Even though the kelvin is the SI base unit of temperature, the degree Celsius will be the unit you use most often in your science studies. The formulas below show the relationships between temperatures in degrees Fahrenheit (°F), degrees Celsius (°C), and kelvins (K).

$$°C = \frac{5}{9}(°F - 32)$$

$$°F = \frac{9}{5}°C + 32$$

$$K = °C + 273$$

See page R42 for help with using formulas.

Examples of Temperature Conversions		
Condition	**Degrees Celsius**	**Degrees Fahrenheit**
Freezing point of water	0	32
Cool day	10	50
Mild day	20	68
Warm day	30	86
Normal body temperature	37	98.6
Very hot day	40	104
Boiling point of water	100	212

LAB HANDBOOK

Converting Between SI and U.S. Customary Units

Use the chart below when you need to convert between SI units and U.S. customary units.

SI Unit	From SI to U.S. Customary			From U.S. Customary to SI		
Length	**When you know**	**multiply by**	**to find**	**When you know**	**multiply by**	**to find**
kilometer (km) = 1000 m	kilometers	0.62	miles	miles	1.61	kilometers
meter (m) = 100 cm	meters	3.28	feet	feet	0.3048	meters
centimeter (cm) = 10 mm	centimeters	0.39	inches	inches	2.54	centimeters
millimeter (mm) = 0.1 cm	millimeters	0.04	inches	inches	25.4	millimeters
Area	**When you know**	**multiply by**	**to find**	**When you know**	**multiply by**	**to find**
square kilometer (km^2)	square kilometers	0.39	square miles	square miles	2.59	square kilometers
square meter (m^2)	square meters	1.2	square yards	square yards	0.84	square meters
square centimeter (cm^2)	square centimeters	0.155	square inches	square inches	6.45	square centimeters
Volume	**When you know**	**multiply by**	**to find**	**When you know**	**multiply by**	**to find**
liter (L) = 1000 mL	liters	1.06	quarts	quarts	0.95	liters
	liters	0.26	gallons	gallons	3.79	liters
	liters	4.23	cups	cups	0.24	liters
	liters	2.12	pints	pints	0.47	liters
milliliter (mL) = 0.001 L	milliliters	0.20	teaspoons	teaspoons	4.93	milliliters
	milliliters	0.07	tablespoons	tablespoons	14.79	milliliters
	milliliters	0.03	fluid ounces	fluid ounces	29.57	milliliters
Mass	**When you know**	**multiply by**	**to find**	**When you know**	**multiply by**	**to find**
kilogram (kg) = 1000 g	kilograms	2.2	pounds	pounds	0.45	kilograms
gram (g) = 1000 mg	grams	0.035	ounces	ounces	28.35	grams

Precision and Accuracy

When you do an experiment, it is important that your methods, observations, and data be both precise and accurate.

low precision

precision, but not accuracy

precision and accuracy

Precision

In science, **precision** is the exactness and consistency of measurements. For example, measurements made with a ruler that has both centimeter and millimeter markings would be more precise than measurements made with a ruler that has only centimeter markings. Another indicator of precision is the care taken to make sure that methods and observations are as exact and consistent as possible. Every time a particular experiment is done, the same procedure should be used. Precision is necessary because experiments are repeated several times and if the procedure changes, the results will change.

EXAMPLE

Suppose you are measuring temperatures over a two-week period. Your precision will be greater if you measure each temperature at the same place, at the same time of day, and with the same thermometer than if you change any of these factors from one day to the next.

Accuracy

In science, it is possible to be precise but not accurate. **Accuracy** depends on the difference between a measurement and an actual value. The smaller the difference, the more accurate the measurement.

EXAMPLE

Suppose you look at a stream and estimate that it is about 1 meter wide at a particular place. You decide to check your estimate by measuring the stream with a meter stick, and you determine that the stream is 1.32 meters wide. However, because it is hard to measure the width of a stream with a meter stick, it turns out that you didn't do a very good job. The stream is actually 1.14 meters wide. Therefore, even though your estimate was less precise than your measurement, your estimate was actually more accurate.

Making Data Tables and Graphs

Data tables and graphs are useful tools for both recording and communicating scientific data.

Making Data Tables

You can use a **data table** to organize and record the measurements that you make. Some examples of information that might be recorded in data tables are frequencies, times, and amounts.

EXAMPLE

Suppose you are investigating photosynthesis in two elodea plants. One sits in direct sunlight, and the other sits in a dimly lit room. You measure the rate of photosynthesis by counting the number of bubbles in the jar every ten minutes.

1. Title and number your data table.
2. Decide how you will organize the table into columns and rows.
3. Any units, such as seconds or degrees, should be included in column headings, not in the individual cells.

Table 1. Number of Bubbles from Elodea

Time (min)	Sunlight	Dim Light
0	0	0
10	15	5
20	25	8
30	32	7
40	41	10
50	47	9
60	42	9

Always number and title data tables.

The data in the table above could also be organized in a different way.

Table 1. Number of Bubbles from Elodea

Light Condition	Time (min)						
	0	10	20	30	40	50	60
Sunlight	0	15	25	32	41	47	42
Dim light	0	5	8	7	10	9	9

Put units in column heading.

LAB HANDBOOK

Making Line Graphs

You can use a **line graph** to show a relationship between variables. Line graphs are particularly useful for showing changes in variables over time.

EXAMPLE

Suppose you are interested in graphing temperature data that you collected over the course of a day.

Table 1. Outside Temperature During the Day on March 7

	Time of Day						
	7:00 A.M.	9:00 A.M.	11:00 A.M.	1:00 P.M.	3:00 P.M.	5:00 P.M.	7:00 P.M.
Temp (°C)	8	9	11	14	12	10	6

1. Use the vertical axis of your line graph for the variable that you are measuring—temperature.
2. Choose scales for both the horizontal axis and the vertical axis of the graph. You should have two points more than you need on the vertical axis, and the horizontal axis should be long enough for all of the data points to fit.
3. Draw and label each axis.
4. Graph each value. First find the appropriate point on the scale of the horizontal axis. Imagine a line that rises vertically from that place on the scale. Then find the corresponding value on the vertical axis, and imagine a line that moves horizontally from that value. The point where these two imaginary lines intersect is where the value should be plotted.
5. Connect the points with straight lines.

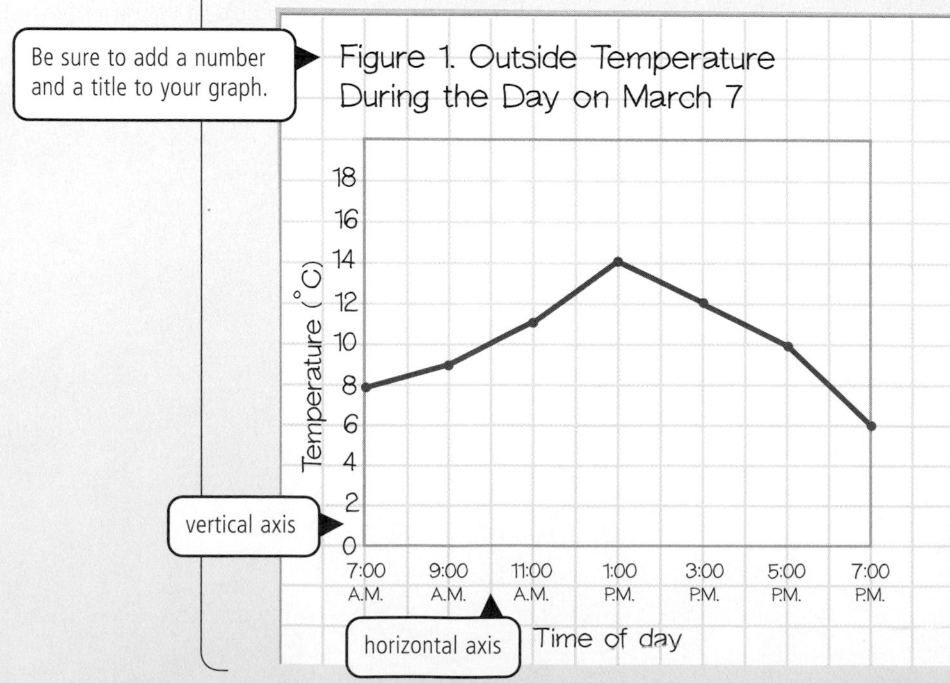

LAB HANDBOOK

Making Circle Graphs

You can use a **circle graph,** sometimes called a pie chart, to represent data as parts of a circle. Circle graphs are used only when the data can be expressed as percentages of a whole. The entire circle shown in a circle graph is equal to 100 percent of the data.

EXAMPLE

Suppose you identified the species of each mature tree growing in a small wooded area. You organized your data in a table, but you also want to show the data in a circle graph.

1. To begin, find the total number of mature trees.

   $56 + 34 + 22 + 10 + 28 = 150$

2. To find the degree measure for each sector of the circle, write a fraction comparing the number of each tree species with the total number of trees. Then multiply the fraction by 360°.

   Oak: $\frac{56}{150} \times 360° = 134.4°$

3. Draw a circle. Use a protractor to draw the angle for each sector of the graph.
4. Color and label each sector of the graph.
5. Give the graph a number and title.

Table 1. Tree Species in Wooded Area

Species	Number of Specimens
Oak	56
Maple	34
Birch	22
Willow	10
Pine	28

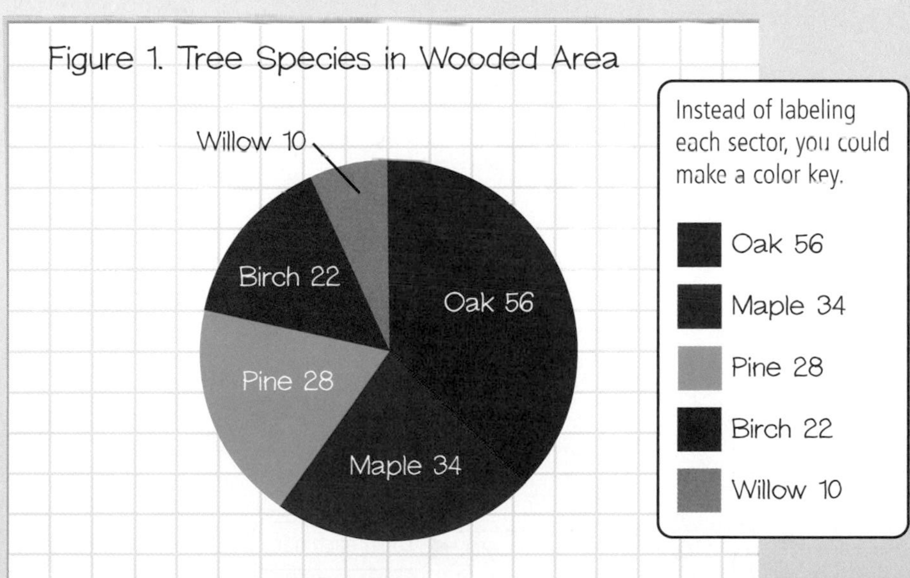

Figure 1. Tree Species in Wooded Area

LAB HANDBOOK

Bar Graph

A **bar graph** is a type of graph in which the lengths of the bars are used to represent and compare data. A numerical scale is used to determine the lengths of the bars.

EXAMPLE

To determine the effect of water on seed sprouting, three cups were filled with sand, and ten seeds were planted in each. Different amounts of water were added to each cup over a three-day period.

Table 1. Effect of Water on Seed Sprouting

Daily Amount of Water (mL)	Number of Seeds That Sprouted After 3 Days in Sand
0	1
10	4
20	8

1. Choose a numerical scale. The greatest value is 8, so the end of the scale should have a value greater than 8, such as 10. Use equal increments along the scale, such as increments of 2.
2. Draw and label the axes. Mark intervals on the vertical axis according to the scale you chose.
3. Draw a bar for each data value. Use the scale to decide how long to make each bar.

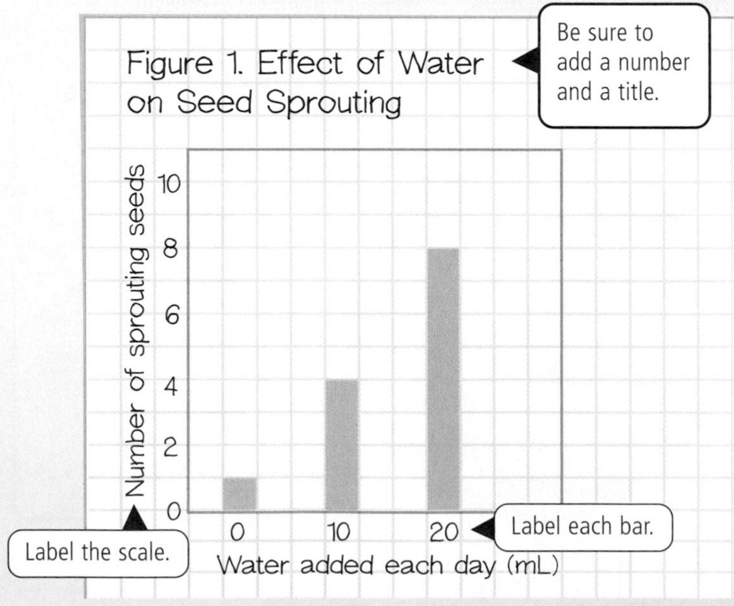

Double Bar Graph

A **double bar graph** is a bar graph that shows two sets of data. The two bars for each measurement are drawn next to each other.

EXAMPLE

The seed-sprouting experiment was done using both sand and potting soil. The data for sand and potting soil can be plotted on one graph.

1. Draw one set of bars, using the data for sand, as shown below.
2. Draw bars for the potting-soil data next to the bars for the sand data. Shade them a different color. Add a key.

Table 2. Effect of Water and Soil on Seed Sprouting

Daily Amount of Water (mL)	Number of Seeds That Sprouted After 3 Days in Sand	Number of Seeds That Sprouted After 3 Days in Potting Soil
0	1	2
10	4	5
20	8	9

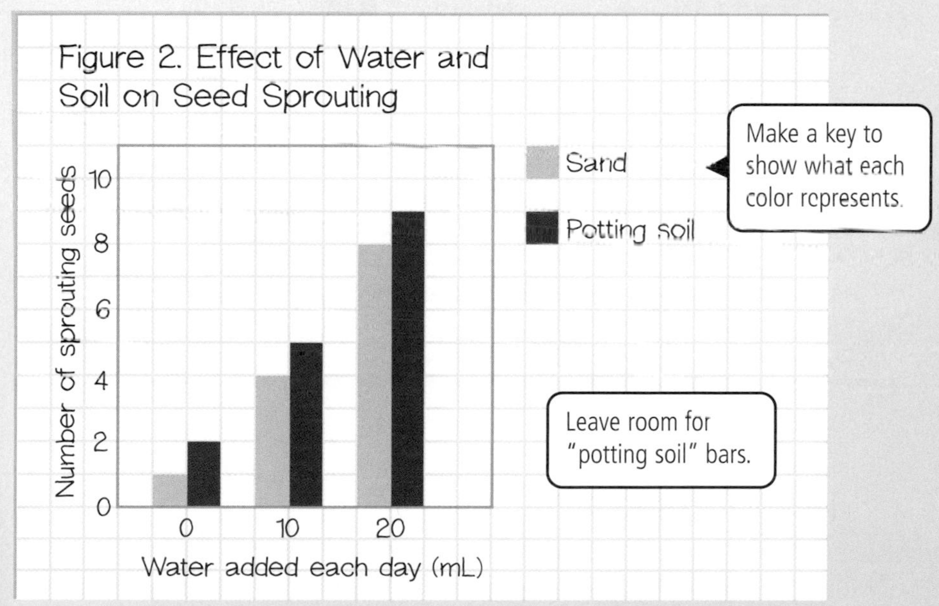

LAB HANDBOOK

Designing an Experiment

Use this section when designing or conducting an experiment.

Determining a Purpose

You can find a purpose for an experiment by doing research, by examining the results of a previous experiment, or by observing the world around you. An **experiment** is an organized procedure to study something under controlled conditions.

Don't forget to learn as much as possible about your topic before you begin.

1. Write the purpose of your experiment as a question or problem that you want to investigate.
2. Write down research questions and begin searching for information that will help you design an experiment. Consult the library, the Internet, and other people as you conduct your research.

EXAMPLE

Middle school students observed an odor near the lake by their school. They also noticed that the water on the side of the lake near the school was greener than the water on the other side of the lake. The students did some research to learn more about their observations. They discovered that the odor and green color in the lake came from algae. They also discovered that a new fertilizer was being used on a field nearby. The students inferred that the use of the fertilizer might be related to the presence of the algae and designed a controlled experiment to find out whether they were right.

Problem

How does fertilizer affect the presence of algae in a lake?

Research Questions

- Have other experiments been done on this problem? If so, what did those experiments show?
- What kind of fertilizer is used on the field? How much?
- How do algae grow?
- How do people measure algae?
- Can fertilizer and algae be used safely in a lab? How?

Research

As you research, you may find a topic that is more interesting to you than your original topic, or learn that a procedure you wanted to use is not practical or safe. It is OK to change your purpose as you research.

Writing a Hypothesis

A **hypothesis** is a tentative explanation for an observation or scientific problem that can be tested by further investigation. You can write your hypothesis in the form of an "If . . . , then . . . , because . . ." statement.

Hypothesis

If the amount of fertilizer in lake water is increased, then the amount of algae will also increase, because fertilizers provide nutrients that algae need to grow.

Hypotheses
For help with hypotheses, refer to page R3.

Determining Materials

Make a list of all the materials you will need to do your experiment. Be specific, especially if someone else is helping you obtain the materials. Try to think of everything you will need.

Materials

- 1 large jar or container
- 4 identical smaller containers
- rubber gloves that also cover the arms
- sample of fertilizer-and-water solution
- eyedropper
- clear plastic wrap
- scissors
- masking tape
- marker
- ruler

Determining Variables and Constants

EXPERIMENTAL GROUP AND CONTROL GROUP

An experiment to determine how two factors are related always has two groups—a control group and an experimental group.

1. Design an experimental group. Include as many trials as possible in the experimental group in order to obtain reliable results.
2. Design a control group that is the same as the experimental group in every way possible, except for the factor you wish to test.

Experimental Group: two containers of lake water with one drop of fertilizer solution added to each
Control Group: two containers of lake water with no fertilizer solution added

Go back to your materials list and make sure you have enough items listed to cover both your experimental group and your control group.

LAB HANDBOOK

VARIABLES AND CONSTANTS

Identify the variables and constants in your experiment. In a controlled experiment, a **variable** is any factor that can change. **Constants** are all of the factors that are the same in both the experimental group and the control group.

1. Read your hypothesis. The **independent variable** is the factor that you wish to test and that is manipulated or changed so that it can be tested. The independent variable is expressed in your hypothesis after the word *if*. Identify the independent variable in your laboratory report.
2. The **dependent variable** is the factor that you measure to gather results. It is expressed in your hypothesis after the word *then*. Identify the dependent variable in your laboratory report.

Hypothesis
If the amount of fertilizer in lake water is increased, then the amount of algae will also increase, because fertilizers provide nutrients that algae need to grow.

Table 1. Variables and Constants in Algae Experiment

Independent Variable	Dependent Variable	Constants
Amount of fertilizer in lake water	Amount of algae that grow	• Where the lake water is obtained • Type of container used • Light and temperature conditions where water will be stored

Set up your experiment so that you will test only one variable.

MEASURING THE DEPENDENT VARIABLE

Before starting your experiment, you need to define how you will measure the dependent variable. An **operational definition** is a description of the one particular way in which you will measure the dependent variable.

Your operational definition is important for several reasons. First, in any experiment there are several ways in which a dependent variable can be measured. Second, the procedure of the experiment depends on how you decide to measure the dependent variable. Third, your operational definition makes it possible for other people to evaluate and build on your experiment.

EXAMPLE 1

An operational definition of a dependent variable can be qualitative. That is, your measurement of the dependent variable can simply be an observation of whether a change occurs as a result of a change in the independent variable. This type of operational definition can be thought of as a "yes or no" measurement.

Table 2. Qualitative Operational Definition of Algae Growth

Independent Variable	Dependent Variable	Operational Definition
Amount of fertilizer in lake water	Amount of algae that grow	Algae grow in lake water

A qualitative measurement of a dependent variable is often easy to make and record. However, this type of information does not provide a great deal of detail in your experimental results.

EXAMPLE 2

An operational definition of a dependent variable can be quantitative. That is, your measurement of the dependent variable can be a number that shows how much change occurs as a result of a change in the independent variable.

Table 3. Quantitative Operational Definition of Algae Growth

Independent Variable	Dependent Variable	Operational Definition
Amount of fertilizer in lake water	Amount of algae that grow	Diameter of largest algal growth (in mm)

A quantitative measurement of a dependent variable can be more difficult to make and analyze than a qualitative measurement. However, this type of data provides much more information about your experiment and is often more useful.

Writing a Procedure

Write each step of your procedure. Start each step with a verb, or action word, and keep the steps short. Your procedure should be clear enough for someone else to use as instructions for repeating your experiment.

If necessary, go back to your materials list and add any materials that you left out.

Procedure

1. Put on your gloves. Use the large container to obtain a sample of lake water.

2. Divide the sample of lake water equally among the four smaller containers.

Controlling Variables
The same amount of fertilizer solution must be added to two of the four containers.

3. Use the eyedropper to add one drop of fertilizer solution to two of the containers.

4. Use the masking tape and the marker to label the containers with your initials, the date, and the identifiers "Jar 1 with Fertilizer," "Jar 2 with Fertilizer," "Jar 1 without Fertilizer," and "Jar 2 without Fertilizer."

5. Cover the containers with clear plastic wrap. Use the scissors to punch ten holes in each of the covers.

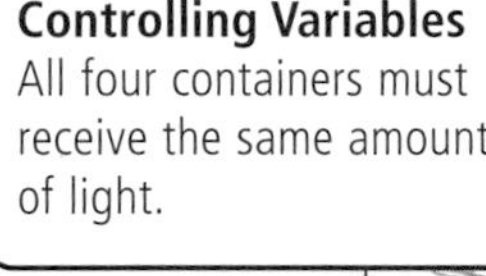

Controlling Variables
All four containers must receive the same amount of light.

6. Place all four containers on a window ledge. Make sure that they all receive the same amount of light.

7. Observe the containers every day for one week.

8. Use the ruler to measure the diameter of the largest clump of algae in each container, and record your measurements daily.

LAB HANDBOOK

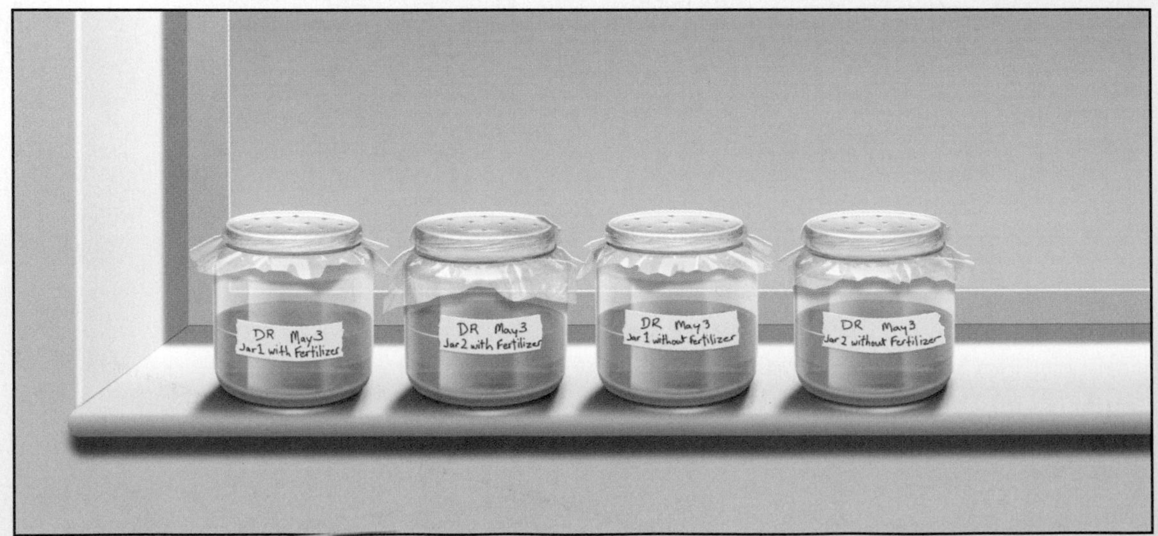

Recording Observations

Once you have obtained all of your materials and your procedure has been approved, you can begin making experimental observations. Gather both quantitative and qualitative data. If something goes wrong during your procedure, make sure you record that too.

Observations
For help with making qualitative and quantitative observations, refer to page R2.

For more examples of data tables, see page R23.

Table 4. Fertilizer and Algae Growth

	Experimental Group		Control Group		
Date and Time	Jar 1 with Fertilizer (diameter of algae in mm)	Jar 2 with Fertilizer (diameter of algae in mm)	Jar 1 without Fertilizer (diameter of algae in mm)	Jar 2 without Fertilizer (diameter of algae in mm)	Observations
5/3 4:00 P.M.	0	0	0	0	condensation in all containers
5/4 4:00 P.M.	0	3	0	0	tiny green blobs in jar 2 with fertilizer
5/5 4:15 P.M.	4	5	0	3	green blobs in jars 1 and 2 with fertilizer and jar 2 without fertilizer
5/6 4:00 P.M.	5	6	0	4	water light green in jar 2 with fertilizer
5/7 4:00 P.M.	8	10	0	6	water light green in jars 1 and 2 with fertilizer and in jar 2 without fertilizer
5/8 3:30 P.M.	10	18	0	6	cover off jar 2 with fertilizer
5/9 3:30 P.M.	14	23	0	8	drew sketches of each container

Notice that on the sixth day, the observer found that the cover was off one of the containers. It is important to record observations of unintended factors because they might affect the results of the experiment.

Drawings of Samples Viewed Under Microscope on 5/9 at 100x

Use technology, such as a microscope, to help you make observations when possible.

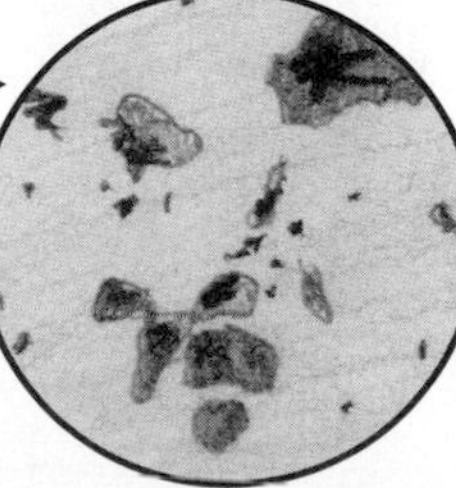
Jar 1 with Fertilizer

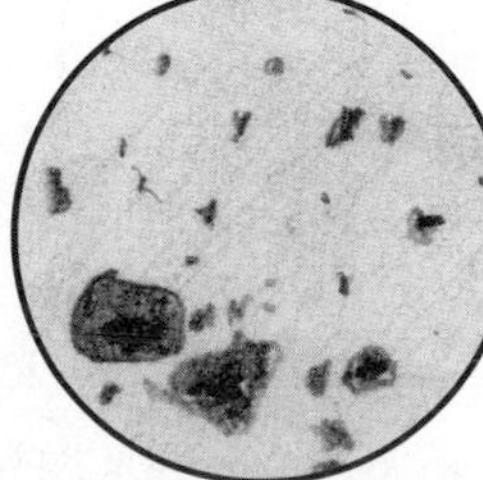
Jar 2 with Fertilizer

Jar 1 without Fertilizer

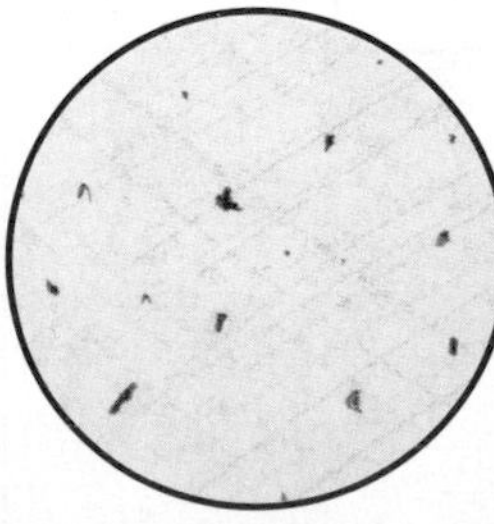
Jar 2 without Fertilizer

LAB HANDBOOK

Summarizing Results

To summarize your data, look at all of your observations together. Look for meaningful ways to present your observations. For example, you might average your data or make a graph to look for patterns. When possible, use spreadsheet software to help you analyze and present your data. The two graphs below show the same data.

EXAMPLE 1

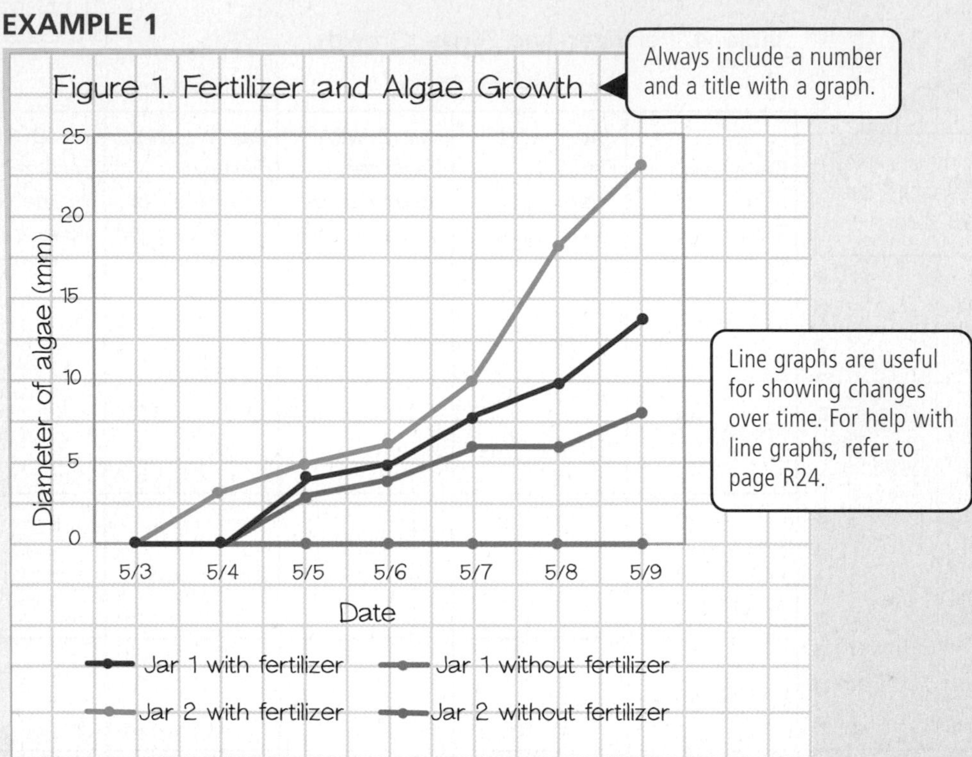

Always include a number and a title with a graph.

Line graphs are useful for showing changes over time. For help with line graphs, refer to page R24.

EXAMPLE 2

Bar graphs are useful for comparing different data sets. This bar graph has four bars for each day. Another way to present the data would be to calculate averages for the tests and the controls, and to show one test bar and one control bar for each day.

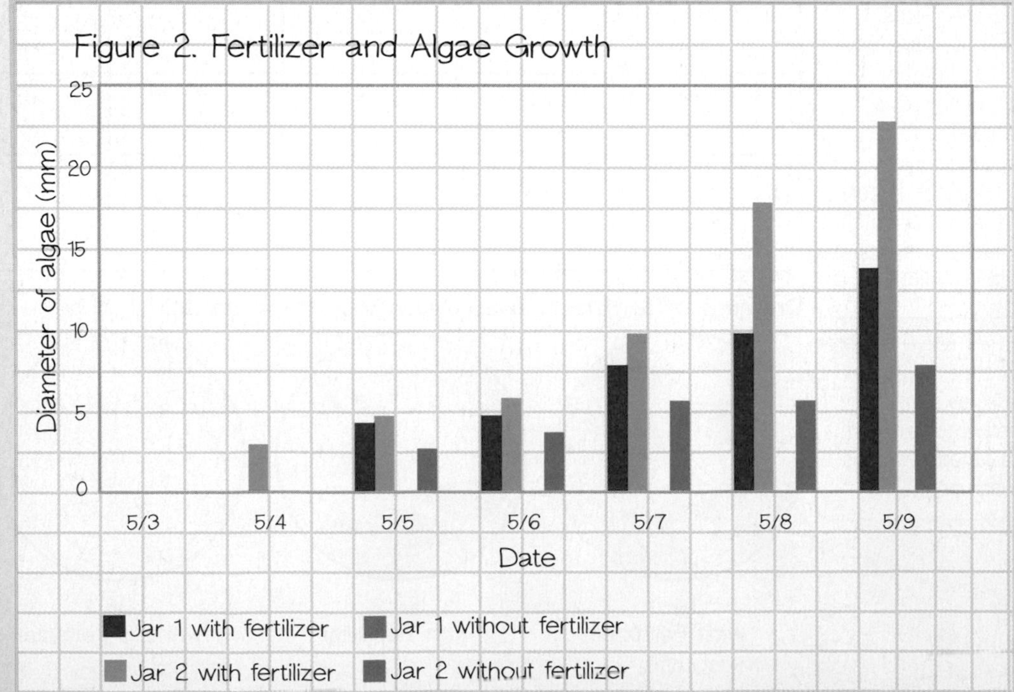

Drawing Conclusions

RESULTS AND INFERENCES

To draw conclusions from your experiment, first write your results. Then compare your results with your hypothesis. Do your results support your hypothesis? Be careful not to make inferences about factors that you did not test.

For help with making inferences, see page R4.

Results and Inferences

The results of my experiment show that more algae grew in lake water to which fertilizer had been added than in lake water to which no fertilizer had been added. My hypothesis was supported. I infer that it is possible that the growth of algae in the lake was caused by the fertilizer used on the field.

Notice that you cannot conclude from this experiment that the presence of algae in the lake was due only to the fertilizer.

QUESTIONS FOR FURTHER RESEARCH

Write a list of questions for further research and investigation. Your ideas may lead you to new experiments and discoveries.

Questions for Further Research

- What is the connection between the amount of fertilizer and algae growth?
- How do different brands of fertilizer affect algae growth?
- How would algae growth in the lake be affected if no fertilizer were used on the field?
- How do algae affect the lake and the other life in and around it?
- How does fertilizer affect the lake and the life in and around it?
- If fertilizer is getting into the lake, how is it getting there?

Describing a Set of Data

Means, medians, modes, and ranges are important math tools for describing data sets such as the following widths of fossilized clamshells.

13 mm 25 mm 14 mm 21 mm 16 mm 23 mm 14 mm

Mean

The **mean** of a data set is the sum of the values divided by the number of values.

Example

To find the mean of the clamshell data, add the values and then divide the sum by the number of values.

$$\frac{13\text{ mm} + 25\text{ mm} + 14\text{ mm} + 21\text{ mm} + 16\text{ mm} + 23\text{ mm} + 14\text{ mm}}{7} = \frac{126\text{ mm}}{7} = 18\text{ mm}$$

ANSWER The mean is 18 mm.

Median

The **median** of a data set is the middle value when the values are written in numerical order. If a data set has an even number of values, the median is the mean of the two middle values.

Example

To find the median of the clamshell data, arrange the values in order from least to greatest. The median is the middle value.

13 mm 14 mm 14 mm 16 mm 21 mm 23 mm 25 mm

ANSWER The median is 16 mm.

Mode

The **mode** of a data set is the value that occurs most often.

Example

To find the mode of the clamshell data, arrange the values in order from least to greatest and determine the value that occurs most often.

13 mm 14 mm 14 mm 16 mm 21 mm 23 mm 25 mm

ANSWER The mode is 14 mm.

A data set can have more than one mode or no mode. For example, the following data set has modes of 2 mm and 4 mm:

2 mm 2 mm 3 mm 4 mm 4 mm

The data set below has no mode, because no value occurs more often than any other.

2 mm 3 mm 4 mm 5 mm

Range

The **range** of a data set is the difference between the greatest value and the least value.

Example

To find the range of the clamshell data, arrange the values in order from least to greatest.

13 mm 14 mm 14 mm 16 mm 21 mm 23 mm 25 mm

Subtract the least value from the greatest value.

13 mm is the least value.
25 mm is the greatest value.

25 mm – 13 mm = 12 mm

ANSWER The range is 12 mm.

Using Ratios, Rates, and Proportions

You can use ratios and rates to compare values in data sets. You can use proportions to find unknown values.

Ratios

A **ratio** uses division to compare two values. The ratio of a value *a* to a nonzero value *b* can be written as $\frac{a}{b}$.

Example

The height of one plant is 8 centimeters. The height of another plant is 6 centimeters. To find the ratio of the height of the first plant to the height of the second plant, write a fraction and simplify it.

$$\frac{8 \text{ cm}}{6 \text{ cm}} = \frac{4 \times \overset{1}{\cancel{2}}}{3 \times \underset{1}{\cancel{2}}} = \frac{4}{3}$$

ANSWER The ratio of the plant heights is $\frac{4}{3}$.

You can also write the ratio $\frac{a}{b}$ as "a to b" or as $a{:}b$. For example, you can write the ratio of the plant heights as "4 to 3" or as 4:3.

Rates

A **rate** is a ratio of two values expressed in different units. A unit rate is a rate with a denominator of 1 unit.

Example

A plant grew 6 centimeters in 2 days. The plant's rate of growth was $\frac{6 \text{ cm}}{2 \text{ days}}$. To describe the plant's growth in centimeters per day, write a unit rate.

Divide numerator and denominator by 2: $\frac{6 \text{ cm}}{2 \text{ days}} = \frac{6 \text{ cm} \div 2}{2 \text{ days} \div 2}$

Simplify: $= \frac{3 \text{ cm}}{1 \text{ day}}$

You divide 2 days by 2 to get 1 day, so divide 6 cm by 2 also.

ANSWER The plant's rate of growth is 3 centimeters per day.

Proportions

A **proportion** is an equation stating that two ratios are equivalent. To solve for an unknown value in a proportion, you can use cross products.

Example

If a plant grew 6 centimeters in 2 days, how many centimeters would it grow in 3 days (if its rate of growth is constant)?

Write a proportion: $\frac{6\text{ cm}}{2\text{ days}} = \frac{x}{3\text{ days}}$

Set cross products: $6\text{ cm} \cdot 3 = 2x$

Multiply 6 and 3: $18\text{ cm} = 2x$

Divide each side by 2: $\frac{18\text{ cm}}{2} = \frac{2x}{2}$

Simplify: $9\text{ cm} = x$

ANSWER The plant would grow 9 centimeters in 3 days.

Using Decimals, Fractions, and Percents

Decimals, fractions, and percentages are all ways of recording and representing data.

Decimals

A **decimal** is a number that is written in the base-ten place value system, in which a decimal point separates the ones and tenths digits. The values of each place is ten times that of the place to its right.

Example

A caterpillar traveled from point *A* to point *C* along the path shown.

A — 36.9 cm — B — 52.4 cm — C

ADDING DECIMALS To find the total distance traveled by the caterpillar, add the distance from *A* to *B* and the distance from *B* to *C*. Begin by lining up the decimal points. Then add the figures as you would whole numbers and bring down the decimal point.

$$\begin{array}{r} 36.9\text{ cm} \\ +\ 52.4\text{ cm} \\ \hline 89.3\text{ cm} \end{array}$$

ANSWER The caterpillar traveled a total distance of 89.3 centimeters.

MATH HANDBOOK

Example *continued*

SUBTRACTING DECIMALS To find how much farther the caterpillar traveled on the second leg of the journey, subtract the distance from *A* to *B* from the distance from *B* to *C*.

$$\begin{array}{r} 52.4 \text{ cm} \\ -\ 36.9 \text{ cm} \\ \hline 15.5 \text{ cm} \end{array}$$

ANSWER The caterpillar traveled 15.5 centimeters farther on the second leg of the journey.

Example

A caterpillar is traveling from point *D* to point *F* along the path shown. The caterpillar travels at a speed of 9.6 centimeters per minute.

MULTIPLYING DECIMALS You can multiply decimals as you would whole numbers. The number of decimal places in the product is equal to the sum of the number of decimal places in the factors.

For instance, suppose it takes the caterpillar 1.5 minutes to go from *D* to *E*. To find the distance from *D* to *E*, multiply the caterpillar's speed by the time it took.

$$\begin{array}{r} 9.6 \\ \times\ 1.5 \\ \hline 480 \\ 96 \\ \hline 14.40 \end{array} \qquad \begin{array}{rl} 1 & \text{decimal place} \\ +\ 1 & \text{decimal place} \\ \hline & \\ & \\ 2 & \text{decimal places} \end{array}$$

Align as shown.

ANSWER The distance from *D* to *E* is 14.4 centimeters.

DIVIDING DECIMALS When you divide by a decimal, move the decimal points the same number of places in the divisor and the dividend to make the divisor a whole number.

For instance, to find the time it will take the caterpillar to travel from *E* to *F*, divide the distance from *E* to *F* by the caterpillar's speed.

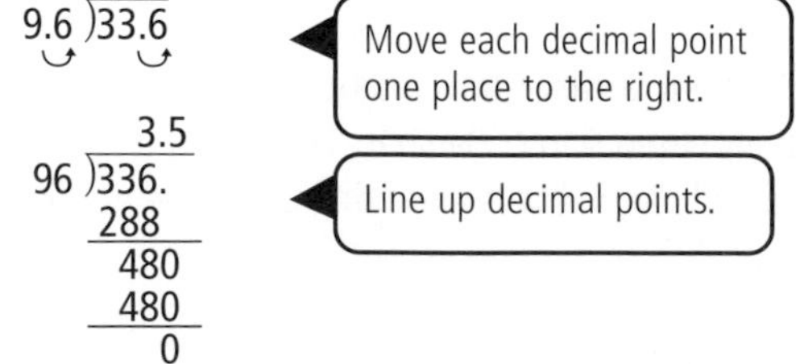

9.6)33.6
Move each decimal point one place to the right.
3.5
96)336.
288
480
480
0
Line up decimal points.

ANSWER The caterpillar will travel from *E* to *F* in 3.5 minutes.

MATH HANDBOOK

Fractions

A **fraction** is a number in the form $\frac{a}{b}$, where *b* is not equal to 0. A fraction is in **simplest form** if its numerator and denominator have a greatest common factor (GCF) of 1. To simplify a fraction, divide its numerator and denominator by their GCF.

Example

A caterpillar is 40 millimeters long. The head of the caterpillar is 6 millimeters long. To compare the length of the caterpillar's head with the caterpillar's total length, you can write and simplify a fraction that expresses the ratio of the two lengths.

Write the ratio of the two lengths: $\frac{\text{Length of head}}{\text{Total length}} = \frac{6 \text{ mm}}{40 \text{ mm}}$

Write numerator and denominator as products of numbers and the GCF: $= \frac{3 \times 2}{20 \times 2}$

Divide numerator and denominator by the GCF: $= \frac{3 \times \cancel{2}^{1}}{20 \times \cancel{2}_{1}}$

Simplify: $= \frac{3}{20}$

ANSWER In simplest form, the ratio of the lengths is $\frac{3}{20}$.

Percents

A **percent** is a ratio that compares a number to 100. The word *percent* means "per hundred" or "out of 100." The symbol for *percent* is %.

For instance, suppose 43 out of 100 caterpillars are female. You can represent this ratio as a percent, a decimal, or a fraction.

Percent	Decimal	Fraction
43%	0.43	$\frac{43}{100}$

Example

In the preceding example, the ratio of the length of the caterpillar's head to the caterpillar's total length is $\frac{3}{20}$. To write this ratio as a percent, write an equivalent fraction that has a denominator of 100.

Multiply numerator and denominator by 5: $\frac{3}{20} = \frac{3 \times 5}{20 \times 5}$

$= \frac{15}{100}$

Write as a percent: $= 15\%$

ANSWER The caterpillar's head represents 15 percent of its total length.

MATH HANDBOOK

Using Formulas

A **formula** is an equation that shows the general relationship between two or more quantities.

In science, a formula often has a word form and a symbolic form. The formula below expresses Ohm's law.

Word Form	**Symbolic Form**
$\text{Current} = \dfrac{\text{voltage}}{\text{resistance}}$	$I = \dfrac{V}{R}$

The term *variable* is also used in science to refer to a factor that can change during an experiment.

In this formula, *I*, *V*, and *R* are variables. A mathematical **variable** is a symbol or letter that is used to represent one or more numbers.

Example

Suppose that you measure a voltage of 1.5 volts and a resistance of 15 ohms. You can use the formula for Ohm's law to find the current in amperes.

Write the formula for Ohm's law: $I = \dfrac{V}{R}$

***Substitute 1.5 volts for* V *and 15 ohms for* R:** $I = \dfrac{1.5 \text{ volts}}{15 \text{ ohms}}$

Simplify: $I = 0.1 \text{ amp}$

ANSWER The current is 0.1 ampere.

If you know the values of all variables but one in a formula, you can solve for the value of the unknown variable. For instance, Ohm's law can be used to find a voltage if you know the current and the resistance.

Example

Suppose that you know that a current is 0.2 amperes and the resistance is 18 ohms. Use the formula for Ohm's law to find the voltage in volts.

Write the formula for Ohm's law: $I = \dfrac{V}{R}$

***Substitute 0.2 amp for* I *and 18 ohms for* R:** $0.2 \text{ amp} = \dfrac{V}{18 \text{ ohms}}$

Multiply both sides by 18 ohms: $0.2 \text{ amp} \cdot 18 \text{ ohms} = V$

Simplify: $3.6 \text{ volts} = V$

ANSWER The voltage is 3.6 volts.

MATH HANDBOOK

Finding Areas

The area of a figure is the amount of surface the figure covers.

Area is measured in square units, such as square meters (m^2) or square centimeters (cm^2). Formulas for the areas of three common geometric figures are shown below.

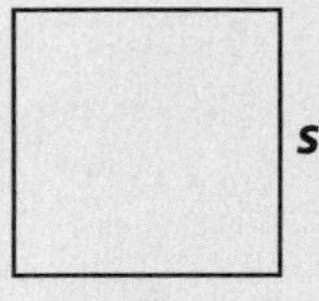

Area = (side length)^2
$A = s^2$

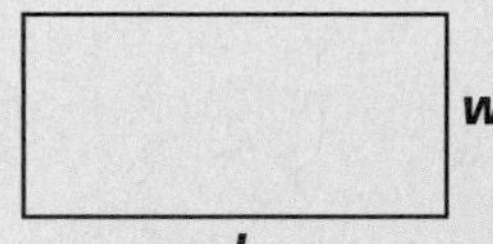

Area = length × width
$A = lw$

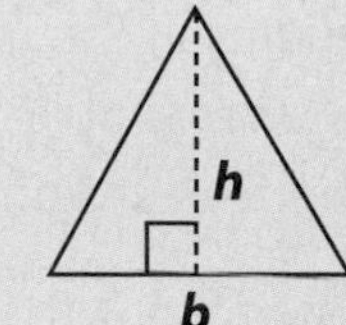

Area = $\frac{1}{2}$ × base × height
$A = \frac{1}{2}bh$

Example

Each face of a halite crystal is a square like the one shown. You can find the area of the square by using the steps below.

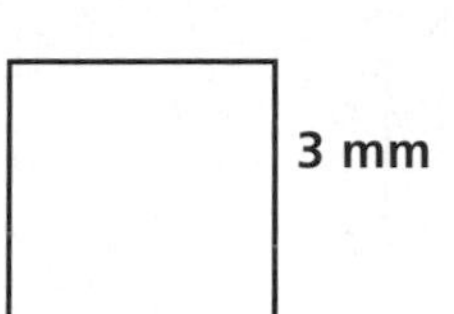

Write the formula for the area of a square: $A = s^2$

Substitute 3 mm for s: $= (3 \text{ mm})^2$

Simplify: $= 9 \text{ mm}^2$

ANSWER The area of the square is 9 square millimeters.

Finding Volumes

The volume of a solid is the amount of space contained by the solid.

Volume is measured in cubic units, such as cubic meters (m^3) or cubic centimeters (cm^3). The volume of a rectangular prism is given by the formula shown below.

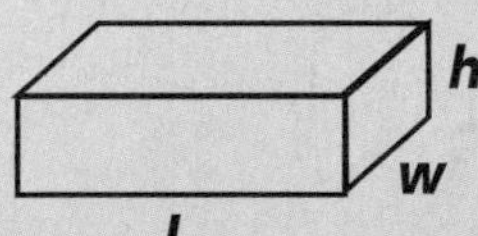

Volume = length × width × height
$V = lwh$

Example

A topaz crystal is a rectangular prism like the one shown. You can find the volume of the prism by using the steps below.

10 mm
12 mm
20 mm

Write the formula for the volume of a rectangular prism: $V = lwh$

Substitute dimensions: $= 20 \text{ mm} \times 12 \text{ mm} \times 10 \text{ mm}$

Simplify: $= 2400 \text{ mm}^3$

ANSWER The volume of the rectangular prism is 2400 cubic millimeters.

Using Significant Figures

The **significant figures** in a decimal are the digits that are warranted by the accuracy of a measuring device.

When you perform a calculation with measurements, the number of significant figures to include in the result depends in part on the number of significant figures in the measurements. When you multiply or divide measurements, your answer should have only as many significant figures as the measurement with the fewest significant figures.

Example

Using a balance and a graduated cylinder filled with water, you determined that a marble has a mass of 8.0 grams and a volume of 3.5 cubic centimeters. To calculate the density of the marble, divide the mass by the volume.

Write the formula for density: $\text{Density} = \frac{\text{mass}}{\text{Volume}}$

Substitute measurements: $= \frac{8.0 \text{ g}}{3.5 \text{ cm}^3}$

Use a calculator to divide: $\approx 2.285714286 \text{ g/cm}^3$

ANSWER Because the mass and the volume have two significant figures each, give the density to two significant figures. The marble has a density of 2.3 grams per cubic centimeter.

Using Scientific Notation

Scientific notation is a shorthand way to write very large or very small numbers. For example, 73,500,000,000,000,000,000,000 kg is the mass of the Moon. In scientific notation, it is 7.35×10^{22} kg.

Example

You can convert from standard form to scientific notation.

Standard Form	Scientific Notation
720,000	7.2×10^5
5 decimal places left	Exponent is 5.
0.000291	2.91×10^{-4}
4 decimal places right	Exponent is –4.

You can convert from scientific notation to standard form.

Scientific Notation	Standard Form
4.63×10^7	46,300,000
Exponent is 7.	7 decimal places right
1.08×10^{-6}	0.00000108
Exponent is –6.	6 decimal places left

MATH HANDBOOK

Note-Taking Handbook

Note-Taking Strategies

Taking notes as you read helps you understand the information. The notes you take can also be used as a study guide for later review. This handbook presents several ways to organize your notes.

Content Frame

1. Make a chart in which each column represents a category.
2. Give each column a heading.
3. Write details under the headings.

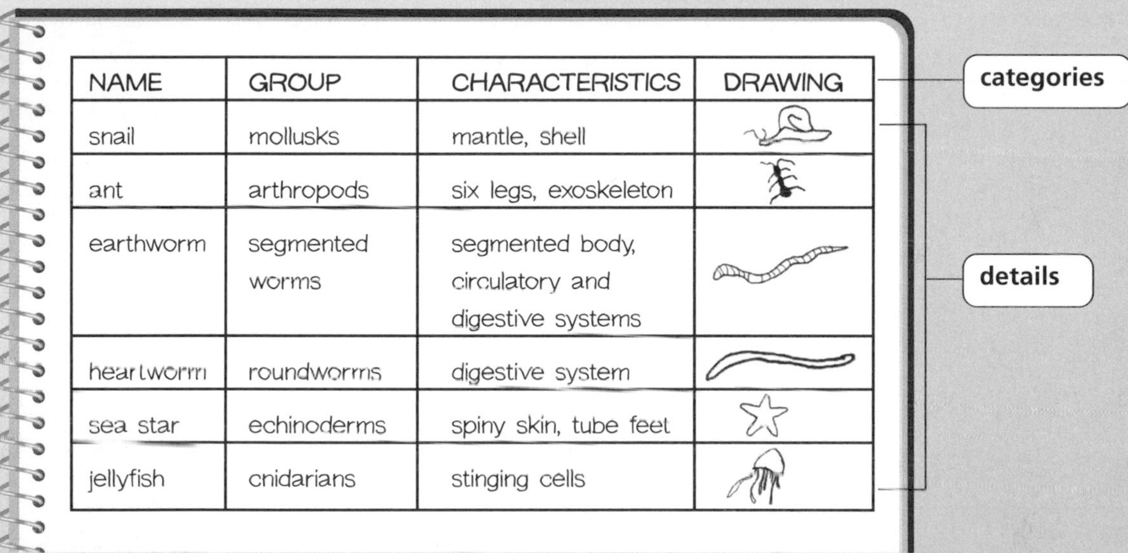

NAME	GROUP	CHARACTERISTICS	DRAWING
snail	mollusks	mantle, shell	
ant	arthropods	six legs, exoskeleton	
earthworm	segmented worms	segmented body, circulatory and digestive systems	
heartworm	roundworms	digestive system	
sea star	echinoderms	spiny skin, tube feet	
jellyfish	cnidarians	stinging cells	

Combination Notes

1. For each new idea or concept, write an informal outline of the information.
2. Make a sketch to illustrate the concept, and label it.

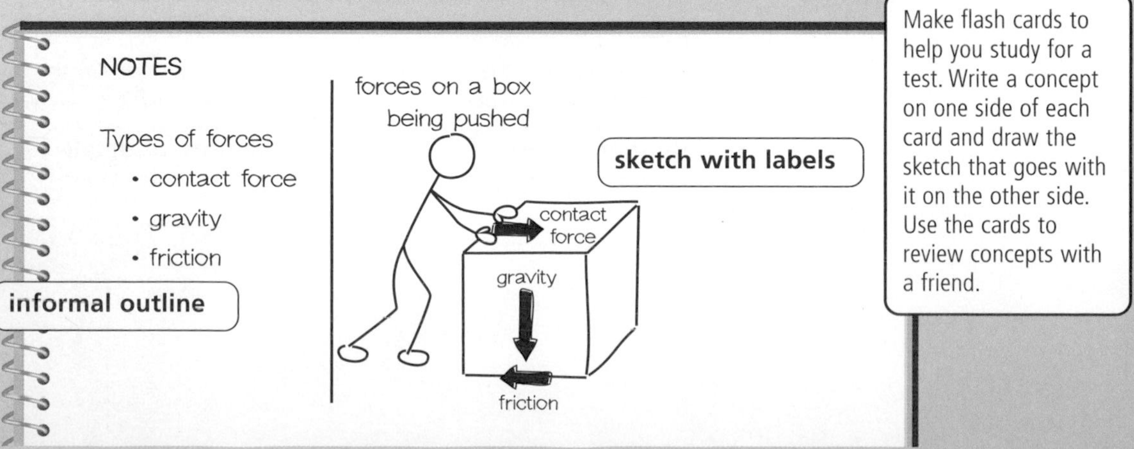

Make flash cards to help you study for a test. Write a concept on one side of each card and draw the sketch that goes with it on the other side. Use the cards to review concepts with a friend.

Main Idea and Detail Notes

1. In the left-hand column of a two-column chart, list main ideas. The blue headings express main ideas throughout this textbook.
2. In the right-hand column, write details that expand on each main idea.

You can shorten the headings in your chart. Be sure to use the most important words.

When studying for tests, cover up the detail notes column with a sheet of paper. Then use each main idea to form a question—such as "How does latitude affect climate?" Answer the question, and then uncover the detail notes column to check your answer.

MAIN IDEAS	DETAIL NOTES
1. Latitude affects climate. (main idea 1)	1. Places close to the equator are usually warmer than places close to the poles. 1. Latitude has the same effect in both hemispheres. (details about main idea 1)
2. Altitude affects climate. (main idea 2)	2. Temperature decreases with altitude. 2. Altitude can overcome the effect of latitude on temperature. (details about main idea 2)

Main Idea Web

1. Write a main idea in a box.
2. Add boxes around it with related vocabulary terms and important details.

You can find definitions near highlighted terms.

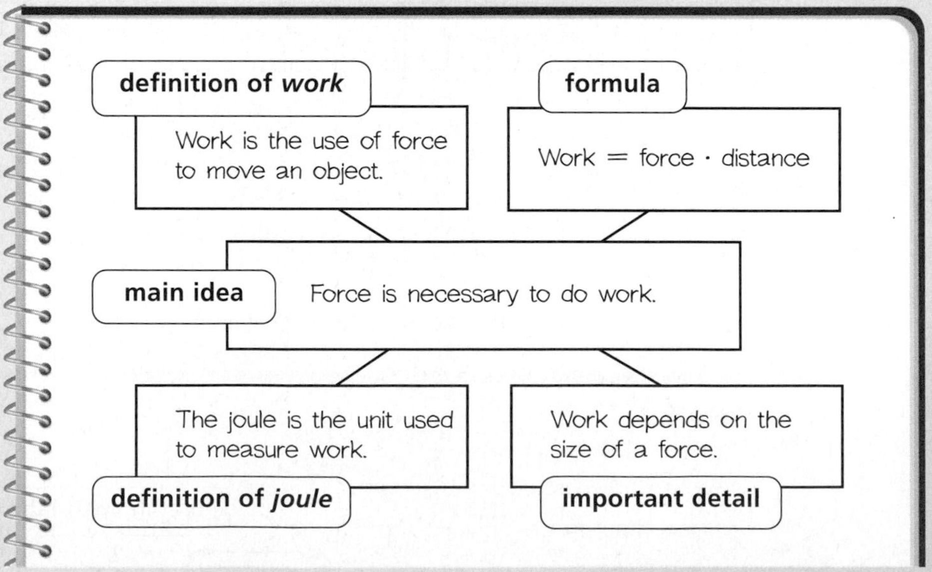

definition of *work*
Work is the use of force to move an object.

formula
Work = force · distance

main idea
Force is necessary to do work.

definition of *joule*
The joule is the unit used to measure work.

important detail
Work depends on the size of a force.

NOTE-TAKING HANDBOOK

Mind Map

1. Write a main idea in the center.
2. Add details that relate to one another and to the main idea.

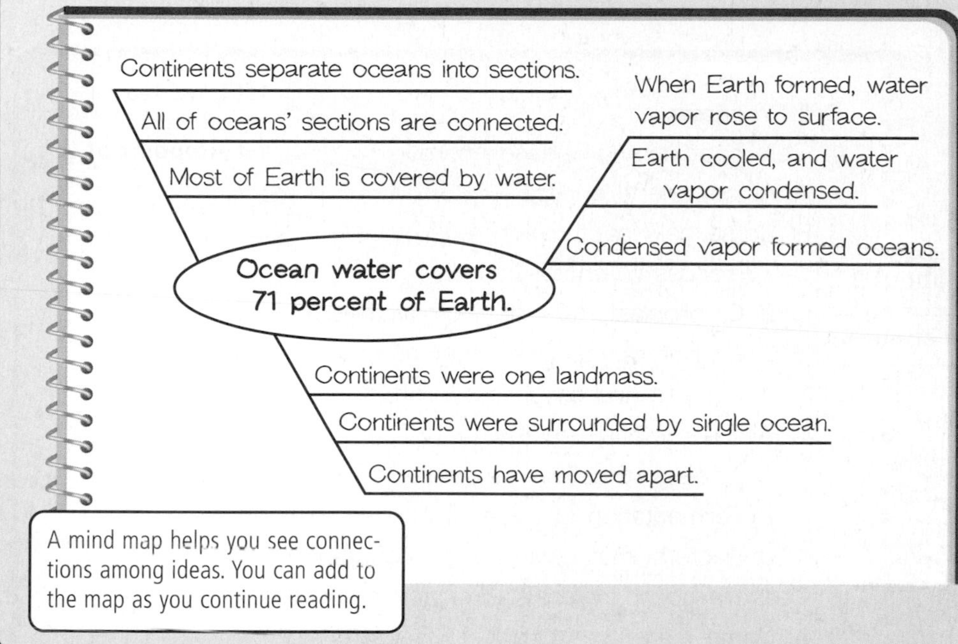

Continents separate oceans into sections.
All of oceans' sections are connected.

When Earth formed, water vapor rose to surface.
Earth cooled, and water vapor condensed.
Condensed vapor formed oceans.
Ocean water covers 71 percent of Earth.
Continents were one landmass.
Continents were surrounded by single ocean.
Continents have moved apart.
A mind map helps you see connections among ideas. You can add to the map as you continue reading.

Supporting Main Ideas

1. Write a main idea in a box.
2. Add boxes underneath with information—such as reasons, explanations, and examples—that supports the main idea.

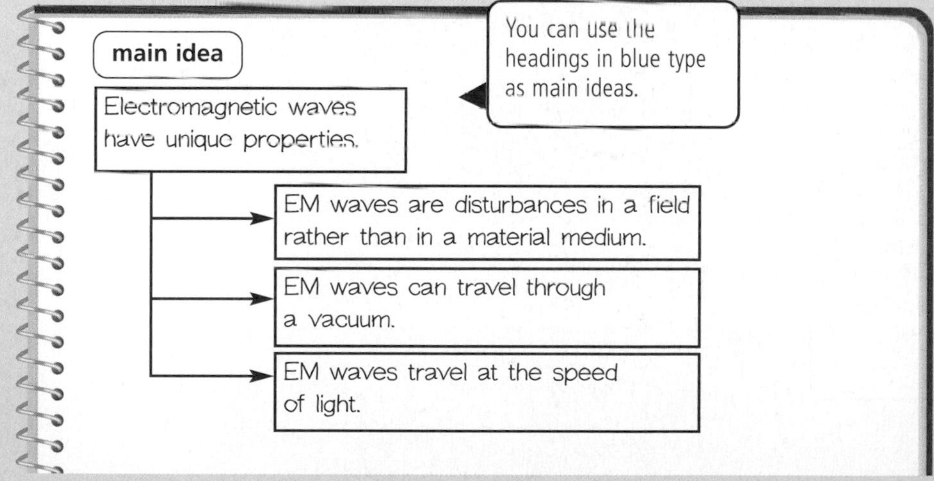

main idea
Electromagnetic waves have unique properties.
EM waves are disturbances in a field rather than in a material medium.
EM waves can travel through a vacuum.
EM waves travel at the speed of light.
You can use the headings in blue type as main ideas.

NOTE-TAKING HANDBOOK

Outline

1. Copy the chapter title and headings from the book in the form of an outline.
2. Add notes that summarize in your own words what you read.

Cell Processes

I. Cells capture and release energy. (1st key idea)
    A. All cells need energy. (1st subpoint of I)
    B. Some cells capture light energy. (2nd subpoint of I)
        1. Process of photosynthesis (1st detail about B)
        2. Chloroplasts (site of photosynthesis) (2nd detail about B)
        3. Carbon dioxide and water as raw materials
        4. Glucose and oxygen as products
    C. All cells release energy.
        1. Process of cellular respiration
        2. Fermentation of sugar to carbon dioxide
        3. Bacteria that carry out fermentation

II. Cells transport materials through membranes.
    A. Some materials move by diffusion.
        1. Particle movement from higher to lower concentrations
        2. Movement of water through membrane (osmosis)
    B. Some transport requires energy.
        1. Active transport
        2. Examples of active transport

Correct Outline Form

Include a title.

Arrange key ideas, subpoints, and details as shown.

Indent the divisions of the outline as shown.

Use the same grammatical form for items of the same rank. For example, if A is a sentence, B must also be a sentence.

You must have at least two main ideas or subpoints. That is, every A must be followed by a B, and every 1 must be followed by a 2.

Concept Map

1. Write an important concept in a large oval.
2. Add details related to the concept in smaller ovals.
3. Write linking words on arrows that connect the ovals.

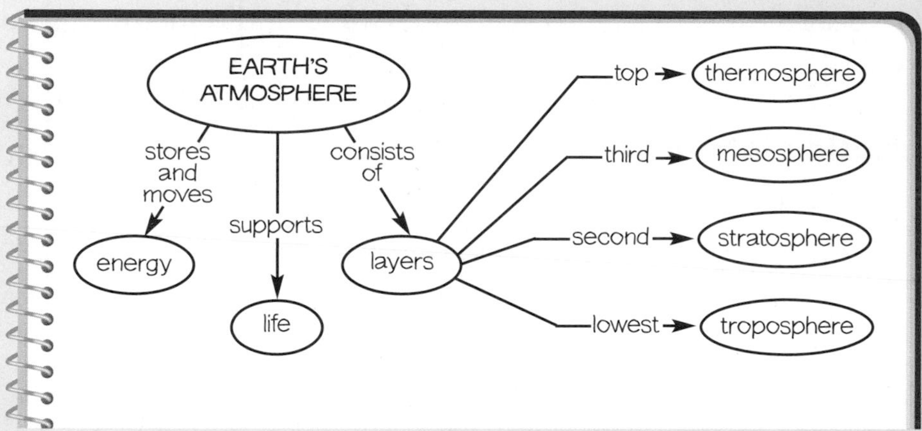

The main ideas or concepts can often be found in the blue headings. An example is "The atmosphere stores and moves energy." Use nouns from these concepts in the ovals, and use the verb or verbs on the lines.

Venn Diagram

1. Draw two overlapping circles, one for each item that you are comparing.
2. In the overlapping section, list the characteristics that are shared by both items.
3. In the outer sections, list the characteristics that are peculiar to each item.
4. Write a summary that describes the information in the Venn diagram.

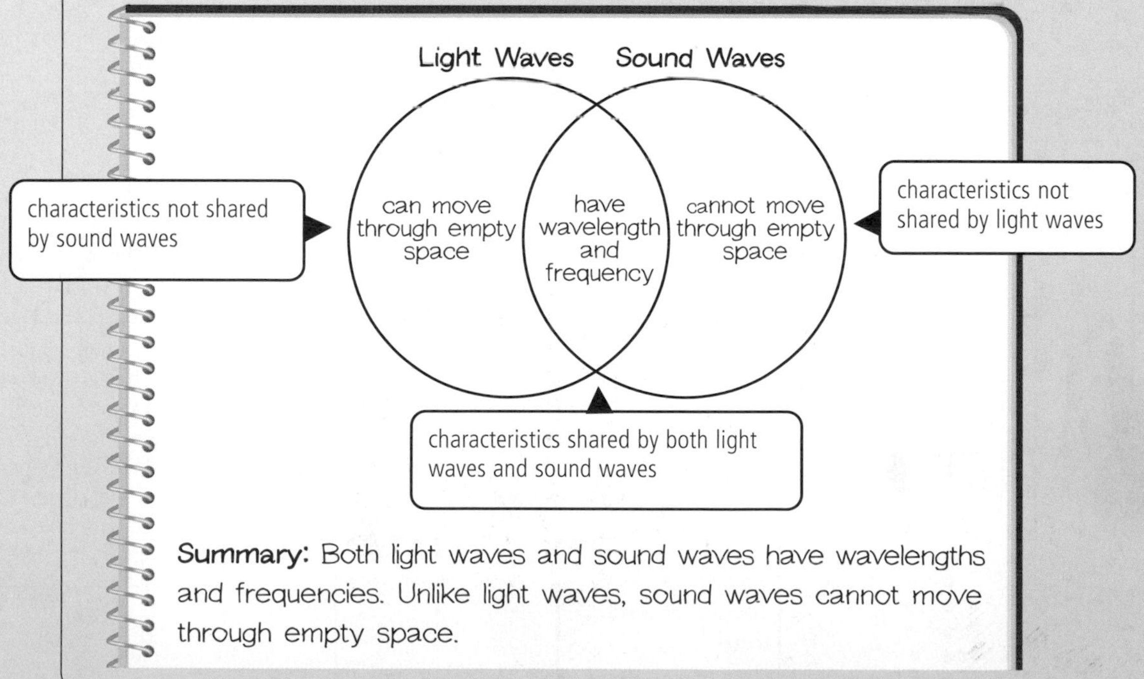

NOTE-TAKING HANDBOOK

Vocabulary Strategies

Important terms are highlighted in this book. A definition of each term can be found in the sentence or paragraph where the term appears. You can also find definitions in the Glossary. Taking notes about vocabulary terms helps you understand and remember what you read.

Description Wheel

1. Write a term inside a circle.
2. Write words that describe the term on "spokes" attached to the circle.

When studying for a test with a friend, read the phrases on the spokes one at a time until your friend identifies the correct term.

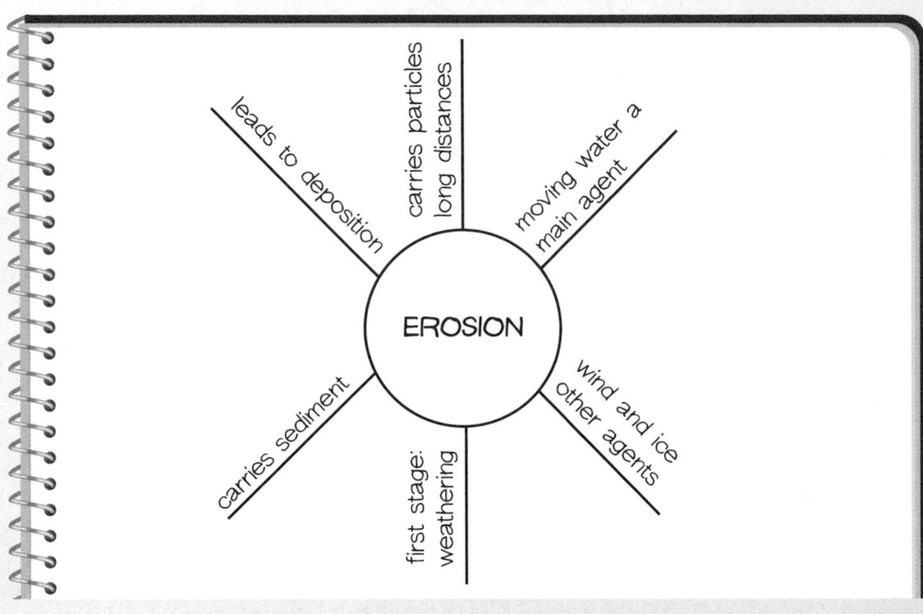

Four Square

1. Write a term in the center.
2. Write details in the four areas around the term.

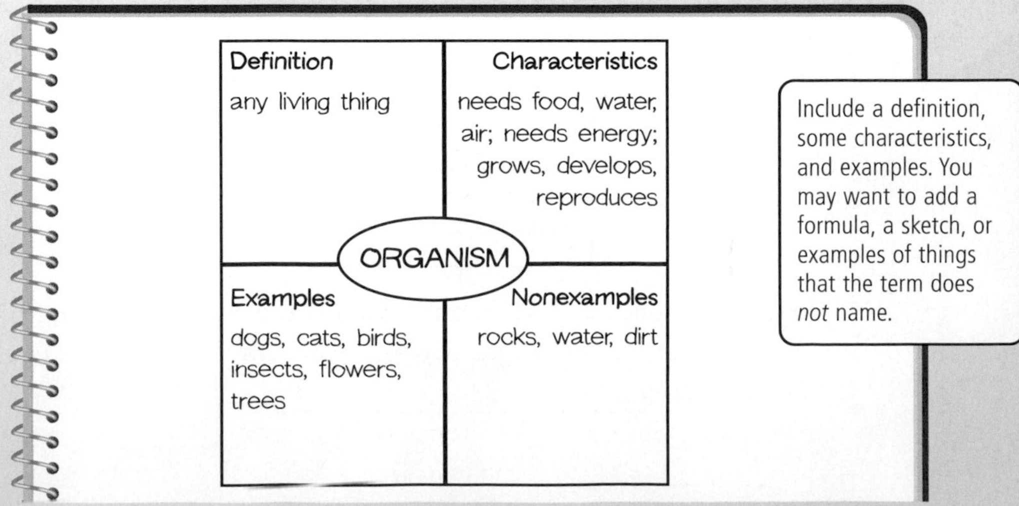

Include a definition, some characteristics, and examples. You may want to add a formula, a sketch, or examples of things that the term does *not* name.

Frame Game

1. Write a term in the center.
2. Frame the term with details.

Include examples, descriptions, sketches, or sentences that use the term in context. Change the frame to fit each new term.

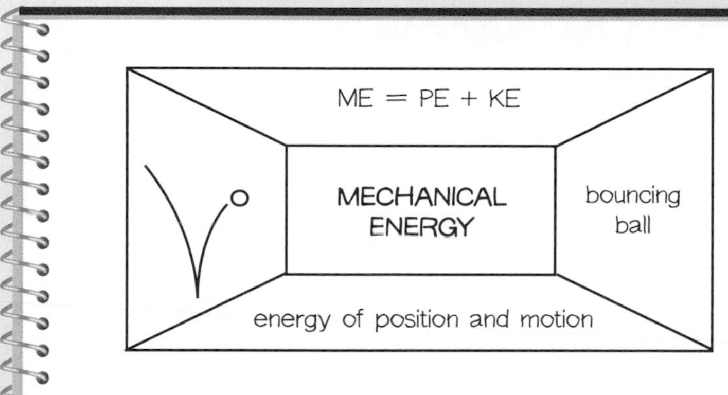

Magnet Word

1. Write a term on the magnet.
2. On the lines, add details related to the term.

You can also use phrases or sentences on the lines.

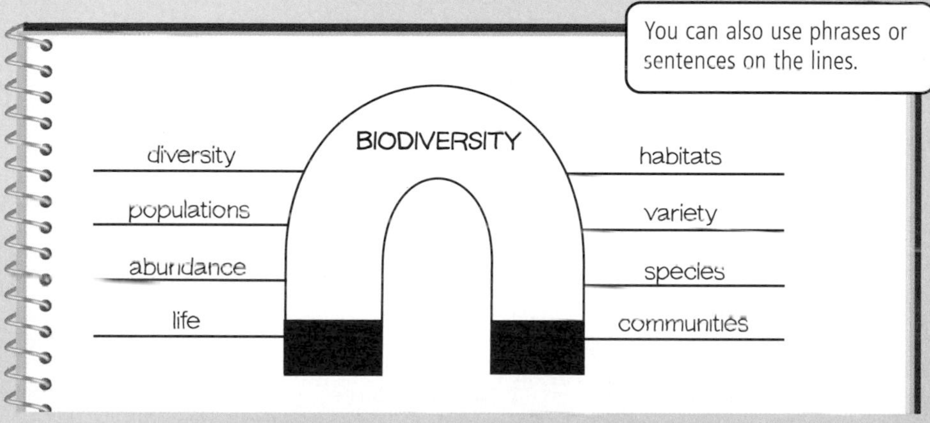

Word Triangle

1. Write a term and its definition in the bottom section.
2. In the middle section, write a sentence in which the term is used correctly.
3. In the top section, draw a small picture to illustrate the term.

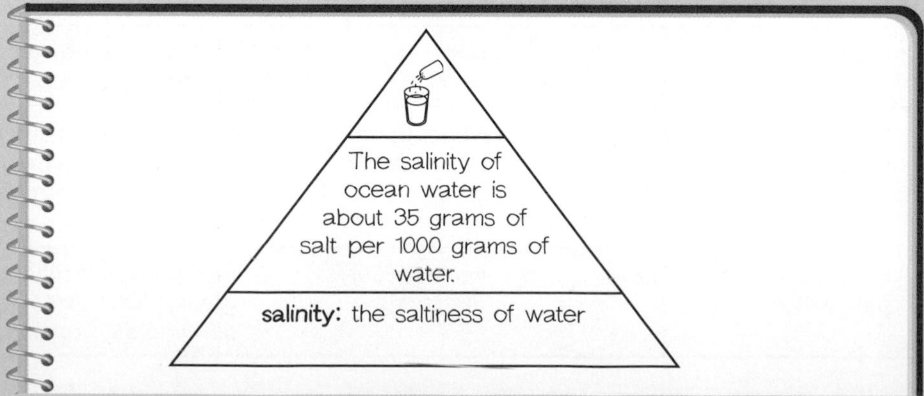

NOTE-TAKING HANDBOOK

Appendix

Properties of Common Minerals

In this table, minerals are arranged alphabetically, and the most useful properties for identification are printed in *italic* type. Most minerals can be identified by means of two or three of the properties listed below. For some minerals, density is important; for others, cleavage is characteristic; and for others, the crystal shapes identify the minerals. The colors listed are the most common for each mineral.

Name	Hardness	Color	Streak	Cleavage	Remarks
Apatite	5	Green, brown	White	Poor in one direction	Nonmetallic (glassy) luster. Sp. gr. 3.1 to 3.2.
Augite	5–6	Dark green to black	Greenish	*Two directions, nearly at 90°*	Nonmetallic (glassy) luster. *Stubby four- or eight-sided crystals.* Common type of pyroxene. Sp. gr. 3.2 to 3.4.
Beryl	7.5–8	*Bluish-green, yellow, pink, colorless*	White	Imperfect in one direction	Nonmetallic (glassy) luster. *Hardness, greenish color, six-sided crystals.* Aquamarine and emerald are gem varieties. Sp. gr. 2.6 to 2.8.
Biotite mica	2.5–3	Black, brown, dark green	White	*Perfect in one direction*	Nonmetallic (glassy) luster. *Thin elastic films peel off easily.* Sp. gr. 2.8 to 3.2.
Calcite	*3*	White, colorless	White	*Perfect, three directions, not at 90° angles*	Nonmetallic (glassy to dull) luster. *Fizzes in dilute hydrochloric acid.* Sp. gr. 2.7.
Chalcopyrite	3.5–4	*Golden yellow*	Greenish black	Poor in one direction	Metallic luster. *Hardness distinguishes from pyrite.* Sp. gr. 4.1 to 4.3.
Chlorite	2–2.5	*Greenish*	Pale green to gray or brown	Perfect in one direction	Nonmetallic (glassy to pearly) luster. *Nonelastic flakes.* Sp. gr. 2.6 to 3.3.
Copper	2.5–3	*Copper red*	Copper	None	*Metallic luster on fresh surface. Dense.* Sp. gr. 8.9.
Corundum	9	Brown, pink, blue	White	None, parting resembles cleavage	Nonmetallic (glassy to brilliant) luster. *Barrel-shaped, six-sided crystals with flat ends.* Sp. gr. 4.0.
Diamond	10	Colorless to pale yellow	White	Perfect, four directions	Nonmetallic (brilliant to greasy) luster. *Hardest of all minerals.* Sp. gr. 3.5.

Sp. gr. = specific gravity

APPENDIX

Name	Hardness	Color	Streak	Cleavage	Remarks
Dolomite	3.5–4	Pinkish, colorless, white	White	*Perfect, three directions, not at 90° angles*	Nonmetallic luster. *Scratched surface fizzes in dilute hydrochloric acid. Cleavage surfaces curved. Sp. gr. 2.8 to 2.9.*
Feldspar (Orthoclase)	*6*	*Salmon pink, red,* white, light gray	White	*Good, two directions, 90° intersection*	Nonmetallic (glassy) luster. *Hardness, color, and cleavage taken together are diagnostic.* Sp. gr. 2.6.
Feldspar (Plagioclase)	6	*White to light gray,* can be salmon pink	White	*Good, two directions, about 90°*	Nonmetallic (glassy to pearly) luster. *If striations are visible, they are diagnostic.* Sp. gr. 2.6 to 2.8.
Fluorite	4	Varies	White	*Perfect, four directions*	Nonmetallic (glassy) luster. In cubes or octahedrons as crystals. Sp. gr. 3.2.
Galena	2.5	*Lead gray*	Lead gray	*Perfect, three directions, at 90° angles*	*Metallic luster.* Occurs as crystals and masses. *Dense.* Sp. gr. 7.4 to 7.6.
Gold	2.5–3	*Gold*	Gold	None	Metallic luster. *Dense.* Sp. gr. 15.0 to 19.3.
Graphite	1–2	*Dark gray to black*	Grayish black	*Perfect in one direction*	Metallic or nonmetallic (earthy) luster. *Greasy feel, marks paper.* This is the "lead" in a pencil (mixed with clay). Sp. gr. 2.2.
Gypsum	*2*	Colorless, white, gray, yellowish, reddish	White	*Perfect in one direction*	Nonmetallic (glassy to silky) luster. *Can be scratched easily by a fingernail.* Sp. gr. 2.3.
Halite	2–2.5	Colorless, white	White	*Perfect, three directions, at 90° angles*	Nonmetallic (glassy) luster. *Salty taste.* Sp. gr. 2.2.
Hematite	5–6 (may appear softer)	*Reddish-brown, gray, black*	*Reddish*	None	Metallic or nonmetallic (earthy) luster. *Dense.* Sp. gr. 5.3.
Hornblende	5–6	*Dark green to black*	Brown to gray	*Perfect, two directions at angles of 56° and 124°*	Nonmetallic (glassy to silky) luster. Common type of amphibole. Long, slender, six-sided crystals. Sp. gr. 3.0 to 3.4.
Kaolinite	2	White, gray, yellowish	White	*Perfect in one direction*	Nonmetallic (dull, earthy) luster. Claylike masses. Sp. gr. 2.6.
Limonite group	4–5.5	*Yellow, brown*	*Yellowish brown*	None	Nonmetallic (earthy) luster. Rust stains. Sp. gr. 2.9 to 4.3.
Magnetite	5.5–6.5	*Black*	Black	None	Metallic luster. Occurs as eight-sided crystals and granular masses. *Magnetic. Dense.* Sp. gr. 5.2.

Sp. gr. = specific gravity

Name	Hardness	Color	Streak	Cleavage	Remarks
Muscovite mica	2–2.5	Colorless in thin films; silvery, yellowish, and greenish in thicker pieces	*White*	Perfect in one direction	Nonmetallic (glassy to pearly) luster. *Thin elastic films peel off readily.* Sp. gr. 2.8 to 2.9.
Olivine	6.5–7	*Yellowish, greenish*	White	*None*	*Nonmetallic (glassy) luster. Granular.* Sp. gr. 3.3 to 4.4.
Opal	5–6.5	Varies	White	None	*Nonmetallic (glassy to pearly) luster. Conchoidal fracture.* Sp. gr. 2.0 to 2.2.
Pyrite	*6–6.5*	*Brass yellow*	Greenish black	None	Metallic luster. *Cubic crystals* and granular masses. *Dense.* Sp. gr. 5.0 to 5.1.
Quartz	*7*	*Colorless, white; varies*	White	None	Nonmetallic (glassy) luster. *Conchoidal fracture. Six-sided crystals common.* Many varieties. Sp. gr. 2.6.
Serpentine	3–5	*Greenish (variegated)*	White	None or good in one direction, depending on variety	*Nonmetallic (greasy, waxy, or silky) luster. Conchoidal fracture.* Sp. gr. 2.5 to 2.6.
Sphalerite	*3.5–4*	*Yellow, brown, black*	Yellow to light brown	*Perfect, six directions*	*Nonmetallic (brilliant to resinous) luster.* Sp. gr. 3.9 to 4.1.
Sulfur	1.5–2.5	*Yellow*	Yellow	Poor, two directions	Nonmetallic (glassy to earthy) luster. Granular. Sp. gr. 2.0 to 2.1.
Talc	*1*	Apple-green, gray, white	White	Perfect in one direction	Nonmetallic (pearly to greasy) luster. Nonelastic flakes, *greasy feel.* Sp. gr. 2.7 to 2.8.
Topaz	*8*	Varies	White	Perfect in one direction	Nonmetallic (brilliant to glassy) luster. *Crystals commonly striated length-wise.* Sp. gr. 3.4 to 3.6.
Tourmaline	7–7.5	*Black; varies*	White	None	Nonmetallic (glassy) luster. *Crystals often have triangular cross sections. Conchoidal fracture.* Sp. gr. 3.0 to 3.3.

Sp. gr. = specific gravity

APPENDIX

Topographic Map Symbols

The U.S. Geological Survey uses the following symbols to mark human-made and natural features on all of the topographic maps the USGS produces.

Primary highway, hard surface
Secondary highway, hard surface
Light-duty road, hard or improved surface
Unimproved road
Trail
Railroad: single track
Railroad: multiple track
Bridge
Drawbridge
Tunnel
Footbridge
Overpass—Underpass
Power transmission line with located tower
Landmark line (labeled as to type) — TELEPHONE

Dam with lock
Canal with lock
Large dam
Small dam: masonry—earth
Buildings (dwelling, place of employment, etc.)
School—Church—Cemeteries — Cem
Buildings (barn, warehouse, etc.)
Tanks; oil, water, etc. (labeled only if water) — Water Tank
Wells other than water (labeled as to type) — Oil — Gas
U.S. mineral or location monument—Prospect
Quarry—Gravel pit
Mine shaft—Tunnel or cave entrance
Campsite—Picnic area
Located or landmark object—Windmill
Exposed wreck
Rock or coral reef
Foreshore flat
Rock: bare or awash

Benchmarks — BM × 671 — × 672
Road fork—Section corner with elevation — 429 — + 58
Checked spot elevation — × 5970
Unchecked spot elevation — × 5970

Boundary: national
State
county, parish, municipio
civil township, precinct, town, barrio
incorporated city, village, town, hamlet
reservation, national or state
small park, cemetery, airport, etc.
land grant
Township or range line, U.S. land survey
Section line, U.S. land survey
Township line, not U.S. land survey
Section line, not U.S. land survey
Fence line or field line
Section corner: found—indicated
Boundary monument: land grant—other

Index contour
Intermediate contour
Supplementary cont
Depression contours
Cut—Fill
Levee
Mine dump
Large wash
Dune area
Distorted surface
Sand area
Gravel beach

Glacier
Intermittent streams
Seasonal streams
Aqueduct tunnel
Water well—Spring
Falls
Rapids
Intermittent lake
Channel
Small wash
Sounding—Depth curve — 10
Marsh (swamp)
Dry lake bed
Land subject to controlled flooding

Woodland
Mangrove
Submerged marsh
Scrub
Orchard
Wooded marsh
Vineyard
Many buildings
Areas revised since previous edition

Source: U.S. Geological Survey

Properties of Rocks and Earth's Interior

Scheme for Sedimentary Rock Identification

TEXTURE	GRAIN SIZE	COMPOSITION	COMMENTS	ROCK NAME	MAP SYMBOL
Clastic (fragmental)	Pebbles, cobbles, and/or boulders embedded in sand, silt, and/or clay	Mostly quartz, feldspar, and clay minerals; may contain fragments of other rocks and minerals	Rounded fragments	Conglomerate	
			Angular fragments	Breccia	
	Sand (0.2 to 0.006 cm)		Fine to coarse	Sandstone	
	Silt (0.006 to 0.0004 cm)		Very fine grain	Siltstone	
	Clay (less than 0.0004 cm)		Compact; may split easily	Shale	

CHEMICALLY AND/OR ORGANICALLY FORMED SEDIMENTARY ROCKS

TEXTURE	GRAIN SIZE	COMPOSITION	COMMENTS	ROCK NAME	MAP SYMBOL
Crystalline	Varied	Halite	Crystals from chemical precipitates and evaporites	Rock Salt	
	Varied	Gypsum		Rock Gypsum	
	Varied	Dolomite		Dolostone	
Bioclastic	Microscopic to coarse	Calcite	Cemented shell fragments or precipitates of biologic origin	Limestone	
	Varied	Carbon	From plant remains	Coal	

Scheme for Metamorphic Rock Identification

TEXTURE		GRAIN SIZE	COMPOSITION	TYPE OF METAMORPHISM	COMMENTS	ROCK NAME	MAP SYMBOL
FOLIATED	MINERAL ALIGNMENT	Fine	MICA	Regional	Low-grade metamorphism of shale	Slate	
		Fine to medium	MICA, QUARTZ, FELDSPAR, AMPHIBOLE, GARNET	(Heat and pressure increase with depth)	Foliation surfaces shiny from microscopic mica crystals	Phyllite	
					Platy mica crystals visible from metamorphism of clay or feldspars	Schist	
	BAND-ING	Medium to coarse	PYROXENE		High-grade metamorphism; some mica changed to feldspar; segregated by mineral type into bands	Gneiss	
NONFOLIATED		Fine	Variable	Contact (Heat)	Various rocks changed by heat from nearby magma/lava	Hornfels	
		Fine to coarse	Quartz	Regional or Contact	Metamorphism of quartz sandstone	Quartzite	
			Calcite and/or dolomite		Metamorphism of limestone or dolostone	Marble	
		Coarse	Various minerals in particles and matrix		Pebbles may be distorted or stretched	Metaconglomerate	

Scheme for Igneous Rock Identification

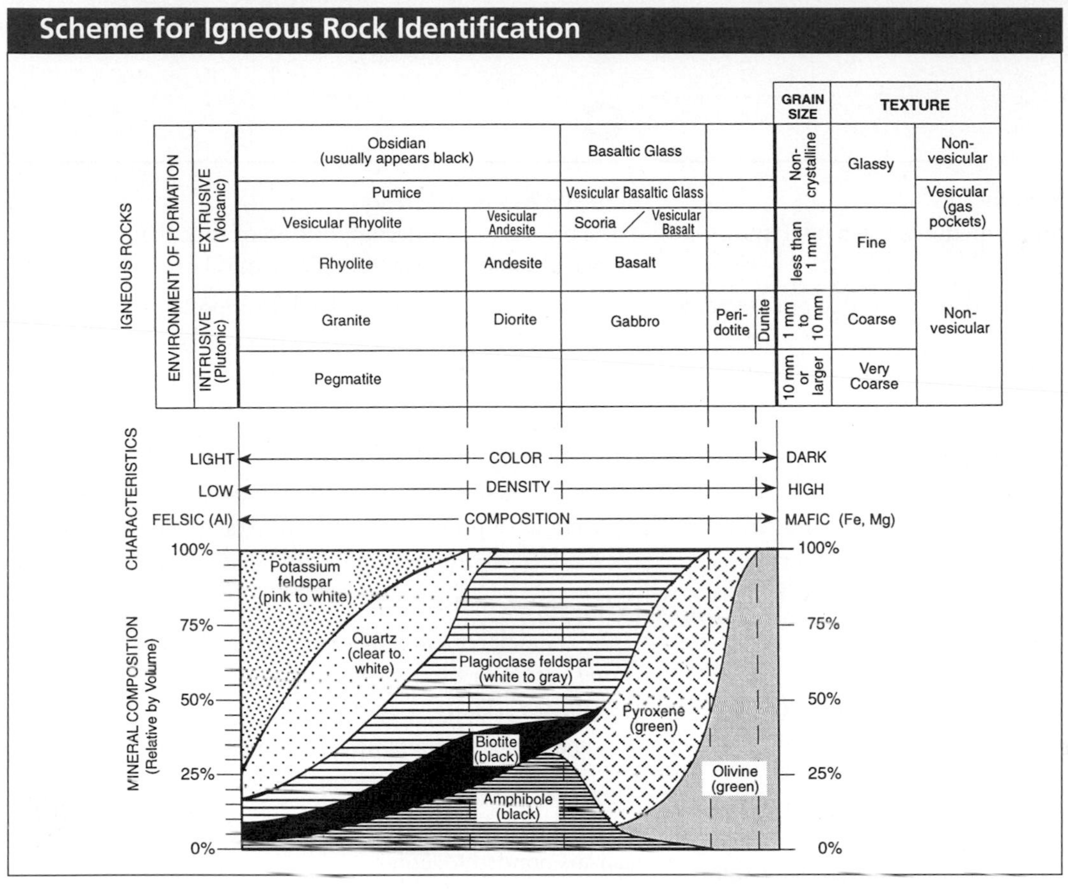

IGNEOUS ROCKS
ENVIRONMENT OF FORMATION
EXTRUSIVE (Volcanic)
INTRUSIVE (Plutonic)
Obsidian (usually appears black)
Basaltic Glass
Pumice
Vesicular Basaltic Glass
Vesicular Rhyolite
Vesicular Andesite
Scoria
Vesicular Basalt
Rhyolite
Andesite
Basalt
Granite
Diorite
Gabbro
Peri-dotite
Dunite
Pegmatite
GRAIN SIZE
TEXTURE
Non-crystalline
Glassy
Non-vesicular
Vesicular (gas pockets)
less than 1 mm
Fine
1 mm to 10 mm
Coarse
Non-vesicular
10 mm or larger
Very Coarse
CHARACTERISTICS
LIGHT
COLOR
DARK
LOW
DENSITY
HIGH
FELSIC (Al)
COMPOSITION
MAFIC (Fe, Mg)
MINERAL COMPOSITION (Relative by Volume)
100%
75%
50%
25%
0%
Potassium feldspar (pink to white)
Quartz (clear to white)
Plagioclase feldspar (white to gray)
Biotite (black)
Amphibole (black)
Pyroxene (green)
Olivine (green)

Inferred Properties of Earth's Interior

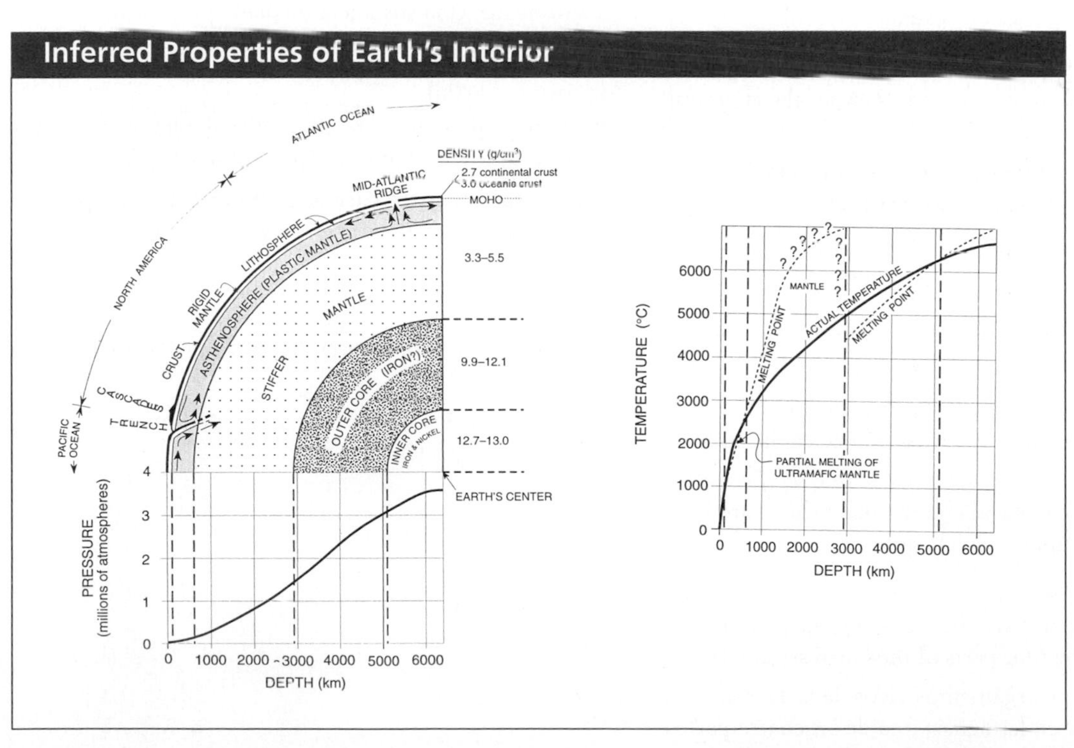

ATLANTIC OCEAN
NORTH AMERICA
PACIFIC OCEAN
CASCADES
TRENCH
CRUST
RIGID MANTLE
LITHOSPHERE
ASTHENOSPHERE (PLASTIC MANTLE)
MID-ATLANTIC RIDGE
MANTLE
STIFFER
OUTER CORE (IRON?)
INNER CORE (IRON & NICKEL)
DENSITY (g/cm³)
2.7 continental crust
3.0 oceanic crust
MOHO
3.3–5.5
9.9–12.1
12.7–13.0
EARTH'S CENTER
PRESSURE (millions of atmospheres)
0
1
2
3
4
0 1000 2000 - 3000 4000 5000 6000
DEPTH (km)
TEMPERATURE (°C)
0
1000
2000
3000
4000
5000
6000
MANTLE
MELTING POINT
ACTUAL TEMPERATURE
MELTING POINT
PARTIAL MELTING OF ULTRAMAFIC MANTLE
0 1000 2000 3000 4000 5000 6000
DEPTH (km)

APPENDIX

Glossary

GLOSSARY

A

abrasion (uh-BRAY-zhuhn)
The process of wearing something down by friction. (p. 116)

abrasión El proceso de desgaste de algo por efecto de la fricción.

alluvial fan (uh-LOO-vee-uhl)
A fan-shaped deposit of sediment at the base of a slope, formed as water flows down the slope and spreads at the bottom. (p. 153)

abanico aluvial Un depósito de sedimentos en forma de abanico situado en la base de una pendiente; se forma cuando el agua baja por la pendiente y se dispersa al llegar al pie de la misma.

atmosphere (AT-muh-SFEER)
The outer layer of gases of a large body in space, such as a planet or star; the mixture of gases that surrounds the solid Earth; one of the four parts of the Earth system. (p. 10)

atmósfera La capa externa de gases de un gran cuerpo que se encuentra en el espacio, como un planeta o una estrella; la mezcla de gases que rodea la Tierra sólida; una de las cuatro partes del sistema terrestre.

atom
The smallest particle of an element that has the chemical properties of that element. (p. xvii)

átomo La partícula más pequeña de un elemento que tiene las propiedades químicas de ese elemento.

B

barrier island
A long, narrow island that develops parallel to a coast as a sandbar builds up above the water's surface. (p. 160)

isla barrera Una isla larga y angosta que se desarrolla paralelamente a la costa al crecer una barra de arena hasta rebasar la superficie del agua.

biosphere (BY-uh-SFEER)
All living organisms on Earth in the air, on the land, and in the waters; one of the four parts of the Earth system. (p. 11)

biosfera Todos los organismos vivos de la Tierra, en el aire, en la tierra y en las aguas; una de las cuatro partes del sistema de la Tierra.

C

chemical weathering
The breakdown or decomposition of rock that takes place when minerals change through chemical processes. (p. 118)

meteorización química La descomposición de las rocas que ocurre cuando los minerales cambian mediante procesos químicos.

cleavage
The property of a mineral that describes its tendency to break along flat surfaces. (p. 53)

clivaje La propiedad de un mineral que describe su tendencia a romperse a lo largo de una superficie plana.

climate
The characteristic weather conditions in an area over a long period of time. (p. xxi)

clima Las condiciones meteorológicas características de un lugar durante un largo período de tiempo.

compound
A substance made up of two or more different types of atoms bonded together.

compuesto Una sustancia formada por dos o más diferentes tipos de átomos enlazados.

contour interval
On a topographic map, the difference in elevation from one contour line to the next. (p. 26)

equidistancia entre curvas de nivel En un mapa topográfico, la diferencia en elevación de una curva de nivel a la siguiente.

contour line
A line on a topographic map that joins points of equal elevation. (p. 25)

curva de nivel Una línea en un mapa topográfico que une puntos de igual elevación.

convection
The transfer of energy from place to place by the motion of heated gas or liquid; in Earth's mantle, convection is thought to transfer energy by the motion of solid rock, which when under great heat and pressure can move like a liquid. (p. xv)

convección La transferencia de energía de un lugar a otro por el movimiento de un líquido o gas calentado; se piensa que en el manto terrestre la convección transfiere energía mediante el movimiento de roca sólida, la cual puede moverse como un líquido cuando está muy caliente y bajo alta presión.

crystal
A solid substance in which the atoms are arranged in an orderly, repeating, three-dimensional pattern. (p. 46)

cristal Una sustancia sólida en la cual los átomos están organizados en un patrón tridimensional y ordenado que se repite.

cycle
n. A series of events or actions that repeat themselves regularly; a physical and/or chemical process in which one material continually changes locations and/or forms. Examples include the water cycle, the carbon cycle, and the rock cycle.

v. To move through a repeating series of events or actions.

ciclo ***s.*** Una serie de eventos o acciones que se repiten regularmente; un proceso físico y/o químico en el cual un material cambia continuamente de lugar y/o forma. Ejemplos: el ciclo del agua, el ciclo del carbono y el ciclo de las rocas.

D

data
Information gathered by observation or experimentation that can be used in calculating or reasoning. *Data* is a plural word; the singular is *datum.*

datos Información reunida mediante observación o experimentación y que se puede usar para calcular o para razonar.

delta
An area of land at the end, or mouth, of a river that is formed by the buildup of sediment. (p. 153)

delta Un área de tierra al final, o en la desembocadura, de un río y que se forma por la acumulación de sedimentos.

density
A property of matter representing the mass per unit volume. (p. 54)

densidad Una propiedad de la materia que representa la masa por unidad de volumen.

deposition (DEHP-uh-ZISH-uhn)
The process in which transported sediment is laid down. (p. 145)

sedimentación El proceso mediante el cual se deposita sedimento que ha sido transportado.

desertification (dih-ZUR-tuh-fih-KAY-shuhn)
The expansion of desert conditions in areas where the natural plant cover has been destroyed. (p. 133)

desertificación La expansión de las condiciones desérticas en áreas donde la vegetación natural ha sido destruida.

divide
A continuous high line of land—or ridge—from which water drains to one side or the other. (p. 151)

línea divisoria de aguas Una línea continua de tierra alta, o un cerro, desde donde el agua escurre hacia un lado o hacia el otro.

drainage basin
An area of land in which water drains into a stream system. The borders of a drainage basin are called divides. (p. 151)

cuenca tributaria Un área de tierra en la cual el agua escurre a un sistema de corrientes. Los límites de una cuenca tributaria se denominan líneas divisorias de aguas.

dune
A mound of sand built up by wind. (p. 161)

duna Un montículo de arena formado por el viento.

E

element
A substance that cannot be broken down into a simpler substance by ordinary chemical changes. An element consists of atoms of only one type. (p. 45)

elemento Una sustancia que no puede descomponerse en otra sustancia más simple por medio de cambios químicos normales. Un elemento consta de átomos de un solo tipo.

elevation
A measure of how high something is above a reference point, such as sea level. (p. 25)

elevación Una medida de lo elevado que está algo sobre un punto de referencia, como el nivel del mar.

energy
The ability to do work or to cause a change. For example, the energy of a moving bowling ball knocks over pins; energy from food allows animals to move and to grow; and energy from the Sun heats Earth's surface and atmosphere, which causes air to move. (p. xv)

energía La capacidad para trabajar o causar un cambio. Por ejemplo, la energía de una bola de boliche en movimiento tumba los pinos; la energía proveniente de su alimento permite a los animales moverse y crecer; la energía del Sol calienta la superficie y la atmósfera de la Tierra, lo que ocasiona que el aire se mueva.

equator
An imaginary east-west line around the center of Earth that divides the planet into the Northern Hemisphere and the Southern Hemisphere; a line set at 0° latitude. (p. 18)

ecuador Una línea imaginaria de este a oeste alrededor del centro de la Tierra y que divide al planeta en hemisferio norte y hemisferio sur; la línea está fijada a latitud 0°.

erosion
The process in which sediment is picked up and moved from one place to another. (p. 145)

erosión El proceso en el cual el sedimento es recogido y transportado de un lugar a otro.

evaporation
The process by which liquid changes into gas. (p. xv)

evaporación El proceso por el cual un líquido se transforma en gas.

exfoliation (ex-FOH-lee-AY-shuhn)
In geology, the process in which layers or sheets of rock gradually break off. (p. 116)

exfoliación En geología, el proceso en el cual capas u hojas de roca se desprenden gradualmente.

experiment
An organized procedure to study something under controlled conditions. (p. xxiv)

experimento Un procedimiento organizado para estudiar algo bajo condiciones controladas.

extrusive igneous rock (ihk-STROO-sihv)
Igneous rock that forms as lava cools on Earth's surface. (p. 83)

roca ígnea extrusiva Roca ígnea que se forma al enfriarse la lava sobre la superficie de la Tierra.

F

false-color image
A computer image in which the colors are not what the human eye would see. A false-color image can assign different colors to different types of radiation coming from an object to highlight its features. (p. 32)

imagen de color falso Una imagen computacional en la cual los colores no son los que el ojo humano observaría. Una imagen de color falso puede asignar diferentes colores a los diferentes tipos de radiación que provienen de un objeto para hacer destacar sus características.

floodplain
A flat area of land on either side of a stream that becomes flooded when a river overflows its banks. (p. 152)

planicie de inundación Un área plana de tierra en cualquier costado de un arroyo que se inunda cuando un río se desborda.

foliation
The arrangement of minerals within rocks into flat or wavy parallel bands; a characteristic of most metamorphic rocks. (p. 100)

foliación La organización de minerales en bandas paralelas planas u onduladas en las rocas; una característica de la mayoría de las rocas metamórficas.

force
A push or a pull; something that changes the motion of an object. (p. xvii)

fuerza Un empuje o un jalón; algo que cambia el movimiento de un objeto.

fossil
A trace or the remains of a once-living thing from long ago. (p. xxi)

fósil Un rastro o los restos de un organismo que vivió hace mucho tiempo.

fracture
The tendency of a mineral to break into irregular pieces. (p. 53)

fractura La tendencia de un mineral a romperse en pedazos irregulares.

friction
A force that resists the motion between two surfaces in contact. (p. xxi)

fricción Una fuerza que resiste el movimiento entre dos superficies en contacto.

G

geographic information systems
Computer systems that can store, arrange, and display geographic data in different types of maps. (p. 33)

sistemas de información geográfica Sistemas computarizados que pueden almacenar, organizar y mostrar datos geográficos en diferentes tipos de mapas.

geosphere (JEE-uh-SFEER)
All the features on Earth's surface—continents, islands, and seafloor—and everything below the surface—the inner and outer core and the mantle; one of the four parts of the Earth system. (p. 12)

geosfera Todas las características de la superficie de la Tierra, es decir, continentes, islas y el fondo marino, y de todo bajo la superficie, es decir, el núcleo externo e interno y el manto; una de las cuatro partes del sistema de la Tierra.

glacier (GLAY-shuhr)
A large mass of ice that exists year-round and moves over land. (p. 165)

glaciar Una gran masa de hielo que existe durante todo el año y se mueve sobre la tierra.

gravity
The force that objects exert on each other because of their mass. (p. xvii)

gravedad La fuerza que los objetos ejercen entre sí debido a su masa.

H

hardness
The resistance of a mineral or other material to being scratched. (p. 55)

dureza La resistencia de un mineral o de otro material a ser rayado.

humus (HYOO-muhs)
The decayed organic matter in soil. (p. 123)

humus La materia orgánica en descomposición del suelo.

hydrosphere (HY-druh-SFEER)
All water on Earth—in the atmosphere and in the oceans, lakes, glaciers, rivers, streams, and underground reservoirs; one of the four parts of the Earth system. (p. 10)

hidrosfera Toda el agua de la Tierra: en la atmósfera y en los océanos, lagos, glaciares, ríos, arroyos y depósitos subterráneos; una de las cuatro partes del sistema de la Tierra.

hypothesis
A tentative explanation for an observation or phenomenon. A hypothesis is used to make testable predictions. (p. xxiv)

hipótesis Una explicación provisional de una observación o de un fenómeno. Una hipótesis se usa para hacer predicciones que se pueden probar.

I, J

igneous rock (IHG-nee-uhs)
Rock that forms as molten rock cools and becomes solid. (p. 78)

roca ígnea Roca que se forma al enfriarse la roca fundida y hacerse sólida.

intrusive igneous rock (ihn-TROO-sihv)
Igneous rock that forms as magma cools below Earth's surface. (p. 83)

roca ígnea intrusiva Roca ígnea que se forma al enfriarse el magma bajo la superficie de la Tierra.

K

kettle lake
A bowl-shaped lake that was formed as sediment built up around a block of ice left behind by a glacier. (p. 169)

lago kettle Un lago en forma de tazón que se formó al acumularse sedimento alrededor de un bloque de hielo que quedó tras el paso de un glaciar.

L

latitude
The distance in degrees north or south from the equator. (p. 18)

latitud La distancia en grados norte o sur a partir del ecuador.

lava
Molten rock that reaches a planet's surface through a volcano. (p. 62)

lava Roca fundida que llega a la superficie de un planeta a través de un volcán.

law
In science, a rule or principle describing a physical relationship that always works in the same way under the same conditions. The law of conservation of energy is an example.

ley En las ciencias, una regla o un principio que describe una relación física que siempre funciona de la misma manera bajo las mismas condiciones. La ley de la conservación de la energía es un ejemplo.

loess (LOH-uhs)
Deposits of fine-grained, wind-blown sediment. (p. 162)

loes Depósitos de sedimento de grano fino transportado por el viento.

longitude
The distance in degrees east or west of the prime meridian. Longitude lines are numbered from 0° to 180°. (p. 19)

longitud La distancia en grados al este o al oeste del primer meridiano. Las líneas de longitud están numeradas de 0° a 180°.

longshore current
The overall direction and movement of water as waves strike the shore at an angle. (p. 159)

corriente litoral La dirección y el movimiento general del agua conforme las olas golpean la costa en ángulo.

longshore drift
The zigzag movement of sand along a beach, caused by the action of waves. (p. 159)

deriva litoral El movimiento en zigzag de la arena a lo largo de una playa, ocasionado por la acción de las olas.

luster
The property of a mineral that describes the way in which light reflects from its surface. Major types of luster are metallic and nonmetallic. (p. 52)

brillo La propiedad de un mineral que describe la manera en la cual la luz se refleja en su superficie. Los principales tipos de brillo son metálico y no metálico.

M, N

magma
Molten rock beneath Earth's surface. (p. 62)

magma Roca fundida que se encuentra bajo la superficie de la Tierra.

map legend
A chart that explains the meaning of each symbol used on a map; also called a key. (p. 17)

clave del mapa Una tabla que explica el significado de cada símbolo usado en un mapa.

map scale
The comparison of distance on a map with actual distance on what the map represents, such as Earth's surface. Map scale may be expressed as a ratio, a bar scale, or equivalent units. (p. 17)

escala del mapa La comparación de la distancia en un mapa con la distancia real en lo que el mapa representa, como la superficie de la Tierra. La escala del mapa puede expresarse como una azón, una barra de escala o en unidades equivalentes.

mass
A measure of how much matter an object is made of.

masa Una medida de la cantidad de materia de la que está compuesto un objeto.

mass wasting
The downhill movement of loose rock or soil. (p. 147)

movimiento de masa El desplazamiento cuesta abajo de suelo o de roca suelta.

matter
Anything that has mass and volume. Matter exists ordinarily as a solid, a liquid, or a gas. (p. xvii)

materia Todo lo que tiene masa y volumen. Generalmente la materia existe como sólido, líquido o gas.

mechanical weathering
The breakdown of rock into smaller pieces of the same material without any change in its composition. (p. 116)

meteorización mecánica El desmoronamiento de las rocas en pedazos más pequeños del mismo material, sin ningún cambio en su composición.

metamorphic rock (MEHT-uh-MAWR-fihk)
Rock formed as heat or pressure causes existing rock to change in structure, texture, or mineral composition. (p. 78)

roca metamórfica Roca formada cuando el calor o la presión ocasionan que la roca existente cambie de estructura, textura o composición mineral.

metamorphism (MEHT-uh-MAWR-FIHZ-uhm)
The process by which a rock's structure or mineral composition is changed by pressure or heat. (p. 96)

metamorfismo El proceso mediante el cual la estructura o la composición mineral de una roca cambia debido a la presión o al calor.

mineral
A substance that forms in nature, is a solid, has a definite chemical makeup, and has a crystal structure. (p. 43)

mineral Una sustancia sólida formada en la naturaleza, de composición química definida y estructura cristalina.

molecule
A group of atoms that are held together by covalent bonds so that they move as a single unit.

molécula Un grupo de átomos que están unidos mediante enlaces covalentes de tal manera que se mueven como una sola unidad.

moraine (muh-RAYN)
A deposit of till left behind by a retreating glacier. Moraines can form along a glacier's sides and at its end. (p. 168)

morrena Un depósito de sedimentos glaciares dejado por un glaciar que retrocede. Las morrenas pueden formarse en los costados de un glaciar o en su extremo.

O

ore
A rock that contains enough of a valuable mineral to be mined for a profit. (p. 64)

mena Una roca que contiene suficiente mineral valioso para ser extraído con fines lucrativos.

P, Q

planet
A spherical body, larger than a comet or asteroid, that orbits the Sun, or a similar body that orbits a different star.

planeta Un cuerpo esférico, más grande que un cometa o un asteroide, que orbita alrededor del Sol, o un cuerpo similar que orbita alrededor de una estrella distinta.

prime meridian
An imaginary north-south line that divides the planet into the Eastern Hemisphere and the Western Hemisphere. The prime meridian passes through Greenwich, England. (p. 19)

primer meridiano Una línea imaginaria de norte a sur que divide al planeta en hemisferio oriental y hemisferio occidental. El primer meridiano pasa a través de Greenwich, Inglaterra.

projection
A representation of Earth's curved surface on a flat map. (p. 20)

proyección Una representación de la superficie curva de la Tierra en un mapa plano.

R

radiation (ray-dee-AY-shuhn)
Energy that travels across distances as certain types of waves. (p. xv)

radiación Energía que viaja a través de la distancia en forma de ciertos tipos de ondas.

recrystallization
The process by which bonds between atoms in minerals break and re-form in new ways during metamorphism. (p. 97)

recristalización El proceso mediante el cual los enlaces entre los átomos de los minerales se rompen y se vuelven a formar de diferentes maneras durante el metamorfismo.

relief
In geology, the difference in elevation between an area's high and low points. (p. 25)

relieve En geología, la diferencia en elevación entre los puntos altos y bajos de un área.

relief map
A map that shows the differences in elevation in an area. Relief maps can show elevations through the use of contour lines, shading, colors, and, in some cases, three-dimensional materials. (p. 16)

mapa de relieve Un mapa que muestra las diferencias en elevación de un área. Los mapas de relieve pueden mostrar elevaciones mediante del uso de curvas de nivel, sombreado, colores y, en algunos casos, materiales tridimensionales.

remote sensing
A method of using scientific equipment to gather information about something from a distance. Most remote sensing methods make use of different types of electromagnetic radiation. (p. 30)

sensoramiento remoto Un método de reunir información sobre algo a distancia usando equipo científico. La mayoría de los métodos de sensoramiento remoto hacen uso de diferentes tipos de radiación electromagnética.

rock
A naturally formed solid that is usually made up of one or more types of minerals. (p. 75)

roca Un sólido formado de manera natural y generalmente compuesto de uno o más tipos de minerales.

rock cycle
The set of natural, repeating processes that form, change, break down, and re-form rocks. (p. 78)

ciclo de las rocas La serie de procesos naturales y repetitivos que forman, cambian, descomponen y vuelven a formar rocas.

S

sandbar
A ridge of sand built up by the action of waves and currents. (p. 160)

barra de arena Una colina de arena que se forma por la acción de las olas y las corrientes.

satellite
A body that orbits a more massive body. A natural satellite is also called a moon.

satélite Un cuerpo que orbita otro de mayor masa. Un satélite natural también se denomina luna.

sediment
Solid materials such as rock fragments, plant and animal remains, or minerals that are carried by water or by air and that settle on the bottom of a body of water or on the ground. (p. 89)

sedimento Materiales sólidos como fragmentos de rocas, restos de plantas y animales o minerales que son transportados por el agua o el aire y que se depositan en el fondo de un cuerpo de agua o en el suelo.

sedimentary rock (SEHD-uh-MEHN-tuh-ree)
Rock formed as pieces of older rocks and other loose materials get pressed or cemented together or as dissolved minerals re-form and build up in layers. (p. 78)

roca sedimentaria Roca que se forma cuando los pedazos de rocas más viejas y otros materiales sueltos son presionados o cementados o cuando los minerales disueltos vuelven a formarse y se acumulan en capas.

sensor
A mechanical or electronic device that receives and responds to a signal, such as light. (p. 31)

sensor Un dispositivo mecánico o electrónico que recibe y responde a una señal, como la luz.

sinkhole
An open basin that forms when the roof of a cavern becomes so thin that it falls in. (p. 155)

sumidero Una cuenca abierta que se forma cuando el techo de una caverna se vuelve tan delgado que se desploma.

slope
A measure of how steep a landform is. Slope is calculated as the change in elevation divided by the distance covered. (p. 25)

pendiente Una medida de lo inclinada de una formación terrestre. La pendiente se calcula dividiendo el cambio en la elevación por la distancia recorrida.

soil horizon
A soil layer with physical and chemical properties that differ from those of soil layers above or below it. (p. 124)

horizonte del suelo Una capa del suelo con propiedades físicas y químicas que difieren de las de las capas del suelo superior e inferior a la misma.

soil profile
The soil horizons in a specific location; a cross section of soil layers that displays all soil horizons. (p. 124)

perfil del suelo Los horizontes del suelo en un lugar específico; una sección transversal de las capas del suelo que muestra todos los horizontes del suelo.

streak
The color of a mineral powder left behind when a mineral is scraped across a surface; a method for classifying minerals. (p. 51)

raya El color del polvo que queda de un mineral cuando éste se raspa a lo largo de una superficie; un método para clasificar minerales.

system
A group of objects or phenomena that interact. A system can be as simple as a rope, a pulley, and a mass. It also can be as complex as the interaction of energy and matter in the four parts of the Earth system.

sistema Un grupo de objetos o fenómenos que interactúan. Un sistema puede ser algo tan sencillo como una cuerda, una polea y una masa. También puede ser algo tan complejo como la interacción de la energía y la materia en las cuatro partes del sistema de la Tierra.

T, U

technology
The use of scientific knowledge to solve problems or engineer new products, tools, or processes.

tecnología El uso de conocimientos científicos para resolver problemas o para diseñar nuevos productos, herramientas o procesos.

theory
In science, a set of widely accepted explanations of observations and phenomena. A theory is a well-tested explanation that is consistent with all available evidence.

teoría En las ciencias, un conjunto de explicaciones de observaciones y fenómenos que es ampliamente aceptado. Una teoría es una explicación bien probada que es consecuente con la evidencia disponible.

till
Sediment of different sizes left directly on the ground by a melting, or retreating, glacier. (p. 168)

sedimentos glaciares Sedimentos de diferentes tamaños depositados directamente en el suelo por un glaciar que se derrite o retrocede.

topography
All natural and human-made surface features of a particular area. (p. 24)

topografía Todas las características de superficie de origen natural y humano en un área particular.

variable
Any factor that can change in a controlled experiment, observation, or model. (p. R30)

variable Cualquier factor que puede cambiar en un experimento controlado, en una observación o en un modelo.

volume
An amount of three-dimensional space, often used to describe the space that an object takes up.

volumen Una cantidad de espacio tridimensional; a menudo se usa este término para describir el espacio que ocupa un objeto.

W, X, Y, Z

weathering
The process by which natural forces break down rocks. (p. 115)

meteorización El proceso por el cual las fuerzas naturales fragmentan las rocas.

Index

Page numbers for definitions are printed in **boldface** type.
Page numbers for illustrations, maps, and charts are printed in *italics.*

INDEX

E

F

G

H

INDEX

INDEX

N

O

P

Q

INDEX

R

S

INDEX

T

U, V

W, X, Y, Z

Acknowledgments

Photography

Cover © Per Breiehagen/Getty Images; **i** © Per Breiehagen/Getty Images; **iii** *left (top to bottom)* Photograph of James Trefil by Evan Cantwell; Photograph of Rita Ann Calvo by Joseph Calvo; Photograph of Linda Carnine by Amilcar Cifuentes; Photograph of Sam Miller by Samuel Miller; *right (top to bottom)* Photograph of Kenneth Cutler by Kenneth A. Cutler; Photograph of Donald Steely by Marni Stamm; Photograph of Vicky Vachon by Redfern Photographics; **vi** © Steve Starr, Boston Inc./PictureQuest; **vii** Stephen Alvarez/National Geographic Image Collection; **ix** *top* Bike Map courtesy of Chicagoland Bicycle Federation. Photograph by Sharon Hoogstraten; *center, bottom* Photographs by Sharon Hoogstraten; **xiv–xv** Doug Scott/age fotostock; **xvi–xvii** © Aflo Foto Agency; **xviii–ix** © Tim Fitzharris/Masterfile; **xx–xxi** AP/Wide World Photos; **xxii** © Vince Streano/Corbis; **xxiii** © Roger Ressmeyer/Corbis; **xxiv** *left* University of Florida Lightning Research Laboratory; *center* © Roger Ressmeyer/Corbis; **xxv** *center* © Mauro Fermariello/ Science Researchers; *bottom* © Alfred Pasieka/Photo Researchers; **xxvi–xxvii** © Stocktrek/ Corbis; *center* NOAA; **xxvii** *top* © Alan Schein Photography/Corbis; *right* Vaisala Oyj, Finland; **xxxii** Screen Grab © The Chedd-Angier Production Company; **2–3** Courtesy of NASA/JPL/Caltech; **3** *top* Carla Thomas/NASA; *bottom* Diamonds North Resources, Ltd.; **4** *top* Carla Thomas/NASA; *bottom* © The Chedd-Angier Production Company; **5** © William Whitehurst/Corbis; **6–7** NASA; **7** *top left* © NASA; *center left* SeaWiFS Project/NASA Goddard Space Flight Center; *bottom left* National Air & Space Museum/Smithsonian Institution; *top right* Courtesy of L. Sue Baugh; *center right* Bike Map courtesy of Chicagoland Bicycle Federation. Photograph by Sharon Hoogstraten; *bottom right* NASA Goddard Space Flight Center; **9** Photograph by Sharon Hoogstraten; **10–11** NASA; **10** *bottom left* © David Parker/Photo Researchers; *bottom center* © R. Wickllund/OAR/National Undersea Research Program; **11** *bottom center* University of Victoria, Victoria, British Columbia, Canada; *bottom right* © Peter and Georgina Bowater/Stock Connection/PictureQuest; **12** © Photodisc/Getty Images; **13** Photograph by Sharon Hoogstraten; **14** © A. Ramey/PhotoEdit/PictureQuest; **15** Photograph by Sharon Hoogstraten;**16** U.S. Geological Survey; **19** © David Parker/Photo Researchers; **20** Photograph by Sharon Hoogstraten; **23** © Jerry Driendl/Getty Images; **24** Photograph by Sharon Hoogstraten; **25** *top* © Stan Osolinski/Getty Images; *bottom* U.S. Geological Survey; **26, 28** *top left* U.S. Geological Survey; *bottom left, center right, bottom right* Photographs by Sharon Hoogstraten; **30, 31** *top right* © Space Imaging; *bottom background* © Paul Morrell/Getty Images; *bottom left* National Oceanic and Atmospheric Administration/Department of Commerce; **32** *top left, top center* Eros Data Center/U.S. Geological Survey; *bottom right* Photograph by Sharon Hoogstraten; **34** Photo courtesy of John D. Rogie, 1997; **35** © Lynn Radeka/SuperStock Images; **36** *top* NASA; *lower center* U.S. Geological Survey; *bottom left, background,* © Paul Morrell/Getty Images; *bottom left* National Oceanic and Atmospheric Administration/ Department of Commerce; **38** U.S. Geological Survey; **40–41** © Steve Starr, Boston Inc./ PictureQuest; **41** *top right, center right* Photographs by Sharon Hoogstraten; *bottom right* © Dan Suzio/Photo Researchers; **43** Photograph by Sharon Hoogstraten; **44** © Andrew J. Martinez/Photo Researchers; **45** *left* © Astrid & Hanns-Freider/Photo Researchers; *center* © Charles D. Winters/Photo Researchers; **46** Photograph by Sharon Hoogstraten; **47** *top left, center* © Charles D. Winters/Photo Researchers; *top right* Photograph by Malcolm Hjerstedt. Courtesy of F. John Barlow/SANCO Publishing; *bottom left* © Biophoto Associates/Photo Researchers; *bottom center* © Dorling Kindersley; *bottom right* © Phil Degginger/Color Pic, Inc.; *top* © David Young Wolff/PhotoEdit; *bottom* © Doug Martin/Photo Researchers; **49** *background* © Joyce Photographics/Photo Researchers; *top* © Dorling Kindersley; **50, 51** Photographs by Sharon Hoogstraten; **52** *top left* © Charles D. Winters/Photo Researchers; *top right* © Mark A. Schneider/Photo Researchers; *bottom* Photograph by Sharon Hoogstraten; **53, 54** Photographs by Sharon Hoogstraten; **55** *top, center right* Photographs by Sharon Hoogstraten; *bottom right* © Thomas Hunn/Visuals Unlimited; **56** Photograph by Sharon Hoogstraten; **57** *top left, center* © Mark A. Schneider/Visuals Unlimited; *top right* Photograph by Sharon Hoogstraten; **58** *top left* © Martin

Miller/Visuals Unlimited; *bottom left, right* Photographs by Sharon Hoogstraten; **59, 60** Photographs by Sharon Hoogstraten; **61** *top left* © Geoff Tompkinson/Photo Researchers; *center left* © A.J. Copely/Visuals Unlimited; *bottom left* © Charles D. Winters/Photo Researchers; *top right* © Charles Falco/Photo Researchers; *center right, bottom right* © Dorling Kindersley; **63** *top right, center left* © Mark A. Schneider/Photo Researchers; *center right* © Andrew J. Martinez/Photo Researchers; *bottom right* © M. Claye/Photo Researchers; **65** *top* © Mervyn P. Lawes/Corbis; *bottom* Photograph by Sharon Hoogstraten; **66** Newmont Mining Corp.; **67** *top left* © Dorling Kindersley; *top right* © Louis Goldman/Photo Researchers; *center left, bottom left* © Dorling Kindersley; **68** *center* © Charles D. Winters/Photo Researchers; *bottom left* © Astrid & Hanns-Freider/Photo Researchers; *bottom right top* © Photodisc/Getty Images; *bottom right middle* © Dorling Kindersley; *bottom right* © Photodisc/Getty Images; **70** *left* NASA/Science Photo Library; right NASA; **72–73** Stephen Alvarez/NGS Image Collection; **73** *top, center* Photographs by Sharon Hoogstraten; *bottom* Courtesy of L. Sue Baugh; **75** Photograph by Sharon Hoogstraten; **76** *top left* © Dorling Kindersley; *top right* © Doug Martin/Photo Researchers; *bottom* © The Image Bank/Getty Images; **77** *top* © James Lyon/Lonely Planet Images; *bottom* Photograph by Sharon Hoogstraten; **79** *center left, bottom* © Andrew J. Martinez/Photo Researchers; *center right* © Arthur R. Hill/Visuals Unlimited; **81** *background* Arne Danielsen, Norway; *left* © Charles O'Rear/Corbis; *right* © Detlev Van Ravenswaay/ Photo Researchers; **82** Photograph by Sharon Hoogstraten; **83** *top left* © Arthur R. Hill/Visuals Unlimited; *top center, top right* © Joyce Photographics/Photo Researchers; *bottom center* © Mark Schneider/Visuals Unlimited; *bottom right* © Dorling Kindersley; **84** *top* © Andrew J. Martinez/Photo Researchers; *bottom* © Breck P. Kent; **85** Photograph by Sharon Hoogstraten; **86, 87** © Francois Gohier/Photo Researchers; **88** *background* © Dr. Juero Aleon/Photo Researchers; **89** Photograph by Sharon Hoogstraten; **91** *left* © Carolyn Iverson/Photo Researchers; *right* © Ted Clutter/Pennsylvania State Museum Collection/Photo Researchers; **92** *top left* Photograph by Sharon Hoogstraten; *center* Courtesy of L. Sue Baugh; *bottom right* © Norbert Wu/Norbert Wu Productions/PictureQuest; *bottom left;* National Oceanic and Atmospheric Administration **93** *top* © Look GMBH/eStockPhotography/PictureQuest; *bottom* © Corbis; **94** Photograph by Sharon Hoogstraten; **95** *left* © 1991 Ned Haines/Photo Researchers; *center* © Wayne Lawler/Photo Researchers; *right* © Jim Steinberg/Photo Researchers; **96** Photograph by Sharon Hoogstraten; **97** *right (top to bottom)* © Andrew J. Martinez 1995/Photo Researchers; © Andrew J. Martinez 1995/Photo Researchers; Boltin Picture Library; © Breck P. Kent; © 1996 Andrew J. Martinez/Photo Researchers; **98** Photograph by Sharon Hoogstraten; **100** *top left* The Boltin Picture Library; *top right* Photograph courtesy of John Longshore; *bottom left* © E.R. Degginger/Color-Pic, Inc.; *bottom right* © Patricia Tye/Photo Researchers; **102** *top* Will Hart/PhotoEdit; *center, bottom* Photographs by Sharon Hoogstraten; **103** © Corbis; **104** *top left, top center* © Andrew J. Martinez/Photo Researchers; *top right; upper center section left* Arthur R. Hill/Visuals Unlimited; *lower center section, left* © Andrew J. Martinez/Photo Researchers; *right* Photograph by Sharon Hoogstraten; *bottom left, center* © Andrew J. Martinez/Photo Researchers; *bottom right* © Breck P. Kent; **106** © G.R. Roberts Photo Library; **108** *top* © Chris Butler/Photo Researchers; *bottom* © Detlev van Ravenswaay/Photo Researchers; **109** *top* © Jim Brandenburg/Minden Pictures; *center* J.W. Schopf/University of California, Los Angeles; *bottom* Japan Meteorological Agency; **110** *top left* © Simon Fraser/Photo Researchers; *top right* © Chase Studios/Photo Researchers; *bottom* Courtesy of the Ocean Drilling Program; **111** *top* NASA Goddard Space Flight Center; *bottom* STS-113 Shuttle Crew/NASA; **112–113** © Wendy Conway/Alamy Images; **113** *top right, center* Photographs by Sharon Hoogstraten; **115** Photograph by Sharon Hoogstraten; **117** *background* © Photodisc/Getty Images; *inset top* © Susan Rayfield/Photo Researchers; *inset center, bottom left* Photographs courtesy of Sara Christopherson; *inset bottom right* © Kirkendall-Spring Photographer; **118** Photograph by Sharon Hoogstraten; **119** *top left* © Bettmann/Corbis; *top right* © Runk/Schoenberger/ Grant Heilman Photography; *bottom* © Cheyenne Rouse/Visuals Unlimited; **121** *background* © Ecoscene/Corbis; **inset** © Michael Nicholson/Corbis; **122** Photograph by Sharon Hoogstraten; **123** *left* © Joel W. Rogers/Corbis; *right* © Barry Runk/Grant Heilman Photography; **124** © Barry Runk/Grant Heilman Photography; **125** *top left* © Sally A. Morgan/Corbis; *top right* © Peter Falkner/Photo Researchers; *bottom left* © Tony Craddock/ Photo Researchers; *bottom left* © Tui de Roy/Bruce Coleman, Inc.; **128** © Barry Runk/Grant Heilman Photography; **129** © Jim Strawser/Grant Heilman Photography; **130** *top left* © Larry Lefever/Grant Heilman Photography; *center right, bottom left* Photograph by Sharon Hoogstraten; **132**

© Cameron Davidson/Stock Connection, Inc./Alamy Images; **133** AP/Wide World Photos; **134** *top* © Steve Strickland/ Visuals Unlimited; *bottom* Betty Wald/Aurora; **135** Photograph by Sharon Hoogstraten; **136** *left* © Charles O'Rear/Corbis; *right* © Larry Lefever/Grant Heilman Photography; **137** *center inset* Courtesy of Teska Associates, Evanston. Illinois; **138** *top right* © Runk/Schoenberger/Grant Heilman Photography; *bottom* © Larry Lefever/Grant Heilman Photography; **140** © Barry Runk/Grant Heilman Photography; **142–143** © A.C. Waltham/Robert Harding Picture Library/Alamy Images; **143** *center right* Photograph by Sharon Hoogstraten; **145** © Bernhard Edmaier/Photo Researchers; **146** Photograph by Sharon Hoogstraten; **147** AP/Wide World Photos; **148** *top* Photograph by L.M. Smith, Waterways Experiment Station, U.S. Army Corps of Engineers. Courtesy, USGS; *bottom* © Thomas Rampton/Grant Heilman Photography; **149** © Troy and Mary Parlee/Alamy Images; **150** Photograph by Sharon Hoogstraten; **151** © Bill Ross/Corbis; **152** *top* © Kevin Horan/Stock Boston /PictureQuest; *bottom* © Yann Arthus-Bertrand/Corbis; **153** © 1992 Tom Bean; **154** © Charles Kennard/Stock Boston/PictureQuest; **155** © Reuters NewMedia, Inc./Corbis; **156** © Peter Bowater/Alamy Images; **158** © John and Lisa Merrill/Getty Images; **159** © Robert Perron; **160** Photograph by Sharon Hoogstraten; **161** © Tim Barnwell/Picturesque/ PictureQuest; **162** © John Shaw/Bruce Coleman, Inc.; **163** *top* © 1994 Tom Bean; *right* © Goodshoot/Alamy Images; **164** *background* © Gustav Verderber/Visuals Unlimited; *inset left* © Gary Meszaros/Bruce Coleman, Inc.; *inset right* © Lee Rentz/Bruce Coleman, Inc.; **165** Photograph by Sharon Hoogstraten; **167** *left* © Bernard Edmaier/Photo Researchers; *right* © ImageState-Pictor/PictureQuest ; **168** *top* © Norman Barett/Bruce Coleman, Inc.; *bottom* © Jim Wark/Airphoto; **169** *top* © 1990 Tom Bean; *bottom* Photograph by Sharon Hoogstraten; **171** © Charles W. Campbell/ Corbis; **172** *top* © Bernhard Edmaier/Photo Researchers; *center* © John and Lisa Merrill/Getty Images; **174** © Tom Bean; **R28** © Photodisc/Getty Images.

Illustrations and Maps

Accurate Art Inc. **39, 107, 175**
Richard Bronson/Wildlife Art Ltd. **83**
Peter Bull/ Wildlife Art Ltd. **160, 162, 167, 169**
Stephen Durke **45, 53**
Chris Forsey **99**
Luigi Galante **127, 138**
David Hardy **12, 84, 86, 104**
Gary Hincks **63, 79, 80, 149, 153**
Mapquest.com, Inc. **17, 18, 23, 32, 33, 34, 36, 64, 88, 110, 125, 166, 170**
Morgan, Cain & Assoc. **128**
Mike Saunders **117, 120, 138**
Dan Stuckenschneider **R11–R19, R22, R32**
Raymond Turvey **159**
Rob Wood **117, 154**